# Integrating
# Traditional Healing
# Practices Into Counseling
# and Psychotherapy

D1202973

# MULTICULTURAL ASPECTS OF COUNSELING AND PSYCHOTHERAPY SERIES

## SERIES EDITOR

Paul B. Pedersen, Ph.D.,
*Professor Emeritus, Syracuse University*
*Visiting Professor, Department of Psychology, University of Hawaii*

## EDITORIAL BOARD

## VOLUMES IN THIS SERIES

# Integrating Traditional Healing Practices Into Counseling and Psychotherapy

Edited by

## Roy Moodley
University of Toronto

## William West
University of Manchester

*Multicultural Aspects of Counseling and Psychotherapy Series 22*

**SAGE Publications**
Thousand Oaks ▪ London ▪ New Delhi

*For information:*

Sage Publications, Inc.
2455 Teller Road
Thousand Oaks, California 91320
E-mail: order@sagepub.com

Sage Publications Ltd.
1 Oliver's Yard
55 City Road
London EC1Y 1SP
United Kingdom

Sage Publications India Pvt. Ltd.
B-42, Panchsheel Enclave
Post Box 4109
New Delhi 110 017 India


*Library of Congress Cataloging-in-Publication Data*

Integrating traditional healing practices into counseling and psychotherapy / editors Roy Moodley, William West.
    p. cm. — (Multicultural aspects of counseling and psychotherapy; v. 22)
Includes bibliographical references and index.
ISBN 978-0-7619-3046-4 (hardcover) — ISBN 978-0-7619-3047-1 (pbk.)
    1. Spiritual healing. 2. Counseling—Religious aspects. 3. Psychotherapy—Religious aspects.
I. Moodley, Roy. II. West, William, 1950- III. Series.
BL65.M45I58 2005
615.8′52—dc22                    2004028861

This book is printed on acid-free paper.

10   11   12   13   14     9   8   7   6   5   4   3   2

| | |
|---|---|
| *Acquisitions Editor:* | Arthur T. Pomponio |
| *Editorial Assistant:* | Veronica Novak |
| *Production Editor:* | Tracy Alpern |
| *Copy Editor:* | Rachel Hile Bassett |
| *Typesetter:* | C&M Digitals (P) Ltd. |
| *Indexer:* | Gloria Tierney |
| *Cover Designer:* | Edgar Abarca |

# Contents

# Foreword

Only since the middle of the last century have anthropologists and transcultural psychiatrists begun to take traditional, folk, religious, and indigenous healing practices seriously. Prior to that period, scholars of sound mind were more likely to regard these practices as superstitious hocus-pocus than as forms of healing, and more likely to regard practitioners as pathologically afflicted than as important contributors to their communities. Eventually scholars began to interpret religious healing by analogy with psychotherapy. A profound and definitive turning point was reached with the publication of Jerome Frank's *Persuasion and Healing*, which over three editions (1961, 1973, 1991) transformed the contemporary understanding of the relation between culture and psychotherapy and prompted us to develop an expanded understanding of psychotherapy as a human endeavor not limited to Euro-American societies. Frank directed our attention to the task of developing the psychotherapy analogy into a truly comparative theory of psychotherapy by formulating its least common denominator in the manner in which interpersonal stress is central to affliction; in the importance of the assumptive world that underlies therapeutic practices; in the way all forms of healing address an underlying state of demoralization; in the relevance of myth and ritual across all forms of psychotherapy; and in the manner in which all these forms of healing have to do with rhetoric, hermeneutics, and the transformation of meaning.

Frank regretted not having updated his chapters on religious healing for the third edition of his book, but his intellectual legacy is the condition of possibility for the new cross-cultural psychiatry developed by Arthur Kleinman and others, as well as for the entire movement of multicultural counseling and psychotherapy represented in this volume. The present work is a landmark effort by those involved with cultural issues in counseling and psychotherapy to move beyond sterile notions of multiculturalism and cultural competency, which—despite the best of intentions—often reduce culture to a series of formulae and seek competence in the form of a recipe. In the first place, it is an attempt to get the "big picture" of diversity across the many forms of healing through history and across cultures that can justifiably fall under the umbrella of the psychotherapy analogy. This aspect of the work contributes to the broad aim of developing a comparative theory of psychotherapy. Second, in a variety of ways it addresses the relations among these different forms of healing in practice. In a pragmatic sense, contributors ask about the ways ritual healing and psychotherapy can and should be integrated or used to complement one another, but they also consider the possible role of spirituality in psychotherapy per se. If ritual healing is a form of psychotherapy, is psychotherapy also inherently a ritual? If certain forms of prayer can be considered to be psychotherapy, can psychotherapy legitimately include prayer as one of its therapeutic techniques?

In sum, this book is about expanding the cultural horizons of counseling and psychotherapy. This is not an optional enterprise undertaken for the sake of allowing practitioners to deepen their professional satisfaction or enhance their ability to reflect on what psychotherapy means to them. In this historical epoch of globalization and constant flow of populations, few therapists today will go through a career without encountering patients who have recourse to ethnic or religious traditions of healing in addition to counseling or psychotherapy. This book is necessary not because psychotherapy can be conceived broadly, but because of the world in which we live and the challenges it presents.

Thomas J. Csordas, Ph.D.
*University of California San Diego*

# Series Editor's Foreword

The functions of counseling have been practiced for thousands of years and are not merely an invention of the last century or two. Roy Moodley and William West do an excellent job of integrating "traditional healing" practices, often from non-Western traditions, into the process of counseling and psychotherapy. It is significant that contemporary counseling practice has rediscovered many of the principles and strategies of indigenous healing in non-Western cultures and applied those insights to contemporary problems quite effectively. This book raises the possibility of a conventional and a traditional healer working together for the ultimate benefit of the client.

This collection, comprising chapters written by different and highly qualified authors, provides a comprehensive and informed perspective to the reader on how healing is conceived across cultures. Only by better understanding the holistic context in which healing and illness function can the modern counselor or therapist identify the most relevant resources for healing. Moodley and West seek to popularize the functional utility of a culture-centered approach and to explain why in the world this approach has not been more popular in the past.

The authors acknowledge the confusion in how multiculturalism is defined and even the ways that multiculturalism has been used to fragment and disempower minority populations, as was the case with apartheid in South Africa. This confusion of meaning has sometimes prevented the effective healing of culturally different clients from multicultural social settings. Previous books on multicultural counseling are cited and discussed and evaluated. The primary weakness that Moodley and West seek to define and address is the lack of multicultural theory and theorizing outside the context of a small constituency of dedicated scholars. This critique of multiculturalism will provoke discussion and demonstrate how the term *multiculturalism* is understood differently in countries such as Canada than it is in the United States.

Moodley and West demonstrate how contemporary counseling can be changed without either underemphasizing or overemphasizing the cultural context. They redefine the healing process itself, pointing out that health is more than the absence of illness. The authors in this book carefully document their positions by reviewing the literature and "doing their homework" successfully. One clear conclusion is that simple answers to complex questions in culture and mental health are dangerous and should be avoided. There is a necessary complexity that must be accommodated. The readers will not always agree with the authors of these chapters, and the book does not avoid controversy, but it will provoke a useful and meaningful discussion.

We are delighted to include the Moodley and West book in the Multicultural Aspects of Counseling and Psychotherapy (MACP) series. The books in this series have not avoided controversy in pointing out gaps in the literature about culture and mental health. This book is right in that tradition. By inclusively understanding both the cultural context and the counseling process, this book adds to the library of other MACP books and continues the tradition for examining multicultural aspects of counseling.

—Paul Pedersen

*Professor Emeritus*
*Syracuse University;*
*Visiting Professor*
*Department of Psychology*
*University of Hawaii*

# Acknowledgments

We offer our sincerest thanks and appreciation to all of the contributors in this book for sharing their expertise in a way that the book demanded, sometimes having to cut much material and edit some wonderful pieces of creative writing. We would like to thank many of our close colleagues and friends in Canada, the United Kingdom, and the United States who have in many different ways contributed directly and indirectly both to this book and to our understanding of traditional healing, culture, and therapy, although they should in no way be held responsible for what has been written here. In particular, we wish to thank Waseem Alladin, Linda Ankrah, Allen Bergin, Niyi Bojuwoye, Joseph Calabrese, Thomas J. Csordas, Kam Dhillon, Shukla Dingra, Jim Fitzgerald, Joanne Grierson, Lovie Grierson, Bill Hall, Susan James, Eunsun Joo, Naila Khan, Arthur Kleinman, Nick Ladany, Vivian Lalande, Pittu Laungani, John McLeod, Sharon Mier, David Orlinsky, Paul Pedersen, Abdullah Popoola, Cecilia Rachier, Wayne Richards, Rebecca Sima, Daniel Schgurensky, David Smith, Anne Solomon, Lana Stermac, Mansor Abu Talib, Clemmont Vontress, Dori Yusef, and Nathalie Zajde. In addition, we would like to acknowledge the following reviewers: Alberta Gloria, University of Wisconsin, Madison; Garrett J. McAuliffe, Old Dominion University; and Natasha Mitchell, University of Maryland, College Park.

We remember with much sadness the death of Dr. Mohammed Aslam (Nottingham University, UK) who so much desired to write a chapter but died before doing so.

We would like to acknowledge the help and support of and offer our sincere thanks to:

- Patricia Poulin, who translated Chapter 3 from the French, and Katie Hinnenkamp for translating Chapter 8 from the Spanish;
- the Ontario Institute for Studies in Education at the University of Toronto for the Connaught Start-up Grant that Roy Moodley received, part of which supported this project;

- Arthur Pomponio, Veronica Novak, and Tracy Alpern of Sage, as well as copy editor Rachel Hile Bassett, for their tremendous help and support;
- the people in our lives who were patient, understanding, and supportive during our absences from them while we edited this book: Roisin, Maya, Tara, Emily, Zina, Daniel, Gay, and Anissa.

Finally, it feels important for us to acknowledge each other's time, patience, and understanding of each other as this project developed. The depth of relationship that evolved over the years for us has now developed into an intimate friendship.

—Roy Moodley and William West

# Introduction

*Roy Moodley and William West*

This book evolved out of a desire to understand the rich healing traditions of various cultures from around the world, several of which are very much in use and are still practiced today, some alongside contemporary health care. A number of these "vernacular and indigenous forms" of healing go back at least a thousand years before the start of the Christian era, and in some cases have even longer histories. Depending how cultural and traditional healing is defined and interpreted, many present-day Christian rituals (often seen as practices aligned to modernity, objectivity, and the West when compared to developing societies)—such as God's healing powers, prayer and incantations, and healing by the saints—are practices that are no different from those that are often regarded as pagan, particularly practices from the cultures of the East.

However, in the last two decades, many traditional healing methods seem to have appeared in reformulated and reconstituted ways in the West, often in an uncoordinated and unplanned way. Away from the public gaze and sometimes in the silence of the night, these practices appear to address some of the many shortcomings of conventional medicine and health care. In counseling and psychotherapy, a number of clients and patients appear to be accessing these traditional methods, sometimes in parallel with conventional therapy, in the same way that many people use a multiple range of cure-seeking methods for physical ailments, that is, seeking the help of a modern physician as well as using acupuncture, massage, yoga, and meditation. For example, Moodley (1998b, 1999) writes about clients who consult traditional healers while at the same time engaging in psychotherapy. It seems that through the traditional healer, clients are able to identify cultural metaphors, symbols, and archetypes that may be outside the parameters of Western counseling and psychotherapy (see also West, 2004, pp. 65–66, for discussion).

The collection of chapters in this volume explores the complexities of the various approaches and argues for the inclusion and integration of traditional and indigenous healing practices in counseling and psychotherapy. This need to look outside the boundaries of Western psychology is a direct result of the failures of multicultural counseling or the way psychotherapy is practiced in a multicultural context. It seems that multicultural counseling and psychotherapy is in crisis.

### ❖ MULTICULTURAL COUNSELING AND PSYCHOTHERAPY: CRISIS COULD LEAD TO CREATIVITY

The lack of a comprehensive definition of *multiculturalism* has led to a great deal of confusion in the practice of psychotherapy (Sue, 1997). Because multiculturalism suffers from a general lack of complex theorizing (Willett, 1998), it seems understandable that it emerges as a confusing site in clinical work. Perhaps it is not the lack of a comprehensive definition that is the problem, but rather the perverse way in which multiculturalism is interpreted in the West. Under the guise of promoting cultural and social equity (and justice), it has fragmented, disempowered, and ghettoized many cultural and ethnic groups, creating barriers and preventing the evolution of a comprehensive multiple-cultural and multiple-ethnic (national) community. In other words, it has remained resistant to changing the status quo of the dominant culture, which is often perceived to be hegemonic. Indeed, this situation contributes much to the confusion that already exists historically in conventional counseling and psychotherapy. It has been extremely problematic for psychotherapy researchers, scholars, and practitioners to find any meaningful understanding of how to apply multicultural ideas in their clinical work.

Since its early beginnings in the 1960s, multicultural counseling, with its emphasis on culture (see Vontress, 1979), has been growing in all sorts of directions. The 1980s and 1990s saw a focus on cultural competencies (see Sue, Arredondo, & McDavis, 1992; Sue et al., 1982, for details) and its (black and white) racial identity theories (see Cross, 1971, 1995; Helms, 1984, 1995). In Ponterotto, Fuertes, and Chen's (2000) analysis of the models of multicultural counseling, they suggest that the models of Cross and of Helms have generated more research than any other framework, and that these models have "brought the status of multicultural counseling to a new plateau of sophistication" (p. 654). However, both the cultural competency and the racial identity models could be seen as narrow and "skin deep," so to speak. They fix the notions of culture and race as independent and objective variables, in the process rarefying these problematic concepts.

Then Pedersen (1991) reminded us that multicultural counseling is the "fourth force" in counseling psychology. Although many scholars agree with this view, there is little discussion of how multicultural counseling fails to theorize early childhood development, conceptualizations of the (multicultural) self, or any analysis on cultural psychopathology. All we seem to have are the cultural competencies as therapeutic techniques, and much of this work has no "force" outside the theorizing and researching by a small constituency of dedicated scholars.

From the 1990s onward, a cultural shift began to emerge, and we saw the inclusion of gender and sexual orientations, which took center stage alongside race, culture, and ethnicity as key variables in multicultural counseling and psychotherapy. As if not to marginalize class and disability issues, they too were added to the list, but this action tends to be more rhetorical and is often confined to an academic/intellectual accommodation rather than indicating any real move to offer training or research in these areas. But the issue of religion and spirituality tends to be outside, in the margins, maybe a footnote in most cases. In the words of Yarhouse and Fisher (2002), "Despite the significance of religion in the lives of most members of the general population and the value of religion in promoting mental health . . . religion remains an often overlooked expression of diversity" (p. 172). There has been much criticism of multicultural and diversity counseling (see Stone, 1993; Weinrach & Thomas, 1996).

With the inclusion of gender, race, ethnicity, sexual orientations, class, and gender as key variables, multicultural counseling and psychotherapy still appears to have failed to seriously address the underrepresentation of black, ethnic-minority, and other disadvantaged groups as clients; as psychologists, psychotherapists, and counselors; as clinical supervisors; and as researchers and scholars. These failures can be explained as stemming from a failure to understand individual cultural healing contexts (Bhugra & Bhui, 1998), mistrust of psychotherapy and its practitioners (Kareem, 1992), negative attitude toward therapists, as well as the perception that therapy has no benefit (Garfield, 1986). Or, could it be that the individualistic, Eurocentric, and ethnocentric nature of the process itself is the problem? Could it be that conventional therapy will always be available to the "WAYVIS" clients (white, attractive, young, verbal, intelligent, single) and that minorities and new immigrants will always be "outside" the supposedly flexible and reflexive places and spaces of counseling and psychotherapy?

What can be done other than advocate the removal of counseling and psychotherapy as mental health care processes for oppressed and disadvantaged groups? We do not think that this is the answer. We believe that a creative move(ment), a small paradigm shift—the inclusion and integration of traditional healing methods into mainstream counseling and psychotherapy—will not only make a difference to (an ailing) multicultural counseling movement but will also add a new lease of life to psychotherapy and counseling generally.

We make this suggestion knowing full well the fantasies, complexities, and confusions that surround the adoption of methods, models, and practices from other cultures.

Our understanding of this is informed by professional as well as personal perspectives—both of us are researchers and psychotherapists, and we both have more than a scholarly interest in this area of practice. William West is a Quaker and a therapist whose research focuses mainly on spirituality and psychotherapy, and he has recently published two books in this area (see West, 2000, 2004). William advocates for the need to incorporate cultural method in counseling, but he cautions us when he says, "It is important that we do not get caught up in the drama of various shamanic healing rituals however engaging. For there is a Western seeking after extreme experiences and quick fixes, which gives shamanism an attractiveness and a glamour. This ignores the cultural context within which the shaman works" (West, 2004, p. 61). In his therapy practice, William uses healing—"laying of hands"—with his clients. Roy Moodley, on the other hand, has witnessed and observed healing through the laying of hands as part of the black South African church experience.[1] Also, as noted above, Roy has argued for the inclusion or integration of traditional healing in psychotherapy, based on his experience of working with patients who sought traditional healing while in psychotherapy with him (see Moodley, 1998b, 1999, for discussion on the case vignettes).

## ❖ PRACTICE OF TRADITIONAL HEALING

Western counseling and psychotherapy, when viewed in the context of the history of healing, is relatively new. Human societies since the dawn of history have "interrogated" their conflicts, illnesses, and diseases with various forms of healing practices. For example, shamanism (see Eliade, 1964; Levi-Strauss, 1967; Vitebsky, 2001), qigong (see Chen, 2003), *Bhuta vidya* (see Rao, 1986), homeopathic or imitative magic (i.e., charms based on the Law of Similarity; see Frazer, 1922), Aesculapian healing rites (see Field, 1990; Kirmayer, 2003), and Salish spirit dancing (see Ward, 1989) are some of the many practices that were responsible for maintaining the psychological and mental well-being of people in the societies that practice these healing methods (Moodley, 1998a). Many of these traditional methods or folk counseling (Tseng & Hsu, 1979) are still practiced in different parts of the world today, sometimes alongside or in conjunction with, and sometimes in place of, the modern Western forms. In Brazil, for example, Hohmann et al. (1990) stated that traditional practices have flourished and complemented a deficient mental health care system. In the São Paulo area alone, for instance, there are more than 75 spiritist psychiatric hospitals, which integrate medical and spiritist techniques based on reincarnation and the use of mediums who mediate the healing process through the concept of spiritual "fluids" around the body (see Hohmann et al.).

For 80% of the African population, according to Ataudo (1985), traditional methods are synonymous with primary health care. Traditional healing seems to reflect a transitional stage in the search for an integrated and indigenous approach to mental health issues arising from the sociocultural and psycho-historical (colonial and postcolonial) experiences of the African continent as a whole. Healing practices that went "underground," so to speak, are now emerging in large metropolitan cities side by side with contemporary Western clinical medicine. For example, Awanbar (1982) identifies several distinguishing features in the mental health strategies in Nigerians, especially among the Yoruba people. These are shamanism and possession; oral legends and mythology; incantations and word-magic; abreaction (cult forms such as rituals, symbolic sacrifices, suggestion, and dancing); and detoxification. One or more of these features appear to be essential ingredients of a successful traditional healing program. It is not clear in Awanbar's analysis whether a modern therapist in Nigeria uses any of these methods or whether they are offered alongside the modern therapies by a traditional healer. It seems highly likely that the latter system is the one that prevails, just as it is in many countries in Africa, Asia, and South America.

Reviewing traditional methods, Tseng and McDermott (1975) write,

> It is becoming more and more clear that such simplistic notions regarding therapeutic approaches as considering one approach universally primary or superior are no longer tolerable and that many techniques seem to be effective with the same problem throughout the world. (p. 378)

Field (1990), in reviewing his own practice in healing, exorcism, and object relations theory, began to reconsider whether what he feared were serious lapses (traditional healing) from "good practice" (scientific models) might in fact have been appropriate, time-honored therapeutic responses (p. 275). Many Indian patients, for example, seek the healing method of *Bhuta vidya*,[2] a magicoreligious procedure, prior to seeking modern treatment. In some cases, the traditional methods are experienced concurrently with or are followed by the modern methods of health care (Rao, 1986). In China, on the other hand, healing has been more influenced by Chinese medicine than by religious thought and movement, as in India. However, Tseng and Hsu (1979) suggest that a form of Chinese divination in which "the client is usually warned not to be too ambitious or aggressive, or to do things that are inappropriate for his role or status" (p. 341) is experienced by Chinese patients. Such divine intervention, according to Tseng and Hsu, reinforces the traditional Chinese way of remaining patient, unaggressive, and accepting.

In North America and Europe, many people from the dominant culture and also those from the diasporic communities actively seek alternative treatments, such as acupuncture, herbalism, yogic meditation, ayurveda, and others. However, anecdotal evidence suggests that many people from immigrant communities—first and second generations—also appear to consult traditional healers, mainly from their communities but also from other cultural groups, who happen to live among them, such as *hougans* (from Haiti), hakims (from Pakistan), obeah men and women (from the Caribbean), shamans (from Asia and Africa), and Voodoo doctors (from Latin America). Many of these practitioners (with the exception of a few who are dubious, dangerous, and untrained) are qualified and legitimate in the eyes of the community. Their professional "calling" has been handed down through "tribal law," religious custom, and cultural traditions, and they seems to have found their way into the homes of both working-class and middle-class clients. A comparative study on alternative healers indicates that middle-class Americans practice beliefs and techniques that include naturopathy, the occult, Christian Science, psychic and faith healing, and New Age therapies (Heber, Fleisher, Ross, & Stanwick, 1989). Although the "diversity of alternative medicine and spiritual healing methods are usually associated with neo-religious cults or charismatic religious movements," many people in the West are seeking traditional healing (Field, 1990, p. 275). More and more people appear to enter the realm of the Other's healing space to find emotional and physical healing, spiritual fulfillment and solitude, and an embodied sense of self.

It seems a paradox that when contemporary Western healing practices appear to be so sophisticated and underpinned by postmodern technology, patients should be turning to traditional healing methods. In Ataudo's (1985) view, traditional healing represents a structured system of ordering, classifying, and explaining illness, comprising equally elaborate concepts of treatment as contemporary Western healing procedures. There is much to commend in the use of traditional methods, according to Majumdar (1944), as long as the people have faith in the system they own, and this depends largely on the way it is integrated into the community. On a more historical scale, we seem to have come full circle regarding the fragmentation of the subject through the Cartesian body/mind division, which presents itself as an absent phenomenon in the philosophy of traditional healing. Therefore, traditional and cultural healing could also be understood as a biopsychosocial concept that organizes a particular illness perception or representation of discomfort of the self, thus making possible a specific form of treatment that is required at the time (Ataudo, 1985). A similar point is made by West (2004), after Cushman (1995), when he says, "Each era has a particular construction of self with characteristic illness, healers and healing methods . . . each is unique and local and not reducible to a universal law" (West, 2004, p. 35). Is this process linear or circular? From recent evidence on the growing awareness and interest in issues of spirituality, contemplative meditation, and well-being, it seems that we have come full circle. Issues of spirituality, divinity, the supernatural, god, and religion are once again appearing to surface in our consciousness. It seems reasonable, perhaps inevitable, that these issues will be part of the healing process in the 21st century, as they were in centuries before the Christian era.

## ❖  HOW THE BOOK IS ORGANIZED

The book is divided into five parts, organized in a sequence beginning with concepts and ideas that form the early beginnings of the development and evolution of cultural and traditional healing and eventually ending with chapters that discuss the links that could be made between traditional healing and psychotherapy and counseling.

Part I, "Indigenous Performances, Cultural Worldviews, and Supernatural Healing," looks at the ideas, philosophies, and practices that supported traditional healing historically. In Chapter 1, "Shamanic Performances: Healing Through Magic and the Supernatural," Roy Moodley explores the relationship between the belief in magic and supernatural healing and the tension that this brings by practices that challenge it. The chapter traces the movement of healing from gods to modern psychological healing. In Chapter 2, "Aboriginal Worldview of Healing: Inclusion, Blending, and Bridging," Anne Poonwassie and Ann Charter first historically contextualize the Aboriginal community, then explore the worldview of the community, which sets the scene for discussion of the Medicine Wheel, storytelling, ceremonies, and the bridging of therapeutic approaches. In Chapter 3, "The *Djinns*: A Sophisticated Conceptualization of Pathologies and Therapies," Tobie Nathan offers an etymological study of the Arabic word *djinn*, meaning "demon spirit." Through a depth analysis and by including the ecology of the *djinn*, Tobie brings to our consciousness the complex and "culture-centered" meanings and interpretations of this term. Finally, William West tempts us to consider crossing the line between conventional counseling and psychotherapy into the unknown yet safe waters of cultural and spiritual healing in Chapter 4, "Crossing the Line Between Talking Therapies and Spiritual Healing." William explores the implications of therapists and their clients who are using and integrating approaches from both the talking therapies and the various forms of spiritual healing.

Part II, "Healing and Curing: Traditional Healers and Healing," considers the healers and healing traditions of a few of the many communities from around the world that are still actively engaging in traditional healing. In Chapter 5, "Indigenous Healers and Healing in a Modern World," Anne Solomon and Njoki Nathani Wane interview three indigenous healers who tell their story of how they became "wounded" healers. This is followed by Chapter 6, "Traditional Healing Practices in Southern Africa: Ancestral Spirits, Ritual Ceremonies, and Holistic Healing," in which Olaniyi Bojuwoye offers us an insight into Zulu cosmology and traditional healing practices. This chapter also addresses the implications for integrating some of these practices into cross-cultural counseling. In Chapter 7, "Caribbean Healers and Healing: Awakening Spiritual and Cultural Healing Powers," Ronald Marshall discusses the relationship between traditional spiritual rituals and their convergence with contemporary religious practice. Ronald reports on a study he conducted in Trinidad on religiosity and health, which focused on the effects of the use of traditional medicine on spiritual and cultural beliefs and how these beliefs bring about healing. The chapter discusses practices such as Voodoo and Shinto. In Chapter 8, "Latin American Healers and Healing: Healing as a Redefinition Process," Lilián González Chévez explores through a client case vignette "the discursive activity of the *curandera*" (of Mexico), whose multiple frames of meanings provide the patient with an explanatory structure so that the patient can understand his or her illness in terms of its organic, social, and cultural origins. We travel to the other side of the globe with Joseph K. So in Chapter 9, "Traditional and Cultural Healing Among the Chinese," which develops the issues in Chinese traditional healing, first from a historical perspective and then by exploring the conceptualization of illness and healing in contemporary Chinese culture. Joseph also discusses the major treatment modalities, such as acupuncture, herbal medicine, and *qigong*. Finally in Part II, Chapter 10, "South Asian (Indian) Traditional Healing: Ayurvedic, Shamanic, and Sahaja Healing," Manoj Kumar, Dinesh Bhugra, and Jagmohan Singh discuss the social and cultural histories that have shaped and informed traditional South Asian (Indian) healing practices. They explore the ayurvedic tradition of healing and briefly discuss spiritual healing practices such as prayers, chanting, meditation, and others.

Part III, "Spirituality, Religion, and Cultural Healing," considers traditional healing from a religious point of view, beginning with Clemmont E. Vontress's discussion in Chapter 11, "Animism: Foundation of Traditional Healing in Sub-Saharan Africa," on the source of African spirituality, the precolonial religious practice of animism. Clemmont's discussion explores a wide range of healers and their healing practices, such as Voodoo and other forms. The chapter also examines the implications for integration of some of these approaches into counseling. In Chapter 12, "Hindu Spirituality and Healing Practices," Pittu Laungani looks at the relationship between Hinduism and healing, exploring the various practices and processes by which Hindus seek cures to their illnesses. Fernando L. Garzon, in Chapter 13, "Inner Healing Prayer in 'Spirit-Filled' Christianity," introduces us to the development of Christian inner healing prayer. Fernando traces its roots historically and through a case study demonstrates the process of this kind of healing in the life of a client. In Chapter 14, "Islam, Divinity, and Spiritual Healing," Qulsoom Inayat explores the philosophy and practices of hakims, mullahs, and other religious and faith leaders. Qulsoom argues that "illnesses" and ailments presented by Muslim clients are often those that have not been successfully treated by Western psychological or medical intervention, and that traditional healing may offer more positive results. In Chapter 15, "Jewish Healing, Spirituality, and Modern Psychology," Laura J. Praglin offers us insight into the history of Jewish healing practices since biblical times. Laura looks at the techniques and processes and considers the pitfalls and possibilities of integrating traditional Jewish healing into modern counseling and psychology. Finally in Part III, Chapter 16, "Buddhist Moments in Psychotherapy," Roshni Daya discusses Buddhist philosophy and its relationship to counseling and psychotherapy.

Part IV, "Traditional Healing and Its Contemporary Formulations," introduces us to a few of the many cultural healing practices that have been reconceptualized or modified to fit into modernity. Part IV begins with Chapter 17, "The Sweat Lodge as Psychotherapy: Congruence Between Traditional and Modern Healing," by David Paul Smith, who presents us with an ethnographic description of a Native American sweat lodge and a detailed account of a ritual conducted by an Ojibwa medicine man. David argues that the sweat lodge has many characteristics in common with modern psychotherapy and many others that can be further incorporated. In Chapter 18, "*Maat: An African-Centered Paradigm for Psychological and Spiritual Healing,*" Mekada Graham brings to our consciousness the depth of spirituality in contemporary black communities and the way spiritual practices work toward well-being. Staying with the contemporary theme, Chapter 19, "Morita Therapy: A Philosophy of Yin/Yang Coexistence" by Charles P. Chen, takes us step by step through the treatment process of Morita therapy and the rationale for each stage. Charles, as a therapist who practices Morita with his clients, is best qualified to bring us close to the possibility of using this method in our work. In Chapter 20, "Pagan Approaches to Healing," Estelle Seymour looks at the history of modern Paganism, its growth, and its relationship to contemporary therapies. This is followed by Chapter 21, "Yoga and Its Practice in Psychological Healing," in which Josna Pankhania discusses a range of physical, psychological, and emotional benefits that can be acquired through yoga *asanas* (physical exercises), *pranayama* (breathing exercises), and *dhyana* (meditation). Josna also offers examples to illustrate how yoga has assisted people in their journey toward well-being and wholeness. Finally in Part IV, Chapter 22, "Holistic Healing, Paradigm Shift, and the New Age," Patricia A. Poulin and William West discuss the newer forms of healing referred to as "holistic," "complementary and alternative," or "New Age." Patricia and William illustrate their scope through the examination of a case study.

Part V, "Finding the Link Between Traditional Healing and Therapy," attempts to make the connection between healing and psychotherapy and counseling. In Chapter 23, "Spiritual and Healing Approaches in Therapeutic Practice," Robert N. Sollod examines how healing can be integrated into psychotherapy. Through a social anthropologist's perspective, Michael Anderson shares with us the ritual structure of therapy in Chapter 24, "Psychotherapy as Ritual: Connecting the Concrete With the Symbolic." Michael explores the notion of *liminality* and its various phases, with possibilities in the therapy room. In Chapter 25, "The Healing Path: What Can Counselors Learn From Aboriginal People About How to Heal?" Rod McCormick explores spirituality in terms of nature, specifically water, trees, sky, and animals, and how such encounters with nature have helped Aboriginal people on their healing journeys. Rod examines how some of these healing approaches can be integrated into contemporary counseling. Chapter 26, "*Herbalistas, Curandeiros,* and *Bruxas*: Valuable Lessons From Traditional Systems of Healing," by Birdie J. Bezanson, Gary Foster, and Susan James, examines healing practices among the Portuguese immigrant community in Ontario, Canada. Finally in Part V, and bringing the book to a conclusion, Chapter 27, "Sharing Healing Secrets: Counselors and Traditional Healers in Conversation" by Rebecca Gawile Sima and William West, focuses on research that Rebecca conducted in Tanzania to explore the process of collaboration between traditional healers and counselors.

Without exception, all of the chapters in this book demonstrate an awareness and sensitivity respecting the vastness of cultural healing and the limitations of a postmodernist social science analysis. Yet, through the receptive characteristics of a poststructuralist and social constructivist paradigm, all the above writers have attempted to interpret and rediscover the tradition of age-old healing practices and their possible contribution to cross-cultural counseling and psychotherapy. Therefore, the chapters in this book seek not only to bring to consciousness multiple configurations of traditional psychological patterns and related behaviors but to engage the reader in a (re)discovery of the Other psychic spaces and places that may be accessible either in parallel to, or in conjunction with, their current clinical practice.

## ❖ NOTES

1. In Greek religion, hands (*cheires*) and divine power were equated (Kerenyi, 1968). According to Kirmayer (2003), "much healing occurs by touch, not only the surgeons cutting and sewing, or the manipulation and massage of physiotherapy and bodywork, but also the gentle touch of solace. In magical therapy, the combination of word and touch (*logos* and *praxis*) is essential" (p. 258). The Atharva Veda (a Hindu text) describes priests who used to touch their patients with their 10 fingers and would recite a prayer beginning "*uta deva avahitam,*" and the sins accrued to the person in his or her past life, which were responsible for the disease, were exorcised (Biswas, 2001).

2. *Bhuta vidya* dates back to 500 BC, as recorded in India's philosophical and religious literature, including the Rig-Veda ("Royal Knowledge"), the Upanishads, and the Bhagavad Gita, as well as in the tradition of yoga. The Atharva Veda, one of the Vedas, refers to devils and spirits as causes of illness and prescribes cures for them. The general belief that the cause of mental maladies lay in the supernatural reinforced the need to seek remedies in religious and magical techniques.

## ❖ REFERENCES

Ataudo, E. S. (1985). Traditional medicine and biopsychosocial fulfillment in African health. *Social Science in Medicine, 21,* 1345–1347.

Awanbar, D. (1982). The healing process in African psychotherapy. *American Journal of Psychotherapy, 35,* 206–213.

Bhugra, D., & Bhui, K. (1998). Psychotherapy for ethnic minorities: Issues, context and practice. *British Journal of Psychotherapy, 14,* 310–326.

Biswas, D. (2001). Some aspects of therapeutic science as found in the Atharvaveda. *Journal of Asiatic Society, 43*(2), 16–23.

Chen, N. N. (2003). *Breathing spaces: Qigong, psychiatry and healing in China.* New York: Columbia University Press.

Cross, W. E. (1971). The negro-to-black conversion experience: Towards a psychology of black liberation. *Black World, 20,* 13–27.

Cross, W. E. (1995). The psychology of nigrescence: Revisiting the Cross model. In J. G. Ponterotto, J. M. Casas, L. A. Suzuki, & C. M. Alexander (Eds.), *Handbook of multicultural counseling* (pp. 93–122). Thousands Oaks, CA: Sage.

Cushman, P. (1995). *Constructing the self, constructing America: A cultural history of psychotherapy.* Reading, MA: Addison-Wesley.

Eliade, M. (1964). *Shamanism: Archaic techniques of ecstasy.* Princeton, NJ: Princeton University Press.

Field, N. (1990). Healing, exorcism and object relations theory. *British Journal of Psychotherapy, 6,* 274–284.

Frazer, J. G. (1922). *The golden bough: A study in magic and religion.* London: Macmillan.

Garfield, S. L. (1986). Research on client variables in psychotherapy. In S. L. Garfield & A. E. Bergin (Eds.), *Handbook of psychotherapy and behavior change* (3rd ed., pp. 213–256). New York: Wiley.

Heber, A. S., Fleisher, W. P., Ross, C. A., & Stanwick, R. S. (1989). Dissociation in alternative healers and traditional therapists: A comparative study. *American Journal of Psychotherapy, 43,* 562–574.

Helms, J. E. (1984). Towards a theoretical explanation of the effects of race on counseling: A black and white model. *Counseling Psychologist, 12,* 153–165.

Helms, J. E. (1995). An update of Helm's white and people of color racial identity models. In J. G. Ponterotto, J. M. Casas, L. A. Suzuki, & C. M. Alexander (Eds.), *Handbook of multicultural counseling* (pp. 181–198). Thousands Oaks, CA: Sage.

Hohmann, A. A., Richeport, M., Marriott, B. M., Canino, G. J., Rubio-Stipec, M., & Bird, H. (1990). Spiritism in Puerto Rico. Results of an island-wide community study. *British Journal of Psychiatry, 156,* 328–335.

Kareem, J. (1992). The Nafsiyat Intercultural Therapy Centre: Ideas and experience in intercultural therapy. In J. Kareem & R. Littlewood (Eds.), *Intercultural therapy: Themes, interpretations and practice* (pp. 14–37). Oxford, UK: Blackwell.

Kerenyi, K. (1968). *Asklepios, archetypal image of the physician's existence.* Princeton, NJ: Princeton University Press.

Kirmayer, L. J. (2003). Asklepian dreams: The ethos of the wounded-healer in the clinical encounter. *Transcultural Psychiatry, 40,* 248–277.

Levi-Strauss, C. (1967). *Structural anthropology.* New York: Basic Books.

Majumdar, D. N. (1944). *Races and cultures of India.* London: Asia Publishing House.

Moodley, R. (1998a). Cultural returns to the subject: Traditional healing in counselling and therapy. *Changes: An International Journal of Psychology and Psychotherapy, 16*(1), 45–56.

Moodley, R. (1998b). "I say what I like": Frank talk(ing) in counseling and psychotherapy. *British Journal of Guidance and Counselling, 26,* 495–508.

Moodley, R. (1999). Challenges and transformation: Counselling in a multi-cultural context. *International Journal for the Advancement of Counselling, 17,* 109–125.

Pedersen, P. (Ed.). (1991). Multiculturalism as a fourth force in counseling [Special issue]. *Journal of Counseling Development, 70*(1).

Ponterotto, J. G., Fuertes, J. N., & Chen, E. C. (2000). Models of multicultural counseling. In S. D. Brown & R. W. Lent (Eds.), *Handbook of counseling psychology* (3rd ed., pp. 639–669). New York: John Wiley.

Rao, A. V. (1986). Indian and Western psychiatry: A comparison. In J. L. Cox (Ed.), *Transcultural psychiatry* (pp. 291–305). London: Croom Helm.

Stone, G. L. (Ed.). (1993). White American researchers and multicultural counseling. *Counseling Psychologist, 21,* 197–277.

Sue, D. (1997). Multicultural training. *International Journal of Intercultural Relations, 21,* 175–193.

Sue, D. W., Arredondo, P., & McDavis, R. J. (1992). Multicultural competencies and standards: A call to the profession. *Journal of Multicultural Counseling and Development, 20,* 64–88.

Sue, D. W., Bernier, J. E., Durran, A., Feinberg, L., Pedersen, P., Smith, E. J., et al. (1982). Position paper: Cross-cultural counseling competencies. *Counseling Psychologist, 10,* 45–52.

Tseng, W. S., & Hsu, J. (1979). Culture and psychotherapy. In J. A. Marsella, R. G. Tharp, & T. J. Ciborowski (Eds.), *Perspectives on cross-cultural psychology* (pp. 333–345). New York: Academic Press.

Tseng, W. S., & McDermott, J. F. (1975). Psychotherapy: Historical roots, universal elements, and cultural variations. *American Journal of Psychiatry, 132,* 378–384.

Vitebsky, P. (2001). *Shamanism.* Norman: University of Oklahoma Press.

Vontress, C. E. (1979). Cross-cultural counseling: An existential approach. *Personnel and Guidance Journal, 58,* 117–122.

Ward, C. A. (Ed.). (1989). *Altered states of consciousness and mental health: A cross cultural perspective.* London: Sage.

Weinrach, S. G., & Thomas, K. R. (1996). The counseling profession's commitment to diversity-sensitive counseling: A critical reassessment. *Journal of Counseling and Development, 74,* 472–477.

West, W. (2000). *Psychotherapy and spirituality: Crossing the line between therapy and religion.* London: Sage.

West, W. (2004). *Spiritual issues in therapy: Relating experience to practice.* Basingstoke, UK: Palgrave Macmillan.

Willett, C. (1998). *Theorizing multiculturalism.* Malden, MA: Blackwell.

Yarhouse, M. A., & Fisher, W. (2002). Levels of training to address religion in clinical practice. *Psychotherapy Theory/Research/Practice/Training, 39,* 171–176.

# PART I

Indigenous Performances, Cultural Worldviews, and Supernatural Healing

# 1

# Shamanic Performances

*Healing Through Magic and the Supernatural*

*Roy Moodley*

It seems that for more than 5,000 years, human beings evolved a set of complex practices that involved religion, magic, and supernatural healing. These practices were to appease the gods and goddesses, who appeared to relieve them of their pain and suffering, and to heal them of their illnesses and diseases. The reverence for and fear of a god or goddess brought health, whereas indifference or hostility brought illness and disease (Weatherhead, 1968). In most societies of the past, religion, magic, and supernatural healing were integral parts of experience, with special ceremonies and events enacted to celebrate the god or goddess. When a state of disequilibrium (illness, disease, or discomfort) was experienced, individually or collectively, help was sought through religion, magic, and supernatural healing. Whereas magic was used to negotiate on behalf of individuals with the supernatural forces, religion attempted to deal with the broader social and cultural issues confronting the community (Rosman & Rubel, 1992). This apparent distinction seems to suggest that religion and magic are separate processes, but although this may be the case in the West, elsewhere, in some other cultures, the two have always been historically connected.

Religion, for thousands of years, was usually understood to be the worship of supernatural beings, and then came Émile Durkheim, who denied that supernatural beings were essential to religion and defined religion as "a unified system of beliefs and practices relative to sacred things," a definition that had a tremendous impact on modern views on religion (Durkheim, 1912/1995, p. 44; cited in Stark, 2004). Perhaps this view also contributed to the more recent position on the separation of religion and magic, especially in the West. The concept of magic is also bedeviled by numerous definitions. According to Stark, the term *magic* "refers to all efforts to *manipulate or compel* supernatural forces *without reference to a God or Gods* or to *matters of ultimate meaning*. Put another way, magic is *limited to impersonal conceptions of the supernatural*" (Stark, p. 116). On the other hand, Whitmont (1983), a Jungian, suggests that confining the process to the supernatural "limits magic to a manipulation of force, rather than to a particular form of consciousness and dynamics. The magical consciousness historically expressed the dynamic of instinctual and affect energy in the context of a field of unitary reality" (p. 44). Understood in this way, magic suggests a "here-and-now" existence without a differentiation of past, present, and future, leading one to contest the idea that religion and magic could be connected.

In the 19th century, many leading social evolutionists thought that religion originated in magic, an idea that goes back at least to Hegel (1840/1996) and that was embraced by Spencer (1896), Frazer (1922), and others. On the other hand, Durkheim (1912/1995) and others embraced the opposite view. Stark (2004) notes that "both the ethnographic and the historical records suggest that religion and magic developed in tandem and were always recognized as different" (p. 9; see Stark for discussion). Clearly, it seems that the evolution of religion and magic (or magic and religion) and later science was part of an attempt to deal with illness and disease. According to Weatherhead (1968), it was religion that first attempted to deal with the misery of disease and suffering, whereas the science of medicine, it seems, had its roots in religion and magic. But only magic and religion depend upon the supernatural, which could be understood as essences, forces, or entities that are beyond or outside nature that can suspend, alter, or ignore physical forces (Stark).

Many have attempted to define and make sense of religion, magic, and supernatural healing (as noted above), and not least among them are the so-called khaki-clad pocket-notebook diarists, the social and cultural anthropologists (e.g., Crawley, 1902; Malinowski, 1948/1992; Taylor, 1871/1958). But it is to James George Frazer, the Scottish classicist, that I turn now to begin the discussion in this chapter. In his mammoth and extensively documented study of magic and religion, *The Golden Bough* (1922), Frazer, through the lenses of the colonial understanding of cultures and societies outside Europe, inscribes and reinscribes narratives of magic, religion, and supernatural healing. In critiquing the work for its particular assumptions and perceptions, it is not Frazer's particular view that is called into question but rather the exotic, erotic, or neurotic projections by the West toward supernatural and shamanic healing of cultures of the diaspora.[1] The second part of the chapter looks at the work of the shaman, such as hakims, *deonras, amagqiras,* obeah men and women, and others. And finally, the chapter attempts to contextualize these healers in particular places and spaces, specifically the holy shrines, marabouts, and sacred temples where they practice their particular "brands" of cultural magic, religion, and supernatural healing, sometimes in communion with ancestral spirits. But first, we turn to *The Golden Bough* and its production and textualization of the "Other."

## ❖ *THE GOLDEN BOUGH:* COLONIAL PERCEPTIONS OF MAGIC AND RELIGION

Frazer's (1922) extensive research on religion, magic, and healing of communities and societies around the world, with examples dating back historically, clearly illustrates that people from these ancient societies felt that illnesses of the body were related to the mind and the soul (see Weatherhead, 1968). Frazer's research indicated that the principles of magic were the foundations of many of the early methods used, especially homeopathic or imitative magic.[2] Through the use of positive and negative charms and the ritual of piercing needles into personal artifacts or images of the enemy (e.g., voodoo dolls), people were able to work through much of their stress and aggression.

Homeopathic or imitative magic is not practiced for spiteful purposes only but can have benevolent uses as well. An example, noted by Frazer (1922), of the Dyaks of Borneo illustrates this type of use. When a woman is experiencing difficulties in labor, a "wizard" is called in to facilitate the delivery by manipulating the body of the woman. At the same time, immediately outside the room another wizard expresses the anguish and pain of labor by imitating the woman in the room. This is achieved by means of a large stone, representing the fetus, which is wrapped around the stomach of the wizard. Although the process is perceived in terms of the reality of homeopathic or imitative magic, the wizard, paradoxically, has to experience the process in physical terms.[3]

The essential requirement for empathy in all healing processes centers on the idea of feeling with the client. The wizard, by experiencing the pain for him- or herself, makes the empathic process more concrete and emotionally possible both for him- or herself and for the patient, but operating under the guise of the metaphysical. For the patient, a fusion of both the physical and the spiritual worlds creates a unity that brings relief from pain and suffering. This kind of treatment by the wizards continues until the infant is born.[4] Crawley (1902) notes that a similar kind of process happened in the Aru Islands, but for different reasons. His research, conducted with similar lenses and much earlier than that of Frazer (1922), seems to focus simplistically on only one aspect of healing in these communities.

Frazer's (1922) research, treatment, and analysis of many of the examples, like much of the colonial writings of the time, reflect the misinformed and biased views on the social, cultural, and religious processes of people from Africa, Asia, South and Central America, and the Caribbean. This encounter with the other culture contributed not only to a particular, singular perspective that these ethnologists constructed, but to a great extent altered the historical and psychological perspectives of those communities' understanding of themselves through these researchers' chosen examples and their recording of them.

Both Frazer's (1922) and Crawley's (1902) responses to traditional healing in these societies show a strong bias toward the theory that "third-world" cultures were uncivilized and primitive. They, like the other colonial commentators of the time, appeared to offer their observations through an essentializing and Eurocentric lens that presented healing and cultural practices either as exotic or "primitive." This in effect led them to ascribe all sorts of interpretations to these people and their experiences. For these writers, the people were ignorant, naive, and superstitious and had primitive thoughts concerning these normal experiences. What seems so obvious now—but was not then to these observers of the Other cultures—was the subtle and sophisticated way in which such complicated medical matters were resolved. This invalidates the simplistic analysis of complex practices (Moodley, 1998). For example, in the case of mothers in difficult labor, Western observers concluded that the people ascribed the cause to be evil spirits and the work of the devil. Although this may be correct in terms of how the people interpreted their experiences, it has to be seen in the context of the sociocultural and religious construct that existed at the time. This is no different from many of the experiences in Europe in a much earlier period. For example,

In Medieval Europe, women who were suffering from a difficult delivery were prescribed words inscribed on communion wafers. This was the general practice where charm formula types were limited to powerful words, names and commands. Powerful names or texts were written on parchment and tied to the body as an amulet. (Olsan, 2003, p. 358)

In some cultures, the banging of drums was used to ward off the "evil spirit" that was said to be the cause of the difficult labor. It seems that externalizing the actual problem to a source that is not human but supernatural offers the possibility for intervention by the known methods and remedies of the time, that is, prayers, magical charms, and amulets.

In *Charms and Prayers in Medieval Medical Theory and Practice*, Olsan (2003) discusses the writings of four medical medieval writers; among them is a cleric and physician to King John, Gilbertus Anglicus (writing around 1200–1250). He utilized the work of Hippocrates, Galen, Avicenna, and others to create the *Compendium Medicinae*, which became a standard reference for physicians for centuries. Cures include dietary regimes, pills, powder, herb waters for baths, and others. Although prayers, charms, and amulets were used at the time, they were not included in his book[5] because he aimed to indicate a "freedom from superstition."[6] Another of these writers was John Gaddesden (ca. 1280–1349), who studied theology and medicine at Oxford and was said to have "cured Edward III of smallpox by wrapping him in a red cloth" (Olsan, 2003, p. 345). If magic, magical charms, prayers, and amulets were accepted by the lawmakers of the day, then it seems that lay members of the society would have had no difficulty in using them. It seemed that for more malignant diseases, discomfort, and distress, people used other ways to exorcise themselves of the assumed cause and origin of the problem. In some cases, it was thought to be an evil force that needed to be literally exorcised.

In this section, I referred to just one example from Frazer's (1922) colossal work but offered a critique that may appear to be ingenuous. Although criticism of Frazer's treatment is quite appropriate regarding the "politics of race and culture," he no doubt made it possible for us to "gaze upon" the complex ways in which traditional healing was experienced. Clearly, to understand the wider relevance of religion, magic, and supernatural healing, one needs a much greater knowledge not of psychology but of the elements of culture. As Steiner (1956) writes, "Frazer . . . found a method and frame of reference almost predestined to lend an air of scientific inquiry to the discussion of homoeopathic or sympathetic magic and the principles of contagion" (p. 94). Much, of course, depended on the shaman and his or her performances and the context (sometimes "played" for the benefit of a particular ethnologist) within which the rituals were conducted. It is to the shaman that we turn next.

## ❖ SHAMANS AND SUPERNATURAL HEALING

The shaman[7] or healer (also called in different cultures by other names, such as hakim,[8] *deonra*,[9] *amagqira*,[10] and obeah man or woman[11]), the client, and sometimes both are said to be possessed by a supernatural power during a therapy session. In this trancelike state, the "problem" is "interrogated," and solutions are offered by the "spirits" acting on behalf of the gods. Some of the problems that appear in the repertoire of a shaman's healing process are object intrusion, retrieval of loss of soul (Field, 1990; Majumdar, 1944), sorcery, object intrusion, spirit intrusion, violation of taboo (Majumdar; Tseng & McDermott, 1975), sudden lapses of memory, or peculiar mental symptoms without specific physical ailments (Kuper, 1960). The shaman seemingly informs the patient that the source of the problem could be a god, devil, another soul, or another person.

It seems that the shaman—by concretizing the experience such that the cause of the problem is located in an external object and outside the individual— creates the perception that the problem can be solved. The person, who is assumed to be possessed by an evil spirit, the devil, or an evil curse, is required to undergo a period of preparation and cleansing before the actual ceremony of healing and exorcism. A successful completion of the cleansing period will be followed by the next stage, the performance of specific ceremonial rituals in relation to the perceived problem. This seems to have been the case among the Ancient Greeks in their Aesculapian healing rites. People would enter the temple of healing, lie on a pallet, and sleep. It is said that the god Aesculapius would come into their dreams and perform the healing rites, advise, or heal the illness himself (see Field, 1990; Kirmayer, 2003; Tseng & Hsu, 1979; Weatherhead, 1968).[12]

Among the Indians in Natal (South Africa), in a slightly different ceremony, a similar phenomenon occurs. In this ceremony, which requires immense preparation under the guidance of the Brahman[13] (priest), the patients go into a trance, and then skewers, needles, hooks, and other instruments are inserted into their skin. In this process, the possessed group of individuals would silently walk or dance rhythmically through the crowd against a background of pipes, drums, and singing of prayer and hymns. At various intervals, attendants would pour rose water on their needled tongues and turmeric water at their feet (Kuper, 1960). Sometimes chariots are dragged by men with chains hooked into the flesh of their backs, as in the Muslim festival of Al Mohurram. A fire pit would be ready for those who needed to walk through the fire. The mantra-chanting crowds participate in this ceremony in both direct and indirect ways (Moodley, 1998). When patients "dance on nailed shoes without pain or have skewers pierced through the flesh without bleeding, or walk through fire without being burnt, or carry unusual and heavy burdens without weariness" (Kuper, 1960, p. 217), the almost-possessed crowd seems to collectively identify with the cathartic experience of the patient. In many cases, where the shaman interprets that the patient is "carrying" or "bearing" the illness for the family or group to which she or he belongs, the patient's family as part of the crowd actively participates in the ritual. Members of such a family could also receive the trance or spirit and act as interpreters where the "speaking of tongues" is experienced (Moodley, 1998).

A similar phenomenon is shared by some Western revivalist Christian denominations. At the end of what seems to be a long and intense supernaturally oriented process, the shaman would offer a solution to the problems diagnosed earlier in the treatment. In some cases, a prescription of a particular diet, a period of rest, or a repetition of the same ritual a year later would be recommended. This prayer and exorcism stage is most complex and elaborate and involves the shaman and the patient at the deepest level of unconscious activity. So it seems that not only is the individual patient's "self" healed, but also the "collective self" of the group undergoes healing. At the physiological level, a change of diet or a period away from the usual ritual of daily life seems to offer time for a readjustment of hormonal and biochemical functions. At the psychological level, the release of tension and stress and the accompanying relief contributes toward an equilibrium of the chaotic and conflicting unconscious states that the individual experiences (Moodley, 1998).

The patient receives the treatment with unquestioning faith in the power of the shaman's divine intervention. The addition of herbal medicine as an ingredient in the solution, although it could be the basis of the actual healing, is accepted in a minor way as the method in which magic, religion, and divination work. It seems that the effectiveness depends to some degree on the "experience and other qualities of the interpreter" (Tseng & McDermott, 1975, p. 379), the strength of the belief in the method, and the compliance with the treatment procedure. Successful treatment reinforces the concept and encourages further consultation and increased participation by the individual, the family, and the group. Although failures in such treatment do not discredit the process or bring it into disrepute, because it is believed that the supernatural has the power to decide whether to heal or not, failures contribute to the search for alternatives within the same method of healing or a transfer to another healer or another god with the same interlocutor. Sometimes the patient is required to go to another sacred or holy location with the same healer. This is explored next.

## ❖  HOLY SHRINES, SACRED RITUALS, AND ANCESTRAL SPIRITS

The method, nature, and location of the delivery of healing can vary depending on the type and intensity of the problem, as well as the circumstances that prevail within that particular family or community and also the quality of rapport among the healer, the patient, and the healing model used. Healing can also be conducted in the client's home by the visiting healer with the active participation of the client's family, as in the case of the practice of *hooponopono*.[14] In some cases, especially in the North African countries, therapy is conducted in special shrines, which sometimes become therapeutic villages where patients may stay for many weeks (Nemec, 1980, as cited in Moodley, 1998). The Zar cult in Ghana, Ethiopia, and Sudan and the Rab cult in Senegal (Asuni, 1986)[15] and the use of marabouts[16] in Algeria are examples of this process. Awanbar (1982) cites the Nigerian Aro village treatment center founded by Lambo[17] as an approach that blends indigenous African psychology and Western psychotherapy. This approach, which apparently is based on the "village system" of cult healing, utilizes the dynamic resources of the community, such as the cult systems mentioned above.

In comparing contemporary Western with African traditional methods, Asuni (1986) suggests that African group ritual healing is more like psychodrama and that patients let loose their feelings in the dances, songs, ceremonies, and rituals. Sometimes the patient's ailment is not removed, but he or she learns to accept it and to come to terms with it by his or her group membership, as in the case of the Zar cult. The objective in traditional healing appears, then, to be to integrate the psychological ailment in the individual and at the same time to include and reinforce his or her membership in the group. Asuni seems to believe that this is the case in African traditional healing, where "the therapist's aim is to unravel social complications while also prescribing a course of treatment" in a public way, engaging all those present (Asuni, p. 315). Ataudo (1985) refers to this approach as the "first contact medicine," which identifies with "cultural fuels" such as belief systems, customs, ancestor consultation, ancestor worship, reincarnation attitudes, behavior, and values of the culture in which it operates.

Concepts such as ancestor consultation, ancestor worship, and reincarnation were among some of the processes that evolved to resolve deep inner conflicts experienced by members of those societies. It seems that the magical power of the gods could be carried by the ancestral spirits to their human relatives so that it could heal and transform them. According to Majumdar (1944), in Indian culture, "the soul became the spirit at death and it is the spirit of the dead ancestors that evoked religious rites or propitiation" (p. 398). Buhrmann's (1986) research among the Zulu people of South Africa found that a symbiotic relationship seems to exist between the people and their ancestral spirits. The mutual protection and well-being of both the living and the dead are objectives of the encounter with the ancestors. There are a number of ways in which the ancestors communicate with the living. Buhrmann's research revealed the following ways this happens: (a) through dreams, which are regarded as fragments of reality (advice and instruction given in the dream are usually acted upon); (b) through somatic sensations and symptoms: aches and pains in the neck, shoulder, and back; disturbances in the urogenital and reproductive systems; and (c) through disturbances of procreation such as sterility, miscarriages, stillbirths, and deaths of children during infancy and early childhood.

Clearly, these signs and symptoms, which can be termed *psychosomatic,* are responses for change. It seems then that the concept of ancestor consultation has a firm base in ascertaining the level of disturbance or disease that is confronting the individual or group in that society. If the ancestors are conceived as living in and out of one's body, then it indicates that solutions to problems that the body is experiencing will be found in the voice or message of the ancestors. If the shaman is the one who experiences the psychosomatic disturbances, then his or her interpretations of the patient's illness and the subsequent "solutions" could well make the whole process magical and supernatural to the patient. So it seems that as far as the Zulu people are concerned, ancestor consultation, dream analysis, and the belief in the supernatural are different ways in which they are able to "interrogate" their illness and conflicts and maintain an equilibrium in their lives and in their society.

## ❖ CONCLUSION

Any understanding of religion, magic, and supernatural healing requires a creative and imaginative shift, suspending any logical, rational, and objective mode of thinking and going beyond the limits of science and into alchemy. It seems that each concept on its own has a certain appeal, understanding, and acceptance. However, the converging of all three can appear to be problematic, because we lack a set of vocabularies, idioms, and phrases to explain the merging of these divergent practices in modern health care.

But not so in the older societies, as Biswas (2001) notes of South Asian communities during the Vedic (ca. 1500 BC, when ayurvedic healing originated) and the pre-Vedic (Atharvadeda) periods, when people were unable to dissociate magic, medicine, and religion. Whenever they would administer medicine, they would apply it in association with spells, amulets, talismans, and recitation of mantras. In African culture, according to Awanbar (1982), the magicoreligious belief system keeps the importance and position of control in balance with the omnipotent supernatural forces on the one hand and the sociocultural and political environment on the other. This is reflected in many examples in *Black Magic: Religion and the African American Conjuring Tradition* by Yvonne Chireau (2003). She writes about the rich Hoodoo, Conjure, and root-working traditions that the slave communities engaged in. Chireau suggests that "Black Americans utilized conjuring traditions not only because they saw them as valuable resources for resistance, but because they believed that the supernatural realm offered alternative possibilities for empowerment" (p. 18).

So it seems that religion, magic, and supernatural healing not only maintain the continuity of the soul or spirit in a temporal-spatial matrix of human life form, but also organize, shape, and control the individual's physical body (and mind) so that "things do not fall apart," and the center of society is held.

❖ NOTES

1. The term *diaspora* originates from the Greek and means a scattering or sowing of seeds. Originally, it was used to refer to the dispersal of the Jews and their exile from Judea in 586 BC by the Babylonians and AD 135 by the Romans. Today, the term *diaspora* refers to any population having to leave their original homelands. The term not only refers to the people but has in recent years been used to describe the socioeconomic and cultural implications of such a dispersal (e.g., diasporic culture). In the late 20th century, *diaspora* has been used to refer to various groups who have been displaced from their land as a result of slavery, economic poverty, discrimination, or persecution (African diaspora, Irish diaspora, the Asian diaspora, the Jewish diaspora, etc.).

2. The term *homeopathic* as used by Frazer (1922) differs markedly from its modern use, which refers to the treatment of diseases by use of herbal medicines. Frazer's use concerns the principles of thought on which magic is based. There is a clear suggestion that through magic, injury or destruction can be caused to another. Although the analysis by Frazer is extremely negative, he does indicate its positive uses.

3. Two examples of the use of narrative charms from Olsan (2003) are worth citing, because they demonstrate the possibility for the patient's problems to be carried by the therapist, or in this case by a saint. The first example is the Veronica charm for chronic bleeding, such as menstrual problems. The narrative charm recalls the woman who was healed of "flux of blood" by touching the hem of Christ's garment (Matthew 9:20; Mark 5:25; Luke 8:44). The other narrative charm is the widely known prayer for toothache addressed to St. Apollonia, who was martyred after being tortured by having her teeth pulled out. Olsan suggests that "in these charms the saints' sufferings correspond to those of the patient . . . but the saints successfully overcame the problem with divine help. In each case, the patient's symptom is linked to the motif of the narrative or historiola in the charm" (p. 361).

4. Another method adopted by homeopathic or imitative magic related to the way in which the cure was experienced. The healer imitates the illness of his or her patient and performs a cure on him or herself. The patient becomes the observer of his or her own illness and cure. The observing patient in turn experiences relief by virtue of the healer's experiencing the problem. The patient, through identification with the healer, disassociates from his or her own illness and in this detached state is able to empathize with the seemingly suffering healer. This mirroring of the illness to the patient allows for the projection of the bad internalized object onto the healer, and the subsequent cathartic separating of these disturbing elements of the ego will begin the process of the reintegration of the true self (Moodley, 1998).

5. But this fact is refuted by "the Montpellier surgeon, Guy de Chauliac, [who] claims that empirical remedies and charms (*empericas et incantaciones*) which he himself 'has taken little of,' can be found in abundance (*copia invenitur multa*) in Gilbertus and the *Thesaurus pauperum*" (Olsan, 2003, p. 345).

6. Gilbertus notes that to ensure the conception of a child a particular ritual was undertaken by "the collection of a herb on the feast of John the Baptist at the third hour, accomplished by three recitations of the Lord's prayer. The juice is then extracted and words are written with the juice. The charm itself involves writing words, some biblical, on a parchment to be hung around the neck of the man or woman during intercourse. If it was hung around the man's neck, a son will be conceived, if around the woman's, a daughter" (Olsan, 2003, p. 352).

7. The word *shaman* comes from a Northern Siberian tribe, the Tungus.

8. Hakims are Muslim healers.

9. This is one of the names given to a shaman in India. The treatments that the *deonra* offers to ward off crises and diseases include *dukidanal* (an examination of the patient's urine—the changes in the color of the urine aid diagnosis) and two kinds of divination known as *daada nam* and *rum nam,* which involve reciting the names of greater and lesser gods and possession by them. Advice is offered as a process of trial and error. Herbal medicine, dietary restrictions, hygiene, and a general sense of social responsibility are prescribed for mental conflicts that afflict the patient (Majumdar, 1944).

10. *Amagqira* are traditional Xhosa healers.

11. Obeah men and women are healers from the Caribbean.

12. Aesculapius, known as the father of the art of healing (religious and scientific) in Greek mythology, was the god of medicine. The Greek Asklepios was the son of Apollo and the nymph Coronis. He learned the art of healing from Chiron, a mentor or spiritual father, who has both human and animal form (Kirmayer, 2003). The Egyptians claimed that he was apotheosized from the human magician Imhotep (which means "he comes in peace"), who worked in the court of King Zoser of the third Egyptian dynasty in 2900 BC. He was invoked as a god and was believed to visit people in their sleep and heal their pain and disease. Imhotep's name and fame passed from Egypt to Persia and then to Greece, where temples were erected to honor him. Hygeia, the daughter of Asklepios, was the Greek goddess of health and was also worshipped in the temples. Patients would sleep all night in the precincts of the temple to receive healing from either the god or the goddess via priests who were acting for them. The cult of Asklepios was introduced into Rome through the Sibylline books (293 BC) to avert a pestilence (see Weatherhead, 1968).

13. Also meaning "magical phrases" (Edwardes, 1969, p. 6).

14. The term *hooponopono* literally means "to make things right," a method practiced by Hawaiian people in dealing with conflict. After a ritual prayer to the gods, the assembled family members discuss and confront each other and resolve the problem, which is then symbolically taken and given to the sea. The therapy culminates in a banquet (Tseng & McDermott, 1975).

15. Zar cults, found in Ethiopia and Sudan, or the Rab cult, found in Senegal, are processes of folk or social therapy (Asuni, 1986). During these group therapy dances, patients tend to be spiritually elevated. The sessions can last for the duration of 3 to 7 days or, in multiples of seven, up to 3 months, depending on the established ritual practices and the severity of the illness (Awanbar, 1982, p. 209).

16. Marabouts are places occupied by a saint (living or dead) where people request help through the process of spiritual meditation. During the process of Islamization, some of these shrines were destroyed.

17. Lambo is regarded as the "father of modern psychotherapy in Africa" (Awanbar, 1982, p. 211).

## ❖ REFERENCES

Asuni, T. (1986). African and Western psychiatry: A comparison. In J. L. Cox (Ed.), *Transcultural psychiatry* (pp. 306–321). London: Croom Helm.

Ataudo, E. S. (1985). Traditional medicine and biopsychosocial fulfillment in African health. *Social Science and Medicine, 21*, 1345–1347.

Awanbar, D. (1982). The healing process in African psychotherapy. *American Journal of Psychotherapy, 36*, 206–213.

Biswas, D. (2001). Some aspects of therapeutic science as found in the Artharvadeda. *Journal of the Asiatic Society, 43*(2), 16–23.

Buhrmann, M. V. (1986). *Living in two worlds: Communication between a white healer and her black counterpart.* Chicago: Chiron.

Chireau, P. Y. (2003). *Black magic: Religion and the African American conjuring tradition.* Berkeley: University of California Press.

Crawley, E. (1902). *The mystic rose.* London: Macmillan.

Durkheim, E. (1995). *The elementary forms of religious life* (K. E. Fields, Trans.). New York: Free Press. (Original work published 1912)

Edwardes, M. (1969). *Everyday life in early India.* London: Batsford.

Field, N. (1990). Healing, exorcism and object relations theory. *British Journal of Psychotherapy, 6*, 274–284.

Frazer, J. G. (1922). *The golden bough: A study in magic and religion.* London: Macmillan.

Hegel, G. W. F. (1996). *Lectures on the philosophy of religion: Vol. 1. Introduction and the concept of religion.* Berkeley: University of California Press. (Original work published 1840)

Kirmayer, L. J. (2003). Asklepian dreams: The ethos of the wounded-healer in the clinical encounter. *Transcultural Psychiatry, 40*, 248–277.

Kuper, H. (1960). *Indian people in Natal.* Westport, CT: Greenwood.

Majumdar, D. N. (1944). *Races and cultures of India.* London: Asia Publishing House.

Malinowski, B. (1992). *Magic, science and religion.* Prospect Heights, IL: Waveland Press. (Original work published 1948)

Moodley, R. (1998). Cultural returns to the subject: Traditional healing in counselling and therapy. *Changes: An International Journal of Psychology and Psychotherapy, 16*(1), 45–56.

Olsan, L. T. (2003). Charms and prayers in medieval theory and practice. *Social History of Medicine, 16*, 343–366.

Rosman, A., & Rubel, P. G. (1992). *The tapestry of culture: An introduction to cultural anthropology* (4th ed.). New York: McGraw-Hill.

Spencer, H. (1896). *Principles of sociology* (2nd ed.). New York: D. Appleton.

Stark, R. (2004). *Exploring the religious life.* Baltimore: Johns Hopkins University Press.

Steiner, F. (1956). *Taboo.* Middlesex, UK: Penguin Books.

Taylor, E. (1958). *Religion in primitive culture.* New York: Harper. (Original work published 1871)

Tseng, W. S., & Hsu, J. (1979). Culture and psychotherapy. In J. A. Marsella, R. G. Tharp, & T. J. Ciborowski (Eds.), *Perspectives on cross-cultural psychology* (pp. 333–345). New York: Academic Press.

Tseng, W. S., & McDermott, J. F. (1975). Psychotherapy: Historical roots, universal elements, and cultural variations. *American Journal of Psychiatry, 132,* 378–384.

Weatherhead, L. D. (1968). *Psychology, religion and healing.* London: Hodder & Stoughton.

Whitmont, E. C. (1983). *Return of the Goddess: Femininity, aggression and the modern grail quest.* London: Routledge & Kegan Paul.

# 2

# Aboriginal Worldview of Healing

*Inclusion, Blending, and Bridging*[1]

*Anne Poonwassie and Ann Charter*

The need for recognition and acceptance of Aboriginal healing methods has been expressed by many Aboriginal and non-Aboriginal authors (e.g., E. Duran & B. Duran, 1995; Krosgrud Miley, O'Melia, & DuBois, 1995; Minor, 1992; V. Morrisette, McKenzie, & L. Morrisette, 1993; Regnier, 1995). Aboriginal peoples in North America have ancient cultures, specific philosophical foundations and practices that continue to provide them with guidance in everyday life. In their healing process, these imperatives provide guidance to those who experience intellectual, physical, psychological, emotional, or spiritual distress—individually, in a family, or in a community. The purpose of this chapter is to provide some understanding of these foundations and practices and to offer some frameworks and practical suggestions for working with Aboriginal clients. The context of the chapter is based predominantly on the Canadian prairies; however, the core principles relevant to the empowering approaches discussed here can be loosely generalized to other regions. Consultation with Elders and traditional teachers in other regions is imperative to understand subtle regional differences.

## ❖ HISTORICAL CONTEXT

Prior to contact with European cultures and colonizers, indigenous nations in North America had social, political, economic, and cultural structures that emerged from their specific worldviews (Charter, Hart, & Pompana, 1996; Hamilton & Sinclair, 1991; Miller, 1997). Most of these structures and perspectives were gradually eroded or replaced through structural and cultural colonization (Kellough, 1980). North American governments utilized the educational system to undermine the tribal system, social organization, religion, health systems, forms of leadership, and economic systems of the Aboriginal peoples. In Canada, for example, these groups found themselves dependent upon provincial services, such as welfare, health care, and education, as well as the federal government, to pay for these services (Tobias, 1990).

The loss of social and kinship structures—including gender, parenting, and social role models—has resulted in a sense of anomie and nemesis for many Aboriginal peoples (Charter et al., 1996; Miller, 1997). In turn, those negative influences have resulted in the marginalization and clientization of these groups in contemporary society (Charter et al.). Systemic racism in social, medical, and educational systems continues to reinforce the assimilation and integration of Aboriginal peoples into the general North American population. Despite overwhelming social, political, economic, and cultural domination and continual interference from North American governments and institutions, Aboriginal peoples have managed to maintain core aspects of their cultures and continue the process of reclaiming autonomy and self-government.

## ❖ WORLDVIEWS

Worldviews emerge from the totality of peoples' social, political, economic, cultural, and spiritual perceptions and beliefs. Ermine (1995) defines Aboriginal and Western worldviews as "diametric trajectories in the realm of knowledge" (p. 101). He describes Aboriginal worldviews as founded on a search for meaning from a metaphysical, implicit, subjective journey for knowledge based on the premises of "skills that promote personal and social transformation; a vision of social change that leads to harmony with rather than control over the environment; and the attribution of a spiritual dimension to the environment" (p. 102).

He contrasts it with the Western worldview of the physical, explicit, scientific, and objective journey for knowledge. Ermine draws upon Engels's (1893/1902) concept of false consciousness and writes, "The Western world has capitulated to a dogmatic fixation on power and control at the expense of authentic insights into the nature and origin of knowledge as truth" (p. 102). It is not surprising that the two worldviews often clash with one another.

"At a fundamental cultural level, the difference between traditional Aboriginal and Western thought is the difference in the perception of one's relationship with the universe and the Creator" (Hamilton & Sinclair, 1991, p. 20). Christian European Canadians believed that they were meant to dominate the earth and its creatures. The Aboriginal peoples believed that they were the least important creatures of the universe and that they were dependent upon the four elements (fire, water, earth, and air) and all of creation for survival (Hamilton & Sinclair). For many Aboriginal peoples today, this belief system continues to be the framework within which they live their lives. Others do not accept traditional worldviews any longer, and some are in the process of returning to traditional ways, seeking meaning and harmony in their lives.

Traditional philosophies are presented by Elders and traditional teachers via the Medicine Wheel in conjunction with many diverse ceremonies (Charter, 1994; Regnier, 1995). Cultural imperatives are learned, integrated, and applied as a result of learning traditional teachings, participating in ceremonies, and seeing the modeling of appropriate behaviors in everyday life.

## ❖ MEDICINE WHEEL

Traditional Aboriginal peoples perceive life as a gift from the Creator. They understand that they have a responsibility to nurture and care for that gift at a personal and collective level. They were also granted medicines, sacred ceremonies, Elders, traditional healers or medicine people, and sacred teachings such as the Medicine Wheel to help maintain or restore life to balance and harmony. A good life, or good health, is perceived to be a "balance of physical, mental, emotional and spiritual elements. All four interact together [to] form a strong, healthy person. If we neglect one of these elements we get out of balance and our health suffers in all areas" (Malloch, 1989, p. 106).

The Medicine Wheel, the Wheel of Life, the Circle of Life, and the Pimaatisiwin Circle are symbolic expressions of similar, ancient, and sacred Aboriginal concepts; they are the philosophical foundations from which similar cultural imperatives emerge. These concepts are symbolic, cyclical interpretations of life and universal connectedness that provide a means for individuals to make sense of their world (J. Bopp, M. Bopp, Brown, & Lane, 1985). Regnier (1995) states that the symbolism represents unity, interdependence, and harmony among all beings in the universe and identifies time as the continual recurrence of natural patterns.

Williams (1989) prefers the Anishinabe (Ojibwa) term *Pimaatisiwin Wheel,* and she describes "the search for pimaatisiwin" as "the aim and hope of living a Good Life on this Earth" (p. 49). Her description of the Pimaatisiwin Wheel includes the following: The four directions—North, East, South, and West—are represented, respectively, by the colors white, red, yellow, and blue. Within these colors are the four races: the White Race, the Red Race, the Yellow Race, and the Black Race; the four Life-givers: air, food, sun, and water; the four seasons: winter, spring, summer, and fall; the four vices: greed, apathy, jealousy, and resentment; and the four moral principles: caring, vision, patience, and reasoning. The North gives us the rocks, which speak to us of strength. The East gives us the animals, which talk to us about sharing. From the South we receive trees, which teach us about honesty, and from the West we are given the grasses, which teach us about kindness. All things in this Life were, and are, given to us by the Mother of us all, the Earth.

Healing—the quest for balance and restoration of harmony—is understood to include either three aspects of the person—the body, mind, and spirit (Williams, 1989)—or four aspects of a person—the physical, the emotional, the intellectual, and the spiritual (Absalon, 1993; J. Bopp et al., 1985; Regnier, 1995). These teachings are both secular and spiritual and are interwoven to include all aspects of life.

The Medicine Wheel philosophy includes all stages of human development, from birth to death and rebirth. It connects all stages with each other, with all living beings, and with all life in the universe, thus providing a place of centering for each person in the cosmos (J. Bopp et al., 1985). An understanding of the Medicine Wheel is a starting point for helpers as well as those seeking healing. An underlying principle that emerges from the Medicine Wheel is that each person travels around the circle of life at his or her own pace and with personal levels of understanding as a result of his or her experiences.

## ❖ CULTURAL IMPERATIVES

All traditional Aboriginal cultures have specific cultural imperatives that influence their actions and beliefs. Because of the diversity of indigenous nations, there is a diversity in the order of importance of cultural imperatives; however, there is a common base of values that should not be indiscriminately applied to all indigenous nations (Hamilton & Sinclair, 1991). Developing an in-depth understanding and respect for the values, beliefs, and practices of Aboriginal peoples in a specific geographical area is vital to support. Such values as "non-interference, sharing, non-competitiveness, acceptance of responsibility for one's actions, the distancing of problems, and acknowledgment of the wisdom of all are expressed through the Medicine Wheel teachings" (Charter, 1994, p. 4; see also Good Tracks, 1989). In addition, these cultural imperatives are reinforced through ceremonies, teachings, and behaviors of Elders, traditional medicine men and women, family members, and community role models and norms. The methods used by Aboriginal communities today frequently reflect traditional approaches to supporting and healing their members.

## ❖ TRADITIONAL APPROACHES TO SUPPORT AND HEALING

It is important to understand that there are no "fixed" Aboriginal approaches to support and healing. Rather, each nation or cultural grouping identifies its own healers and defines its healing process (Malloch, 1989). Generally, however, the approaches to healing have emerged from cultural imperatives, and these values have remained intact and accepted by individuals and tribal groupings. Storytelling, teaching and sharing circles, participation in ceremonies, role modeling, the sweat lodge, and the vision quest are among traditional Aboriginal approaches to helping and healing.

## ❖ STORYTELLING

Storytelling is one of the most effective and influential ways of incorporating many cultural values into the helping process (Charter, 1994; Dion Buffalo, 1990; Tafoya, 1989). It provides a venue for sharing information and noninterfering problem solving; it helps the listener understand how to accept responsibility for his or her actions and how to acknowledge the wisdom of others; and it is noncompetitive and noncoercive.

Dion Buffalo (1990) discusses the importance of storytelling from a Plains Cree healing perspective, asserting that "healing through stories is but one aspect of synthesizing our relationship with ourselves and with the entire universe" (p. 120). She adds:

The storyteller is a healer or synergizer within an Indian community whose function is to produce sound-words for the listeners so that constricted energy can be released. The synergizer uses picture words to awaken in the listeners the awareness that they have within themselves all the elements necessary for their own healing. Synergizers are also the seed bearers; they plant images in our consciousness that take root and flower. A seed-thought is the conscious impression that comes into being that liberates our mind and livens our imagination. Seed-thoughts have transformation energy because they surprise our consciousness into a new way of seeing. Storytelling is the vehicle used by synergizers to communicate seed-thoughts. (Dion Buffalo, p. 120)

## ❖ PARTICIPATION IN CEREMONIES

Most Aboriginal nations hold traditional ceremonies. However, not all Aboriginal people participate in or accept the validity of traditional ceremonies as a component of life or healing. In accordance with traditional values, respect is afforded to those who do not choose a traditional path to healing. Participation in traditional ceremonies is a personal choice that is not to be influenced by coercion of any form. Such ceremonies are considered to be a part of healing in contemporary Aboriginal societies, because they either confirm or reconnect Indigenous Peoples with their ancestral roots and belief systems (Hart, 1997; McCormick, 1994).

Traditional ceremonies may include attendance or participation in sun dances, medicine lodges, fasts, sweats, sharing circles, talking circles, pipe ceremonies, moon ceremonies, giveaways, or potlatches. Participation is at the level and degree with which the participant is comfortable. However, in some ceremonies, in addition to developing a deeper spiritual understanding of oneself and how one is connected to the universe, individuals or the community may be developing specific attributes such as courage, confrontation of personal fears, or meeting difficult personal goals. Participation in these ceremonies often requires major physical, emotional, intellectual, and spiritual sacrifices. These sacrifices are not only for the development of the individual but also for the healing of the community.

These ceremonies, in addition to many others, help confirm indigenous cultures in a variety of ways. Ceremonies are the means and the method for establishing social networks, connecting with the natural environment, reconnecting personally and anchoring oneself, helping others and being helped by them in return, developing a sense of spiritual connectedness, learning traditional teachings, and storytelling. Attendance and participation in traditional ceremonies provide opportunities to practice some of the most sacred values, such as sharing, caring, and honesty, and to develop a sense of spiritual connectedness.

Ceremonies have been introduced into urban settings as a result of (a) urbanization, (b) the natural evolution of traditional cultures in a contemporary context, and (c) social problems and issues that have resulted from past and current social influences. The need for ceremonies for urban Aboriginal peoples is growing rapidly as they relocate from home communities to urban centers in order to meet personal and professional goals.

Hart (1997) reviews 15 family violence projects "conceived, developed and implemented by Aboriginal people" (p. 5), several of which were based in the largest urban centers in Canada. He notes that the core components of these projects were characterized by the valuing of tradition and culture; inclusion of Elders; connectedness; restoration of balance; an attitude of caring; a preference for forgiveness rather than punishment; a sense of equality; nurturing and mutually respectful relationships; acceptance of the client as a whole person; and a need for a holistic connection of the body, mind, and spirit.

## ❖ ISSUES IN COUNSELING AND THERAPY WITH ABORIGINAL CLIENTS

Ideally, all communities would have adequate local resources to provide counseling and therapy services for all community members. That is not the reality for most Aboriginal communities, and not all Aboriginal clients have access to Aboriginal helpers. "Ethnic matching" is not always possible, and it does not eliminate all value conflicts (Merali, 1999, p. 30). Merali notes that counselors and therapists must develop the understanding and the skills to work effectively with clients from different cultures.

D. W. Sue and D. Sue (1990) suggest that an effective and helpful counselor will use a process that is consistent with the client's values, life experiences, and culturally conditioned communication and will work with the client to define suitable goals. Techniques for facilitating empowerment include accepting the individual's definition of the problem, building upon his or her identified strengths, analyzing with the individual his or her power in the situation, teaching needed skills, and collaboratively mobilizing resources and advocating for the individual (Gutierrez, 1990).

Both Aboriginal and non-Aboriginal helpers must also understand that many "Native American clients have been so acculturated that many times the focus of the therapy is merely to reconnect them to a traditional system of beliefs and make sense of their lifeworld from a traditional perspective" (E. Duran & B. Duran, 1995, p. 19). For some Aboriginal clients, decolonization may include the validation of traditional and cultural practices, if they wish to return to those value and belief systems. Others, however, may no longer value traditional approaches because of assimilation or personal choice (Charter et al., 1996; V. Morrissette et al., 1993). This may also apply to Aboriginal counselors and therapists who have been trained or educated in non-Aboriginal systems. In order to begin to meet the needs of all Aboriginal clients, it is important to identify the critical components of the counseling process or method that help facilitate decolonization and empowerment.

Counselors and therapists who work in cross-cultural settings must also (a) be aware of the sociopolitical factors that affect the client, (b) understand that culture and language may present barriers in the counseling process, (c) acknowledge that feeling different may influence the client's openness to change, (d) emphasize the importance of worldviews and cultural identity in the counseling process, (e) understand cultural and communication style differences among various groups, and (f) become aware of one's own cultural biases and assumptions (D. W. Sue & D. Sue, 1990).

## ❖ BRIDGING OF THERAPEUTIC APPROACHES

The need for bridging of Aboriginal and Western therapeutic approaches has long been recognized by Aboriginal leaders and Elders, as well as by contemporary Aboriginal and non-Aboriginal authors. Many decades ago, Chief Sitting Bull advised his people, "Take what is good from the White Man and let's make a better life for our children" (quoted in E. Duran & B. Duran, 1995, p. 19), and Shingwauk asked for teaching lodges so that the children of his people could learn to survive in a changing world (Miller, 1997). Today, many Aboriginal and non-Aboriginal authors, as well as practitioners, strongly advocate for the recognition, acceptance, and inclusion of Aboriginal cultural and spiritual healing practices in general Canadian society. They assert that Aboriginal peoples have practiced effective healing methods for centuries and that these methods are as valid as Western therapeutic modalities. They continue to be proven, viable, balanced, harmonious, and holistic approaches to living, healing, and helping (Absalon, 1993; Mignone, O'Niel, & Wilkie, 2003; Minor, 1992; Regnier, 1995).

In bridging therapeutic approaches, counselors and therapists must consider modalities that are client centered (least intrusive) and holistic (incorporating the mind, body, spirit, and emotions). Rice (2003) points out that indigenous healing practices center on the psychospiritual domain of personality. Rice suggests that existential and transpersonal approaches that deal with the implicit rather than the explicit self must be seriously considered as appropriate and viable alternatives in the helping process. An example of such a technique is focusing-oriented psychotherapy, a client-centered approach to healing based on humanistic principles. Focusing facilitates access to the deepest level of spiritual awareness in the body, where unresolved problems and issues can be sensed implicitly and where they can be resolved gently and completely (Gendlin, 1981, 1996). It is a holistic and a deeply spiritual process that allows clients to have total control of the pace and direction of their healing journey.

The focusing movements resonate with the wisdom of a traditional Aboriginal vision quest, one of ancient indigenous personal growth, development, and healing practices. Although experiential approaches such as focusing are considered relatively contemporary, they bring the "evolution" of therapeutic approaches full circle, back to the indigenous values of respect and noninterference and back to the ancient wisdom of connecting the mind with the body, the spirit, and the emotions. Aboriginal communities, faced with the need to resolve a legacy of multigenerational trauma brought on by years of colonization and culturally inappropriate and damaging interventions, find approaches such as focusing familiar, helpful, and effective (Poonwassie & Charter, 2001; Turcotte, 1998, 2002).

## ❖ CONCLUSION

Aboriginal peoples have long argued that the solutions that have originated from within their own cultures have been "more effective than the disastrous 'solutions' imposed by the majority culture" (Couture, 1987, p. 184). Initiatives that originate in Aboriginal communities and that espouse those communities' worldviews, cultural imperatives, and traditional approaches have proven to be most successful in meeting their peoples' holistic health needs and in facilitating change.

Counselors who collaborate with Aboriginal communities in healing initiatives must incorporate Aboriginal peoples into their work, including traditional resources as needed and utilizing holistic and implicit modalities. They must critically examine their role as experts and be prepared to relinquish control and learn, understand, and accept realities and worldviews other than their own (Borg, Brownlee, & Delaney, 1995). We present these ideas in the spirit of sharing and respect.

## ❖ NOTE

1. This chapter is adapted with permission from Poonwassie, A. and Charter, A. (2001). An Aboriginal Worldview of Helping: Empowering Approaches. *Canadian Journal of Counselling, 56*(1), 63–74.

## ❖ REFERENCES

Absalon, K. (1993). *Healing as practice: Teachings from the medicine wheel* (Paper commissioned for the WUNSKA network). Ottawa, Ontario, Canada: Canadian Association of Schools of Social Work.

Bopp, J., Bopp, M., Brown, L., & Lane, P. (1985). *The sacred tree.* Lethbridge, Alberta, Canada: University of Lethbridge.

Borg, D., Brownlee, K., & Delaney, R. (1995). Postmodern social work practice with Aboriginal people. In R. Delaney & K. Brownlee (Eds.), *Northern social work practice* (pp. 505–514). Thunder Bay, Ontario, Canada: Lakehead University.

Charter, G. A. (1994). *A Medicine Wheel approach to working with men who batter* (Paper commissioned for the WUNSKA network). Ottawa, Ontario, Canada: Canadian Association of Schools of Social Work.

Charter, G. A., Hart, M., & Pompana, Y. (1996). *Aboriginal people and social work.* Winnipeg, Manitoba, Canada: University of Manitoba, Continuing Education Division.

Couture, J. E. (1987). What is fundamental to Native education? Some thoughts on the relationship between thinking, feeling and learning. In L. L. Stewin & J. H. McCann (Eds.), *Contemporary and educational issues: The Canadian mosaic* (pp. 178–191). Mississauga, Ontario, Canada: Copps, Clark & Pitman.

Dion Buffalo, Y. R. (1990). Seeds of thought, arrows of change: Native story telling as metaphor. In T. A. Laidlaw, C. Malmo, & Associates (Eds.), *Healing voices* (pp. 118–142). San Francisco: Jossey-Bass.

Duran, E., & Duran, B. (1995). *Introduction: Native American postcolonial psychology.* Albany: State University of New York Press.

Engels, F. (1902). *The mark.* New York: New York Labor News Company. (Original work published 1893)

Ermine, W. (1995). Aboriginal epistemology. In M. Battiste & J. Barman (Eds.), *First Nations education in Canada: The circle unfolds* (pp. 101–112). Vancouver, British Columbia, Canada: University of British Columbia Press.

Gendlin, E. T. (1981). *Focusing.* New York: Bantam Books.

Gendlin, E. T. (1996). *Focusing-oriented psychotherapy: A manual of the experiential method.* New York: Guilford Press.

Good Tracks, J. G. (1989). Native American non-interference. In D. R. Burgest (Ed.), *Social work practice with minorities* (2nd ed., pp. 30–35). Metuchen, NJ: Scarecrow Press.

Gutierrez, L. M. (1990). Working with women of color: An empowerment perspective. *Social Work, 35,* 149–153.

Hamilton, A. C., & Sinclair, C. M. (1991). *Aboriginal concepts of justice: Vol. 1. Report of the Aboriginal justice inquiry of Manitoba: The justice system and Aboriginal people.* Winnipeg, Manitoba, Canada: Queen's Printer.

Hart, R. (1997). *Beginning a long journey.* Ottawa, Ontario, Canada: Minister of Public Works and Government Services; Health Canada, National Clearinghouse on Family Violence, Family Violence Prevention Division.

Kellough, G. (1980). From colonialism to economic imperialism: The experience of the Canadian Indian. In J. Harp & J. Hofley (Eds.), *Structured inequality in Canada* (pp. 343–377). Scarborough, Ontario, Canada: Prentice Hall.

Krosgrud Miley, K., O'Melia, M., & DuBois, B. L. (1995). *Generalist social work practice: An empowering approach.* Needham Heights, MA: Allyn & Bacon.

Malloch, L. (1989). Indian medicine, Indian health: Study between red and white medicine. *Canadian Women Studies, 10*(2 & 3), 105–113.

McCormick, R. (1994). *The facilitation of healing for the First Nations people of British Columbia.* Unpublished master's thesis, University of British Columbia, Vancouver, British Columbia, Canada.

Merali, N. (1999). Resolution of value conflict in multicultural counselling. *Canadian Journal of Counselling, 33,* 28–36.

Mignone, J., O'Niel, J., & Wilkie, C. (2003). *Mental health services review: First Nations and Inuit health branch, Manitoba region.* Winnipeg, Manitoba, Canada: University of Manitoba Centre for Aboriginal Health Research.

Miller, J. R. (1997). *Shingwauk's vision: A history of native residential schools.* Toronto, Ontario, Canada: University of Toronto Press.

Minor, K. (1992). *Issumatuq: Learning from the traditional healing wisdom of Canadian Inuit.* Halifax, Nova Scotia, Canada: Fernwood.

Morrissette, V., McKenzie, B., & Morrissette, L. (1993). Towards an Aboriginal model of social work practice. *Canadian Social Work Review, 10,* 91–108.

Poonwassie, A., & Charter, A. (2001). Counselling of Aboriginal students: Bridging of conflicting worldviews. In K. P. Binda & S. Calliou (Eds.), *Aboriginal education in Canada: A study in decolonization* (pp. 121–136). Mississauga, Ontario, Canada: Canadian Educators' Press.

Regnier, R. (1995). The sacred circle: An aboriginal approach to healing education at an urban high school. In M. L. Battiste & J. Barman (Eds.), *First Nations education in Canada: The circle unfolds* (pp. 313–329). Vancouver, British Columbia, Canada: University of British Columbia Press.

Rice, B. (2003). Articulating Aboriginal paradigms: Implications for Aboriginal social work practice. *Native Social Work Journal, 5,* 87–97.

Tafoya, T. (1989). Circles and cedar: Native Americans in family therapy. *Journal of Psychotherapy and the Family, 6,* 71–98.

Sue, D. W., & Sue, D. (1990). *Counselling the culturally different: Theory and practice.* Toronto, Ontario, Canada: John Wiley & Sons.

Tobias, J. L. (1990). Protection, civilization, assimilation: An outline of Canada's Indian policy. In J. R. Miller (Ed.), *Sweet promises: A reader on Indian-White relations in Canada* (pp. 127–144). Toronto, Ontario, Canada: University of Toronto Press.

Turcotte, S. (1998). The mission of the Pacific Centre for Focusing. *The Folio: A Journal for Focusing and Experiential Therapy, 16,* 1–4.

Turcotte, S. (2002, March). *Impact of family violence on individuals, families and communities: Issues and approaches to treatment.* Keynote address presented at "Impact of Family Violence on Individuals, Families and Communities: Issues and Approaches to Treatment," University of Manitoba, Winnipeg, Manitoba, Canada.

Williams, A. (1989). The spirit of my quilts. *Canadian Women Studies, 10,* 49–51.

# 3

# The *Djinns*

## *A Sophisticated Conceptualization of Both Pathologies and Therapies*[1]

*Tobie Nathan*

This chapter attempts to convey the popular and clinical implications of the use of the concept *djinn*.

*Djinns* could be defined as invisible beings capable of occupying the body and controlling the psychological functioning of a person or a family with the goal of obtaining a compensation from human beings. This compensation can take the form of an offering, a sacrifice, an altar, or even a cult. *Djinn* is an Arabic word derived from a prolific root.

## ❖ *DJINN*: RELATED WORDS

### Uterus

*Janna* is the womb, the uterus, the internal space where fertility originates, and is therefore probably associated with the earth. *Djinns* come from both the belly and the earth; they arise from women and spring forth from gardens. The word *janna* evokes the mystery of fecundity. What is it, in the earth, that makes plants grow? What is it, in a woman's uterus, that allows the fetus to develop? *Janna* refers not only to the container but also to the principle that acts from within—a force necessarily hidden. *Djinn*, first and foremost, refers to an "invisible being" (Guedmi, 1984).

## Madness

In Arabic, as in other Semitic languages, the plural of a word signifies a general concept. For instance, the word *lailat* means "nights" or, more accurately, the concept of *night*. It is associated with the Hebrew mythical figure Lilith. In essence, it is the night personified. The plural of *djinn, jenoun,* or *jnoun* yields *junan* or *jenan*, which means "madness." This implies a compelling idea clinicians should reflect upon: "To know every single *djinn* would make one the master of madness." And how can one come to know every *djinn*? By treating the insane!

## "Indjinned"

*Majnoun* means to be under the control of a *djinn*—to be "indjinned."[2] It is commonly used to refer to madness, with all the allusive, derogatory, ludicrous, and insulting connotations that are associated with it.

## Fetus

*Janin,* "the fetus," is the product or tenant of the *janna*. The fetus is as much the tenant of the womb as the *djinn* is of the woman it possesses. *Janin* also means "little *djinn*," probably because the fetus is always hidden—the *djinn* is hidden in the night and in the earth in the same way a fetus is hidden in the womb. *Janin*—both fetus and little *djinn*—reminds us also that without the help of *djinns*, human beings could not reproduce. And we know how prone these invisible beings are to appear to pregnant women (Nathan & Moro, 1989).

## Garden

*Jénéna* means "garden," the place of all the *jnoun* (plural of *djinn*), of all the active and hidden principles, where the constant work of these invisible forces is most manifest. *Jénéna*, the garden, is a paradise for *jnoun*.

## Paradise

The word *jennat* can be translated as "paradise." This is probably associated with the idea that once we arrive in heaven, the secret of trees—not only the secret of the tree of knowledge, but of all the trees, hence of all the *jnoun*—will be revealed to us. It is the place where all *jnoun* are visible.

## Cadaver

*Janan* means both "cadaver" and "tomb," where the unceasing activity of the dead, resulting from metamorphoses of the world of the living, manifests. Thus, it is not surprising to hear that cemeteries house *jnoun*. And according to the Quran, *jnoun* feed on bones.

## ❖ *JNOUN'S* ECOLOGY

Although they live "in the hidden world" and also in gardens, deserts, forests, bushes, garbage piles, ruins, sewage pipes, and the blood of animals (I even heard of a *djinn* that had settled inside the mechanism of a watch!), *jnoun* are similar to humans. There are males and females, and they reproduce through sexual activity. However, little is known of their mating behaviors.

They may also have a religious affiliation. The Muslim *jnoun* are the least dangerous of all, because it is possible to negotiate with them by invoking Allah's name. Christians *jnoun* are more difficult but less so than Jewish *jnoun,* who are almost beyond hope. As for pagan *jnoun* (*kafrin*), they are the most feared because of their deafness to Muslim "arguments" and because they are the most violent of all. A diagnosis of a *Kafar* ("pagan") *djinn* always indicates fear for the patient's life.

The *jnoun* are thus invisible beings whose existence is largely accepted, including by the Prophet, who converted several tribes. From a historical and cultural standpoint, *jnoun* is a generic term undoubtedly referring to the divinities of the populations converted to Islam prior to their conversion (similar to how descriptions of "the devil" referred to the pagan practices of the Christianized populations in Europe). Nevertheless, more than 12 centuries after Islamization, the *jnoun* are still present not only in the countries of Maghreb, but also in Arabia, in Yemen, in Somalia, in Djibouti, in India, in Pakistan, and in all of Africa. They are still there when it comes to interpreting the negativities of existence, and they often constitute the soul of traditional therapeutic practices.

### ❖ OTHER NAMES

**Stranger–Visitor**

Instead of the word *djinn,* the words *afritt* and *zar* are used in Egypt and in Sudan. In my understanding, the *affrit* differs from the *djinn* by its location. An *afritt* is not a garden being like the *djinn* but a water being who likes to hide in the whirlpool of the Nile.

The word *zar* in Arabic, Amharic, and Hebrew is always embedded within a chain of meaning around the concepts of "stranger" or "visitor." *Jnoun* are radically different from us humans—not our fellow men, yet still our brothers, brothers of a different species, made of a different substance.

The *zars* are feared strangers to whom we offer our bodies with the hope of understanding them, much in the same way men have intercourse with women in order to understand women's logic, and women with men to untangle men's sexuality. Thanks to *zars,* we learn of another species' way of knowing.

Merchants are the most likely people to encounter *jnoun. Jnoun* appear wherever strangers are bound to meet one another, such as at the *souk*—the market. Evidently, they abound in metropolitan cities. A Malian healer asked me once, "How can you treat patients in Paris; there are so many *jnoun* there!"

The words are not equivalent, however. In each case, a universe emerges in the background: *Djinn* calls forth the invisible, *zar* calls forth the stranger, and *afrit* the whirlpool.

**Winds**

Another interesting series of words is derived from *Ria',* which has the same meaning as *jnoun* but evokes very different associations. The singular word *ri'ha* means "smell," *ri'h* means "breathe, wind," and *ro'h* refers to the soul (in Hebrew, *roua'h*). The life of a human being, his or her identity, is associated with the breathing, the specific smell that emanates from him or her. We understand thus that the Ethiopian and Sudanese masters of *zars* are masters of perfumes. For them, healing means changing a person's smell, the sign of the active principle that makes a living being. This active principle is hidden in the blood. The specialists of *zar* seem to have acquired its mastery in order to use the blood animals. First, the animal principle must be removed before introducing the perfume, the soul reconstructed by the master of the soul, professor of perfumes.

**Landlords**

*Melk,* used for example by the *gnaouas* in Morocco, refers to "landlord." It is close in significance to *malek,* "the king" (in Hebrew, *melekh*). The concept suggests a world so full of landlords that if we could see them, we would not dare to set a foot on the ground for the fear of trampling one, a world far from the one suggested by modern republics composed of citizens transparent to themselves and autonomous! We should consider the gathering rites of *melk* as a sophisticated form of democracy, a parliament of the invisibles that allows us to summon the owners to whom we belong. We can indeed pretend to be emancipated, yet those thoughts that cross our minds or the mood that suddenly overwhelms us remind us that we are the property of interests whose intentions are very difficult to decipher, even for ourselves.

## Master

In Hebrew, the word *ba'al* signifies "landlord," but also suggests master and husband. We can say "your *ba'al*," to signify "your husband," but the "*ba'al*" are the gods of the past, those animal gods with whom, according to the Bible, people committed so many immoral acts.

What the *jnoun* do to humans today is precisely what was depicted in the Mesopotamian, Babylonian, and Canaanite cults to the *ba'als*: copulation with divinities, service, and sacrificial offerings. Interestingly, there are also similarities with Beninese descriptions of their relationships with their Voodoo divinities: for example, *voduno*, "slave of the *vodún*," and *vodúnsi*, "priestess of the *vodún*" or "the *vodún*'s spouse." If we want a correct rendition of the word *ba'al*, we have to combine "master," "landlord," and "husband," as well as "force" and "animal." These are all characteristics that we find in reference to demons in the Bible.

## Demons

In Hebrew, *shed* (plural *shedim*) can be translated into "demon." But the same word in Arabic, *shed,* means "the force" and "to pull." We find the same root in Hebrew, in one of God's names, the one referring to His strength—*el shaddai,* "The Almighty."

## S'hur

Spells are profoundly connected to *jnoun*. No one can cast a spell on someone without the help of a *djinn*; conversely, no one can undo a spell without penetrating the world of *jnoun*. A person can be the target of a *s'hur* as a result of a spiteful act perpetrated against him or her, either by someone jealous or envious who made himself or herself the magical object—the *s'hur*—destined to destroy the victim or by a *sh'har,* a "sorcerer," enlisted to achieve this goal. The symptoms of such an affliction can range from feelings of apathy and weakness to a madness episode.

The *s'hur* refers both to the action of the sorcerer and the object by which the sorcerer achieves his goals. The efficacy of the *s'hur*, demonstrated by an infinite number of testimonies, is unquestionable. What remains to be understood, however, is the concrete processes through which they affect people (on the same topic, see Mauss, 1902, especially his discussion of the notion of Mana).

## ❖ ECOLOGY OF *DJINNS*

An attack by a *djinn* is a complex event. The vocabulary and therapies used carry many meanings that are sometimes contradictory.

### Quranic Therapies

Quranic therapists (*cheikh, fkih,* or *taleb*) do not negotiate with the *djinn,* because doing so would entail associating oneself with pagan forces. Instead, they pray, call forth God, and threaten or beat the *djinn* in order to get it to leave. This can be equated to an exorcism.

A North African patient describes the treatment a *taleb* provided to his son:

He takes the thumb of the child and prays until the child falls. He throws water with the Koran on the woman or the man, and the devil can come out. He speaks with the devil. The devil who took my son went to his place, not in a dream but in reality! He even appeared to my wife and said to her: "You have hurt me and the child." He started calling forth his own, the other devils.

### Congregations of Possessed

Other therapies, often practiced by women, seek to tame the *djinn.* Here, the sick one is initiated into a congregation, a *zaouia.* These patients are future seers suffering from an initiatory illness. The therapeutic rite is a sort of religious ritual.[3]

### Therapists Associated With *Djinns* by Personal Contracts

A third category includes therapists who have at their service auxiliary spirits (also *jnoun*) that they send to fight or convince the *djinn* responsible for the affliction to leave the sick one.

### The Price of Treatment

To heal their 10-year-old son, the 'Hok family requested help from the three types of therapists, as is generally the case in similar situations.

The Quranic healer was ineffective, as is often the case. Those working in congregations were not able to make Souleyman enter a trance state. These attempts were very expensive for the family (~$13,500 USD).

The last therapist consulted called forth his own *jnoun* and ordered them to find the spell that caused the affliction.

> Mrs 'Hok: He wrote a scripture that he then burned . . . he wrote with ink made of sheep's wool . . . he burned the scripture until the *jnoun* appeared. Then, he started speaking to them. He said to me: "put your hand on the basin; I will count until three . . . put your hand on the basin . . . if you find something. And I found it. He took the object out. In a sleeve of one of the child's t-shirts, something written in red, with blood . . . and also pieces of bent iron, two scriptures in the sleeve . . . eleven knots on a silk thread . . . so that he would be sick for eleven years, it seems. . . . And a piece of wire in the shape of a hook—like a fish-hook—all of this in a t-shirt with earth on it and fresh grass. (Nathan, 1998)

### The Unfolding of a Therapy

The healer thus made a piece of cloth from a shirt recognized by the parents as belonging to their son appear under a basin, associated with a number of objects. The consultation presented here took place in the Paris metropolitan area in 1999. The child, who had not gone to school since he was 4 years old, was starting to show severe disabilities. Psychological interventions were systematically refused by both the child and the parents. This treatment was the only one that proved to be effective.

Confronted with such a case, a clinician faces a number of difficult problems: (a) the language of the parents; (b) their universe—including their conceptions, reasoning, and certainties; (c) the reality, the coherence, and the efficacy of the professionals acting in parallel with this universe—French and North African healers, in France as well as in their home country.

Ethnopsychiatry seeks to address these clinical problems, as much in theory as in technique, taking care not to disqualify any of the professionals connected together by the affliction of the person who is "possessed" (Hacking, 1988).

## ❖ THE *DJINN* MACHINERY

### A Necessary Notion: The Ecological Niche

It is not sufficient to classify disorders. Indeed, when a disorder exists within a culture, it is always associated with beings, objects, professionals, a network of professionals, a vocabulary, and a language. Thus, the disorder takes on a life of its own and becomes incomprehensible. Hence, I follow Hacking (1988) and consider an ecological niche rather than a syndrome (see, e.g., Abdelhafid, 1995; Brunel, 1926; Crapanzano, 1973; Pâques, 1976, 1991).

*Djinn* thus encompasses all of the following: beings possessing given characteristics, disorders, and therapies; cults to pay tribute to *jnoun*, then referred to as *mlouk*, "landlords" (Deleuze & Parnet, 1977, p. 104); networks of congregations (*zaouias*) devoted to the same spirit, extending all over the country and meeting every year for a ceremony and animal sacrifices; as well as perfumes, networks of solidarities, hierarchies, constraints to invention, a market, and so on.

*Djinn* is a "machine" (in Deleuze and Parnet's [1977] sense):

Machine . . . this does not mean either mechanical or organic. . . . The machine . . . is a "proximity" grouping between independent and heterogeneous terms. . . . What defines a machine assemblage is the shift of a center of gravity along an abstract line. (Deleuze & Parnet, 1977, p. 2)

It is a machine that pushed a human society to "marry," to borrow Deleuze and Parnet's (1977) terms, with strangers. We can posit that the consequences of such a union include an identification of these strangers and an in-depth knowledge of their nature, of their habitat, and of their ways of being and acting.

For as someone becomes, what he is becoming changes as much [as] he does himself. Becoming are not phenomena of imitation or assimilation, but of a double-capture, of non-parallel evolution, of nuptials between two reigns. Nuptials are always against nature. Nuptials are the opposite of a couple. (Deleuze & Parnet, 1977, p. 51)

A society that is passionate about the existence of *djinns*—interested in their sexuality, their habits, and their intent—is also profoundly intrigued and preoccupied by otherness. There are only two ways of knowing *jnoun*: through ancient texts, presumably written following encounters with such beings, and through the afflictions that currently affect human beings.

The world of *jnoun* is a world of thoughts, not a world of belief. It is both supported by and different from philosophy and religion. It resembles philosophy in its search for the characteristics of these beings, in the same way philosophers seek to identify new concepts. But it also resembles religion, because the beings in question are alive and have intentions. Interacting with such beings has consequences. Where religion builds groups, contributing to the creation of social spaces and to the intelligence of the weak and the deprived, the world of *jnoun* leads those who venture in it to explore the margins, the other side, the escape hatches. Religion sets up order; the world of *jnoun* gathers those who are excluded from this order, treats them, and facilitates their reintegration in specific niches. If religion builds walls, the world of *jnoun* creates openings. The philosophical world resembles the world of the *jnoun* by its obligation to create, but it is less accountable to life's demands. Identifying the right *djinn* leads to the healing of the patient or the worsening of the patient's illness. The construction of a "good" concept has much less obvious results in life. But philosophy is able to disintegrate worlds by emptying them of meaning, by deconstructing them. In the end, a healer, an ally of the *jnoun,* is a religious person without a religion, a philosopher lacking that hatred for the world as it is.

Hakim (pseudonym) turned to the Centre Georges Devereux after many problems with other therapists. The following case report is from an ethnopsychiatric consultation at the Centre Georges Devereux. The clinical observation was that Hakim's affliction stemmed from having the heart of a female *djinn* in his male body.[4]

The *djinn* speaks to him: He hears her within himself—her voice giving him absurd orders: "repeat 9999 times the *fatiha,*" "rape yourself as though you were a woman," "throw away the bread upon which you pronounced the *bismillah.*"[5] She also gives him doubts (*wesswesses* in Arabic): "You thought about God while going to the washroom," and so on.

He feels his thoughts are controlled by her. His reflexes and automatic manifestations are animated by incomprehensible intentions. And apparently, his actions also belong to another.

She acts: She hates his wife. She swears at her, even hits her at times. She stops him from making love with her, makes him leave the bed when she is there. God only knows why, but she gets angry at him and hits him, too. His body curls up in impossible postures, his face grimaces, and he groans from the pain.

She cheats on him: When she desires a man, she makes him have an erection and pushes him to look at the man with enamored eyes. She speaks to him about the people he meets. She promises to leave him alone if he fulfills such and such obligation—for instance, to apply a sticky and smelly substance to his hair or to pull up his left sleeve. He complies, but *she* remains, imposing more rules.

He tries to defend himself.

He listens to a tape with Quranic verses for hours.

He has consulted dozens of therapists, Muslim healers (*fkih, taleb, cheikh*). One of them diagnosed him: a female *djinn*, a *djenneia*, is living in his body. The remedy? Quranic scriptures, purification rituals, and fumigation. Nothing specific to this particular being. This treatment yielded no results.

It is easy to guess what his psychiatrists thought: unconscious homosexuality and delusions. They prescribed neuroleptic medication and recommended psychotherapy.

The side effects from the drugs were unbearable, and he threw them away after 2 weeks. As for psychotherapists, he consulted with at least 10 different ones, but none of these "believed" in *djinns*.

A *djinn* forces the afflicted to reconstruct part of the world; it calls for the introduction of a new name. No one was able to give Hakim the name of the female *djinn*.

What one should do to really help Hakim:

Treat the *djinn* (find the invisible)—get him to settle in, identify the objects he prefers, the actions that calm him, the words that capture him and allow the *djinn* to control him.

Treat the *zar*—identify the "stranger," find out his name, his ancestry, his tribe, his religion.

Treat the *ri'h,* his "smell," his affections, his passions; find out where his intentions are nourished.

Treat the *shed,* the force—identify the benefits that the patient can derive from marrying with the invisible.

Refrain from thinking that Hakim is homosexual, hysterical, schizophrenic, or borderline; but do not think either that possession by a *djinn* could be a sort of item in a new semiology—the treatment would lead to a catastrophe. Hakim is a place, a location—the location of a union, to borrow from Deleuze and Parnet (1977):

> There are no longer binary machines: question-answer, masculine-feminine, man-animal, etc. The wasp and the orchids provide the example. The orchid seems to form a wasp image, but in fact there is a wasp-becoming of the orchid, an orchid-becoming of the wasp, a double capture since "what" each becomes changes no less than "that which" becomes. [We could add here: a becoming-*djinn* of the man; a becoming-man of the *djinn*]. The wasp becomes part of the orchid's reproductive apparatus at the same time as the orchid becomes the sexual organ of the wasp. One and the same becoming, a single bloc of becoming, or, as Rémy Chauvin says: an "a-parallel evolution of two beings who have nothing whatsoever to do with each other." (p. 2)

Practitioners, researchers, theologians, and philosophers sometime describe *djinns* exclusively in terms of their objective characteristics, thus transforming them into objects of belief, and recognizing their existence only in the realm of the human psyche. I hope to have demonstrated here how such a position, though it may appear reasonable, in effect releases us from the obligation to understand and unfold the process in its complex entirety. Thus, to say that "*djinns* are imaginary beings in which North and West African populations believe" would be both a crime against the mind, depriving us of the subtle chain of reasoning that pushes us to search, and an act of aggression against the populations in question.

### ❖ WHAT *DJINNS* WANT FROM HUMANS

Muslims consider *djinns* as vestiges of a long-gone past. Many commentators, anthropologists, and specialists of the history of religions are following their lead (see, e.g., Doutté, 1908/1984, an excellent monograph despite the trappings of the typical thinking in those days). However, what characterizes *jnoun* in contrast to divinities is their a priori indetermination. Whereas a god is honored in the ways that suit the god, no one knows in advance the identity and the specific demands of a *djinn,* and these are never known in advance. *They are a perfume* requiring a specific fabrication, which is at once a creation and a creature. *They are a color,* mixed by hand from specific ingredients. *They are objects*—not a generic amulet, but one created *ex nihilo* for the occasion. And the actions that will be ritualized must be created for each *djinn. They are demons.*

Creating concepts—such would be the work of the philosopher. Identifying new *djinns,* never encountered before; naming them, defining their demands, organizing specific rituals—such would be the work of the therapist in the world of *djinns.*

And finally, what do *jnoun* want? They want to stop the movement of the world, to freeze life; they dream of being like their human brothers: settled down, territorialized. But they want to stop the world to their benefit, to become the only organizing principle of the universe, from which all the others would be derived. Here is the secret: The *jnoun* want to become God. Sometimes, they succeed.

For instance, Dionysos can be considered a sort of *djinn,* one who has succeeded in becoming a god. Indeed, after setting up his cult in Asia, he moves on to Thebes, seeking recognition as a god:

> And so, along all Asia's swarming littoral of towering cities where Greeks and foreign nations, mingling, live, my progress made. There I taught my dances to the feet of living men,
> establishing my mysteries and rites that I might be revealed on earth for what I am: a god.
> And thence to Thebes. (Euripides, 1959, p. 156)

## ❖ NOTES

1. Chapter translated from the French by Patricia Poulin.
2. *Majnoun*, "taken by a *djinn*," "indjinned"; *madroub*, "hit" [by a *djinn*]; *markoub*, "mounted" [by a *djinn*]; *mamlouk*, "possessed"—as when we are the owner of land or of an apartment—[by a *djinn*]; *masloukh*, "rubbed until blood is shed" [by a *djinn*]; *malbouss*, "worn" [by a *djinn*]—as a piece of clothing is worn—[by a *djinn*], and so forth.
3. Examples of the same type of ritual abound: Moroccan congregations—*Gnawa, Hamadchas, Aissaouas*; the *ndop* in Senegal; the *djina don* in Mali, and so forth.
4. The names of people and locations as well as any details that could lead to the identification of the family have been modified.
5. *Bismillah*, "in the name of God," a Muslim conjuration widely used to keep beings from other worlds at bay—both nonbelievers and spirits.

## ❖ REFERENCES

Abdelhafid, C. (1995). *La thérapie syncrétique des Gnaoua marocains.* Unpublished doctoral thesis, Université de Paris VII.

Brunel, R. (1926). *Essais sur la confrérie religieuse des Aîssâoûa au Maroc.* Paris: Geuthner.

Crapanzano, V. (1973). *The Hamadsha: A study in Moroccan ethnopsychiatry.* Berkeley: University of California Press.

Deleuze, G., & Parnet, C. (1977). *Dialogues.* London: Athlone Press.

Doutté, d'E. (1984). *Magie et religion dans l'Afrique du Nord.* Paris: J. Maisonneuve et P. Geuthner. (Original work published 1908)

Euripides. (1959). *The Bacchae.* In W. Arrowsmith (Ed. & Trans.), *Three tragedies.* Chicago: University of Chicago Press.

Guedmi, J. (1984). Rêve des doubles ou Fatiha l'oubliée. *Nouvelle revue d'ethnopsychiatrie, 2,* 13–34.

Hacking, I. (1988). *Mad travelers: Reflections on the reality of transient mental illness.* Charlottesville: University Press of Virginia.

Mauss, M. (1902). Esquisse d'une théorie générale de la magie. *L'année sociologique.* Retrieved January 10, 2005, from http://www.uqac.uquebec.ca/zone30/Classiques_des_sciences_sociales/classiques/mauss_marcel/socio_et_anthropo/1_esquisse_magie/esquisse_magie.pdf

Nathan, T. (1998). Georges Devereux et l'ethnopsychiatrie clinique. *Nouvelles revue d'ethnopsychiatrie, 34,* 7–18, 35–36.

Nathan, T., & Moro, M. R. (1989). Enfants de djinné: Evaluation ethnopsychanalytique des interactions précoces. In S. Lebovici, P. Mazet, & J. P. Visier (Eds.), *L'évaluation de interactions précoces entre le bébé et ses partenaires* (pp. 307–339). Geneva, Switzerland: EHSEL.

Pâques, V. (1976). Le monde des gnawa. In J. Poirier & R. Raveau (Eds.), *L'autre et l'ailleurs: Hommage à Roger Bastide* (pp. 169–182). Paris: Berger-Levreault.

Pâques, V. (1991). *La religion des esclaves, recherche sur la confrérie marocaine des gnawa.* Bergamo, Italy: Moretti and Vitali.

# 4

# Crossing the Line Between Talking Therapies and Spiritual Healing

*William West*

T his chapter explores the implications for counselors, counseling psychologists, psychotherapists, and their clients of using and integrating approaches from both the talking therapies and the various forms of spiritual and cultural healing. It draws on my doctoral and postdoctoral studies (West, 1995, 1997, 1998, 2000a, 2004) and focuses on the context of therapy and healing, the transition from therapist to therapist-healer, the models of therapist-healer integration, and implications and future developments.

There is much debate about the overlaps and differences between the training and practice of counselors and psychotherapists. Indeed, an increasing number of practitioners are trained and registered as both, which was one compelling argument for the British Association for Counselling's decision to add Psychotherapy to its title in 2001, becoming the British Association for Counselling and Psychotherapy. I will use the word *therapist* to cover both. Having trained and practiced both as a therapist and as a spiritual healer, it seemed natural to me to investigate how the two might be integrated. Not wishing to close down any discussions that

**Table 4.1**    Healing Phenomena in Respondents' Work ($n = 27$)

| Healing Phenomena | Number of Respondents | % |
|---|---|---|
| Healing energies present | 23 | 86 |
| Feeling part of something bigger than you and your client | 21 | 78 |
| Hands-on healing | 20 | 74 |
| Spiritual counseling | 16 | 59 |
| Feeling Grace is present | 15 | 56 |
| Feeling God is present | 10 | 37 |
| Aura work | 10 | 37 |
| Spirit guides | 8 | 30 |
| Noncorporeal presence | 8 | 30 |
| Seeing auras | 6 | 22 |
| Channeling | 6 | 22 |

might arise as to what constitutes healing, I deliberately used a catch-all description of healing in my letter to would-be participants in my research: "The use of one or more of the following: intuition; presence; inspiration; psychic; shamanic; altered states; (spiritual) healing methods; subtle energy work; mediumship; channelling; use of spirit guides; and transpersonal work" (West, 1997, p. 291).

Rather than get caught up in the futile debate of what spiritual healing is and whether it works (see Benor, 1993, for a review of the evidence), I was more interested in exploring how therapists might integrate spiritual healing in their practice, what issues arose from such integration, how therapists conceptualized such integration, and their experience of becoming healers. This inevitably suggested a qualitative study involving in-depth, semistructured interviews or dialogues. I also decided to use a human inquiry group (West, 1996) to which all of the 30 people I interviewed were invited. Six people became regular participants in this human inquiry group, in which the integration of therapy and healing could be more fully explored and experienced. Of the 30 people I was able to interview (out of the 40 people who initially contacted me), 27 of them indicated (as shown in Table 4.1) what healing phenomena they actually encountered in their work. Clearly, this group of respondents is not necessarily typical of the wider group of talking therapists, though it is possible that therapists' practice is more spiritual than is generally recognized. Certainly there is a difference between therapists' public discourse about their practice, including what they discuss in supervision (West, 2000b, 2003), and what actually happens behind the closed door of the therapy room.

Large numbers of therapists are engaged in prayer for their clients. Such prayer may involve therapists praying silently for clients within and outside of therapy sessions, vocal prayer during sessions, or encouragement to clients to pray outside of sessions (discussed in Gubi, 2001, 2002; Richards & Bergin, 1997). Gubi (2001), in a survey into the use of prayer in counseling, contacted just over half of the practitioners accredited by the British Association for Counselling and Psychotherapy, and 43% (247) responded. Of these, 59% had used prayer covertly in their work with clients (Christian or otherwise), and 12% had used prayer overtly with Christian clients. Only 24% who used prayer overtly or covertly had ever discussed it in supervision. Gubi (2002) speculates that this may be "because prayer is perceived to be a culturally unacceptable aspect of their work," with the result that they fear "their competence, professionalism and credibility [will be] questioned, or in case it is badly received or not understood" (p. 6).

Richards and Bergin (1997) advise spiritually minded therapists to pray and contemplate about their clients while engaged in client assessment and case conceptualization. For such therapists, this can result in "spiritual impressions and insights that deepen their understanding of their clients and increase their ability to help them" (pp. 198–199).

Thorne (2002) advocates that counselors hold their clients in mind on a regular basis and also that they seek an appropriate spiritual discipline to practice: "To put it as succinctly as possible, the person-centred therapist who commits himself or herself to the living out of the core conditions is exercising the spiritual discipline which is the expression of a practical mysticism" (p. 84). So the assumption that counseling and psychotherapy are, and can be construed as, largely secular activities is open to challenge on the basis of what therapists actually do in their consulting rooms, even if the dominant discourse within the profession still largely ignores spirituality.

If we examine Table 4.1, it is striking how many of my respondents (23 out of 27) are comfortable with and acknowledge healing energies to be present in their work. An almost equal number (21) acknowledge sometimes feeling part of something bigger than themselves and their clients. Perhaps not surprising is the fact that nearly three quarters (21) on occasion use hands-on healing techniques. Over half acknowledge the possibility of Grace occurring, and more than one third would claim that God is present at times in their work. What is notable is how underrepresented traditional psychic and healing phenomena are. For example, only a minority acknowledges the use of spirit guides or channeling.

❖  THE CONTEXT OF THERAPY AND HEALING

It was clear from my research that there were three ways in which the word *healing* was being used: (a) as a blanket term for the outcome of any caring activity by care workers, be they medical (e.g., doctor, nurse) or social (e.g., social worker, probation officer, therapist); (b) as intentional activity by someone calling him- or herself a healer, which may or may not involve energy exchange (see Courtenay, 1991; Willis, 1992); and (c) as unintentional experiences, similar to (b), that can occur within the work of therapists, which are well described by Rogers' (1980) concept of *presence* (Kirschenbaum & Henderson, 1990), Thorne's (1991) concept of *tenderness,* or Buber's (1970) *I/Thou relationship.* It should be noted that Shari Geller's recent research into Rogers' (1980) presence (Geller, 2001; Geller & Greenberg, 2002) has changed matters, because she insists that presence can be taught; if so, this would add a fourth possibility, conceptually unavailable to my respondents, of deliberately creating the possibility of healing.

Any consideration of spiritual healing has to take into account the cultural context. For instance, in Britain, spiritual healing was illegal until the late 1950s under the Witchcraft Act, and the laying of hands as a form of spiritual healing remains illegal in many part of Europe. There is also a strong link made in people's mind between spiritual healing and madness. This is strengthened when one explores the *Diagnostic and Statistical Manual of Mental Disorders,* 4th edition (American Psychiatric Association, 1994), in which diagnoses of psychosis may overlap with mystical and spiritual experiences (West, 2000a). Many of those having spiritual emergencies (Ankrah, 2002) know that the phenomena experienced—hearing voices, seeing human auras, and so forth—will be seen as abnormal.

We can connect this with McLeod's (2001) view of counseling as a liminal activity in which counselors are on the edge of institutions and on the edge of society and deal with madness and with people's struggles to find their place in modern society. McLeod suggests that "counselling represents one of many ways in which cultural norms and values of a society are affirmed, and operates as a means of helping individuals to negotiate their own relationship with these cultural norms" (p. 589).

Spiritual healing remains on the edge of mainstream Christianity, perhaps because it is seen as having something of the devil and something of the Pagan about it. This is despite the paradox that early Christians were often engaged in spiritual healing, as are charismatic Christians today. However, Christianity is currently in a huge decline in Britain, in terms of church attendance, and most people, in Davie's (1994) memorable words, believe but don't belong. Hay has explored religious, paranormal, and ecstatic experiences for more than 25 years (Hay, 1982; Hay & Hunt, 2000; Hay & Morisy, 1978), and his work leads him to conclude that such experiences are more common than usually acknowledged, that spiritual experiences are as common as ever, and that people continue to believe in some form of divinity.

It seems that in Britain, as in parts of North America, people can be seen as leading postmodern lives of New Age and Do-It-Yourself spirituality, where yoga, meditation, and therapy have replaced the pastor and priest and where there is crossover into Eastern spiritual ideas drawn from Hinduism, Buddhism, and Taoism.

## ❖ THE TRANSITION FROM THERAPIST TO THERAPIST-HEALER

The transition from being a therapist to being a therapist and healer was not easy for many of my respondents. Not all of them experienced a dramatic emergence into being a healer. Indeed, one of the key factors in many people's development was contact with a healer. The factors involved were as follows:

Contact with a healer (11)

Illness or midlife crisis (9)

Bereavement (4)

A natural extension of their therapy work (3)

Healing experience since childhood (2)

Personal therapy (2)

Obeying a dream (1)

For some respondents, more than one factor was involved. There is not room to go fully into these factors (for further details, see West, 1997, 2004), but I will give some examples here. The illnesses connected to healers' emergence can last for a number of years. One person interviewed had had a breakdown followed by a divorce, became very depressed, attempted suicide, and then developed bulimia. Taking part in analytic group therapy for 2 years helped for a while, but then her depression returned.

She saw herself as being at that time "generally . . . very lost in my life. I didn't have a direction. I'd lost any sort of spirituality . . . I'd become very disillusioned and embittered, a lost soul really." She was also suffering from chronic lower back pain from a bad fall. Someone suggested that she consult a healer about her chronic pain, and this had a powerful effect on her both physically and psychologically. She reported experiencing "all these streams of movement and energy . . . moving in my body, and he wasn't even touching me. And I thought, 'What the hell is going on?' And I had this feeling, like so many healers, that I'd come home . . . and I was totally fascinated by the experience of having healing."

The death of individuals close to us can often be the harbinger of change, causing us to question what we are doing with our lives and sometimes leading to an interest in the spiritual and in healing. One person I interviewed used her newfound healing skills to "more or less assist at my father's death. He was assuaged by whatever I was able to transmit to him. His pain was taken away and so on. But after that I just went completely flat."

Another woman spoke movingly of the death of her father and reported that it triggered a state within which she had hallucinations: "I thought of it as a nervous breakdown, after that I gave up teaching. It was after that that I finished the relationship, it was like everything stopped at that point. It was like a death . . . got into therapy . . . I swam around for about 5 years not knowing what I was going to do . . . and then I became a therapist."

Becoming a healer is no guarantee of good health, nor is it the end of the process of spiritual emergence; further transitions are possible. One woman was clearly going through a deep transition at the time of her interview: "I'm being stripped of things I have relied on, spiritually stripped. So I had to start all over again with absolutely nothing and it felt like death. And now I'm feeling I have to drop everything, like everything that I'm working in, that has to go too; just being stripped." She was moved to describe her experiences in shamanic terms: "It feels like [the] death of everything that I am, everything I've ever believed, like a shaman's death if you want to put it into grandiose terms. I had it thrust upon me whether I liked it or not."

## ❖  MODELS OF THERAPIST-HEALER INTEGRATION

By examining how respondents spoke of their therapy and healing work, it was possible to map their perceptions of the relationship between healing and therapy (Figure 4.1).

Through reflection on this mapping, a developmental model for the integration of therapy and healing was devised (Table 4.2), and each respondent was assigned to a stage of it. However, it seems clear from my research that stage 4 is not necessarily achieved once and for all; indeed, the way a practitioner works might well vary between clients and during the course of any one client's therapy.

The first step in integrating therapy and healing is usually an attempt to encompass one inside the other (Figure 4.1, d and e). Although this may well bring feelings of relief, it is usually not a satisfactory solution. The practitioner will tend to be driven to achieve a clearer and more equal integration. Once this is accomplished, it is often difficult for practitioners to label their new role, as a number of respondents discovered. Such difficulties represent one major area

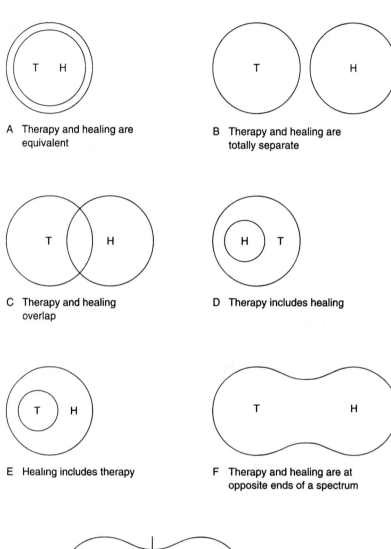

A  Therapy and healing are
   equivalent

B  Therapy and healing are
   totally separate

C  Therapy and healing
   overlap

D  Therapy includes healing

E  Healing includes therapy

F  Therapy and healing are at
   opposite ends of a spectrum

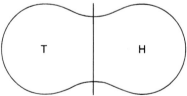

G  A barrier exists between therapy and healing, which can be
   dissolved by healer emergence

**Figure 4.1**    Developmental Model of Integration of Therapy and Healing

**Table 4.2**        Developmental Model of Integration of Therapy and Healing

| | |
|---|---|
| Stage 1 | Practitioner is initially either a therapist or a healer |
| Stage 2 | Practitioner becomes both therapist and healer and uses both modalities separately with differing sets of clients (position B) |
| Stage 3 | Practitioner begins to integrate one with the other (positions C, D, and E) |
| Stage 4 | True integration occurs and transcends both positions (position F) |

that supervision could address, but unfortunately, effective supervision can also prove difficult to obtain (which is discussed further in the next section).

## ❖ PROBLEMS ARISING FROM THE RESEARCH

Two key areas of difficulty emerged from my research. The first centered around language and the second around supervision. There were two aspects to this issue of language: how to talk about the experiences of spiritual healing and how to label the new type of practitioner that was emerging.

This first issue of how to talk about spirituality and spiritual healing experiences is an age-old problem (Wilber, 1979). It is a challenge to put into words experiences that are beyond our usual consciousness, such as feeling merged with our clients, having the sense of forming a third entity with our clients, or experiencing God or another presence in the therapy room. One respondent, struggling to convey his experience of an I/Thou moment with his client, said, "In the 'I/Thou' in which we are one, yet there's also a sense in which we are still separate. I think it may be a problem where . . . we're trying to use language to define things that aren't easily defined" (West, 1995, p. 303). Another respondent told me, "I'm very aware that when I'm with clients, there's a third party present, if you like. It's very difficult to explain, but I am aware of another that makes sense and helps what's going on. . . . It's difficult to put into words" (West, 1995, p. 303).

This language issue is compounded by the increasing alienation from religion, religious traditions, and religious language. As one respondent told me, "The problem with our present society and why we're having problems with people having spiritual emergencies is because we don't have a language or a concept here in mainstream society" (West, 1995, p. 304). People having spiritual emergencies fear they are going mad and that no one else has ever had such an experience (Ankrah, 2002). The communication of some basic information about such experiences can greatly reduce the fear, anxiety, and terror involved.

The second language issue centers around what to call one's practice. Four of my respondents experienced difficulties over what to call their practice, and three of these distinguished between how they personally see their work and the labels they publicly adopt for it. One told me that she did not know what to call her work in her own mind, but she described herself to others as a therapist—"the most low-key and invisible label" she could choose. Another acknowledged that she identified most with the term *healer* but admitted that when "I think in terms of making a living I find it easier to present myself as a psychotherapist" (West, 1995, p. 305).

This dilemma of what to call the helping role and the therapeutic practice involved can be understood in terms of Wilber's (1979) 10-stage model of human spiritual development. Wilber identifies forms of therapy and spiritual development most suited to what level and what problems a person has. He suggests that Western forms of therapy are most helpful in the early stages of his model. However, the later, more explicitly spiritual stages need a helper who works explicitly within a spiritual framework. Of course, Wilber is not without his critics, even from within the spiritual healing community, but his model does help us to think about therapy and spirituality in a useful way (further discussed in Rowan, 1993; West, 2000a, 2004).

With regard to supervision issues, I will focus on the findings of both my doctoral study into integrating therapy and healing and my later study into the spirituality of Quaker therapists (West, 1998). Out of the 48 interviewed in both studies combined, supervision difficulties were present for 14 respondents—nearly 30% (West, 2000b). In a situation where people volunteer to be interviewed, it is likely that those with difficulties may well be more likely to offer themselves as research participants. Nevertheless, a key theme of the studies concerned the taboo that exists against talking about spirituality. Perhaps like clients, supervisees are waiting to be given permission to talk of spirituality. Those facing the problems were as likely to be seasoned therapists as those not reporting such difficulties, both averaging over 10 years in practice as therapists.

The following are some examples from my respondents:

I'd often come out quite angry, because I feel in some way my client has been degraded by exposing their vulnerability. I don't feel the client has been helped, and I feel in some way there's some sacred thing that has happened that has been exposed to the [supervision] group, that has not affirmed the sacredness of what was going on in the therapist-client relationship. (West, 2000b, pp. 115–116)

There does seem a tenderness around how clients and their therapists relate to their experience of spirituality (West, 2000b).

I found that when I did have one client for whom the spiritual was very important, it was quite difficult to deal with, being supervised by someone who had no sense of the spiritual. Either I took what I'd done to supervision and got it rubbished or I left it outside supervision, protected it increasingly by not getting it supervised, being quite sure that with this client that was the right way to go. (West, 2000b, p. 118)

I found this unethical behavior most disturbing, and I was left wondering why the practitioner could not seek some sort of consultative supervision for this one particular client. The practitioner had been proactive in establishing a group of trainee therapists who met to discuss the spiritual dimensions of their work.

## ❖ IMPLICATIONS AND CONCLUSION

If we take seriously the increasingly expressed need by clients (and, indeed, of therapy trainees as well) to have their spirituality honored and included in the therapeutic encounter, and if we allow their therapists to make the most creative use possible of spiritual and healing insights and methods, then there are some profound implications for training, practice, supervision, research, and our theory making. My respondents were a very experienced group of practitioners who had worked on average more than 10 years as therapists. However, this did not prevent supervision difficulties from arising. This may well be the tip of a bigger iceberg of inadequate supervision (see West, 2002) and some supervisors' negative views of spirituality and healing. A clear way forward is for the training of supervisors and therapists to include the spiritual and allow for the possibility at the very least that incidental healing can arise within therapy.

Becoming a therapist is not the end of any practitioner's professional and spiritual development. Our lives and our clients' lives unfold. How can we honor these processes, how can we remain open to whatever will most benefit ourselves and our clients, however bizarre it may seem? Spiritual healing has been around for thousands of years, and it will continue. Appropriately used, it can aid the client's therapeutic process.

## ❖ REFERENCES

American Psychiatric Association. (1994). *Diagnostic and statistical manual of mental disorders* (4th ed.). Washington, DC: Author.
Ankrah, L. (2002). Spiritual emergency and counselling: An exploratory study. *Counselling and Psychotherapy Research, 2,* 55–60.

Benor, D. J. (1993). *Healing research: Holistic energy medicine and spirituality: Vol. 1. Research in healing.* Munich, Germany: Helix.

Buber, M. (1970). *I and thou.* Edinburgh, Scotland: Clark.

Courtenay, A. (1991). *Healing now.* London: Dent and Sons.

Davie, G. (1994). *Religion in Britain since 1945.* Oxford, UK: Blackwell.

Geller, S. (2001). *Therapists' presence: The development of a model and a measure.* Unpublished doctoral dissertation, York University, Toronto, Ontario, Canada.

Geller, S., & Greenberg, L. (2002). Therapeutic presence: Therapists' experience of presence in the psychotherapy encounter. *Person-Centred and Experiential Therapies, 1,* 71–86.

Gubi, P. (2001). An exploration of the use of Christian prayer in mainstream counselling. *British Journal of Guidance and Counselling, 29,* 425–434.

Gubi, P. (2002, June). *Practice behind closed doors: Challenging the taboo of prayer in mainstream counselling culture.* Paper presented at the Annual Conference of the Society for Psychotherapy Research (International), Santa Barbara, CA.

Hay, D. (1982). *Exploring inner space: Scientists and religious experience.* Harmondsworth, Middlesex, UK: Penguin.

Hay, D., & Hunt, K. (2000). *Understanding the spirituality of people who don't go to church.* Nottingham, UK: Centre for the Study of Human Relations, Nottingham University.

Hay, D., & Morisy, A. (1978). Reports of ecstatic, paranormal, or religious experiences in Great Britain and the United States—A comparison of trends. *Journal for the Scientific Study of Religion, 17,* 255–268.

Kirschenbaum, H., & Henderson, V. (1990). *The Carl Rogers reader.* London: Constable.

McLeod, J. (2001). Counselling as a social process. In P. Milner & S. Palmer (Eds.), *Counselling: The BACP reader* (Vol. 2, pp. 589–598). London: BACP/Sage.

Richards, D. S., & Bergin, A. E. (1997). *A spiritual strategy for counseling and psychotherapy.* Washington, DC: American Psychological Association.

Rogers, C. R. (1980). *A way of being.* Boston: Houghton Mifflin.

Rowan, J. (1993). *The transpersonal, psychotherapy and counselling.* London: Routledge.

Thorne, B. (1991). *Person centred counselling: Its therapeutic and spiritual dimension.* London: Whurr.

Thorne, B. (2002). *The mystical power of person-centred therapy: Hope beyond despair.* London: Whurr.

West, W. S. (1995). *Integrating psychotherapy and healing.* Unpublished doctoral thesis, Keele University, Keele, UK.

West, W. S. (1996). Using human inquiry groups in counselling research. *British Journal of Guidance and Counselling, 24,* 347–355.

West, W. S. (1997). Integrating psychotherapy and healing. *British Journal of Guidance and Counselling, 25,* 291–312.

West, W. S. (1998). Developing practice in a context of religious faith: A study of psychotherapists who are Quakers. *British Journal of Guidance and Counselling, 26,* 365–375.

West, W. S. (2000a). *Psychotherapy and spirituality: Crossing the line between therapy and religion.* London: Sage.

West, W. S. (2000b). Supervision difficulties and dilemmas for counsellors and psychotherapists around healing and spirituality. In B. Lawton & C. Feltham (Eds.),

*Taking supervision forward: Enquiries and trends in counselling and psychotherapy* (pp. 113–125). London: Sage.

West, W. S. (2002). Being present to our clients' spirituality. *Journal of Critical Psychology, Counselling and Psychotherapy, 2*(2), 86–93.

West, W. S. (2003). The culture of psychotherapy supervision. *Counselling Psychotherapy Research, 3,* 123–126.

West, W. S. (2004). *Spiritual issues in therapy: Relating experience to practice.* Basingstoke, UK: Palgrave Macmillan.

Wilber, K. (1979). A developmental view of consciousness. *Journal of Transpersonal Psychology, 11*(1), 11–21.

Willis, R. (1992). Initiation in healing. *Doctor-Healer Network Newsletter, 3,* 9–11.

# PART II

# Healing and Curing

*Traditional Healers and Healing*

# 5

# Indigenous Healers and Healing in a Modern World

*Anne Solomon and Njoki Nathani Wane*

I s there a space in our contemporary society for indigenous healers and healing? Do Indigenous and non-Indigenous Peoples require the services of indigenous healers? These are some of the questions we consider in this chapter, which explores the healing practices of Indigenous Peoples. Indeed, indigenous healing practices are not homogeneous, being in some cases very specific to a particular group, and therefore facile generalizations are problematic. Clearly, our interpretations are colored by our own personal experiences and contexts. However, the general backdrop against which our analysis takes place is within the context of the colonial experience, as well as the cultural specificity of the people. We also offer a broad overview and analysis of conversations we had with three indigenous healers—two Canadians and one African American. We begin by asking if it is at all possible for indigenous healing to be conducted in a colonial context.

## ❖ COLONIALISM AND INDIGENOUS HEALING

In recent decades, Indigenous Peoples[1] have suffered from the consequences of some of the most destructive aspects of global "development." However,

Indigenous Peoples over many centuries have maintained a unique and judicious balance between human needs and the needs of nonhuman nature. Many indigenes have growing interest in returning to their sacred teachings and ceremonies and will continue to follow their traditions to sustain themselves and to help the generations to come. Many of us are beginning to more fully recognize that the ancient ways of our Ancestors are valuable, reliable, and more sustainable than the present-day methods of living in the universe.

However, we must ask ourselves: What are the implications of using indigenous methods in contemporary times? Are these methods transferable to nonindigenous therapists who want to employ them? Indigenous healing practices are usually accompanied by certain rituals, and each methodology has within it specific relevance to sacred teachings held by the Indigenous Peoples. This is not to say that some things cannot be shared; however, it is important to understand that the practices and lessons learned by centuries of colonized, oppressed Indigenous Peoples are different than the practices and lessons of the dominant society.

It is paramount to acknowledge that our societies have gone through tremendous change as a result of colonization, and this affects present practices (Churchill, 1995, 1998; Drinnon, 1997; see also Poonwassie & Charter, Chapter 2 in this volume). This chapter attempts to make understanding these interrelationships more accessible to people in the helping professions and introduces some of the concepts of orality used to maintain and sustain Indigenous Peoples as individuals, communal groups, and nations. During the preparation of this chapter, its coauthor, Anne Solomon, was given specific instructions on what she could share about her indigenous sacred teachings. It is therefore with the consent and approval of her Elders that she shares enough information for others to understand indigenous ways of healing without breaking protocol on sacred teachings and the processes of sacred ceremonies. In many indigenous societies, some of the questions they are constantly asking are, How much of the sacred healing practices can they share? Would these practices work out of context? Is it possible to re-create rituals of healing outside the healers' community? Each healing practice is unique to the individual requiring healing and to the healer.

One of the problems with sharing practices is that indigenous methodologies are not always respected for the integrity inherent in them. Scientific paradigms are often used to deny or refute our time-tested, reliable, valuable, and successful practices. People may not understand the significance and responsibility associated with an invocation to the spirit of a plant, an animal, or an ancestor. When the spirits of the beings respond, if untutored, unapprenticed people are performing the invocation, they may not understand the manner of language, the process, or the practice of communication. They may not understand that a distinct and defined ritual is to take place, or they may not fully understand the consequences of not carrying out the ceremony or practice properly. Furthermore, they may not fully understand the responsibility, the necessity, or the appropriate methodology to bring closure to the process invoked. Our traditional healers, on the other hand, will be aware of the intricacies of these practices and the contexts in which they could be applied.

It is safe to say that our indigenous healers are interdimensional interceders who carry the responsibility and the directions to intervene on our behalf, with our consent and awareness, to help bring healing, balance, peace, and harmony in the present, with the Ancestors, and for the generations of the future. For the Anishinabe and Embu traditions (respectively, of the authors) and in most Indigenous Peoples' traditions, this responsibility extends for at least seven generations (Cajete, 2000; Dei, Hall, & Rosenberg, 2000; Tuhiwai-Smith, 1999; Wane, 2000). The words of renowned Elder and Carrier First Nation woman Maggie Hodgson (personal communication, 2004)[2] assure us that reclaiming and maintaining our old ways must continue. "It's known that on a global scale, the First Nations Peoples of Canada are the fastest growing group of peoples doing their healing work, and it's making a difference. And, we are doing it *our* way. This is amazing."

## ❖ INDIGENOUS WORLDVIEW

There is a communal ideology and unique worldview between and among the Indigenous Peoples of the world. This common thread is inherent in most indigenous cultures despite the severity and sustained duration of the colonial impact or the variance of spiritual practices. In Indigenous Peoples' worldview of societal and cosmological relationships, there is an acute understanding of respect for self, other people, and all of nature, especially the land and the water. This philosophy is the pivotal element of sustainability and balanced harmonious living, grounded in a spiritual relationship to the land. We are taught, shown, and instructed in our responsibility to learn to (re)connect with the land. We are held responsible for the care of the water. It is through this understanding that we are able to support each other with the sacred medicines, ceremonies, and the use of our indigenous methods of traditional counseling.

World Indigenous Peoples manifest a magnificent diversity in sound, size, culture, custom, practice, ritual, ceremony, and domain. However, there is a mysterious and powerful "homophonic rhythm" (Provost-Turchetti, 2002) to the practices and the purpose of the practices we have sustained and maintained since time immemorial. This way of knowing, understanding, and being in the world originates in the simplicity and complexity of our psycho-spiritual-socio, behaviorist-ecological cosmological worldview (Solomon, 1994) commonly known in North America as the Medicine Wheel philosophy (Gunn Allen, 1986; Solomon, 1990). Indigenous Peoples the world over follow the rhythm of the cosmos with distinct relationships to the sun, moon, stars, animals, plants, sound, wind, water, electrical and vibrational energy, thunder, lightning, rain, all creatures of the land and water, the air, and the rhythm of the land itself. Relationship to the spirit world has been a primary value to tribal people to maintain relationships with our ancestors (Gunn Allen, 1986; Yellow Horse Brave Heart, 1995).

Our foreparents introduced us to the spiritual legacy left to us by their Ancestors. The ancestral teachings provide spiritual guidance embodied in the Creator, the giver of life, harmony, balance, cosmic order, peace, and healing. Our spiritual guidance is also embodied in the Great Mother Earth, spirit and culture giver, who represents truth, balance, harmony, law, and cosmic order (Solomon, 1990; Wane, 2002).

❖  INDIGENOUS KNOWLEDGES

Our Ancestors have taught that if any of our actions results in disequilibrium, we have to find ways of healing and purifying the environment, our relations, and ourselves (Solomon, 1990; Wane, 2002). This understanding and the teachings that carried the wisdom were and are so valued that the Indigenous Peoples scripted the knowledge within their hearts to be shared with each other and with future generations. In reality, this knowledge is embodied because it is committed to memory. "Memory is recorded literally in the viscera, in the flesh" (Jousse, 2000, p. 279). "Knowledge" for Indigenous Peoples means *know*-ing the legend stories. Consequently, one must know the legends completely, to the ends of the stories, or the knowledge is incomplete. When we speak of legends, we are also speaking of what are known as sacred teachings and the mythological foundations of our cultures. We maintain relationships with the cosmos through stories. The stories and memories are held in the bodies of people, the bodies of water, and the bodies of land. Consequently, it is pivotal to know the stories of the land in order to attain healing in the indigenous ways (Solomon, 1990).

It is our responsibility to know, understand, and respect the healing power of the "performed knowledges" (Chamberlain, 2003) used by the traditional teachers, Elders, ceremonialists, and traditional healers. Performed knowledges, therefore, relate to indigenous ways of healing, which are living texts. Our performed knowledges and texts, in orality, exist in three-dimensionality, compared to the two-dimensionality of written knowledge and texts in literacy. The songs, dances, ceremonies, sacred medicines, and traditional languages serve as the vehicle and tools of the healer. Consequently, it is with certainty and caution that the Elders and spiritual teachers remind us not to write or record the ceremonies: To do so would take the life out of them. We now turn to three of these healers and spiritual teachers with whom we talked.

## ❖ HEALERS

**Terry Swan,** a Cree-Saulteaux woman originating from Cold Lake First Nation in Alberta, Canada, who identifies herself as a two-spirited lesbian woman (Gunn Allen, 1986; Roscoe, 1988), was, at 2 years of age, taken away from her single-parent mother and adopted by a Dutch family who came to Canada after World War II. Terry grew up totally immersed in non-Native culture. While living in Nova Scotia, she began, with the help of a Mi'kmaq woman, her search for her birth mother. Eventually, Terry's maternal uncle came forward.

After meeting her uncle, and with the help of other Natives, Terry became acquainted with her traditions. Tom Swan was a medicine man. Terry reports, "After hearing my voice on the telephone, he went into the sweat lodge and put up flags, and he asked the spirits about me." Through the ceremonies, Terry's uncle learned about the kind of difficulties she had experienced. Over the years, Terry came to know herself and many of the sacred teachings. She later committed to follow the path of Native spirituality, because "that's where I get my courage and my strength." Through the development of a relationship with her uncle, Terry inherited a sacred item she uses for personal healing. She goes out onto the land to fast; regularly attends sweat lodge ceremonies; and participates in a variety of other ceremonies, such as the purification ceremony, which is intended to open the mind, heart, and feelings of the individual(s). It is used to symbolically wash the negativity and pain from the body, mind, and spirit of a person and of the room or space. When Terry does her ceremonies with clients, by herself, or with her community, she uses the four sacred medicines of sage, sweetgrass, cedar, and tobacco. Each of the medicines can be used in ceremony on its own or in conjunction with any of the others. Frequently, sacred feathers from an eagle or another special bird will also be used while sharing, to remind participants of the sacrifice of the eagle as a special helper to the people.

**David Gehue,** a Mi'kmaq man from Indian Brook First Nation in Nova Scotia and 1 of 13 siblings, learned of his ability to do healing work at the age of 9. At 17, a wrestling accident with his brother caused total blindness. When he lost his eyesight, it was predicted he was going to do special work and that he had to be blind to do it. Consequently, it is believed the loss of sight served to direct and speed up his spiritual training. He remembers that as a child he had different privileges and responsibilities than his siblings. He recalls that the "Indian schooling" he got from his grandmothers and grandfathers was valued more than the compulsory mainstream education. He received subtle and specific spiritual training from his grandparents in their traditional language. He also received specific training from other renowned traditional healers. In addition, after he was introduced to the traditional fasting[3] ceremony, he went into the sacred sweat lodge every day for 1 year and did many more sacred fasts without consciously knowing why. He acquired an inexplicable, insatiable interest and unquenchable thirst for traditional ceremonies.

One of the foremost pieces of information shared by David was that in spite of his interest in and attendance at ceremonies, he did not begin to practice the specific ceremony he has been given—the shake-tent lodge—until after a period of 11 years. Although he does not speak his traditional language, he still has clear recall and use of the language when doing ceremonies. David's gift and ability to be an "empath," also known in the Sioux traditions as a "translator," informs him on what is happening to others; for example, he has been able to work with people who have been comatose for 3 to 5 years. Through his intervention in ceremony, the people became conscious enough to say their final good-byes.

David is a medicine man. He is a sweat lodge keeper, has X-ray vision, and carries the shake-tent lodge. He is also a certified hypnotist, has the ability to communicate telepathically, and interprets dreams. Each of these gifts and responsibilities can be used independently or together. As a medicine man, David is able to determine the client's ailment and its cause and advise a remedy. As a shake-tent keeper, he can directly intervene with the spirits and the Creator on behalf of the client(s). Requiring total darkness, the shake-tent lodge is known to be the highest of sacred ceremonies, in which all manner of healing is possible.

**Zulu**, a woman of African ancestry, is a traditional healer. She explained in her interview that her ability to heal is a gift passed down to her from her grandmother. She can still recall the many times she witnessed her grandmother healing people through touch. Zulu explained that indigenous healing takes different forms depending on each situation. She said that some healers might prescribe a spiritual bath, which is a formal acknowledgment that something needs to be done about your physical, mental, or emotional well-being. She explained, "Beyond the submission in the water and the candles, there has begun a submission for help for oneself. The spiritual bath is not just a beginning for help, but a solution of help." She continued to explain, "The type of bath taken depends on healing needed. Whether it is bath salts; floral herbs; gem stones; spices; nature items such as rocks, pebbles, sand, or leaves, et cetera, all depended on the healing needed." She concluded the interview by stating: "I cannot give you a step by step prescription of what needs to be done because you may apply some of these sacred practices without the respect and integrity passed down by our Ancestors."

## ❖ CONCLUDING COMMENTS

The first two healers spoke of their own personal healing as having been the pathway to becoming healers. Both Terry and David have made great personal sacrifices with the understanding that this is simply the route they must follow to fulfill their responsibilities. Zulu has undergone great transformation through not succumbing to the oppression she has experienced growing up in North America.

It is difficult to convey how the transfer of the gifts of these healers might happen, because each of them has been apprenticed in a variety of ways according to ancient traditions. Their apprenticeships have taken place over a number of years and will continue for several years to come. It is atypical within mainstream culture to instruct a person on a life path as a result of listening to a dream. Becoming a traditional healer is not a conscious independent personal decision: It is a responsibility inherited or determined by the community. It is also a gift that is earned. Each culture and society must determine their own healers based on the commitment, sacrifice, skills, abilities, and gifts of the prospective healers. They must also seek to learn the ancient ways of their ancestors. Finally, in closing, we cite the words and wisdom of Maurice Strong, who reminds us of the following: "As we awaken our consciousness that humankind and the rest of nature are inseparably linked, we will need to look to the world's more than 250 million indigenous peoples" (quoted in Burger, 1990, p. 6) for the sustainability of peace, health, and healing. This does not mean that we have the liberty to appropriate, assimilate, or acculturate ourselves to the ways of Indigenous Peoples: It means we must take individual and collective responsibility for ourselves, each other, the earth, and the universe if we are to sustain life and the universe. The universe is not ours to destroy.

## ❖ NOTES

1. The term *Indigenous Peoples,* wherein both words are capitalized and "Peoples" is plural, was adopted by the United Nations after long, hard discussions just prior to the Decade of Indigenous Peoples 1994–2004. We are capitalizing the word *Ancestors* out of respect and reverence for our origins.

2. Elder Maggie Hodgson, former director of Nechi Institute in Edmonton, Alberta, Canada, is a Carrier Indian with the notable distinction and recognition of Elder and is one of the recipients of the National Aboriginal Achievement Awards.

3. The fasting ceremony can last from 1 to 4 days. It entails abstaining from eating or drinking in order to reach a heightened level of awareness known as "visiting the spirit world," and it occurs four times a year or once a season.

## ❖ REFERENCES

Burger, J. (1990). *The Gaia atlas of first peoples: A future for the indigenous world.* New York: Doubleday.

Cajete, G. (2000). *Native science: Natural laws of interdependence.* Santa Fe, NM: Clear Light.

Chamberlain, J. E. (2003). *If this is your land, where are your stories? Finding common ground.* Toronto, Ontario, Canada: Alfred A. Knopf Canada.

Churchill, W. (1995). *Since predator came.* Littleton, CO: Aigis.

Churchill, W. (1998). *A little matter of genocide: Holocaust denial in the Americas 1492 to present.* Winnipeg, Manitoba, Canada: Arbeiter Press.

Dei, G., Hall, B., & Rosenberg, D. (2000). *Indigenous knowledges in global contexts: Multiple readings of our world.* Toronto, Ontario, Canada: University of Toronto Press.

Drinnon, R. (1997). *Facing west—The metaphysics of Indian-hating and empire building.* Norman: University of Oklahoma Press.

Erodes, R., & Ortiz, A. (Eds.). (1984). *American Indian myths and legends.* New York: Pantheon Books.

Gunn Allen, P. (1986). *The sacred hoop—Recovering the feminine in American Indian traditions.* Boston: Beacon Press.

Jousse, M. (2000). *The anthropology of geste and rhythm.* (E. Sienaert [with J. Conolly], Ed. & Trans.). Durban, South Africa: Mantis.

Kulchyski, P., McCaskill, D., & Newhouse, D. (Eds.). (1999). *In the words of Elders—Aboriginal cultures in transition.* Toronto, Ontario, Canada: University of Toronto Press.

Provost Turchetti, L. (2002). *"Areito" foundations of traditional knowledge touching Taino and Tinne (Dene) indigenous philosophy for aural-oral/kinetic learning of wholeness as wellness.* Unpublished master's thesis, Ontario Institute for Studies in Education, University of Toronto, Toronto, Ontario, Canada.

Roscoe, W. (Ed.). (1988). *Living the spirit—A gay American Indian anthology.* New York: Palgrave, St. Martin's Press.

Sienaert, E., & Conolly, J. (2004). *Holism and education: Seven lectures by Marcel Jousse.* Cape Town & Durban, South Africa: Mantis.

Solomon, A. J. (1990). *Songs for the people—Teachings on the natural way.* Toronto, Ontario, Canada: New Canada Press.

Solomon, A. M. (1994). *Study of Native adolescent males: Their successes in education and life and their familial relationships.* Unpublished master's thesis, University of Toronto, Toronto, Ontario, Canada.

Some, M. P. (1993). *Ritual: Power, healing, and community.* New York: Penguin Books.

Tuhiwai-Smith, L. (1999). *Decolonizing methodologies: Research and Indigenous Peoples.* New York: Zed Books.

Wane, N. (2000). Indigenous knowledge: Lesson from the Elders—A Kenyan case study. In G. Dei, B. Hall, & D. Rosenberg (Eds.), *Indigenous knowledges in global contexts: Multiple readings of our world* (pp. 54–69). Toronto, Ontario, Canada: University of Toronto Press.

Wane, N. N. (2002). African women and spirituality: Connection between thought and education. In E. O'Sullivan, A. Morrell, & M. O'Connor (Eds.), *Expanding the boundaries of transformative learning: Essays on theory and praxis* (pp. 135–150). New York: Palgrave, St. Martin's Press.

Yellow Horse Brave Heart, M. (1995). *The return to the sacred path: Healing from historical trauma and historical unresolved grief among the Lakota.* Unpublished doctoral dissertation, Smith College, Northampton, MA.

# 6

# Traditional Healing Practices in Southern Africa

## Ancestral Spirits, Ritual Ceremonies, and Holistic Healing

*Olaniyi Bojuwoye*

❖ ❖ ❖

Despite very strong foreign Western cultural influences, a majority of indigenous African people of Southern Africa hold on to their traditional cultural values. Western medicine is accepted only superficially, and many patients routinely consult traditional healers after hospitalization (Rudnick, 2000). Traditional healing cultural legacies remain the realities people have come to understand and assimilate.

The root of traditional healing among the people of Southern Africa today can be traced back to the time when the foundations of their cultures were being laid. The development of systems to respond to diseases and restore health to individuals who are ill can certainly not be separated from the social, cultural, and historic contexts in which they occur. Traditional healing, as an integral part of culture, represents a sum total of beliefs, attitudes, customs, methods, and established practices indicative of the worldview of the people.

61

## ❖ THE WORLDVIEW CONSTRUCT

The interconnectedness of phenomenal worlds (which inform collective living) and spirituality are two major aspects of the traditional African worldview that are relevant to health care delivery. The worldview holds that the universe is not void but is filled by different elements that are held together in unity, harmony, and totality by life forces, which maintain firm balance, or equilibrium, between them (Crafford, 1996). A typical traditional Zulu cosmology is an undivided universe in which plants, animals, humans, ancestors, earth, sky, and the entire universe all coexist in varying states of balance between order and disorder, harmony and chaos (Edwards, 2000). The traditional African worldview makes no distinction between living and nonliving, natural and supernatural, material and immaterial, conscious and unconscious. Instead, these sets of phenomena are understood as unities. Seen and unseen exist in dynamic interrelationship, and past, present, and future harmoniously weave into one another (Lambo, 1978).

Communal living represents the collective consciousness reality by which the people are identified. This way of life is referred to as *ubuntu* in South Africa, meaning collectivity, communality, oneness, or cooperation and sharing (Nefale & Van Dyk, 2003). This principle of living emerges poetically in the Xhosa saying: "*umuntu ngumuntu ngabantu,*" which can be translated as: "A human becomes a person through others," "Only through you do I become an I," or "I am because we are" (Edwards, 2000). Thus human personality is believed to be shaped by and developed in community with others. Human nature is viewed as an interdependent, inseparable whole (Nefale & Van Dyk, 2003), and the group is seen as the embodiment of reality and the only framework within which the individual can hope for any degree of self-actualization.

The traditional African worldview is also characterized by animism—the belief that the world is animated by spiritual entities. The rich spirit world of Zulu incorporates an originator, the first Being (God), and other spirit-beings regarded as those of the ancestors (Rudnick, 2000). When someone dies, the person is believed to transform into an ancestral spirit. Death doesn't make a person cease to belong to his or her social unit, family, clan, tribe, village, or nation. The Tswana (and other Southern African indigenous groups such as the Xhosa, Zulu, Sotho, Venda, Ndebele, and others) believe that their ancestors lead similar lives as spirits as they did while alive and that these ancestors are actively involved in the lives of their descendants and have powerful influences on their behaviors. There is a tightly woven interdependency between the living and the dead (Gumede, 1990). The ancestors, though invisible, reside in the household like everyone else (Ngubane, 1977), interceding in virtually all aspects of life, including helping with marital and interpersonal relationship conflicts, bringing about good health, averting illness, assisting in obtaining good fortune, and averting natural disasters and accidents.

## ❖ CONCEPTION OF HEALTH

Traditional Africa views "good health," or "ideal" human functioning, as synony-mous with harmonious relationship with the universe and the local ecology, including plants, animals, and interpersonal relationships (Straker, 1994). The traditional Zulu view of health is that of continuing balance in environmental and social relations within the family, society, peers, ancestors, or deity (Edwards, 2000). Health is considered to have greater meaning, balance, connectedness, and wholeness both within the individual and between individuals and the environ-ment (Katz, 1982). Thus, "ideal" human functioning from the traditional Zulu perspective is that of a person who integrates in, and contributes to, the com-munity and continues to work at maintaining the balance, renewing order, and re-creating new forms of harmony (Edwards, 2000). Traditional Africa's view of the goal of a psychologically healthy person is that of striving to be in harmony with the forces of nature impinging on him or her.

Ill health, or "dis-ease," is viewed as an indication of disharmony or dis-alignment in nature, especially between people (including the ancestral spirits). Dis-ease is like what Gilligan (1998) refers to as "a break in relatedness," or disharmony within the individual (break between body and spirit) and dishar-mony between the individual and the rest of the universe or the reality beyond the individual existence. The individual therefore feels isolated, anxious, tense, confused, frustrated, and annihilated. These feelings do manifest in the body, hurting quite literally in the entrails.

The traditional African worldview also views disease not only as evidence of microbiological infection, but also as a breakdown in the physical, social, and spiritual mechanisms of the individual and the community. Disease is more of a social construction, with the focus on the person-environment relationship, thus stressing the significance of interrelationship in healing (Kleinman, 1980). Disease is not just a physical fact but is associated with other aspects of life (including intellectual, emotional, social, familial, occupational, and spiritual dimensions), making this view consistent with the World Health Organization's (WHO) (1993) conception of health as more than the absence of disease and infirmity but also including complete physical, mental, and social well-being.

Traditional Africa also believes in multiple origins of diseases, with particu-lar emphasis on external causes and with humans and supernatural and ances-tral spirits as agents of diseases. Straker (1994) notes three main external causes—mystical, animistic, and magical. Magical and animistic causation refers to illness inflicted by others either in the material world or the supernatural world, through human employment of witchcraft (magical) or through ancestors (animistic). Mystical causation of illness is regarded as the result of pollution (infiltration or intrusions). Illness caused by pollution may be viewed as arising from ritual impurities (Hammond-Tooke, 1989) and subsequent admonishment from ancestral forces. Disease is also believed to be transmitted from one generation to another as long as the stains of a fault have not been cleared.

Ngubane (1977) notes further that Africans recognize some illnesses as natural ones that "just happen," particularly illnesses such as influenza, measles, chicken pox, diarrhea, fever, headache, and others that are seen as requiring simple treatment by home remedies. Generally, every disease is eventually traceable to spiritual agents—the grief of ancestors or divinities, the practice of sorcery, and various evil spells. The most satisfactory form of explanation is that which explains the purpose of an event and also identifies the force behind it, and these are the steps in the process employed to diagnose diseases, plan treatment strategies, and promote good health.

## ❖ SOUTHERN AFRICAN TRADITIONAL HEALERS

WHO (1993) considers *traditional healers* to mean individuals who are recognized by their communities as competent to provide health care services, using a range of substances and methods based on the community's social, cultural, and religious systems. Southern African traditional healers who fit this definition are the herbalists (*iyanga*) and diviners (commonly known by their Zulu name, *sangoma*, but also called *amagqirha* [Xhosa], *ngaka* [Sotho], and *nanga* [Venda]). The herbalist specializes in using herbs to treat diseases. The diviners (the traditional healers proper) combine the role of herbalist with the roles of psychotherapists, community or tribal historians, priests (who offer sacrifices to gods), fortune tellers, and even judges (by virtue of their reconciling roles in damaged human relationships, including marital conflicts). The traditional healer-diviners are believed to have closer relationships or to be in constant communication with the ancestral spirits. The traditional belief is that ancestral spirits are the ones who actually give guidance in healing practices, whereas the traditional healers act only as "conduit pipes" or as "middlemen" standing between ancestral spirits and human beings. The *sangomas* are reputed for their clairvoyance, their astounding abilities to read patients' minds, and their power to manipulate and use cosmic energy to ensure health and wealth.

## ❖ SELECTION AND TRAINING OF TRADITIONAL HEALERS-DIVINERS

Becoming a *sangoma* (a diviner-priest) in the traditions of the Nguni-speaking peoples (Zulu, Xhosa, Ndebele) of Southern Africa is not a choice. The ancestral spirits are responsible for the selection. The would-be diviner is first possessed by the ancestral spirits, who make their presence known by inflicting on their host serious illnesses, which are best understood by other *sangomas* experienced in the art of divination. One feature of the illness-experiences is excessive dreaming, which may be vague and confusing. Other symptoms are general body pains, severe headache, or general breakdown in bodily functions; sometimes there are unexplained misfortunes such as sudden loss of job, destruction of properties, or an accident that defies all possible explanations. The physiological manifestations of a calling to be a *sangoma* are very severe, dramatic, and, in Western terms, pathological, because some symptoms may include somatoform disorders, involuntary twitches, or episodic dissociation not unlike schizophrenia (Hammond-Tooke, 1989). Swelling of legs, blindness, and inability to walk (Mufamadi & Sodi, 1999) and various other physical and psychological complaints (numbness of some body parts, restlessness, irritability, aggression, and social withdrawal) (Buhrmann, 1990) have also been reported.

It is the job of an experienced master *sangoma* to determine whether or not illness-experiences (referred to as *u thwasa*) are indeed "proof" of being called to become a traditional healer (*sangoma*). The physical, psychological, and financial demands of the treatment of the illnesses and the subsequent training to become a full-fledged *sangoma* are unsavory and life-threatening, making many reluctant at first to accept the call. However, when an experienced *sangoma* is consulted, the illness-experience, debilitating as it may appear to the individual concerned, is redefined as meaningful, especially in terms of spirituality (as a potential source of power or personal strength) and as a vocation or as a way of acquiring valuable diagnostic and therapeutic skills both for employment purposes and for the benefit of one's community (Mufamadi & Sodi, 1999). Treatment of the illness-experience may be said to lead to good mental health, because the traditional healer helps the individual concerned to integrate his or her personality, thus affording the individual the opportunity to attain new and higher levels of homeostatic functioning.

Actual training to become a traditional healer takes place through becoming an apprentice to a renowned traditional healer. The period of apprenticeship varies from a few months to 5 or more years. The training consists of special exercises for the acquisition of skills in divination, diagnosis, and treatment. Trainees spend a lot of time in the field studying different plants to know their uses (visionary, magical, and medicinal uses, including the sociocultural context of their uses). A major feature of training is helping trainees understand and communicate with the spirit world inhabited by ancestors. This is done through altered states of consciousness, such as dreams, which trainees are helped recognize and understand as avenues for the establishment of a link with the ancestors. The gift of possession by ancestral spirits is usually handed from one generation to the next, and therefore many would-be *sangomas* already can dream and recognize messages from dreams. Trainees without such a heritage are assisted by their teacher to first perform appropriate rituals and then to cultivate dreams and recognize their spirit-guides in dreams. They are sensitized to messages and signals from the ancestors or spirits, who teach them to acquire spiritual powers to diagnose illness and to know the cause(s) of the illness and the uses of herbs for visionary experiences and treatment of illnesses.

Training is believed to be done by ancestral spirits and live traditional healers. It is generally agreed that diagnostic skills are acquired through direct dealings with the ancestral spirits, whereas therapeutic skills are acquired through a didactic teaching-learning process with the master trainer. Trainee *sangomas* are required to withdraw from society and are subjected to strict discipline, including abstinence from sex, smoking, and alcohol; consumption of certain kinds of food; observance of taboos and rituals; and avoidance of practices that can "defile" trainees (Ngubane, 1977). Various exercises are employed to evaluate the progress of trainees, and when the master trainer is satisfied that trainees are ready to practice on their own, the training ends with an elaborate initiation ceremony to mark graduation.

## ❖  THE TRADITIONAL HEALING PROCESS

The general procedure for treatment of diseases involves the patient consulting with the healer, who diagnoses the patient's problem and sets a treatment. In Southern Africa, patients don't present their problems to healers; rather, the traditional healer tells patients about their problems when consulted. The process of healing starts with the healer going into an altered state of consciousness by entering a trance, meditating, or becoming possessed by the ancestral spirits, which helps the healer determine what has happened and why it has happened.

When a patient consults a traditional healer, diagnosis of the problems starts first by the healer communicating with the spirits through divination to relate messages from the ancestors. Specially shaped bone pieces and other objects (stones, shells, tortoise scales, tree barks, money, and dice) make up the divination instruments; these are cast, and the positions of the falling objects are used in interpreting the factors associated with the patient's problems. The falling objects' positions in relation to one another are believed to indicate various human relationships and are seen as communication from ancestral spirits concerning the client's problems and what is responsible for the problems. The diviner communicates with the ancestors, dancing, singing praises of the ancestors, and addressing them by requesting their assistance.

Problem diagnosis involves a series of guesses as to why a patient has come for consultation and what has caused the afflictions or diseases. The diviner is careful with his or her choice of words so as not to be perceived as making obvious guesses, but as providing direct communication from ancestral spirits. The patient and relatives are expected to communicate encouragement by handclaps, which help the healer to know if she or he is going in the right direction regarding the disease (and associated factors) or the distressing events the patient is experiencing. The handclaps intensify when the diviner is on the right track, but become less intense when she or he is not on the right track. However, many traditional healers may not need much encouragement from clients, because they are extremely clever and gifted with the ability to read patients' minds. Therefore, such communication may appear to patients as directly guided by the spirits, especially because the patients are usually made to experience ecstatic trance (though inhaling fumes of burnt psychoactive plants) and perceive themselves as journeying to the spirit world with the healer.

Trance and dreams are very important to Southern African traditional healers, and many methods are employed to elicit the altered state of consciousness, or visionary experiences, with drumming, dancing, and singing being the most common. However, Hammond-Tooke (1989) reports that Southern African diviners employ ingestion of psychoactive plants or inhalation of fumes of burnt psychoactive plants for ecstatic trance and associated altered states of consciousness for spiritual contact and to make "soul journeys" to access the world of the spirits, death, and dreams. Many plants in South Africa are said to have dream-inducing properties (NGOMA, 2003), and these plants play a prominent role in training and initiation of traditional healers and generally for the development of divination abilities.

Dreams are believed to be the primary medium through which ancestors communicate with diviners. It is believed that there are other worlds, supernatural worlds, where gods or spirits are alive and active, and it is through dreams (or other forms of altered states of consciousness) that healers link up with these worlds and communicate with spirits or ancestors. It is further contended that it is through dreams that ancestral spirits direct, teach, and pass knowledge of healing to healers. Dreams, therefore, serve as connective links between the mental and physical spheres of humans and are vehicles to be told what to do or to come to an understanding of the process of healing, as in psychoanalysis.

Information dissemination is an integral part of divination and diagnosis of patients' problems. The information disseminated from the spirits to patients is about the world people live in (including the place of humans in relation to other elements in the universe), about the cultural theories of diseases patients suffer from, and about cure. This information helps patients to develop an attitude of acceptance toward the cultural meanings of health and diseases as well as the cultural beliefs about the cause(s) and theories of cure. The education, therefore, becomes very enlightening to patients and helps not only to develop better insight, or self-awareness, but also to place patients on the road to recovery.

African traditional healing is holistic. Healing is applied to the whole person. No distinction is made between physical and mental ailments, and treatment deals with both the symptoms and the root cause, or whatever is underneath causing the symptoms. A major factor in the African traditional view of disease is the belief in the "intentional stance" of the universe, which in turn informs the external locus of control of illnesses (Ray, 1993). Traditional Africa believes that whatever happens to humans in the universe has meaning and purpose. Illnesses, misfortunes, broken relationships and other interpersonal conflicts, physical injuries, and even death are all attributable to inscrutable acts of the spirits, because of violations of some taboos or ritual rules of conduct or disobedience to or disrespect for the ancestors.

The conditions of life in many indigenous communities make the theories of external causes (evil mechanization of some human and spiritual agents) of diseases plausible. Living in circumstances where people compete for limited resources, as in polygamous families; in families with small landholdings, or no land at all; marginalized and disenfranchised communities with attendant poverty and economic, political, and social repressions; perceived inequality and unfairness: All breed rivalry, ill feelings, and ill health. These negative forces that individuals fight hard to defeat or remove usually lead individuals to experience inner crises of emotions and sensations that disrupt normal consciousness. Gilligan (1998) refers to these inevitable inner crises as "demons" of inner feelings (anger, fear, depression, hatred, self-loathing, abuse, addictions, compulsion) buried in the unconscious. This inner chaos, or the apparent disconnection within the individual's deep self, manifests as symptoms of unpleasant somatic experiences. It is the feeling of something wrong deep within the center of the body, that center being the spirit (soul, or mind). After all, we all refer to the area of our body where every thought originates as the spirit. The spirit is the citadel where all forces continually contend, and therefore, it is at the realm of the spirits that resources for the empowerment needed to deal with different forces one faces in daily living must be cultivated. Thus, by going into the spirit world, healers apply collective unconscious energy to reduce the negative powers of unconscious factors, making patients achieve new integration and individuation (Schoeman, 1985).

The negative forces undermining human integrity, making people ill, or destroying people's lives may indeed be parts of the essence of life that people have to live with through processes of negotiation and accommodation. Hence, African traditional healing is not just for symptom removal or exorcism. Apart from the prescription of herbs (or medicines) to deal with physical symptoms of diseases, traditional healers also prescribe rituals to restore harmony, especially between people.

Rituals are symbolic group activities or procedures prepared in a natural way in societies and families to guide and facilitate social and individual change (Ochoa de Eguileor, 1997). Rituals are culturally organized, symbolically meaningful activities that provide standardized therapeutic experiences for reduction of anxiety and emotional distress (Kiev, 1989). A ritual ceremony brings people and all elements (living and nonliving) of the universe together. Rituals unite people together and are avenues for mediating relationship behaviors to influence the way individuals and families treat each other.

Several Zulu rituals involve slaughtering animals (cattle or goats) (Hammond-Tooke, 1989). Some parts of the animal are separated as the ancestors' share, some parts are smeared on the sick person, and everybody present partakes in the eating of the cooked remaining parts. The ceremony is completed with beer brewed specially for the occasion.

The potency of a ritual as a health-promoting strategy is in the social contacts it provides. Traditional Africa believes that the power to ensure harmony in nature is not self-generated but is gained through personal community with other people. Personal empowerment comes in ritual ceremonies, and people are helped break their isolation and find some degree of identity through common observance and experience as they eat, dance, and rejoice together. People also support each other, share a bit of each other's burden, and communalize their grief, thus finding outlets for their anxiety and ridding themselves of problems.

The social contacts offered by a ritual ceremony are related to the existential-phenomenological principle of healing (Spinneli, 1994). According to this theory, each individual defines him- or herself in relation to others, and the self is the product of, or that which emerges from, relational experience. The social contact principle of healing also finds explanation in systems therapy, central to which is the idea of the relational aspect of problems. The assumption is that problems are dyadic in nature, and using relationship to address some problems may be a good strategy to modify disordered beliefs or behaviors (Parrott, 1999).

Forgiveness and reconciliation feature prominently in rituals. Because sacrifices have costs, payment for purchase of animals for sacrifices is a form of punishment (Rudnick, 2000). Once it is recognized that an individual has served some punishment, the road to forgiveness is clear, with the feeling that whoever has been offended is likely to choose to abandon resentment and anger toward the offender and to be prepared to reconcile and adopt a friendlier attitude. It is also psychological healing to know that one has served a just punishment and has been forgiven and reintegrated into the community.

## ❖ CONCLUSION

All human groups have developed culturally appropriate systems by which they respond to diseases and restore health. Southern African traditional healers, from the rich knowledge base of their traditional values, philosophies, and institutions, have been able to serve their communities adequately by relating their patients to their traditions, the herbs, ceremonies, and rituals that determine and frame the culture and the people. Therefore, an immediate implication of the foregoing discussion for cross-cultural counseling is the need to give consideration to contextual factors in service delivery. Through understanding the local environmental beliefs and attitudes to ill health, acceptance and utilization of the service by the target population can be facilitated. In this regard, counselors need to equip themselves with knowledge of the cultures of their clients and operate from the perspective of the realities they and their clients understand.

It is generally agreed that many health-promoting traditional practices cannot be transferred from one culture to another, because all cultures share the inability to read symbolic writing of others. This is in agreement with those who are opposed to integration of different approaches to health care delivery and who argue that practitioners of different approaches should respect each other and give room for dialogue between them to enhance their common purpose in service delivery. However, all successful therapies (Western or non-Western) share common elements, virtues, or principles, which can be identified and integrated even though the different concepts and methods may not. For instance, although practices of ritual are not expected to be incorporated into conventional psychotherapeutic practices, their underlying principles, such as ensuring high-level activity, physical exercises, emotional arousal, and interpersonal exchanges and support, all of which make for personal empowerment and are health promoting, can be incorporated into counseling. These principles feature prominently in group counseling, and therefore, a group approach to therapy with clients from culturally diverse backgrounds will be an important principle in cross-cultural counseling. Certainly, many clients, irrespective of their cultural leanings, have a good chance of experiencing relief if given opportunities to partake of spirit-lifting exercises and interpersonal exchanges offering opportunities for sharing in a communalized way, as in group counseling.

## ❖ REFERENCES

Buhrmann, M. V. (1990). Psyche and soma: Therapeutic considerations. In G. Saayman (Ed.), *Modern South Africa in search of soul: Jungian perspectives on the wilderness within* (pp. 203–218). Boston: Sigo Press.

Crafford, D. (1996). The African religions. In P. Meiring (Ed.), *World of religions—A South African perspective*. Pretoria, South Africa: Kagiso.

Edwards, S. D. (2000). Developing community psychology in Zululand, South Africa. In S. N. Madu, P. K. Baguma, & A. Pritz (Eds.), *Psychotherapy and African reality* (pp. 149–159). Pietersburg, South Africa: UNN Press (The University of the North, for World Council for Psychotherapy, African Chapter).

Gilligan, S. (1998). Listening to our demons—When new identities struggle to emerge. *NETWORKER—Family Therapy, 24,* 41–45.

Gumede, M. V. (1990). *Traditional healers: A medical doctor's perspective.* Braamfontein, South Africa: Skotaville.

Hammond-Tooke, W. D. (1989). *Rituals and medicines.* Johannesburg, South Africa: AD Donker.

Katz, R. (1982). The utilization of traditional healing system. *American Psychologist, 37,* 715–716.

Kiev, A. (1989). Some psychotherapeutic factors in traditional forms of healing. In P. Karl & P. Ebigbo (Eds.), *Clinical psychology in Africa—South of the Sahara, the Caribbean and Afro-Latin America.* Enugu: University of Nigeria.

Kleinman, A. (1980). *Patients and healers in the context of culture: An exploration of borderland between anthropology, medicine and psychiatry.* Berkeley: University of California Press.

Lambo, T. A. (1978). Psychotherapy in Africa. *Human Nature, 1*(3), 32–39.

Mufamadi, J., & Sodi, T. (1999). The process of becoming an indigenous healer among Venda speaking people of South Africa. In S. N. Madu, P. K. Baguma, & A. Pritz (Eds.), *Cross-cultural dialogue on psychotherapy in Africa* (pp. 172–183. Pietersburg, South Africa: UNN Press (The University of the North, for World Council for Psychotherapy, African Chapter).

Nefale, M. C., & Van Dyk, G. A. J. (2003). Ubuntu therapy—A psychotherapeutic model for African clients. In N. S. Madu (Ed.), *Contributions of psychotherapy in Africa* (pp. 76–99). Sovenga, South Africa: UNN Press (The University of the North, for the World Council for Psychotherapy, African Chapter).

NGOMA. (2003). *Traditional healing in South Africa: Culture and substance abuse.* Retrieved March 19, 2003, from http://www.wits.ac.za/izangoma/part3.asp

Ngubane, H. (1977). *Body and mind in Zulu medicine.* London: Academic Press.

Ochoa de Eguileor, I. A. (1997). Rituals in family therapy. In P. J. Hawkins & J. N. Nestoros (Eds.), *Psychotherapy: New perspectives on theory, practice and research.* Athens, Greece: Ellinika Grammata.

Parrott, C. (1999). Towards an integration of science, art and morality: The role of values in psychology. *Counselling Psychology Quarterly, 12,* 5–24.

Ray, C. B. (1993). Aladura Christianity: A Yoruba religion. *Journal of Religion in Africa, 23,* 266–291.

Rudnick, H. (2000). *Traditional healing in South Africa.* Johannesburg, South Africa: Rand Afrikaans University Press.

Schoeman, J. B. (1985). Vera Buhrmann's approach to cultural psychiatry. *Psychotherapeia and Psychiatry in Practice, 36*(1), 7–12.

Spinneli, E. (1994). *Demystifying therapy.* London: Constable.

Straker, G. (1994). Integrating African and Western healing practices in South Africa. *American Journal of Psychotherapy, 48,* 455–467.

World Health Organization. (1993). *World health statistical manual: 1992.* Geneva, Switzerland: Author.

# 7

# Caribbean Healers and Healing

*Awakening Spiritual and Cultural Healing Powers*

*Ronald Marshall*

The English-speaking Caribbean is also regarded as the British West Indies (Gopaul-McNicol, 1993). It is comprised of, but not limited to, a number of territories, namely: Anguilla, Antigua, Barbados, Dominica, Grenada, Montserrat, Jamaica, St. Kitts and Nevis, St. Lucia, St. Vincent, Guyana, Trinidad, and Tobago. The Caribbean is undergoing demographic changes, which are reflected in its population pattern (Theodore & Edward, 1997), and these have implications for distribution of diseases, such as cancers, diabetes, and heart disease, which are very prevalent throughout the region. Patients tend to employ various healing methods, including traditional healing, to alleviate or mitigate their conditions, because from a medical point of view there appear to be no cures.

This chapter explores the issues of traditional healing in the Caribbean, first by recounting the Caribbean experience of slavery and indentureship in an effort to explain the impact of traditional medicine on chronic diseases. Then follows a discussion on the integration of traditional healing practices with contemporary religious faith, the results of which may often lead to cultural and spiritual awakening. The chapter also presents results from a qualitative study that attempted to uncover the experiences of a number of people belonging to various religious groups (in Trinidad) regarding how they deal with their health problems (if they experience any) and what outcomes these experiences may have had on their beliefs about health and illness. The findings also shed some light on the way traditional customs, values, and spirituality converge and are sustained in the Caribbean.

Any understanding of the connection between traditional healing and cultural and spiritual awakening has to acknowledge the significance of the society and the culture, which is filtered and finds expression through individual families and community organizations. Organizations such as religious organizations have a direct affinity with the family, not only with respect to order and fear of God, but also in terms of relationships with each other and the perceptions that people hold about illness, health, and cure.


## ❖ THE DEVELOPMENT OF HEALTH CARE IN THE CARIBBEAN

The development of health care in the Caribbean may have started because of the opinions that European slave masters had of their slaves. Observers believed that the health care of slaves was not taken seriously by the slave masters and that this might have led to the belief that blacks were immune to certain diseases. It must be noted that slaves lived in terrible conditions that exacted a severe toll on their physical and mental health. For example, Handler and Jacoby (1993) reported that "the working and living conditions of the plantation . . . were hostile to slave health, and no slave settlement was exempt from health problems" (p. 74). Further, following Emancipation of these communities, the question of allocation of resources was prioritized in terms of commercial development, heavily slanted in favor of the European markets.

Under these circumstances, religion and folk medicine might have been used increasingly to deal with health disorders, because very little attention was paid to the health of ex-slaves and rural communities from an institutional perspective.

According to Handler and Jacoby (1993), slaves often had to rely on the capacity of the body to heal itself or to use herbs or plants to aid the recovery process. For example, the authors recorded that arrowroot was used both internally and externally for the relief of illnesses. The crushed root was used as a poultice for treating yaws, scorpion and spider bites, in addition to sores and ulcers. Alternatively, its juices were taken for dysentery.

In addition, slaves also used ginger tea to counteract the effects of cold and damp. In these and other ways, slave societies turned to herbs and traditional ways to deal with care and cure for their health. Similarly, the ex-slaves, with the use of prayers, mounted an assault upon many illnesses and diseases in an uncertain and torturous health environment. However, it must be pointed out that the overarching social structures of government, politics, and culture were the conduits through which these practices struggled to find expression and acceptance.

It must also be noted that the 1930s slave revolts in the Caribbean included as part of their genesis the overriding concerns for better health care and improved medical attention, in addition to concerns about rising prices, low wages, and inadequate housing. These demands were met in varying degrees over the ensuing years, but the stage had been set for the manner in which health care would be conceptualized, articulated, and delivered. In sum, the health system involved an emerging constellation of health care providers comprising the individual healer, the religious leaders, and the culture in Caribbean society.

## ❖ RELIGION AND FAITH HEALING IN THE CARIBBEAN

McGuire (1997) argues that religion remains an important factor in societal integration. For one thing, it establishes unity among the group, represents a communion of believers, and contributes to consensus and moral values. For another, it wields powerful negative sanctions for noncooperation, and these appear to be more potent than earthly punishments. This position can be argued for all the different cultural and religious groups that make up Caribbean culture. Of particular importance is how the influence of the various religious groups that came to the Caribbean following Emancipation (e.g., the Muslim faith) came to be fused with more modern or prevailing aspects of Caribbean culture. The Hindu religion, on the other hand, has been present in the Caribbean since Emancipation, but only within the past 30 years has the Hindu presence been felt throughout the island of Trinidad or in the Caribbean, for that matter. According to Vertovec (1992), throughout the 1970s and the 1980s Hinduism started to flourish, and many Hindus became more self-conscious of who they were, their position in the social structure, and their religious practices. Filtering later into the Caribbean religious matrix were the Seventh-Day Adventists and the Jehovah's Witnesses. According to Thomas-Hope (cited in Gates, 1980), these groups hailed mainly from North America. But the predominant religion in the Caribbean is Christianity. Both the French and the English had a certain amount of influence in this regard. The English especially used religion to capture the hearts and souls, emotions and minds of a body of people (slaves) in order to control their lives, both from an educational and a social and cultural perspective. In sum, Caribbean religions are represented by Christians, Hindus, Muslims, Seventh-Day Adventists, and Jehovah's Witnesses. In addition, there is the practice of Voodoo and Rastafarianism in Jamaica. Shango, a fusion of African and Christian religions, has also flourished more in Trinidad than in any other Caribbean territory. I will touch briefly on two of these religions, Shango and Voodoo.

### The Practice of Shango

Shango, as practiced in Trinidad, is derived from the Yoruba religion, and many of its worshipers were imported to Trinidad as slaves. The overwhelming majority of Trinidadian Shangoists are "relatively uneducated, lower class persons, mainly of dark skin color" (Simpson, 1970, p. 17). Shango combines aspects of Yoruba traditional religion, Catholicism, and the Baptist faith and comes out of Haiti, Cuba, and Brazil. Shango healers occasionally communicate with the spirits of the dead to locate the appropriate cure for a client who might be desperately ill (Simpson, 1970).

They hold dear to their faith the sacred act of cleansing. A wrongdoer must spend 7 or 9 days in different churches cleansing himself or herself. Shangoists also use dreams to guide their lives. Some dreams are direct, whereas others need interpretation. Shangoists also "catch the power," a manifestation of a spiritual and gratifying experience. As Simpson (1970) writes,

When a "power" manifests on him, a follower bows and swirls in front of the drummers, dances to the rhythms played by the drummers in honor of the god that has possessed him, shakes his shoulders vigorously, runs, sings, falls to the ground, pours water from a jar, embraces other participants whether or not they are possessed . . . groans, and seizes and shakes both hands of another person, possessed or unpossessed. (p. 24)

### The Practice of *Vodoun*

*Vodoun* (Voodoo) came into existence in Haiti following a mixture of African tradition and French culture. Haiti's contact with France occurred around 1697 when it came to be known as Saint Domingue. African slaves were brought to Haiti to work on the sugar plantations, and they brought with them their culture. The word *Vodoun* means "spirit" or "deity" and has a similar meaning to the word *Orisha* in the Yoruba language (Courlander, Bastien, & Schader, 1966). *Vodoun* is a mixture of various entities: a relationship between the *loa* (Afro-Haitian deity), the *houngan* (the cult priest), the spirit of dead ancestors, the followers, and the community. Thus, *Vodoun* is a socioreligious activity possessing magical features.

As Courlander et al. explain, *Vodoun* has a strong presence in Haiti, influencing almost all aspects of its daily life, but its roots run deep within the peasantry, as their way of surviving their environment. It is more than a ritual. "It is an integrated system of concepts concerning human activities . . . between the natural world and the supernatural . . . between the living and the dead" (Courlander et al., p. 12).

A *Vodoun* ritual takes the form of dancing, offering gifts, and making animal sacrifices to appease the spirits. The spirit takes control of the body, and the dancer falls to the ground. The blood of the sacrificed animal is then given to the possessed person to satisfy the hunger of the spirits. Rituals are also held to appeal to the various *loas* (deities) to make the land more fertile, to improve health, or to make one lucky in some undertaking. In *Vodoun*, a dead person has a human personality, retaining all the privileges he or she has had on earth; he or she is prone to jealousy and has easily wounded feelings; further, since the spirit can confer blessings, care must be taken not to offend him or her (Courlander et al., 1966).

Whereas the *loa* (Afro-Haitian deity) depends on followers for food and material things, the followers depend on the *loa* for blessings. The *houngan* (cult priest), on the other hand, protects individuals from demons and evil spirits that roam the country. The *houngans* must also be able to see into the future. In this regard, the Caribbean islands' religious future was fashioned out of slavery, and their contact with the metropolis formed a fusion of cultures, reflected in the various religious organizations and setting the stage for traditional healing practices and the much sought-after spiritual awakening.

❖ TRADITIONAL HEALING, CONTEMPORARY
  RELIGIOUS PRACTICE, AND SPIRITUAL AWAKENING

According to Matcha (2000), traditional healing had to do with how an individual's constitution, personal habits, the cosmic forces, and the local environment interacted to effect cure or relief. Present-day traditionalists (e.g., acupuncturists, herbalists, and masseurs) have continued in this vein. Such healing has to do with "the long-standing aspect of dealing with diseases representing an indigenous type of health care in developing countries and among the indigenous populations of industrialized countries" (Matcha, p. 282). Like other developing societies and those that had an indigenous population, traditional medicine in the Caribbean is used alongside Western medicine.

In the Caribbean, severe illnesses are still interpreted by a large section of the community as being associated with evil spirits, which have to be cast out by traditional medicine and prayers. Herbs and various oils were used by Shango

Baptists, and the beating of drums and hand clapping are still features of healing in varying degrees. Hunter and Stephen (1986, pp. 6, 128) remind us that "religion is a reality that inevitably draws on cultural materials" that are filtered over personal experience and what these experiences come to mean to us. "Moreover, it is maintained through the sound interaction of individuals" (p. 123). The evolving practices are subsequently played out in cultural healing practices involving traditional medicine and prayer.

Singer (1977) argues that cultural explanations are the reason behind the type of health care one receives in a country (p. 12). He sees it as a colonial system (representing the survival of the colonial in a social system) that creates contradictions and antagonisms.

> All underdeveloped countries that I know of, while citing the need for more physicians, still cite the fact that what physicians they have are concentrated in the urban areas. There we see at once the survivals of colonialism and contradictions and antagonisms in a social system. . . . In all these countries, folk medicine and traditional healing are very powerful. (Singer, 1977, p. 19)

In this regard, Singer (1977) argumentatively sets the stage for our understanding of the continued existence of folk and traditional medicine in ex-colonial Caribbean territories.

The integration between traditional healing and contemporary religious practices is highly evident in the Caribbean. As Oosthuizen, Edwards, Wessels, and Hexham (1998) state,

> Sorcery, witchcraft and spirit possession are realities for many Christians in the established churches and the African independent churches. . . . In the past, it was even taboo in many cases to mention such diseases in the presence of a missionary. Yet, there are churches, which acknowledge the effectiveness of the rituals utilized in the indigenous healing of typical African type of diseases. (p. 76)

Also, McLeod (1998) points to Africa as an example of a place where "the office of the prophet/prayer healer in the African Independent Churches fulfils a much felt need because of the traditional society's age-old role of the diviner and herbalist" (p. 75).

Medicine was first of all born out of the necessity that was magic, followed by prayer; then it became an art and only recently became a science (Bromberg, 1937, cited in Oosthuizen et al., 1998). This underlines the significance of prayer and bush medicine and the continued use of these, particularly in developing countries. This is illustrated, for example, in the excerpt below of a 27-year-old woman of African descent who was diagnosed with liver cancer. She was torn between having the operation (which the doctors felt might not save her life) and following the advice of her spiritual Sister. In the end, she followed the Sister's advice and proceeded to have the operation. She had this to say:

> I felt myself moving above the trees. It was a cool feeling . . . I felt really relaxed and that there was nothing to fear. At the time of the operation, I could see Sister Garcia hovering above the physicians who were operating on me. I felt good, really good.
>
> Yes, I now feel like a whole person and I must thank Sister for her prayers and her intercession on my behalf. Yes, I have gone back to thank her but we drifted apart over the years. I used to attend her Church. . . . However, I have a deep respect for her powers and the power of prayer.[1]

Today, she confesses that she is well healed and speaks in glowing terms of the value of prayer.

There is another example of a man in his 60s who felt that he had too much to bear. He had been married three times and was in a live-in relationship at the time of his interview. He had this to say:

> I was in mental and physical pain. Yes, I think I was going out of my mind. Then someone told me "why don't you go to Father X, he casts out spirits?" I thought, what does all of this have to do with my illness . . . Unless it was punishment . . . for all that I did . . . I toyed with the idea. I had gone to almost every specialist that I knew . . . but I had not been to Church for the past 20 years.
>
> It was a week later, I faced Father X . . . I can't remember what happened but I started to yell uncontrollably. The next thing I realized that I was being pulled from under the table by Father X and his assistant . . . Today, I am all right . . . I continue to go to Church but not as often as I would like . . . My prayers have been answered.[2]

He seemed to be quite relaxed and believed that he had found something spiritual that he had been looking for all of his life. After all that he had been through, he had now found meaning to his life.

According to Mkhwanazi (cited in Oosthuizen et al., 1998), healing rituals go through three separate stages: (a) the illness is labeled with an appropriately sanctioned cultural category; (b) the ritual is culturally transferred; and (c) a new label, such as "cured" or "well," is applied. This is seen in the excerpts just presented. Basically, there are therapeutic effects, and these, according to Mkhwanazi, emanate from the client's belief that the healer has supernatural powers. The diviner would ease the frustration experienced by chronic disease sufferers and would find a "cure" for the incurable. This relationship and behavior take place against the backdrop of prayers, group or family involvement, cultural relatedness, and an atmosphere of expectation and spirituality. It is argued that these processes produce therapeutic effects and make the client believe in the possibility of what had hitherto been perceived as impossible.

## ❖  CULTURE, RELIGION, AND FAITH HEALING

In a semistructured interview that took place among Christians, Hindus, and Muslims in Trinidad among members of the middle- to lower-upper class and the middle-middle class, the effects of culture, religion, and faith healing and the use of traditional medicine to bring about relief and good health were investigated.

Respondents ($N = 65$) were asked a number of questions ranging from the use of traditional medicine to frequency of praying. Respondents were also asked to indicate whether they felt that healing practices effected a cure and how significant or reliable they thought it to be. The research found that those who prayed regularly (three or more times a day) spent an equal amount or slightly more time paying visits to their physician than their counterparts who prayed infrequently (at least once a week or less). Both the frequent worshipper and the infrequent worshipper believed that prayers were a powerful source of healing that came from above. Members of all three religious groups—Christians, Hindus, and Muslims—felt this way. Muslims felt that all diseases came from an unclean life and that diseases were God's way of demonstrating to man what happens when he departs from the life God has made for him. The Christians (Roman Catholics) felt the same way. Indeed, they believed that diseases were a form of punishment, which the Creator alone could relieve. In fact, those who prayed regularly had a greater belief that they would be cured of their chronic disease (heart disease, diabetes, and hypertension) than those who did not pray as frequently, even as they visited the physician.

However, those who prayed regularly accepted death readily as opposed to those who did not pray as frequently. Those who did not pray frequently (at least once per week or less) reportedly spent a greater amount of time with traditional healers than did those who prayed frequently (three or more times a day). The ethnographic study showed that the use of herbs to relieve chronic diseases such as hypertension, diabetes, and heart ailments amounted to 23% or 35% of the frequently worshipping respondents compared with 42% or 65% for the infrequent worshippers.

In addition, those who prayed regularly believed that faith healing and Western medicine are all that matters: "My mother always say, faith without work is dead." Indeed, the vast majority of respondents believed that faith is stronger than traditional medicine. Almost all the respondents (85%) believed that healing takes place through faith and medicine. In fact, Shorter (1985) notes that prayers and the application of physical remedies are indications that we are entering into the absolute and comprehensive healing action of God.

Those who use traditional medicine (herbal healers), on the other hand, pour scorn on Western medicine, claiming that Western medicine misleads the public and that practitioners of Western medicine are guilty of using traditional medicine themselves. When asked about dosage and measurement of their concoctions and the ill effects the concoctions might have on their patients, the herbalists point to the long years that their foreparents were using herbs, during which time "nothing went wrong."

The traditional healer lays claim to having connection with the spiritual forces. The use of herbal medicine is considered to be divine. Some herbalists claim that they experience a certain amount of divine presence in their work. Although the current investigation has not uncovered any tangible evidence of this, it was observed that patients experienced some form of bonding bordering on reverence for the traditional healer.

Many clients interviewed (50%) claimed that they had "seen the light." They had awakened to a new meaning and understanding of life by accessing the intervention of the traditional healer. In the Caribbean, the Shango and similar religiously oriented groups are actually worshipped by their followers and feared by nonenthusiasts, who believe that those individuals can hurt them spiritually if they cross their paths.

## ❖ TRADITIONAL HEALERS AND CONTEMPORARY THERAPISTS

The literature and observation tend to lend support for the view that patients suffering from some forms of chronic diseases may be in need of counseling services. In many instances the goal is psychotherapy. The patient goes to the traditional healer because in his or her estimation it is the "right" thing to do, either because Western medicine has failed to bring about the desired result or because the patient is overwhelmed by the problem and needs "expert" advice or intervention. McLeod (1998) points out that the need for psychotherapy results from the fact that moral controls in modern society tend to be internalized as opposed to being externalized. When this occurs, people are "confused" as to what is right or wrong and seek out ways to relieve guilt or stress brought about by the lack of a common code. This leaves the door open for the emergence of counseling services by the traditional healer to his client.

According to Dube (cited in Oosthuizen et al., 1998), during prayer time the patient's body is touched, and dreams are related and explained by the healer. The client's therapeutic experience emanates from the client's belief in the power of the healer (Dube, cited in Oosthuizen et al., 1998). This is an informal form of counseling, whereas the psychotherapist operates under formal guidelines mapped out by his or her profession.

In the traditional healer's practice, he or she tends to carry out healing within the whole cultural setting including the client, the healer, the group, and the world of the supernatural (Mkhwanazi, as cited in Oosthuizen et al., 1998). Both the traditional healer and the counselor have the predisposition to reclaim the client's sense of self-worth. Above all, they must demonstrate a high level of caring for the client's problem or condition.

Some observers believe that the time has come for the integration of these two systems—those of the traditional healer and the counselor. One of the underlying reasons for this may be found in the common relationship that the two systems share, namely the Judeo-Christian religious tradition, which has many of the values and practices of counseling (McLeod, 1998).

In one study (Propst et al., 1992, as cited in McLeod, 1998), behavioral therapy was administered to a group of depressed Christian clients, and "religious arguments [were] supplied to counter irrational thoughts." A comparison group was given the same behavioral treatment but without the religious arguments. It was found that both groups reported significant benefits from the therapy but in varying degrees.

This finding is consistent with the qualitative research finding from the present qualitative study, which found that those who did not pray frequently still believed in the power of prayer to help and guide them through their illnesses.

Again, the question of multiculture has provided counselors with the opportunity "to give serious consideration to the psychological significance of the religious belief and practices of people from other cultures" (McLeod, 1998, p. 255). In this regard, a rich cross-fertilization of psychotherapeutic techniques remains to be untapped in Caribbean societies.

In the study, a number of people (15%) expressed conditions that warranted psychotherapy, but most used prayers; others combined prayer with counseling services as a feature of counseling strategy in a multicultural Caribbean society. Those seeking counseling services mainly utilized counseling for "problems" with their husbands or for children experiencing conflicts at home.

## ❖ CONCLUSION

Illness represents the sociocultural experiences of the individual exposure in the form of diet, religion, ethnic makeup, and education. Such behavior tends to reflect the cultural options in health recovery available within the culture. Further, in reacting to those symptoms, the patient may use local social networks in addition to compliance with medical advice (Conrad & Kern, 1986, p. 90).

The Caribbean region, like other regions around the world, tends to use both traditional and Western medicine. The difference may lie in the use of prayers combined with Western and traditional medicine. However, it may be similar to places in Asia and Africa. This blend of religion and folk medicine is also practiced by the Mexican American healers called *curanderos*. In the end, these practices set the stage for a fusion of concepts and traditions that are psychotherapeutic in nature, resulting in not only the transformation of counseling and therapy but also the changing and ongoing relations between the diviner, client/follower, and counselor.

## ❖ NOTES

1. These comments were made during an interview by the author with a spiritual healer in Curepe, Trinidad, February 20, 2004.

2. This quote comes from Patrick, one of my research subjects, whom I interviewed March 24, 2004, at Saint Charles Church in the district of Tunapuna.

## ❖ REFERENCES

Conrad, P., & Kern, R. (1986). *Medical sociology.* New York: St. Martin's Press.

Courlander, H., Bastien, R., & Schader, R. P. (1966). *Religion and politics in Haiti.* Washington, DC: Institute for Cross-cultural Research.

Gates, B. (1980). *Afro-Caribbean religion.* London: Ward Lock Educational.

Gopaul-McNicol, S. (1993). *Working with West Indian families.* New York: Guilford Press.

Handler, J., & Jacoby, J. (1993). Slave medicine and plant use in Barbados. *Journal of the Barbados Museum and Historical Society, 41,* 74–98.

Hunter, J. D., & Stephen, C. A. (Eds.). (1986). *Making sense of modern times: Peter Berger and the vision of interpretive sociology.* London: Routledge and Kegan Paul.

Matcha, D. A. (2000). *Medical sociology.* Boston: Allyn & Bacon.

McGuire, M. (1997). *Religion: The social context.* Belmont, CA: Wadsworth.

McLeod, J. (1998). *An introduction to counseling.* Philadelphia: Open University Press.

Oosthuizen, G. C., Edwards, S. D., Wessels, W. H., & Hexham, I. (Eds.). (1998). *Afro-Christian religion and healing in Southern Africa.* Lewiston, NY: Edwin Mellen Press.

Shorter, A. (1985). *Jesus and the witchdoctor: An approach to healing and wholeness.* London: Geoffrey Chapman.

Simpson, G. E. (1970). *Religious cults of the Caribbean* (Rev. ed.). Rio Piedras, Puerto Rico: University of Puerto Rico.

Singer, P. (1977). *Traditional healing: New science or new colonialism?* New York: Conch Magazine Limited.

Theodore, K., & Edward, G. (1997). Socioeconomic and political contest. In *Health conditions in the Caribbean* (Scientific publication No. 561). Washington, DC: Pan American Health Organization, Pan American Sanitary Bureau, Regional Office Washington.

Vertovec, S. (1992). *Hindu Trinidad: Religion, ethnicity and socio-economic change.* London: Macmillan Academic and Professional.

# 8

# Latin American Healers and Healing

*Healing as a Redefinition Process*[1]

*Lilián González Chévez*

This chapter discusses Latin American traditional healers and healing by using an example from Mexico. As part of a tradition and an object of constant reconfiguration, traditional healing in Mexico is widely used by indigenous people and rural *campesinos* as well as by large sectors of the urban population (Fagetti, 2003, p. 6). Historically, traditional healing is rooted in the Meso-American worldview and in a tradition of specialists dedicated to healing activity (López Austin, 1976, p. 16). At the end of the pre-Hispanic epoch there were 40 classes of sorcerers among the Nahua (a relevant indigenous population group of Mexico and part of Central America) whose primary activities were healing and casting spells (López Austin, 1967, p. 87). Many of these specialties have been maintained into the present era, and those skilled in them continue to fully exercise their duties (Zolla, 1994a, p. 306).

Under colonization, elements derived from the evangelizing impulse of the Spanish missionaries were incorporated into the Meso-American worldview to such an extent that few healing practices in contemporary Mexico have not been deeply permeated by syncretic forms of folk Catholicism. At the same time, the Spanish population, by means of the common people, brought with it ideas and patterns of action from peninsular folk healing. In addition, with the consolidation of colonial power, slave labor began to be imported, and with it were introduced African traditional healing practices. These played a decisive role in the configuration of colonial folk healing, greatly contributing to the enrichment of indigenous healing in those places where black populations were established (Aguirre Beltrán, 1980a, p. 264; 1994, p. 109).

Traditional healing in modern Mexico is an amalgam of cultural content inherited from both indigenous healing and from the cultures shaped during the colonial period, from diverse forms of folk religion and from the galenic tradition introduced by Europeans. It continues to be nourished in open, pluralistic, and heterologous ways by devices from the biomedical model and by the urban *curanderos* (healers), who have begun adding "New Age" elements of alternative healing symbols and paraphernalia from the Far East.

However, this particular dynamism does not keep traditional healing from remaining deeply rooted in the current belief systems of broad sections of the population, forming an integral part of their culture (Zolla, Del Bosque, Mellado, Tascón, & Maqueo, 1992, p. 98). Its persistence demonstrates its effectiveness in assigning order to episodes of illness, giving them form and sense, as well as its ability to communicate and confirm ideas about the reality of the world (Young, 1976, p. 19). In that sense, traditional healers—understood to be specialists in ritual—play a role that mediates or articulates a certain view of the world, and when turning to them, social groups appeal to cultural forms that belong to the people themselves (Bartolomé, 1997, p. 120). Nevertheless, it is insufficient to state that the social groups that seek treatment from the world of the *curandero* are instilled with a culture that identifies with that of the healer, and that for that reason, and no other, they request his or her services. In social groups with low education levels that have been more or less marginalized from modernity and the worldwide process of Westernization and globalization, traditional healing is a way of reclaiming their cultural heritage. These communities carry culture backward in time in order to solve their enormous health problems, and this also becomes in part a response to their virtual, partial, or limited access to "well-being" and to scientific-positivist language and its associated resources and promises of modernity.

It is also important to emphasize that indigenous groups, which consistently have the highest levels of marginalization in the country (Rubio & Zolla, 2000, p. 269), are not only living under social inequality, but are also the principal carriers of cultural otherness—that is to say, of difference. There appears, then, a paradox in which the cultural and social richness that nourishes health care strategies is upheld in large part by those living in a context of scarcity and precariousness with respect to their most pressing needs. It is precisely within the borders of these marginalized people's culture that traditional healing is continually preserved, deepened, and enriched, so that it is not by chance that in Mexico—a country of great social inequalities but also of a great ethnocultural diversity—cultural diversity and social inequality continually converge among ethnic minorities.

## ❖ FROM FOLK NOSOLOGY TO STRUCTURAL PATHOGENIC DEVICES

In a survey about people's principal motives for requesting traditional health care, as recorded with 13,067 traditional healers in marginalized rural populations in Mexico (Zolla et al., 1992, p. 72), among the 10 most frequent reasons for a consultation, 4 were found in which the line between the natural and the supernatural orders is blurred, and magicoreligious causality is strongly linked to the emotive sphere and the relational world: *mal de ojo* (evil eye), *susto* (a shock or scare), *aires* (winds), and *daño* (a harmful form of *brujería*, or witchcraft).[2] Four other motives for requesting health care were in line with morbidity statistics recognized by health institutions—diarrhea, dysentery, angina (amigdalytis), and sprains—which allows us to corroborate that the activity of traditional healers is also associated with a level of primary care linked to common illnesses (Lozoya, Velásquez, & Flores, 1988, p. 64).

It is revealing that the cultural-ideological basis in 40% of the requests for care from traditional healers cannot be reduced to the rational-positivist logic of the biomedical model and that these requests appear as dominant models of interpretation with respect to the etiology of illnesses, in particular when they turn out to be insidious, serious, or difficult to resolve. Therefore, the ultimate causes of *susto, mal de ojo, daño,* and *aires* are in a direct relation to the supernatural world but are attributed to emotions and feelings that one experiences or that are projected onto one by others. Other requests for care involve a lesser emotional impact, and their causality can be attributed to natural phenomena, such as an imbalance between heat and cold, excessive work, various nutritional problems, microbes, accidents, or displacement of organs (Aguirre Beltrán, 1980a, p. 38; Álvarez, 1987, p. 76; Erasmus, 1952, p. 411; Kroeger, 1988, p. 29; Queiroz, 1986, p. 314). Nevertheless, folk nosology does not normally allow a clear compartmentalization of concepts. That is to say, the folk explanatory model encompasses ever-widening margins of meaning, so that each nosological entity interconnects in a way that is dynamic and compatible with other entities, without it being quite possible—or even desirable—to exactly outline its margins. Therefore *susto, daño,* and *aires,* as syndromes with multiple meanings, span several relational planes— natural, social, and supernatural—in a contextual spiral whose margins blur. In this sense, the narrative of a patient who complains of *mal aire*[3]—one of the most frequently registered causes of illness in traditional healing—will serve us as a lens to focus on the web of links that organize the system of signs, meanings, and actions in this contextual spiral.

### The Contextual Spiral in Folk Symptomatology

When María, on my first home visit, asks me why a rash has appeared on her skin, I have no reason to suspect an underlying meaning in her question; it seems natural, casual, and without ulterior motives that the layperson is asking the professional (in this case myself, a physician) the cause of her affliction. She shows me her arms, and after a brief examination of her symptoms I explain to her that it appears to be caused by an allergy, so I inquire, "What do you think caused the rash?" "Umm . . . I ate some *chorizo* [spicy sausage]," she answers. "And do you usually have a bad reaction to *chorizo*?" I ask again. "No, but that's what I blame. I had *chorizo* for lunch and in the afternoon I started—a rash started to appear, but it didn't itch. Now it does itch and even more at night. That's why I put aloe vera ointment on it."

In my role as a physician, I then recommend that she continue her aloe vera treatment, prescribe a medication for the itching, indicate some hygienic and dietetic measures, and consider the consultation finished. We continue the conversation without me noticing that the original subject of conversation remains active, beyond my comprehension, in the realm of meaning where the patient's ailment makes sense to her:

"My sister Lorenza, the one that lives over there, had the same thing. . . . She was covered with a rash! With her face and body all discoloured, but she was like that because she was scratching!"

"Do you think it was caused by the sun?"

"Umm, no . . . she doesn't go out in the sun. . . . I took her to Oacalco with the *señora* that heals, and when she came back, she was fine."

"And how long did your sister have the rash?"

"*Ay, doctora,* for a month! We just went last Sunday. The *señora* did a *limpia* [cleansing] for her. First she did it with an egg, then she cleansed her again with another egg. But *doctora,* it's really effective! The glass showed that someone had infected her with a *porquería* [filth], in other words, a *mal aire.*[4] You know, *porquerías!* And she caught it. The *señora* told her, 'It wasn't for you, but you went by at that moment, you caught it.' And yes, she says that when she went out into the street to say good-bye to someone, she felt something like a *mal aire* . . . and then it all started."

"So it's not that the person sent her that *mal aire,* or did they?"

"Well . . . yes. But it was because they were envious, because . . . you know now, she doesn't have a husband, and even though she has five children, now she's becoming really successful, all by herself! . . . she's building a house, she sends her kids to school, and she works all the time . . . And yes . . . the *señora* cured her: she did a *limpia* for her, she *gathered her pulse* and she did an *amarre* [a tying up] so that the trouble wouldn't continue. . . . And she put some healing on her. . . . She cried because it burned, but the next day the rash was gone."

"And then did she believe?"

"No. She didn't go back. But the *señora* told her to boil *coahuilote, arnica, cuachalate,* and *golondrina,* and with that it would be gone. She was bathing with those plants and that made it go away."

María's story gives us some clues to help our interpretation of the semiological systems and folk explanations. The first clue is part of the dual reasoning employed by María herself in order to explain her own illness. In retrospect, it is evident that when María asks me to explain her affliction, she has already contemplated an etiology similar to that which she attributes to her sister's affliction as a possible cause.

When I ask her about her causal interpretation, she goes along with the etiological premises that my own biomedical logic suggests. Perhaps this logic sounded convincing to her or reduced her anxiety about the probable cause of the *mal aire,* or maybe she simply followed my discourse parallel to her own logic—a logic that, to understand its significance, requires knowledge of the cultural keys with which this logic makes sense.

The first key, then, is part of the patient's management of a parallel, polylogical discourse whose wording is used discretionally according to whether the interlocutor is a member of one's cultural group or not. In this case, although the layperson is familiar with the cognitive-rational logic of the professional in a partial and fragmented way, the professional lacks the cultural keys that would allow him or her to even notice the dimensions of the layperson's argument. That is to say, the professional has not accessed the conceptual and linguistic apparatus on which these restricted codes are based.

María's narrative provides us with the second key, which indicates the cause to which she attributes her sister's illness—a *cochinada*[5] or *mal aire.* María's

**Table 8.1**    Semantic Areas Included in the Narrative About the Cause of Affliction

| Folk Explanatory Model (A Summary of the Narrative) | Semantic Area Involved |
|---|---|
| Envy . . . | Emotional |
| provokes in others . . . | Relational |
| favorable social and material conditions in which *ego* is found, despite her having a matrifocal family, which would theoretically give her a comparative disadvantage . . . | Material and social |
| this attracts to her and makes her receptive to supernatural forces . . . | Magic/supernatural |
| which cause or unleash illnesses. | Organic |

reasoning is part of a set of premises on the etiology of the illness, radically distinct from the causal ordering of positive rationality, which is broken down and decoded in Table 8.1.

With striking logical coherence, the folk explanatory model followed by María weaves together diverse planes (natural-supernatural) and spheres of reality (individual-material-social) that are apparently unconnected, joining, in a social representation such as the *mal aire/cochinada,* a semantic area that articulates the emotional, relational, material, magical, and organic causes that she attributes to the illness. The multiple meanings this social representation contains bring to mind two of the properties of ritual symbols referred to by Turner (1980, p. 30): that of the "condensation" of a spectrum of meanings (many things and actions represented in a single symbol) and that of the "unification of disparate meanings" (because they have in common analogous qualities or because they are in fact associated in thought). A third property that Turner (1980) attributes to the dominant ritual symbols is the "polarization of meaning," that is, the ability that symbols have to evoke emotions, determining to a great extent the external form of the symbol, which he calls a "sensory pole," as well as the ability of symbols to link with the norms and values that guide and control people as members of a group, which he refers to as an "ideological pole."

In María's narrative, the unifying thread along which the illness is explained is a feeling of envy, so we designate this as the "sensory pole" of her explanation. The sensory field in this folk representation must be sought in the Meso-American belief that others' hostile emotions or desires have, under certain circumstances, the capacity to tear at people's natural protection, projecting themselves and materializing as illness (see Aguirre Beltrán, 1980b, p. 45).

Such a capacity can stem, among other things, from the manipulation of supernatural forces such as *aires,* sent by some *brujo* (witch doctor) at the wishes of a customer. It can also stem from the fact that upon maneuvering these forces, the *brujo* has set them free to act as they will or under the orders of negative feelings able to bring about an illness (Hermitte, 1970, p. 104; Kearney, 1971, p. 74; Signorini & Tranfo, 1991, p. 239). When the *brujo* manipulates these supernatural forces with the conscious intention of hurting someone, the process is known as *daño* or *cochinada;* when someone unknowingly "catches" it or is "hit" by it, it is known as *mal aire.* In this case, the sensory plane and its meaning are not intelligible for the professional who is consulted, because the professional lacks understanding inherited from the indigenous worldview and from magicoreligious elements still present among the *mestiza* (part Spanish, part indigenous) population. In summation, with respect to the "sensory plane," the folk explanatory model manages to integrate as a coherent and well-articulated cultural system traces of a complex Meso-American worldview in which, as López Austin (1996, p. 137) notes, "invisible beings reverberate their presences in fields, in fountains, in homes, and in the hills . . . and where some—such as the sorcerer—work with a highly developed soul entity, invisible, upon the invisible substances of things" (López Austin, 1996, p. 199). On the other hand, with respect to the problem's "ideological pole," the folk explanatory model hides in the deepest crevices of folk logic those structural pathogenic devices[6] that configure this social drama.

Analyzing María's case, the hostile feelings attributed to the aggressor, such as envy, have as a background disruptions in those aspects of daily life that touch us most as individuals, those dimensions that have to do with personal or family wholeness or survival—such as money, work, housing, general health, and well-being—and the affect that orients interpersonal contacts—in other words, relational life.[7] Such fundamental disruptions implicitly bring with them a transgression of normative rules about the relationships between people—such as codes of reciprocity, redistribution, faithfulness, loyalty, honor, and competition among equals for material goods, affect, or symbols—in a group whose survival as a social subgroup, as well as that of the domestic groups that comprise it, can be seen as a "cohesive social unit" (Douglas, 1976, p. 69). As Finkler (1994) notes, it is "the vital events for people, especially their relationships, their moral dilemmas, and the unresolved contradictions that they confront in daily life" (p. 14) that become fixed in their memories as the causes of illness and anxiety.

❖ DIAGNOSIS

In the context of Mexican traditional healing, establishing the "cause" from which the affliction originated constitutes the essential step for constructing meaning with respect to the illness, and this is achieved in three ways: (a) using the information supplied by the patient and his or her family; (b) to a lesser extent, detecting certain physical signs (a step that is not always taken); and (c) most important, using magicoreligious processes, such as reading the arrangement of kernels of corn that are dropped in a gourd filled with water (a Meso-American tradition), the laying out of cards or *rifa* (a method introduced during the colonial dominion), or the "reading" of an egg with which the patient has previously undergone a *limpia*.[8] The importance that patients and their healers assign to this process of causal determination appears then to be the main operating concept upon which criteria are established to classify afflictions in folk nosology.

To begin with, diagnosis in the ritual activity of the healer is "an act of creative retrospection in which meaning is ascribed to the happenings and the parts of the experience" (Turner, 1982, p. 17). In our example, the healer attempts to decode whether the cause of the illness is "good" (*espanto* [a shock or scare; similar to *susto*], *sombra* [shadow], *latido* [pulse or (heart)beat], or *aire*) or "bad" (*daño* or *mal aire*). Based on this determination, the healer will direct his or her prayers and petitions to the saints in the Christian tradition. Doña Teodora, the *curandera* to whom María went to help her sister, takes the incense and lays out the ritual space by bathing the altar and the patient in purifying smoke. Then she takes a fresh egg out of the plastic bag that she has on the table that functions as an altar and makes the sign of the cross three times on the patient's forehead with the egg.

Teodora breaks the egg into half a glass of water and places it against the light of the window to observe it. The poured-out egg forms white patches with lumps and traces of blood. She interprets it and explains it to the patient and her sister:

> Here we can see a *mal aire*, a *porquería*. Sometimes due to carelessness, ill will, or envy, these *cochinadas* are left for others to catch[9] . . . that's why it comes out looking like that, like a cloudy patch, like a shadow . . . *Ay*, my dear! Be careful!

If the illness is "bad," from the moment that she makes the sign of the cross on the patient's forehead, she can feel that "her brain shrinks up" or she has a feeling of disgust, whereas if it is something "good" or "normal," it means that what is ill is "only" the patient's *latido*. The reading of the egg with which the patient has received a *limpia* "is the same as an x-ray, it is a question of *visualizing* what is being healed." Therefore, if it is something "bad," the egg white may show three long candles, which represent a funeral (death). Other harbingers of death are the appearance of the *Santa Sombra* (Holy Shadow) or the *Santa Muertecita* (Little Holy Death), or when "the water becomes cloudy." In addition, "you can see whether it was sent intentionally [*daño*] or whether you just 'caught it' in the street [*mal aire*]." On the other hand, if it is something "good," "it looks like a cloud" or "it's just *aire*."

## ❖ HEALING THERAPY

*Mal aire* as an ailment with multiple meanings involves all the various planes of the folk explanatory model referred to in Table 8.1. However, it is important to highlight that the multicausal spectrum with which the problem was originally configured is not taken into account when the treatment is performed, because the *curandera* will act exclusively on the *sensory* and *supernatural* planes by means of the ritual representation, and on the *organic* plane by relying on manual maneuvers and plant-based resources. All this occurs without the *curandera* or the patient needing to intervene or directly confront the *material* and *relational* planes that originally acted as the causes that discharged the illness. As Turner (1980) notes, the execution of an instrumentally symbolic act suppresses in the official or verbal meanings the conflict situation present in the interpretation (p. 43). In this way, the connection is blurred between the behavioral expression of the conflict and the normative components. Thus, María's sister receives the following as part of the ritual of the treatment:

*1. A physical maneuver to "gather her pulse in her abdomen"*
    Before carrying out the cure for the *mal aire*, Teodora lays the patient down on a bed and executes a maneuver whose objective is to "center her pulse" in her stomach. According to Teodora,

> When someone is suffering from *daño*, when she has a *mal aire*, first of all you have to find her *latido* in order to help her. You have to cure the pulsing of her stomach and her arm so that they are all right and you save yourself some healing work.

This maneuver attempts to restore the "main pulse" to the navel center by means of the symbolic movement of a vital substance: the blood. Its objective is to relocate the *tonalli*—one of the energy entities of the body, according to the Meso-American worldview (López Austin, 1984, p. 223)—using as an ordering pattern a Meso-American religious symbol, the *Quincunce*[10] (González, 1999, p. 323). This symbolic operator seeks to harmonize the center of the body with its extremes, as well as to harmonize the sick person situated in the terrestrial plane with the cosmos and the subearthly world (López Austin, 1984, p. 285; Tibón, 1981, p. 224).

*2. Prayers and petitions that allow the* mal aire *to be expelled*

Most of the prayers of traditional healers are Catholic, and it is common for them to invoke various saints or patron protectors from the Christian tradition in their petitions. Many healers, even some indigenous ones, verbalize these prayers in Latin to make them more effective. Their function then is to intercede on behalf of the patient, acting as a communicative vessel between the human and the divine—in other words, performing the function of a priest. The home altars of the *curanderos* can also give an idea of their religious resources and loyalties; for example, Teodora has more than a dozen saints and deities spread out on the table that functions as her altar, among them *Señor Santiago, San Martín Caballero, el Niño Doctor* (the Child Doctor), *el Señor de la Columna* (Lord of the Spine), *Santa Clara,* and *San Ramón Nonato.*[11]

In the case described here, Teodora accompanied the above petition with a *limpia,* which consisted of rubbing the patient's body once again with an egg. The *limpia* began by crossing the afflicted woman's forehead with the egg. Her entire body was then rubbed from top to bottom, with special emphasis on the temples, the crown of the head, the neck, the hand and elbow joints, the chest and the back, the backs of the knees, and the ankles. In each of these areas the healer once again made the sign of the cross with the egg. She paid special attention to the feet, as "these are what pick things up." She again broke the egg into half a glass of water, confirming that the image in the egg had come out "clean" through the performed maneuvers, in other words, this time there were no lumps or blood.

*3. The* limpia

The goal of a *limpia* is to purify and symbolically "sweep away" hostile feelings, *aires,* or negative charges that the patient has "picked up." *Limpias* are carried out by passing eggs, plants, scissors, crosses, knives, "dislodging" lotion, or other objects along the patient's body in order to "cut" the *daño* (using scissors or knives), "transfer" the "evil" to the object (through contagion or impregnation), or symbolically "repel" the *cochinada* (using crosses or "dislodging" lotion). Other *limpias* are prepared with boiled mixtures of aromatic plants, which are given to the patient so he or she can apply them to the body, bathe with them, or sprinkle them in his or her house, "cleansing" it of evil spirits. The parts of the body on which the *curandera* places special emphasis during the *limpia* are minor energy centers where *tonalli* resides and where the body's vital force is also concentrated (López Austin, 1984:217).

*4. The* amarre

An *amarre* is a "fix," a covenant that the patient makes with the *curandero* so that the latter, through petitions and prayers and even in the absence of the afflicted person, can symbolically detain or constrict the magical-supernatural forces that others have unleashed upon the patient. The *amarre* happens by means of a candle that the *curandera* burns on her altar until it is completely consumed. On certain days of the week—Mondays, Wednesdays, and Thursdays—the *curandera* "works" the candle with her prayers, tightening around it day after day a red and white ribbon until it is smothered entirely, so that the sacred symbolically contains and immobilizes the evil.

### 5. Rubbings, baths, and fomentations made from medicinal plants

To conclude the cure, Teodora rubs the patient's body with a lotion that makes her cry from the pain and recommends that she bathe with and apply fomentations made from a series of plants: *cuachalalate, arnica, coahuilote,* and *golondrina.* At a topical level these plants act pharmacologically as antiseptics, anti-inflammatories, cellular regenerators, and astringents.[12]

### ❖ CONCLUSION

The traditional medical system contributes to and is reconstituted in the context of a cultural system, and it elaborates its cognitive strategies within the context of this cultural system (see Kleinman, 1980, p. 172). In that sense, the discursive activity of the *curandera* has provided the patient with an organizing frame—an explanatory structure—so that the patient can resituate her experience of illness by activating a cultural code that makes explicit the interconnection between organic illness and emotional and social experience.

As the protagonist or mediator of healing power, the *curandera,* through her discursive activity and concrete corporeal practice, has done a "performance ritual" that activates in the patient a range of sensorial experiences that are retained in the body's memory as an integral part of what she has lived. Such experiences incorporate codified information, acting as catalysts of a symbolic production that takes multiple forms (Leach, 1993, p. 57). This "cultural saturation of experience"—as Good (1994) refers to it—constitutes a way for the patient to resemanticize his or her illness, to give form and meaning to this episode of illness in accordance with socially shared codes that operate as an organizing grammar of the reconstitution of the world, rescuing a space of her own in the affective and social order of things.

### ❖ NOTES

1. Original chapter (longer version) translated by Katie Hinnenkamp.

2. These 10 causes are *mal de ojo,* indigestion, *susto, caída de mollera* (fallen fontanel), dysentery, *aires,* diarrhea, sprains, harm caused by witchcraft, and angina (Zolla et al., 1992, p. 74).

3. *Mal aire:* "harmful wind: an incorporeal entity perceived as a living specter that causes illness. The essences that unleash this danger are several: the breath of the gods that guard the earth; spirits of those dead or murdered; or emanations from people who participate in illicit sex acts, who have an intense stare, or who are envious." *Mal aire* can be placed in or transmitted to the victim's body by one of his or her enemies (Kearney, 1971, p. 74) or manipulated by sorcerers with the intention of harming the victim (Zolla, 1994a, p. 561).

4. A person can become ill with a *mal aire* from being near a dead body, from passing by a place where bunches of herbs that were previously used to do a *limpia* have been thrown, from going walking at night, or simply from having someone who "envies or talks badly about him [or her]" (Romero, 2003, p. 99).

5. *Cochinada: porquería* or filth. A mean, vulgar, unseemly act that is a product of witchcraft.

6. Gilles Bibeau (1992, p. 60) uses the term *structural pathogenic devices* when referring to elements of the macrocontext that shape a culture from outside and that place limits on the game played among the social actors. In the case of Latin America, he situates violence and inequality, historically configured since the colonial period, as the main pathogenic devices.

7. The attitudes of orientation such as love, hate, and indifference have an essential function in everyday interaction and of course constitute a decisive factor in interpersonal relations (Heller, 1977, p. 380).

8. Healing by means of *limpia* in Mexico is a diagnostic-therapeutic principle of Meso-American origin that also has parallels in the Andean region (López Austin, 1976, p. 15; Polia, 1996, p. 566).

9. The objects that were used to perform the *limpia*, if they are not then adequately handled by the *curandero*—buried or burnt, for example—can become a contagious source and can pass on a *mal aire* "because someone else comes by and picks it up again."

10. A Nahua hieroglyphic that represents the "Law of Centre." This is a figure that is found in infinite variants, always with four points joined by a center, a disposition known as *quincunce*. This symbol is found in all the religious manifestations of the Aztec people (Séjourné, 1992, p. 102).

11. On the table there is a plastic bag containing more than 2 kilograms of eggs to be used in diagnosis sessions for the rest of the day. There is also a collection of candlesticks tied with one red and one white ribbon and several glasses with eggs submerged in water, the product of diagnoses done by Teodora with her previous patients. Under the table is an assortment of commercial containers with different liquids and lotions, such as *"Loción de siete machos"* (Seven Machos Lotion), *"Loción de desalojo"* (Dislodging Lotion), and *"Loción para las envidias"* (Lotion for Envies).

12. *Cuachalalate* (*Amphypterigium adstringens*) and *arnica* (*Heterotheca inuloides*) in particular are plants with potent anti-inflammatory and cellular regenerating effects (Lara & Márquez, 1996, p. 43).

## Acknowledgments

This work would not have been possible without the financing received from the Consejo Nacional de Ciencia y Tecnología (National Council on Science and Technology), projects 30489-S and 34581-S. I thank Petra Roldán, Sara Montoya, Guadalupe Meraz, Guadalupe Torres, Elpidia Martínez, Paul Hersch, Eduardo Menéndez, Joseph Ma. Comelles, and Oriol Romaní.

## ❖ REFERENCES

Aguirre Beltrán, G. (1980a). *Medicina y magia: El proceso de aculturación en la estructura colonial.* Mexico City, Mexico: Instituto Nacional Indigenista.

Aguirre Beltrán, G. (1980b). *Programas de salud en la situación intercultural.* Mexico City, Mexico: Instituto Mexicano del Seguro Social.

Aguirre Beltrán, G. (1994). *El negro esclavo en Nueva España: La formación colonial, la medicina popular y otros ensayos* (No. XVI). Mexico City, Mexico: Universidad Veracruzana, Instituto Nacional Indigenista, Gobierno del Estado de Veracruz, Centro de Investigaciones y Estudios Superiores en Antropología Social, and Fondo de Cultura Económica.

Álvarez, L. (1987). *La enfermedad y la cosmovisión en Hueyapan Morelos.* Mexico City, Mexico: Instituto Nacional Indigenista.

Bartolomé, M. A. (1997). *Gente de costumbre y gente de razón: Las identidades étnicas en México.* Mexico City, Mexico: Siglo XXI—Instituto Nacional Indigenista.

Bibeau, G. (1992). Hay una enfermedad en las Américas? Otro camino de la antropología médica para nuestro tiempo. In C. Pinzón, R. Suárez, & G. Garay (Eds.), *Cultura y salud en la construcción de las Américas* (pp. 41–70). Bogotá, Colombia: Colcultura-Comité Internacional para el Desarrollo de los Pueblos.

Douglas, M. (1976). Brujería: El estado actual de la cuestión. In M. Gluckman, M. Douglas, & R. Horton (Eds.), *Ciencia y brujería* (pp. 31–72). Barcelona, Spain: Anagrama.

Erasmus, C. J. (1952). Changing folk beliefs and the relativity of empirical knowledge. *Southwestern Journal of Anthropology, 8,* 411–428.

Fagetti, A. (Ed.). (2003). *Los que saben: Testimonios de vida de médicos tradicionales de la región de Tehuacán.* Puebla, Mexico: Benemérita Universidad Autónoma de Puebla and Consejo Nacional para el Desarrollo de los Pueblos Indígenas.

Finkler, K. (1994). *Women in pain: Gender and morbidity in Mexico.* Philadelphia: Universty of Pennsylvania Press.

González, L. (1999). *El pulso de la sobrevivencia: Estrategias de atención de salud en un colectivo de mujeres del subproletariado urbano.* Unpublished doctoral dissertation, Departamento de Sociología y Metodología de las Ciencias Sociales, Universidad de Barcelona, Spain.

Good, B. J. (1994). *Healing, rationality, and experience: An anthropological perspective.* Cambridge, UK: Cambridge University Press.

Heller, A. (1977). *Sociología de la vida cotidiana.* Barcelona, Spain: Península.

Hermitte, E. H. (1970). *Poder sobrenatural y control social en un pueblo maya contemporáneo* (Ediciones Especiales No. 57). Mexico City, Mexico: Instituto Indigenista Interamericano.

Kearney, M. (1971). *Los vientos de Ixtepeji: Concepción del mundo y estructura social de un pueblo zapoteco.* Mexico City, Mexico: Instituto Indigenista Interamericano.

Kleinman, A. (1980). *Patients and healers in the context of culture: An exploration of the borderland between anthropology, healing and psychiatry.* Berkeley: University of California Press.

Kroeger, A. (1988). Enfoque popular de la enfermedad: Explicaciones, diagnósticos y tratamientos populares. In A. Kroeger & W. Ruiz (Eds.), *Conceptos y tratamientos populares de algunas enfermedades en Latinoamérica* (pp. 23–36). Cuzco, Peru: Centro de Medicina Andina.

Lara, F., & Márquez, C. (1996). *Plantas medicinales de México: Composición, usos y actividad biológica.* Mexico City, Mexico: Universidad Nacional Autónoma de México.

Leach, E. (1993). *Cultura y comunicación: La lógica de la conexión de símbolos* (5th ed.). Madrid, Spain: Siglo XXI de España Editores.

López Austin, A. (1967). Cuarenta clases de magos en el mundo náhuatl. *Estudios de Cultura Náhuatl, 7,* 87–117.

López Austin, A. (1976). Cosmovisión y medicina náhuatl. In C. Viesca (Ed.), *Estudios sobre etnobotánica y antropología médica* (pp. 13–28). Mexico City, Mexico: Instituto Mexicano para el Estudio de las Plantas Medicinales, Asociación Civil.

López Austin, A. (1984). *Cuerpo humano e ideología las concepciones de los Antiguos Nahuas.* Mexico City, Mexico: Universidad Nacional Autónoma de México.

López Austin, A. (1996). *Los mitos del tlacuache.* Mexico City, Mexico: Universidad Nacional Autónoma de México.

Lozoya, X., Velásquez, G., & Flores, A. (1988). *La medicina tradicional en México: Experiencia del programa IMSS-COPLAMAR 1982–1987.* Mexico City, Mexico: Instituto Mexicano del Seguro Social.

Polia, M. (1996). *"Despierta, remedio, cuenta . . .": Adivinos y médicos del Ande* (Vol. 2). Lima, Peru: Pontificia Universidad Católica del Perú.

Queiroz, M. S. (1986). O paradigma mecaniscista da medicina ocidental moderna: Una perspectiva antropológica. *Revue Saude Pública, 20,* 309–317.

Romero, L. (2003). Casilda Valdivia Ramírez, tepopova la que hace limpias. In A. Fagetti (Ed.), *Los que saben: Testimonios de vida de médicos tradicionales de la región de Tehuacán* (pp. 85–107). Puebla, Mexico: Benemérita Universidad Autónoma de Puebla and Consejo Nacional para el Desarrollo de los Pueblos Indígenas.

Rubio, M. A., & Zolla, C. (Eds.). (2000). *Estado del desarrollo económico y social de los Pueblos Indígenas de México, 1996–1997* (Vol. 1). Mexico City, Mexico: Instituto Nacional Indigenista and Programa de Naciones Unidas para el Desarrollo.

Séjourné, L. (1992). *Pensamiento y religión en el México antiguo.* Mexico City, Mexico: Fondo de Cultura Económica and Secretaría de Educación Pública.

Signorini, I., & Tranfo, L. (1991). Enfermedades, clasificación y terapias. In I. Signorini (Ed.), *Los huaves de San Mateo del Mar*. Mexico City, Mexico: Instituto Nacional Indigenista and Consejo Nacional para la Cultura y las Artes.

Tibon, G. (1981). *El ombligo como centro cósmico. Una contribución a la historia de las religiones*. Mexico City, Mexico: Fondo de Cultura Económica.

Turner, V. (1980). *La selva de los símbolos aspectos del ritual Ndembu*. Madrid, Spain: Siglo XXI.

Turner, V. (1982). *From ritual to theatre. The human seriousness of play*. New York: PAJ Publications.

Young, A. (1976). Some implications of medical beliefs and practices for social anthropology. *American Anthropologist, 78*, 5–24.

Zolla, C. (Ed.). (1994a). *Diccionario enciclopédico de la medicina tradicional Mexicana* (Vol. 2). Mexico City, Mexico: Instituto Nacional Indigenista.

Zolla, C., Del Bosque, S., Mellado, V., Tascón, A., & Maqueo, C. (1992). Medicina tradicional y enfermedad. In R. Campos (Ed.), *La antropología médica en México* (Vol. 2, pp. 71–105). Mexico City, Mexico: Instituto Mora and Universidad Autónoma Metropolitana.

# 9

# Traditional and Cultural Healing Among the Chinese

*Joseph K. So*

All cultures have their own unique explanatory models of health and illness that can be best understood within their respective worldviews. The Chinese culture's understanding of health is complex, rooted in its history and philosophy and in the relationship of the people to nature. Despite the increasing globalization of biomedicine, traditional Chinese medical beliefs remain a potent force in illness perception, explanation, and treatment, a model that is continuously undergoing transformations, both within China and among Chinese immigrants overseas. This chapter examines Chinese medical beliefs and healing practices in the larger cultural and historical contexts, focusing on their applications to psychiatry, psychotherapy, and counseling psychology.

Any discussion of Chinese cultural healing must acknowledge that there is no such thing as a single, homogeneous, easily definable "Chinese culture" in the geopolitical sense. Within China's political borders are several hundred *minzú* (ethnic groups), 56 of which are officially recognized by the government. The largest group, the Han Chinese, originated from the Hua-Xia area in north-central China and spread to the south and west and across to Taiwan, Singapore, and overseas. There are six major dialects spoken in China but only one written Chinese language. The Yangtze River historically demarcated the Han population into northern and southern subgroups. Most of the Chinese diaspora to Southeast Asia and the Americas consists of people from the southern coastal regions of China (Djao, 2003). Any discussion of "Chinese culture" must take into account this diversity.

## ❖ HISTORICIZING HEALING IN CHINESE CULTURE

In traditional Chinese medicine (TCM), "health" centers on the harmonious relationship between "heaven," "earth," and *ren* (people), as expressed in the primal forces that exist in each individual, as well as in the larger cosmos. The driving forces behind this relationship are the entities of *qi* (vital energy) and *li* (order). The oft-cited concepts of yin and yang, oppositional yet complementary in nature, are characteristics of the primordial *qi* circulating along the meridians (channels) that correspond to specific organs of the body. These channels are not demonstrable by Western scientific methods, yet they exist within the framework of TCM beliefs. Together with water, fire, wood, metal, and earth, collectively known as the five "elements" or "phases," these entities exist in a delicate balance. Each individual represents a microcosm of the macrocosm (cosmos), and if these forces in a person are out of balance, illness will result (Kaptchuk, 1983).

Chinese medical theory bears no resemblance to biomedicine, the latter subscribing to a germ-based, naturalistic explanatory model. In Chinese medicine, mental illnesses are said to result from an imbalance of yin and yang forces, a stagnation of the *qi* and blood in various body organs, or both. Exogenous forces contributing to illness are the "six excesses," namely wind, cold, summer heat, dampness, dryness, and fire. "Seven emotions" (joy, anger, melancholy, anxiety, sorrow, fear, and fright) are intrinsic causes that can also bring on ill health. For example, anger is bad for the liver, excessive joy harms the heart, anxiety the spleen, melancholy the lungs, fear the kidneys, and so on. Other factors, such as dietary excess or deficiency, fatigue, or injury, may also bring on illness.

The beginning of Chinese medicine is generally attributed to Emperor Shennong, who experimented with plants to discover their medicinal properties and introduced the practice of acupuncture. An ancient compendium of medicinal substances, *Shennong Bencaojing,* was compiled in the 1st and 2nd centuries BC. It contains 365 substances of plant, animal, and mineral origins found to have curative powers, a number of them useful in treating mental illnesses. All "classical" traditional Chinese materia medica can be found in this ancient text (Xie & Huang, 1985).

Two words exist in the Chinese language to describe "psychiatric conditions"—*kuang*, translated as "insanity" or "mania," and *dian*, which is "insanity without excitation" or "epileptic episode." The earliest references to *kuang* can be found as early as 1100 BC in *Shangshu*, or the *Book of Historical Documents*. The term *dian* first appeared in *Shi* (*The Book of Songs*), written in the 7th century BC (Liu, 1981). But no descriptions of the symptoms could be found. By the 2nd century BC, in *Huangdi Neijing* (*Yellow Emperor's Manual of Corporeal Medicine*), limited references to psychiatric disorders are documented, with brief descriptions of symptoms that are attributed to psychosis today.

Documented cases of mental disorders and their treatment in ancient Chinese literature are scarce. Several contemporary writers have attempted to analyze cases of mental illness from the classical literature. Tien (1985) analyzed characters in a number of literary works, the most famous example being *Hong Lou Meng* (*Dream of the Red Chamber*). It is a work populated by highly dysfunctional members of an extended family in feudal China, with many characters exhibiting symptoms of mental disorders. Wang (as cited in Cheng, 1991) identified examples of "psychotherapy" in classical writings. Treatments tended to be short, including *qigong* and herbs, with no mention of the patients' unconscious or past experiences. Typically any "psychotherapy" that took place was of a directive and contextualized nature, involving the patient's family relations and social world. This didactic approach dominated much of contemporary Chinese psychotherapy. During the Cultural Revolution (1966–1976), the teachings of Mao Zedong's *Little Red Book* were deemed therapeutic. Cultural attributes from Confucian and Taoist teachings affect perceptions of self and society, such as ideas about the importance of harmony with nature, balance, moderation and conservation, family support, harmonious interpersonal relations, and a certain pragmatic and adaptable attitude toward problems of living (Yip, 2004).

## ❖ CONCEPTUALIZING ILLNESS AND HEALING

Despite the increasing dominance of biomedicine, TCM continues to offer a viable alternative to many Chinese. With the establishment of the People's Republic of China (PRC) in 1949, the new government viewed TCM as an important heritage and actively promoted its use and fostered research. TCM colleges were established to train Chinese and later foreign practitioners. Medical students in China routinely receive basic training in TCM as part of their core curriculum. The Chinese attitude toward healing is pluralistic and pragmatic, showing a propensity toward multiple treatment modalities. In the PRC, patients can choose either biomedicine or TCM, based on long-held perceptions of the relative efficacies of each system. For example, Western medicine is used for acute diseases and TCM for certain chronic conditions. Since the 1950s, an integrated form of TCM–Western medicine has been in practice. In recent decades, Western diagnostic technologies have been increasingly used, but the etiological explanations remain rooted in Chinese medical theory. The patient often receives a combination of traditional medicines and Western drugs. In ethnographic fieldwork carried out at a psychiatric outpatient clinic in Suzhou, China, in the late 1980s, treatment included a combination of Western psychotropic medication, traditional Chinese herbal remedies, "stress management" techniques such as biofeedback, *qigong*, and occasionally limited psychological counseling (So, 1990).

## ❖ HELP-SEEKING BEHAVIOR

Chinese help seeking is typically circuitous, reflecting long-held cultural beliefs. There is a reluctance to seek outside intervention and a preference for coping within the family for as long as possible. This results from cultural and language barriers or from a lack of culturally appropriate services for immigrants. Equally significant is the failure to recognize the warning signs in the early stages of the illness episode, as well as the social stigma associated with mental illness (Lin, Tardiff, Donetz, & Goresky, 1978). The pattern of intrafamilial coping has not changed significantly over time. Respondents to a survey of the Chinese, Vietnamese, and Korean ethnocultural communities in Toronto showed a preference to seek help from family members over health care professionals. This pattern is consistent among the Chinese from Hong Kong, mainland China, and Taiwan who participated in the survey (R. Y. Wong, J. P. H. Wong, Fung, & Chung, 2003).

According to TCM, emotional disturbances are caused by imbalances of vital forces in the target organs; these imbalances are then expressed as physical malaise, a view at odds with Western science. The idea that physical symptoms can be relieved by Western-style "talk therapy" is essentially alien to Chinese culture. It is often stated that whereas Westerners "psychologize" distress, the Chinese "somatize" distress (Kleinman, 1980; Tseng, Lu, & Yin, 1995). This is explained by the perceived denial and suppression of emotions in Chinese culture, the lack of a vocabulary to express emotions, and the strong mind-body connection previously mentioned. Cheung (1985) disputes this contention, because somatization of psychological distress has also been observed in many other cultures (Singer, 1975). Indeed, somatization appears to be related more to the social, economic, educational, and religious backgrounds of the patient. The level of acculturation to Western values is also a significant determinant. There it can best be understood as a form of coping behavior, one that reflects a more integrated, holistic view of the mind and the body.

## ❖ EVIDENCE-BASED RESEARCH ON THE USE OF TCM

Efforts have been made since the 1950s by the PRC government to conduct clinical trials to demonstrate the efficacy of TCM. Acupuncture, which is the most popular TCM treatment modality in the West, has received the most attention. It is used in conjunction with herbs and other treatment modalities for a number of mental disorders, including schizophrenia, depression, bipolar affective disorders, anxiety disorder, fibromyalgia, and obsessive-compulsive disorders (Flaws, 2000; Flaws & Lake, 2001; Shannon, 2002).

Western science has historically attributed the benefits of TCM to the placebo effect. It can be argued that there are multiple factors for its efficacy that go beyond the placebo effect, such as a patient's willingness and openness to treatment and a positive relationship engendered by an attentive and sympathetic caregiver. A double-blind randomized controlled trial was conducted on acupuncture and depression (Schnyer, 2001). Significant alleviation of symptoms—comparable to other treatments such as medication and psychotherapy—was reported. Other studies have suggested that a combination of treatment modalities may be the most effective. Herbs routinely used in psychiatry are ginkgo (*Ginkgo biloba*), kava (*Piper methysticum*), and valerian (*Valeriana officinalis*). Clinical trials were conducted to assess their effectiveness by breaking these substances down to their biochemical constituents to identify the active ingredients that produce the desired pharmacological results. Some findings suggest that ginkgo may be effective in treating dementia and kava effective for anxiety. Efforts to demonstrate the efficacy of herbal medicine are continuing (Cass & Cott, 2002).

## ❖ THERAPEUTIC ENCOUNTER IN TCM

A TCM consultation bears little resemblance to biomedicine. A typical session involves four diagnostic techniques: observation, questioning, smelling/listening, and pulse taking. Observations include the overall appearance, the "spirit" (*shen*), and the "color" of the patient. In addition, detailed observations of the eyes, lips, and particularly the tongue are noted. Questioning extends well beyond typical medical history taken in Western medicine, including a detailed account of the patient's daily habits and physical and emotional states, down to minute details of symptoms. Smelling odors and listening to the patient's voice and breathing are equally important. Perhaps the most important technique is pulse taking, with dozens of pulses identified, the qualities of each pulse giving clues to the illness. A formal diagnosis is then given based on TCM theory, followed by a prescription, usually of herbs, sometimes in conjunction with acupuncture treatment and dietary advice.

As Csordas and Kleinman (1996) point out, the distinction between diagnosis and treatment in Western medicine is artificial. The healer-patient session in TCM endows the ill person with the power of knowing, which is in itself therapeutic through the removal of fear and anxiety of the unknown. A typical encounter in a Chinese medical clinic in the PRC is a rather public affair, which Csordas and Kleinman see as therapeutic. In ethnographic fieldwork at a psychiatric outpatient clinic in a general hospital in Suzhou, China, sessions were conducted in cramped facilities that necessitated two simultaneous consultations across the table, with waiting patients often in plain view listening in on the session. Together with the didactic nature of the therapeutic advice, these supposedly one-on-one sessions became a form of group therapy (So, 1996).

Much has been made of the unequal relationship between the physician and the patient in biomedicine. In Chinese culture, the position of the healer has always been revered, and the patient expects the healer to assume a directive, didactic, and rather authoritarian stance. At the risk of generalization, Chinese patients tend to prefer a more directive approach from the therapist, whereas insight-oriented, client-centered approaches are viewed as unhelpful. Sue and colleagues (Sue, 1990; Sue, Fujino, Hu, Takeuchi, & Zane, 1991) suggest healer credibility and "ethnic matching" as important issues. Others have countered that the Chinese client/non-Chinese therapist dyad may actually allow the client to be more open to someone outside his or her culture (Tang, 1997). Professional reputation, or "ascribed credibility," is an important incentive for the client to enter treatment. Likewise, a psychoeducational approach with some immediate, tangible benefits will likely encourage the client to remain in treatment.

### ❖ MAJOR TREATMENT MODALITIES

#### Acupuncture

The earliest references to acupuncture can be found in *Huangdi Neijing* (Unschuld, 1986). It involves the use of thin needles inserted at specific points along a system of 12 meridians, each corresponding to a specific organ in the body. Acupuncture stimulates the flow of *qi* and removes stagnation of blood. Inserted at varying depths and with a twisting motion, patients often report a sensation of heat and swelling, which is said to represent the release of *qi*.

Used in China to treat depression, anxiety, and schizophrenia, the most common acupuncture points in psychiatry are located at the top of the head, forehead, on the trunk below the liver, dorsal surface of the foot, wrist, elbow, and medial side of the ankle (Motl, 2002). Acupuncture has also been used successfully in treating addiction and attention deficit disorders. Traditionally mugwort (*Artemisia vulgaris*) is burnt to stimulate circulation, but in recent years, this practice has been replaced by electrostimulation. Multiple treatment sessions are the norm. Ancillary modalities such as *tui-na* (Chinese therapeutic massage) also help stimulate the flow of *qi* through manipulation and finger pressure on the acupuncture points. It is also believed that the physical contact in *tui-na* leads to a transmission of healing energies from the therapist to the patient.

### Herbal Medicine and Nutritional Therapy

Herbal medicine, used in conjunction with dietary counseling, is an integral part of the TCM toolkit. Prescriptions, typically with many ingredients, are tailored to each patient based on specific symptoms. The prescriptions are boiled with water in a clay pot for several hours, and the fluid is consumed. In recent decades, this laborious process has been replaced by factory-packaged "patent medicines," usually in pill form. Chinese medical theory also holds that food has preventive and curative properties. Energies that exist in the cosmos can also be found in food, and thus its consumption can affect the balance of these forces within the person. Some of the most common medicinal herbs can be found in Chinese cuisine. Their selection, preparation, and consumption follow strict principles of balance in the form of color, fragrance, and taste. Fundamental to the practice of nutritional therapy is the belief in balance and moderation of consumption. The therapeutic value of food is widely known and practiced, even for nonpractitioners of TCM (Buell, 2000; Engelhardt, 2001; Farquhar, 2002).

### *Qigong*

*Qigong*, or the "exercise of vital energy," is highly popular in China, reportedly practiced by an estimated 100 million people in a population of 1.3 billion. It involves a precise series of physical movements, regulated breathing, and the consciously directed intention to regulate the flow of *qi* to balance the yin and yang forces in the body. Its precise origin is unclear, but it likely comes from a Tibetan Buddhist tradition. *Qigong* can be "active," involving body movements, or passive, which is more meditative in nature. The Chinese believe that practicing *qigong* helps maintain overall wellness. Lake (2002) recommends the use of *qigong* as an adjunct to psychotherapy. But it has also been reported that the "incorrect" practice of *qigong*, called "*qigong* deviation," can exacerbate a preexisting condition, especially in patients suffering from psychosis (Lake). *Qigong* deviation can occur as uncontrolled *qi*, abnormal sensory perceptions (auditory or visual hallucinations), or "*qigong* possession." The PRC government takes a dim view of some forms of *qigong* practice, such as the controversial *falun gong*, which it sees as thinly disguised cultism and subversion, and the practice of *falun gong* is currently prohibited (Chen, 2003).

## ❖ WESTERN DERIVATIVES OF TCM

Several psychologically based treatments have been developed in the West with origins based on the principles of TCM. Thought Field Therapy, developed by Roger Callahan, and the Emotional Freedom Techniques, developed by Gary Craig, are said to be efficacious in the treatment of phobias, anxiety, attention deficit disorder, and depression. These methods have been likened to a type of "psychological acupuncture without needles." Both use a technique of tapping with two fingertips on specific meridian points with the patient focusing on a negative thought. The tapping process releases the blocked energy and restores its flow. Typical of many alternative treatment modalities, these techniques are still in the experimental stages, with strong adherents as well as detractors (Phillips, 2000).

## ❖ BEYOND TCM: RELIGION AND SPIRITUALITY IN CHINESE CULTURAL HEALING

The mind-body connection fundamental to Chinese medical beliefs is a natural fit for the use of TCM in psychiatry. However, the wholesale application to Chinese clients of Western-style, nondirective "talk therapy" focusing on emotions and feeling is problematic. Many have questioned the appropriateness and efficacy of Western-style psychotherapy for Chinese immigrants. Cheng (1991) found an essential incompatibility between the basic assumptions of Western psychotherapy and Chinese cultural beliefs and suggested modifying therapeutic techniques to be more congruent with the Chinese worldview. The degree of acculturation to Western culture is likely key to the effectiveness of this approach.

Historically, spirit possession by ghosts and demons was an important explanatory model for mental illness in China. It was commonplace for the Chinese patient to visit a Buddhist temple, consult a fortune-teller or feng shui master, or even engage the service of a spiritual healer utilizing possession trance (AvRuskin, 1988; Barnes, 1998). There are examples in the literature documenting spiritual healing among Chinese immigrants (Jordan, 1972; Tsoi, 1985). A study of Singaporean Chinese showed that a majority of mental patients had consulted spiritual healers prior to hospitalization (Tsoi). A recent study showed that almost half of the respondents in a mental health survey of Southeast Asian immigrant and refugee women in Canada rated the clergy, minister, priest, monk, or other religious leader as "helpful" (R. Y. Wong et al., 2003).

The PRC government considers spiritual healing to be superstitious, and its use is actively discouraged. Psychiatric symptoms once attributed to spirit possession are now given the alternate explanation of "incorrect" *qigong* practice, a more "empirical" explanatory model, even though calling *qigong* "empirical" is problematic in Western minds. The decline of spiritual healing among the urban and educated Chinese immigrants reflects a gradual acceptance of a Western view of the mind. An informal survey of case managers at an ethnospecific community health agency in Toronto found the use of spiritual healing to be rare (A. Tse & D. Yang, personal communication, 2004).

In the broadest context, healing in Chinese culture extends beyond what is defined as traditional medicine. Much in the Chinese cultural belief systems is drawn from Confucian, Taoist, and Buddhist teachings that advocate certain guiding principles of living. These principles are considered therapeutic when they aid in restoration of the individual to more "ordered" and "righteous" ways of living. Confucianism, with its belief in the primacy of harmonious social relations, has a strong influence on illness and coping. Its teachings of respect for authority, emotional self-control, importance of family and society over self, and the virtue placed on the ability to endure life's difficulties tend to undermine individual assertiveness when a person is faced with mental health issues. Taoist teachings similarly value self-restraint and the virtue of moderation. Expression of feelings is considered a sign of weakness and poor judgment. Far from being old-fashioned, these philosophical tenets form a significant and integral part of the cognitive world among many contemporary Chinese, and many Chinese incorporate some aspects of these philosophies into their daily lives.

An interesting facet of Chinese cultural healing is the use of Buddhism in psychotherapy. The goal of Buddhism is to end suffering and achieve a state of nirvana, or peace and tranquility, through the practice of "the bodhisattva way." Some clinicians incorporate Buddhist philosophy into counseling, stressing individual responsibility for one's own actions. The Chinese are fond of quoting proverbs, with many incorporating Confucian or Buddhist philosophies as guiding principles. The Buddhist concepts of karma, birth, death, reincarnation, compassion, and wisdom, with their inherent empowering potential for the individual to make life changes, fit well within the principles of cognitive and behavioral therapies. These concepts are useful as coping mechanisms and to achieve a more positive outlook. The application of Buddhist stories as part of "talk therapy" has been found to be effective (Yeung & Lee, 1997).

## ❖ CONCLUSION

Given the complexity and diversity of Chinese cultures, the best—and arguably the only—approach toward an understanding of traditional and cultural healing is from a holistic, integrated perspective, taking into account historical antecedents and their subsequent transformations (Tseng & Wu, 1985). Although some find inherent incompatibilities between the mind-body holism of TCM and the Western, psychologically based, insight-oriented counseling and psychotherapy (Cheng, 1991), others have argued that there has already been a gradual transformation toward a psychologically based TCM practice in North America, recasting the tradition of "demonology" in TCM diagnosis into spiritually based explanatory models (Barnes, 1998). It is safe to say that therapeutic success depends on a thoughtful and appropriate delivery of culturally competent care that acknowledges individual life histories and unique illness experiences and that incorporates the client's social and relational worlds. Staying away from the formulaic and focusing on the individual often makes the difference between success and failure. This critical-interpretive and experiential approach may appear to be at odds with the more empirical, objectified, outcome measurement–oriented approach typical of biomedicine, but ultimately it may prove more meaningful than the striving for a clinically demonstrable efficacy based on Western bioscience.

### Acknowledgments

The author gratefully acknowledges the assistance of Dr. H.-T. Lo, who, as a culturally competent psychiatrist, generously provided material and offered insights.

## ❖ REFERENCES

AvRuskin, T. L. (1988). Neurophysiology and the curative possession trance: The Chinese case. *Medical Anthropology Quarterly, 2,* 286–302.

Barnes, L. L. (1998). The psychologizing of Chinese healing practices in the United States. *Culture, Medicine and Psychiatry, 22,* 413–443.

Buell, P. D. (2000). *A soup for the Qan: Chinese dietary medicine of the Mongol era as seen in Hu Szu-Hui's Yin-shan chengyao: Introduction, translation, commentary and Chinese text.* New York: Kegan Paul International.

Cass, H., & Cott, J. (2002). Herbal medicine. In S. Shannon (Ed.), *Handbook of complementary and alternative therapies in mental health* (pp. 377–400). San Diego, CA: Academic Press.

Chen, N. N. (2003). *Breathing spaces: Qigong, psychiatry, and healing in China*. New York: Columbia University Press.

Cheng, L. Y. C. (1991). Sino-therapy: Is it necessary? Is it possible? *Bulletin of the Hong Kong Psychological Society, 26/27,* pp. 71–80.

Cheung, F. (1985). Facts and myths about somatization among the Chinese. In T. Y. Lin, W. S. Tseng, & E. K. Yeh (Eds.), *Chinese societies and mental health* (pp. 156–166). Hong Kong, China: Oxford University Press.

Csordas, T. J., & Kleinman, A. (1996). The therapeutic process. In C. F. Sargent & T. M. Johnson (Eds.), *Medical anthropology: Contemporary theory and method* (pp. 3–20). Westport, CT: Praeger.

Djao, W. (2003). *Being Chinese: Voices from the diaspora*. Tucson: University of Arizona Press.

Engelhardt, U. (2001). Dietetics in Tang China and the first extant works of material dietetica. In E. Hsu (Ed.), *Innovation in Chinese medicine* (pp. 173–191). Cambridge, UK: Cambridge University Press.

Farquhar, J. (2002). *Appetites: Food and sex in postsocialist China*. Durham, NC: Duke University Press.

Flaws, B. (2000). *Curing fibromyalgia naturally with Chinese medicine*. Boulder, CO: Blue Poppy Press.

Flaws, B., & Lake, J. (2001). *Chinese medical psychiatry: A textbook and clinical manual*. Boulder, CO: Blue Poppy Press.

Jordan, D. K. (1972). *Gods, ghosts, and ancestors*. Berkeley: University of California Press.

Kaptchuk, T. J. (1983). *The web that has no weaver*. New York: Congdon & Weed.

Kleinman, A. (1980). *Patients and healers in the context of culture*. Berkeley: University of California Press.

Lake, J. (2002). Qigong. In S. Shannon (Ed.), *Handbook of complementary and alternative therapies in mental health* (pp. 183–207). San Diego, CA: Academic Press.

Lin, T., Tardiff, K., Donetz, G., & Goresky, W. (1978). Ethnicity and pattern of help seeking. *Culture Medicine and Psychiatry, 2,* 3–14.

Liu, X. H. (1981). Psychiatry in traditional Chinese medicine. *British Journal of Psychiatry, 138,* 429–433.

Motl, J. M. (2002). Acupuncture. In S. Shannon (Ed.), *Handbook of complementary and alternative therapies in mental health* (pp. 431–451). San Diego, CA: Academic Press.

Phillips, M. (2000). *Finding the energy to heal*. New York: Norton.

Schnyer, R. (2001). *Acupuncture in the treatment of depression: A manual for practice and research*. Edinburgh, Scotland: Churchill Livingstone.

Shannon, S. (Ed.). (2002). *Handbook of complementary and alternative therapies in mental health*. San Diego, CA: Academic Press.

Singer, K. (1975). Depressive disorders from a transcultural perspective. *Social Science and Medicine, 9,* 289–301.

So, J. (1990, June). Traditional Chinese medicine (TCM) in psychiatry: A review of history, status, and prospects. In *Proceedings of the Fifth Conference of Health Problems Related to the Chinese in North America: Psychiatric treatment in the Chinese: An eclectic approach* (pp. 15–17). Toronto, Ontario, Canada: Federation of Chinese American and Chinese Canadian Medical Societies.

So, J. (1996). Cultural belief systems and mental health: Chinese culture. In J. So (Ed.), *East + West = Culture-sensitive care: Proceedings of the 7th Hong Fook Mental Health Conference* (pp. 23–32). Toronto, Ontario, Canada: Hong Fook Mental Health Association.

Sue, S. (1990). Serving the ethnic community client: Theoretical and practical considerations. In J. So (Ed.), *Breaking the barrier: Serving the reluctant client: Proceedings of the Fifth Hong Fook Mental Health Conference* (pp. 1–39). Toronto, Ontario, Canada: Hong Fook Mental Health Association.

Sue, S., Fujino, D. C., Hu, L. T., Takeuchi, D., & Zane, N. (1991). Community mental health services for ethnic minority groups: A test of the cultural responsiveness hypothesis. *Journal of Consulting and Clinical Psychology, 59,* 533–540.

Tang, N. M. (1997). Psychoanalytic psychotherapy with Chinese Americans. In E. Lee (Ed.), *Working with Asian Americans* (pp. 323–341). New York: Guilford Press.

Tien, J.-K. (1985). Traditional Chinese beliefs and attitudes toward mental illness. In W.-S. Tseng & D. Y. H. Wu (Eds.), *Chinese culture and mental health* (pp. 67–81). Orlando, FL: Academic Press.

Tseng, W. S., Lu, Q. Y., & Yin, P. Y. (1995). Psychotherapy for the Chinese: Cultural considerations. In W. S. Tseng & E. K. Yeh (Eds.), *Chinese societies and mental health* (pp. 281–294). Hong Kong, China: Oxford University Press.

Tseng, W. S., & Wu, D. Y. H. (Eds.). (1985). *Chinese culture and mental health.* Orlando, FL: Academic Press.

Tsoi, W. F. (1985). Mental health in Singapore and its relation to Chinese culture. In W.-S. Tseng & D. Y. H. Wu (Eds.), *Chinese culture and mental health* (pp. 229–250). Orlando, FL: Academic Press.

Unschuld, P. U. (1986). *Nan Jing: The classic of difficult issues.* Berkeley: University of California Press.

Wong, R. Y., Wong, J. P. H., Fung, K. P., & Chung, R. C. Y. (2003). *Promoting mental health among East and Southeast Asian immigrant/refugee women in Ontario* (Ontario Women's Health Council Final Report). Toronto, Ontario, Canada: Hong Fook Mental Health Association.

Xie, Z., & Huang, X. (Eds.). (1985). *Dictionary of traditional Chinese medicine.* Hong Kong, China: Commercial Press.

Yeung, W. H., & Lee, E. (1997). Chinese Buddhism: Its implications for counseling. In E. Lee (Ed.), *Working with Asian Americans: A guide for clinicians* (pp. 452–463). New York: Guilford Press.

Yip, K.-S. (2004). Taoism and its impact on mental health of the Chinese communities. *International Journal of Social Psychiatry, 50,* 25–42.

# 10

# South Asian (Indian) Traditional Healing

*Ayurvedic, Shamanic, and Sahaja Therapy*

*Manoj Kumar, Dinesh Bhugra, and Jagmohan Singh*

The aim of achieving and maintaining an optimal state of health has exercised the minds of humans since the earliest of times, and as a consequence, various systems of healing developed in different parts of the world. The history of Indian civilization clearly highlights a parallel journey of incessant explorations, experimentations, and numerous developments in the field of alleviating human suffering. The Indian healing tradition is one of the oldest in the world. It is quite remarkable that even as early as 1300 BC, physicians and healers had a holistic concept of health in which mental and spiritual health was given significant importance (Ramachandra Rao, 1990). The diversity of these traditions in India and the astonishing variety and number of practitioners can make a stranger to the country feel that healing—in its manifold aspects—is a central individual and cultural preoccupation (Kakar, 1982).

A vast majority of patients with psychic distress approach traditional physicians—the *vaids* of Hinduism's ayurveda and *siddha* systems and the hakim of the Islamic *unani* tradition—many of whom practice what we today call "psychological medicine." There are also palmists, horoscope specialists, herbalists, diviners, sorcerers, and a variety of shamans, whose therapeutic efforts combine elements from classical Indian astrology, medicine, alchemy, and magic with beliefs and practices from the folk and popular traditions. Ayurveda evolved in India as the natural way of healing, or naturopathy. For centuries, it was the only system of medicine. Around the same time as ayurveda developed, other variations were being developed elsewhere, such as the concept of yin and yang in China; also *unani* had its beginning in Greece and later spread throughout the Middle East, eventually reaching the Indian subcontinent in a much modified form. More recent, the major Indian systems of medicine have been grouped under the acronym AYUSH, which stands for ayurveda, yoga, *unani, siddha,* and homeopathy. In addition to herbal and other traditional medicines, healers and healing temples are seen as providing curative and restorative benefits.

In India, many people troubled by emotional distress or more serious mental illnesses go to Hindu, Muslim, Christian, and other religious centers. The healing power identified with these institutions may reside in the site itself, rather than in the religious leader or any medicines provided at the site (Raguram, Venkateswaran, Ramakrishna, & Weiss, 2002). In a survey conducted by Campion and Bhugra (1996) in 1993 to 1994, 45% of the psychiatric patients surveyed had consulted a religious healer before attending a hospital (in Tamil Nadu, South India). We do not propose to describe in detail every existing healing practice and all types of practicing healers in India. In this chapter we will instead attempt to discuss South Asian traditional healing in terms of traditional Indian psychotherapies conducted through shamans and mystics. We follow this discussion with the healing and medical traditions, such as ayurveda and the spiritual and ritualistic ceremonies in temples and shrines. Finally, we consider the implications for counseling and psychotherapy.

❖ TRADITIONAL INDIAN PSYCHOTHERAPIES

The highly diverse activities of Indian healers share a certain family resemblance in that, as compared to Western psychotherapies, the role of the "sacred" is more prominent in India. It is the sacred that links the guru concerned with the malaise of the spirit to the shaman treating illness due to machinations of the spirits (Kakar, 1982). It is beyond the scope of this chapter to go into detailed description of all the traditional healing practiced in India. However, we'll try to highlight common principles and a few relatively more widely practiced methods.

An exploration of Indian psychotherapeutic traditions not only tells us about certain social values and pressures operating in Indian society but also affords a glimpse into the symbolic universe of Indian culture in which its various healing traditions are embedded.

## Shamanic Healing (Healing the Possessed)

There is a large group of healers with a ubiquitous presence throughout India, including small villages and towns. These shamanic practitioners are known by different names in different places and settings. A Muslim healer is called *pir* or *sayana,* and a Hindu healer may be known as a *baba, ojha,* or tantric healer. They share the same modus operandi, in that they use certain ascribed divine or special powers to heal psychic distress, which can present itself in various forms including depression, anxiety, conversion symptoms, psychosomatic symptoms, and possession illness. In addition, marital and relationship problems, psychosexual difficulties, social disputes, and a range of other difficulties are often presented. Only rarely would such healers attempt to heal nonneurotic (i.e., psychotic) presentation. These healers often conduct rituals, such as chanting of sacred verses, sprinkling of "holy water," preparing a talisman infused with special healing qualities, and so forth. They generally consider themselves to be conduits between god or the supernatural and the patient. The process of exorcism may often involve inducing a possession state, which in itself provides an outlet for unconscious conflicts, without any criticism or punishment (Perera, Bhui, & Dein, 1995).

A different approach to psychic healing is tantra and tantric practices, which involve mantras, meditation, yoga, and rituals. The healing system of tantra is based on a modest theory of the causes and relief of certain forms of mental distress. Its analysis of human disease does not differ from similar analyses by psychoanalysis and other modern "depth" psychologies. However, solutions offered for psychic distress are radically different in their theoretical and practical aspects in tantra. Emphasis is clearly on enactment of unconscious fantasies and conflicts concretely within a ritualistic framework, albeit under the guidance of an expert tantric healer. The healer is believed to be endowed with superhuman power and is thought to be able to successfully heal the afflictions with the right mantra.

## Mystics as Healers

The *Oxford English Dictionary* (Pearsall, 1999) defines *mystic* as a person who seeks by contemplation and self-surrender to attain unity with the deity or the absolute, and so reaches truths beyond human understanding. There has been a long tradition of mystics in India, and Indian mystics have a large following of disciples who generally seek solutions for psychological distress. Often, when a following is large enough, the group may transform into a well-established sect of which the master or guru is the head. A common goal of self-realization, self-transformation, and ultimate unification with the supreme through meditation, prayers, rituals, sacrifices, and lifestyle changes is laid down. There is also an implied promise to remove the suffering, mental and otherwise, during the journey. Obvious mechanisms of healing seem to be initial surrender to the master and projection of all positive qualities onto him or her. This is followed by idealization of the guru/master and identification with him or her, which provides the follower with a new sense of centrality and integration with the whole.

## ❖ HEALING AND MEDICAL TRADITIONS

In modern parlance, the major alternative Indian treatments are brought together under the acronym AYUSH, which stands for ayurveda, yoga, *unani, siddha,* and homeopathy, as described earlier. We shall briefly describe the most ancient of these systems, namely the systems of ayurveda and *siddha.*

### Ayurveda

The ayurvedic tradition (which traces its lineage to the early Vedic civilization and systems of thought in India, around 1700 BC), as described in the classical texts of *Susruta* and *Caraka* (200 BC–400 AD), avoids a strict body-mind dualism and instead emphasizes the interaction of mind and body in the causation of the human condition (in health and disease) (Ramachandra Rao, 1990). *Unani* medicine is an ancient form of medicine, first developed by the Greeks in 460 BC, that was introduced to India in the 13th century. *Unani* philosophy believes that the body is made of three parts: a solid part (termed *organs*), a liquid part (termed *humors*), and a gaseous part (termed *pneuma*). However, it is the disequilibrium in either the quantity or quality of any of the four humors that leads to a diseased state.

According to ayurvedic principles, perfect health can be achieved only when body, mind, and soul are in harmony with each other and with other cosmic surroundings. The second dimension in this holistic view of ayurveda is at the social level, where the system describes the ways and means of establishing harmony with and in the society. Ayurveda lays special emphasis on individual constitution, and a person's health as well as treatment are decided accordingly. Mental equilibrium is sought by bringing in harmony three qualities of mind: *sattva, rajas,* and *tamas* (see Bhugra, 1992).

Ayurveda is an integral part of Indian culture. Without some awareness of the theory of ayurvedic medicine, it's not possible to understand much of what goes on in the minds of people in the South Asian world (Obeyesekere, 1977).

The diagnosis is made by the therapist, called a *vaid,* through a history of symptoms and lifestyle, particularly questions about diet, examination of pulse (*nadi*), and questions about dreams, which are then interpreted with reference to psychic life as well as physiological functions, because in ayurveda "psyche" cannot be separated from "soma" (body). Mental illnesses are classified into three groups:

1. Diseases of primarily mental origin with predominantly mental symptoms, such as *unmada,* a generic term that includes almost all the psychotic as well as neurotic disorders

2. Diseases of primarily mental origin with predominantly physical symptoms, such as epilepsy (*iapasmara*), hysterical fits (*apatantraka*), insomnia (*nidranasa*), and "fever from grief and sexual desire" (*sokaja* and *kamaja jvara*)

3. Diseases of primarily physical origin and predominantly mental symptoms, such as certain delusional states (*attatvabhinivesa*) and alcohol or drug intoxication (*mada*)

Treatment of mental disorders in ayurveda follows along the same lines as the treatment of bodily illnesses. The therapeutic repertoire comprises the following treatments:

1. *Purification:* This traditionally consisted of purges, emetics, enemas, and bleeding along with instructions for personal hygiene.

2. *Pacification:* This consists of topical application of ointments, ingestion of decoctions prepared from plants and metals, or both.

3. *Removal of the cause:* This includes removal of predisposing, maintaining, and precipitating factors for the mental illness through changes in lifestyle (e.g., dietary changes, regular sleep, abstinence from alcohol) and changes in environment, which may involve instructions for the family members.

The *vaid* takes an active role in the patient's life in an effort to make the patient follow the rules of "proper conduct" (in the socially desirable sense) through advice, suggestions, and exhortations to stop a particularly harmful activity or to start a particularly desirable one.

### *Siddha* System

*Siddha* medicine, which dates back to around 5000 BC, originated in the southern parts of India. The word *siddha* means "an object to be attained," "perfection," or "heavenly bliss." *Siddhars* were saintly figures who achieved results in medicine through the practice of yoga. The principles and doctrines of this system, both fundamental and applied, have a close similarity to ayurveda, with specialization in iatrochemistry. According to this system, the human body is a replica of the universe, and so are food and drugs, irrespective of their origin. The diagnosis of disease involves identifying its causes. Identification of causative factors is done through pulse reading, urine examination, examination of eyes, study of voice, color of body, examination of the tongue, and assessment of the status of the digestive system. Diagnosis involves the study of the person as a whole, as well as the person's disease.

The treatment is mainly directed toward restoration of equilibrium of the three humors (*vattam, pittam,* and *kapham*), and for this purpose various cleaning procedures are used, such as *vanthi* (vomiting), *piccu* (enema), and others. After these procedures, the patient is ready for the treatment, which involves 12 types of medicated oils and five methods of application on "vital points" (*varmanilaigal*), using a specialized pressure technique. The *siddha* system of medicine emphasizes that the medical treatment shall not be oriented merely to disease but must take into account the patient, the environment, the meteorological consideration, age, sex, race, habits, mental frame, habitat, diet, appetite, physical condition, physiological constitution, and so forth and that treatment should be individualized according to the patient's needs.

### ❖ TWO MODELS FOR PSYCHOTHERAPY IN INDIA

#### Guru-*Chela* (Teacher-Pupil) Relationship

Neki (1975a) points out that ancient psychotherapies are shrouded in mystical and pseudomystical terminologies. He recommends that in order to be fully effective, they need to have simpler terminology, and they must be reinterpreted with scientific scrutiny while being culturally relevant. He proposed two models of psychotherapy for use in India, namely the guru-*chela* (teacher-pupil) relationship and *sahaja* therapy. Of this, the guru-*chela* model of the psychotherapeutic relationship was considered ideal for Indian patients (Neki, 1973).

Regarding the guru-*chela* relationship, the word *guru*, in the Indian tradition, has twin connotations, of being a teacher and a spiritual preceptor. The guru acts as a physician of mind and soul with objectivity and competence. The guru takes the disciple (*chela*) through an experiential journey of self-exploration with an aim to liberate the disciple from all suffering.

The guru-*chela* relationship as a therapeutic paradigm was suggested by Neki (1973) and appears to be tenable where self-discipline, rather than self-expression, is to be inculcated in the patients and where creative harmony is sought between patient and society. More activity and direct guidance and advice by the therapist is adopted in this form of relationship.

The guru-*chela* relationship is polyvalent, polyvariant, and multidimensional and therefore much wider than the transference relationship of Western psychotherapy.

### *Sahaja* Therapy

Etymologically, *sahaja* is derived from *saha* (together) and *ja* (born), thereby meaning "born together," that is, with one self, hence congenital or innate. It signifies the "innate nature" that is born along with a person. Because conditioning influences cramp the "soul" and hold the mind in bondage, *sahaja* becomes the state of renascent freedom or liberation. It is closer to the humanistic school of psychology and aims to achieve an "ideal" state of being by attaining the ultimate human potential. However, the emphasis here is not on "success" in the social sense but rather on insight into real self: equipoise, spontaneity, freedom from all conflicts, and harmony with one's inner self and the environment. Neki (1975b) proposed *sahaja* as an ideal of mental health, which according to him could be suitably merged with the concept of guru-*chela* for psychotherapy in the Indian context.

### ❖ PATHWAYS TO THE INTRODUCTION AND INTEGRATION OF INDIAN HEALING PRACTICES AND THEIR UNDERSTANDING IN THE CULTURAL CONTEXT

With the rapidly changing composition of Western society, with globalization and migration from the developing world, there is an urgent need to revisit various models of psychotherapy. It is crucial to be aware of those cultural differences that are psychologically significant if we wish to avoid stumbling into areas that can be taken for granted in dealing with patients from Western cultures but that may have unanticipated consequences in patients from other cultures (Slote, 1992). Creating a forum where therapists can exchange ideas with community leaders and experts to enhance understanding of traditional Indian healing systems would be a step in that direction, as would developing a culture of awareness about patients' health beliefs and the influence of cultural aspects on the process and outcome of the therapy. A careful preliminary negotiation of treatment targets with individual clients and a willingness to work within the same set of expectations, which may not be those of the therapist, are prerequisites (MacCarthy, 1988). One approach is to learn about indigenous systems of healing and explanatory models that are common to specific cultural groups so that an understanding of distress that is closer to the patient's experience can be achieved before attempts are made to map these to specific biomedical diagnostic categories and related care pathways (Patel, 1995). It is important to acknowledge the importance of the role of the family and issues with and within the family and, where appropriate, to actively involve the family in the therapeutic process.

In general, training psychotherapists in cultural, racial, and ethnic norms should be incorporated into the routine curriculum. The contents of training must include general principles of cross-cultural assessments and interaction; understanding of cultural norms, mores, and taboos prevalent within the Indian community; and an understanding of principles of indigenous healing practices, religious and spiritual formulation, and the impact of migratory experience. Therapists also need to be aware of intergenerational conflicts between primary migrants and subsequent generations.

There are elements in the guru-*chela* relationship that can be successfully applied in a therapeutic transaction with Indian patients as well as at times with non-Indian clients. An attempt must be made, therefore, to isolate these elements and to reconstruct a suitable therapeutic paradigm. In attempting to do so, it is necessary to understand the traditional image of the Indian physician, who, like a guru, has been a highly respected member of the society. The outcomes of these traditional therapies then should be scientifically evaluated through clinical assessment and monitoring, patient and caregiver feedback, audits, and quantitative as well as qualitative research.

❖ CONCLUSION

There are fundamental differences among the Eastern and Western societies, cultures, and mindsets. The divergent concepts of self in relation to society, religion, and culture and differing health beliefs highlight the need for improved understanding of effective patient-specific therapeutic paradigms. The repeated failure of rigid and purely Western psychotherapeutic models when dealing with patients from the Indian subcontinent is largely caused by a limited understanding of cultural influences and a "one size fits all" approach with little consideration to individual needs. The vast repertoire of traditional healing practices prevalent in India reflects certain common, shared philosophies and therapeutic methodologies. These practices mirror the health belief and explanatory models of the Indian population. These models vary significantly from the Western health belief model, which excludes the spiritual dimension and promotes body-mind dualism to some extent.

Culture plays an extremely important role in an individual's development and in defining his or her internal world as well as perception of external realities and environment. According to the cultural and historical evaluation, a behavior, illness, or symptom can be given a different significance (Pesechkian, 1990). When an individual migrates to a different society, he or she brings along a repertoire of traditions, values, perceptions, expectations, and mindsets, which can significantly vary from those of the adopted society or culture. Therefore, the person's response to local practices can be markedly different. There are clinical implications of bringing traditional healing practices into mainstream psychotherapies. Certain concepts, such as mindfulness, are already gaining acceptance among indigenous populations. Some other practices promoting self-awareness and discipline resonate well with mainstream psychotherapies, cognitive therapy in particular. Various other useful and benign aspects of traditional practices could be usefully applied with indigenous populations, for example, *sahaja* therapy. There are greater implications for immigrant and ethnic Indian populations. Besides facilitating increased accessibility, therapists need to understand the needs of a patient on an individual basis. Empirical evidence suggests that patients are more likely to trust and be satisfied when their psychiatrist shares their model of understanding distress and treatment. An integrative approach that incorporates therapeutic elements of traditional Indian healing systems into the Western model of psychotherapy and counseling will improve the efficacy and acceptability of treatment for patients of Indian ethnic origin. Of course, increased flexibility and enhanced understanding of a vastly rich healing tradition would reciprocally contribute to the wider applicability of psychotherapy.

## ❖ REFERENCES

Bhugra, D. (1992). Psychiatry in ancient Indian texts: A review. *History of Psychiatry, 3*, 167–186.
Campion, J., & Bhugra, R. (1996). Experiences of religious healing in psychiatric patients in South India. *Social Psychiatry & Psychiatric Epidemiology, 32*, 215–221.

Kakar, S. (1982). *Shamans, mystics & doctors*. Oxford, UK: Oxford University Press.

MacCarthy, B. (1988). Working with ethnic minorities. In F. N. Watts (Ed.), *New developments in clinical psychology* (pp. 123–139). Chichester, UK: Wiley.

Neki, J. S. (1973). Guru-chela relationship: The possibility of a therapeutic paradigm. *American Journal of Orthopsychiatry, 3*, 755–766.

Neki, J. S. (1975a). Psychotherapy in India: Past, present & future. *American Journal of Psychotherapy, 29*, 92–100.

Neki, J. S. (1975b). Sahaja: An Indian ideal of mental health. *Psychiatry, 36*, 1–11.

Obeyesekere, G. (1977). The theory and practice of psychological medicine in the Ayurvedic tradition. *Culture, Medicine and Psychiatry, 1*, 155–171.

Patel, V. (1995). Explanatory models of mental illness in sub-Saharan Africa. *Social Science Medicine, 40*, 1291–1298.

Pearsall, J. (Ed.). (1999). *Oxford English dictionary* (10th ed.). Oxford, UK: Oxford University Press.

Perera, S., Bhui, K., & Dein, S. (1995). Making sense of possession states: Psychopathology and differential diagnosis. *British Journal of Hospital Medicine, 53*, 582.

Pesechkian, N. (1990). Positive psychotherapy: A transcultural and interdisciplinary approach to psychotherapy. *Psychotherapy Psychosoma, 53*, 39–45.

Raguram, R., Venkateswaran, A., Ramakrishna, J., & Weiss, M. G. (2002). Traditional community resources for mental health: A report of temple healing from India. *British Medical Journal, 325*, 38–40.

Ramachandra Rao, S. K. (1990). *Mental health in Ayurveda: Source book of charaka & sushruta samhita* (National Institute of Mental Health and Neuro Sciences). Bangalore, India: Nimhans Publications.

Slote, W. (1992). Oedipal ties and issues of separation—Individuation in traditional Confucian societies. *Journal of the American Academy of Psychoanalysis, 20*, 435–453.

# PART III

## Spirituality, Religion, and Cultural Healing

# 11

# Animism

## Foundation of Traditional
## Healing in Sub-Saharan Africa

*Clemmont E. Vontress*

This chapter explores the concept of animism, the foundation of the African way of life and conception of well-being. Africans consult a variety of individuals when they encounter physical, psychological, social, and spiritual problems. In this chapter, they are described under six headings: indigenous doctors, herbalists, fetish men, mediums, religious healers, and sorcerers. Although they are known by different names in the various ethnic and national languages on the continent, the belief in animism seems to be common to all. In fact, it appears to unify the whole of sub-Saharan Africa. Finally, implications of traditional healing practices for counseling are discussed.

## ❖ ANIMISM

The term *animism* derives from the Latin word *anima*, meaning "breath" or "soul." It is one of humankind's oldest creeds. From its earliest beginnings, it was the belief that a soul or spirit existed in every object, even inanimate ones (Hefner & Guimaraes, 2003). According to Heraclitus (ca. 500 BC), the soul is a finite phenomenon of the natural world (Wheelwright, 1959). Marcus Aurelius (AD 121–180), Roman emperor from AD 161 to 180, declared that everything in the universe is interconnected (Wolff, 1976). Plato maintained that all nature is kin and knows everything (Levy, 1967).

In sub-Saharan Africa, the view that everything in the universe is of one source, mind, and will is called *animism*. In the West, it is usually called *panpsychism*, a construct advocated and articulated by numerous thinkers, including German philosophers Wilhelm Gottfried Leibniz (1646–1716), Friedrich Schiller (1759–1805), and Arthur Schopenhauer (1788–1860) and their British counterpart Alfred North Whitehead (1861–1947). Levy (1967) declared that the universe itself is like a human being: living, conscious, and divine. Blackburn (1994) indicated that the world, or nature, ought to be considered alive and animated. Human beings are a microcosm or small version of the cosmos. Levy added that the universal soul is eternal and divine. Because the human soul is a "fragment" of the main soul, it also is eternal and divine. It passes not only between humans, but also into plants and inanimate objects as well. Although the human body dies and disintegrates, the soul is forever in the universe (Donceel, 1961). It may inhabit other humans, animals, plants, inanimate objects, and the like.

In the animist view of the world, humans are a link in the cosmic chain of events that summons lower orders (minerals, plants, and animals) to join higher ones (spirits, ancestors, and gods). All of them must be called on in efforts to heal human sufferers (Cisse, 1999). In most sub-Saharan African countries, healers are "called" to their profession (Hahn, 1995). Their clients believe that the healers possess special powers to communicate with a great universal force.

Animism ought to be viewed as a religion that is basic to all other religions (Bon, 1998). As such, it influences the behavior of the living. It is a family affair in the sense that if an individual is out of source, the whole family is out of source. The general health and well-being of an individual depend on connection to a community. A person cannot achieve them solitarily. Healing, ritual, and community welfare are all interrelated (Somé, 1999).

## ❖ THE WORLD OF AFRICAN WELL-BEING

In much of Africa, animism is a religion that significantly affects the inhabitants' way of life (Bon, 1998). As an aspect of culture, it is also related to a group's healing system. The way patients conceive the origin of their illness, the treatment process, and reactions to symptoms are all intrinsically related to an individual's heritage. Cultural assumptions also determine how a sufferer relates to a healer (Alarcón, Foulks, & Vakkur, 1998).

In traditional sub-Saharan Africa, people are expected to live in harmony with the cosmos (Diallo & Hall, 1989). All things are connected, and the rules that protect the integrity and viability of the whole and its parts must be preserved. Anyone who violates the rules that secure harmony among humans, spirits, ancestors, animals, and plants risks psychological disturbance. A physical, psychological, social, or spiritual problem is always linked to a breakage in this important relationship (Somé, 1999).

Ancestors play a significant role in controlling the conduct of the living. Though invisible, they are the glue that holds intact the culture. As omniscient, omnipresent, and perpetual monitors, spirits of the departed are perceived to be valuable members of the community. Their mission is to guarantee the well-being of the living (Bon, 1998). People are expected to adhere to their traditions. Failure to do so may cause the invisible overseers to exact punishment with a vengeance by sending trouble, illness, or death to wrongdoers (Somé, 1999).

The role of the head of the family is to keep vigil over its members (Diallo & Hall, 1989). Family members are expected to abide by the rules and expectations of the group in order to avoid offending members of the invisible community. The family unites against or wards off evil spirits (Bon, 1998). When a member falls sick, the head of the unit is very concerned. He knows that ancestors, the group's disciplinarians, keep a watchful eye on everybody's behavior. Sickness or misfortune means that an ancestor is displeased with the sufferer's behavior. Therefore, the family patriarch seeks to understand the reason for the displeasure and wants to find an immediate way to correct the problem. Failure to act promptly is apt to cause his neighbors to censure him and his family. If he is unable to resolve the situation himself, he consults someone outside his family, usually an indigenous healer.

## ❖ TRADITIONAL HEALERS

Traditional healers are known by various names in different parts of sub-Saharan Africa. Each ethnic group has a culture-specific understanding of healers and their roles. Often the understanding is influenced by the size of the village and the number of available healers. In small communities, there may be a single person who attends the health needs of all residents. In large settlements, healers may specialize in a particular service, such as bone fractures or snakebites. Sometimes the specialists conjoin to help clients. Below, six healing agents are listed and discussed.

**Indigenous Doctors**

Indigenous doctors have been important to Africans for thousands of years (Dickinson, 1999). In francophone Africa, they are called *les guérisseurs* ("healers"). In the anglophone counterpart, they may be called "juju men" or by some other name. In Nigeria, Edo people use the general term *obos* to refer to native doctors. The Yoruba word for them is *babalawo*. Whatever they are called, their services are important to millions of people.

The doctors relate to their clients as authority figures. Often, they may not even talk to the client, choosing instead to talk with the head of the family. In some cases, the client is invited to stay with the healer and his family for several days or weeks. The brief stays allow the healer to monitor the progress of his client. He may touch or massage the client's body as he wishes. On the other hand, the doctor may not even see the client. Some parents come for medical consultation on behalf of the client (Vontress, 1991, 1999).

Because healers presume conjuncture with the universal soul, they resort to several techniques to diagnose the presenting problems of their clients. Some divine the client's situation through a wall or from a great distance. Others probe the head of the family about the client's behavior at home or in the community to ascertain whether the individual has offended an ancestor. Indigenous doctors commonly throw lots (cowrie chips, sticks, stones, etc.) and "read" their landing configuration, which is a kind of problem inventory. Some doctors go to the forest to "consult" plants and trees to diagnose the problem and to determine the best treatment for it (Vontress, 1999). One of the oldest diagnostic methods is the healer's observing the movement of caged mice to derive diagnostic information about human beings. Some healers prefer to look into a natural source of water or a container of water to "see" the client's problem. Finally, a doctor may also touch the garments of their clients to determine the nature and source of their problem. These, then, are just a few diagnostic techniques used by indigenous doctors.

Indigenous doctors use diverse intervention strategies to eradicate, alleviate, or counteract evil forces affecting the lives of their clients. People who seek their help assume that they are able to connect with a universal therapeutic power. In order to transfer the power to their clients, healers may pray with them; give them direct advice, fetishes, or herbs; or consult the spirits on their behalf. When they suspect that someone has put a hex on one of their clients, some healers go to the client's home in order to search for malevolent objects that enemies may have hidden there. When a couple is unable to conceive, a healer may massage their bodies with special lotions while they have intercourse. Often, wives concerned about wayward husbands consult the local healer to get a love potion to put in their spouse's food in order to keep his fidelity. Finally, indigenous doctors may be sorcerer-fighters. That is, they undo spells or hexes that sorcerers have placed on their clients.

## Herbalists

The medicinal use of plants and herbs is as old as mankind (Kubukeli, 1999). Throughout recorded history, writers have referred to the healing qualities of plants (Bricklin, 1983). In view of the widespread belief in animism in Africa, herbal medicine is especially important to its inhabitants. According to the World Health Organization, 80% of the people in countries from South Africa to Ethiopia rely on herbs (Green, 2002). They use them in one form or another for almost everything that ails them (Twitchell, 1982). Some are sewn into bags and worn to ward off evil spirits. Some are boiled to make tea to drink to expel worms and parasites. There are also expectorant plants that can be eaten raw to loosen mucous secretions and to facilitate their expulsion. There are many other ailments for which herbs are used as healing agents. Their consumption promotes universal harmony and well-being. It is understandable that there is a strong demand for them in Africa.

Although each household has its store of herbs, people consult herbalists when their home remedies are ineffective. Herbalists know what plant, bark, or root is most beneficial and what form of it is best for each malady. They are aware of the nosology of sickness and can predict the course of each illness when a specific herb is introduced into the body (Hahn, 1995). Because of their ability to connect with the universal soul or power, they also know the correct dosage and frequency of ingestion or application of selected herbs for each patient.

Herbs are so important to the people of sub-Saharan Africa that they have become an important part of commerce in many African countries. In Côte d'Ivoire, the planting, cultivating, and harvesting of medicinal plants and roots constitutes a veritable industry (Sylla, 1988). In South Africa, more than 400 species of indigenous plants are sold commercially as medicine (Kubukeli, 1999). On market day throughout Africa, plant stalls enjoy brisk sales. In large cities, pharmacies stock and sell traditional herbs, barks, roots, and other healing products alongside Western drugs.

## Fetish Men

As already indicated, animism is the belief that a single spirit animates the entire universe. The universal force inhabits water, trees, stones, mice, humans, and all other things. Everything is divine (Bon, 1998). Thus, a cow, a tree, or the act of people moving in unison in a dance can be sacred. A river or stream of water is sacred and may be used for therapy when necessary. For example, a fetish man may advise the head of a family to immerse briefly in a cold stream a family member who has "gone out of his mind," in order to restore him or her to sanity. As experts on natural beneficial forces, fetish men are educators, doctors, priests, and magicians all in one person (Tchetche, 1998).

In general, all segments of the sub-Saharan population respect the *féticheur*, as he is called in francophone Africa. On lazy Sunday afternoons on the highway running near Grand Bassam, the old French colonial coastal capital city of Côte d'Ivoire, a foreigner may be surprised by the number of expensive cars, seemingly out of place, parked on the glistening sandy shoulder of the road at a site where a sign reads "*Féticheur*" and an arrow points to a shack off the road under a canopy of trees. Sometimes, liveried chauffeurs patiently stand by their vehicles while inside the stalls their passengers inspect and buy objects hanging from the ceiling, spread on tables, or standing on the ground. Masks, stones, snakeskins, bones, leather pouches for powder, phalluses carved from mahogany, and countless other items are available to empower, make whole, or protect the possessor from evil spirits. The fetish man advises his customers which ones are most apt to meet their specific needs. In the big market at Plateau, the center of Abidjan, the commercial capital of Côte d'Ivoire, a larger selection of fetishes is available. In some stalls, customers can read on posted boards the spiritual and medicinal benefits of each object.

An area of life in which fetish men are especially important is soccer, a passionately beloved sport throughout Africa. Each team may have its own *féticheur*, somewhat like American professional football and basketball teams that have their own physicians. According to Asia (1996), the fetish man aims to ensure his team's victory by providing each player with an amulet to wear, a special potion to drink, or a lotion to spread over his body before a match. Hebga (1979) indicates that some fetish men invite players to their home or another place, where they perform rituals over them before a competition. Sometimes they sit on the sideline or stand elsewhere in the stadium, ready to perform rituals and to supply fetishes as needed. Owners and managers of soccer teams take seriously the work of fetish men, as do most people in sub-Saharan Africa (Bon, 1998). Christoph and Oberländer (1996) point out that fetishes are frequently placed, as guardian spirits, on the outskirts of villages.

## Mediums

Although the spirits of departed ancestors are believed to look after the best interests of their descendants, they can also send them illness and misfortune when they are moved to wrath (Hammond-Tooke, 1989). Mediums are individuals who have the power to communicate with the spirits of the invisible world, or the "living dead" of the community, as Rouget (1985) called them. They act as intermediaries between the invisible and visible worlds to determine which spirits are at work and to bring the sick person back into harmony with them ("The human soul or spirit," 2003). Mbiti (1988) indicated that mediums are like radio sets functioning between terminals: the source (spirits or divinities) and recipients (diviners, medicine men, or priests) of the broadcast.

Ancestors seem to use mediums in different ways in order to communicate with their living descendants (Castellan, 1987). First, the medium may summon the dead, who materialize or make their presence known by tapping noises. Second, the medium may become the person through whom the dead person speaks with the voice he used when alive. Third, a medium may become the vehicle that allows the spirit of the deceased to write out a message for someone still alive. Fourth, there are mediums whose bodies are used as a relay to enable the spirits of departed ancestors to touch the sick in order to heal them.

Mediums are at their best during emotionally charged group healing ceremonies involving the whole community. Often referred to as "possession dances," these festive occasions take days to plan and may go on nonstop for up to 72 hours (Stoller & Olkes, 1987). Stoller (1989) indicated that the world of possession takes on the aura of a carnival with its bright costumes, energetic dancing, pulsating music, and frenetic energy. An electrifying drumbeat is an essential part of the ceremony. The spirits are summoned by the continuous, hypnotic rhythm of the "healing drum," as Diallo and Hall (1989) called the percussion instrument. They communicate with the assembled audience via the mediums.

In the Songhay region of Niger, there are possession troupes consisting of mediums, praise singers, musicians, and support staff that rove the countryside, moving from one village to another (Stoller, 1989). The mediums are the central figures, because their bodies are "taken over" by the spirits who communicate through them. During a typical ceremony, a multitude of problems may be presented for consultation. These include individual illnesses, failing crops, family discord, miscarriages, and marriage aspirations. In each case, the medium goes into a hypnotic trance (Ezembe, 1997). The spirit of the departed ancestor speaks through the medium in his own voice to counsel his descendants. Although the advice is directed to one person or family, the entire audience leaves the charged atmosphere with a sense of completion and well-being. Indeed, mediums are an important part of the health system of Africa.

## Spiritual Healers

Healing has always been associated with religion. Stone (1997) indicated that psychiatry was religion before it was psychiatry. The word *psychiatry* comes from the Greek words *psyche* (soul) and *iatreia* (healing). In many non-Western societies, healers are generally believed to have acquired their abilities from a higher power (Hahn, 1995). In Africa, there are approximately 270 million Muslims, 183 million Christians (Catholics and Protestants), and about 130 million animists (Hayes, 1995). In each group, the clerics practice some form of healing.

North African merchants introduced Islam into sub-Saharan Africa in the seventh century (*"Langues et religions,"* 2003). Today, a number of West African countries, including Mauritania, Senegal, Guinea-Bissau, Guinea, Mali, Niger, and the Northern part of Nigeria are predominantly Muslim (Mazrui, 1975). In each of them, almost everybody consults marabouts (clerics) regarding problems in living. People who want to expel evil spirits or want more happiness, glory, or power consult the local marabout (*"Les marabouts,"* 2003). Those who are troubled physically, mentally, socially, or spiritually also seek his assistance. Although marabouts employ some of the same techniques used by indigenous doctors, they differ from them in their use of the Quran as a healing agent. Often, they write a verse from it on a piece of paper or wood. Then they wash it off and boil it as tea. Clients drink it to cure themselves of maladies.

Christianity was introduced into Africa in the 4th century (*"Langues et religions,"* 2003). It spread throughout sub-Saharan Africa during the European colonization beginning in the 15th century. Today, Catholicism and Protestantism have nominally permeated much of the continent. The Bible has been translated into 400 African languages (Rosy, 1992). Religious healing is deeply rooted in the Christian tradition (Ehrenwald, 1976). Descriptions of healing miracles can be found in the Old and New Testaments. Today, the heavily Protestant countries in Africa are Ghana, Nigeria, and Kenya (Rosy). Although congregations present themselves as Catholic or Protestant, most of the priests and ministers mix traditional beliefs and practices into their services, which often are energized by chanting, drumming, and traditional dancing (*"Langues et religions,"* 2003). In assuming the role of healer, pastors pray with or for their clients to help them resolve problems. They also use many of the techniques used by indigenous doctors to intervene on behalf of parishioners presenting physical, psychological, social, and spiritual problems.

Vodoun, sometimes called Voodoo, is a religion whose roots go back 6,000 years in African traditions. In modern history, it can be traced to the West African Yoruba people who lived in 18th- and 19th-century Dahomey, a country that occupied parts of what is now known as Togo, Benin, and Nigeria (Christoph & Oberländer, 1996). It derives from the word *vodu* in the Fon language of Dahomey and means "spirit" or "god" (*"Voodoo zombies,"* 2003). More than 60 million people practice it not only in Africa, but also in the Caribbean, South America, in large cities of the United States, and elsewhere in the world (Handwerk, 2002). In Benin, there are 4 million adherents of Vodoun.

Vodoun priests are prominent and respected community figures. People perceive them to have strong connections with the spirits, who are called on to heal the sick, help the needy, and provide practical solutions to life's problems (Handwerk, 2002). As healers, Vodoun priests use a variety of therapeutic methods. Many of them are the same ones used by indigenous doctors already discussed. Fetishes, herbs, special powders, and roots are employed to restore individuals to normalcy. However, the most powerful healing occurs in a group or congregational setting. The priest-healer may orchestrate rituals and sacrifice animals (Christoph & Oberländer, 1996). During religious ceremonies, loud syncopated drumming, chanting, and preaching electrify the atmosphere in preparation for the visit of spirits of departed ancestors and other entities of nature. The bodies of certain members of the audience are taken over by the spirits, during which time they dance, jump, whirl, and emit various sounds. At the end of the event, the participants retire to their homes, all feeling revitalized and in harmony with themselves, their fellows, and nature at large.

### Sorcerers

The word *sorcery* derives from the Latin *sors* and means "spell" (Guiley, 1999). It refers to the casting of spells or the use of charms to influence love, fertility, luck, health, and wealth. The French word *sorcier* means "witch." In general, the terms *witchcraft* and *sorcery* are used interchangeably (Hayes, 1995). An old idea discussed by ancient scholars and described in the Bible, today sorcery often is associated with the human being's electrochemical system (Lightman, 1999). Cross-culturally, the system is held to be the essence of the universal spirit-energy. It is reflected in language such as "divine light," the "light of the Holy Spirit," and the "Enlightenment."

A sorcerer is an individual who is born with or has acquired the knowledge and capacity to control, channel, or otherwise manipulate another person's vital force (Diallo & Hall, 1989). In many parts of the world, it is believed that the sorcerer robs people of this force, causing them to fall sick or die. Such a belief is especially widespread in Africa. Some religious scholars and anthropologists estimate that as many as 75% of sub-Saharan Africans of all educational and socio-economic levels believe in sorcery (Tucker, 1999). In communities across the region, endless stories of witchcraft abound. People are so afraid of it that they often take matters into their own hands when they suspect that a sorcerer is in their midst. In South Africa during the last part of the 20th century, villagers killed several hundred of their neighbors whom they suspected of being sorcerers (Hayes, 1995). The fear and related killings became so widespread that the federal government made a legislative inquiry into the matter. In 1995, it issued a

285-page report detailing and confirming the murders (Tucker). However, it failed to verify the existence of sorcery.

Guiley (1999) indicates that the belief in sorcery fulfills various needs in African societies beset with poverty and related problems. When resources are limited, people frequently mistrust their neighbors and may be jealous of them (Tucker, 1999). Out of frustration and desperation, some turn to witchcraft to hurt others whom they wrongfully perceive to be the source of their problems and therefore their enemies. In small communities, individuals who stand out in any way—intelligence, wealth, and so forth—are most apt to be targets of sorcery (Tucker).

Although sorcerers who reportedly hurt people get most of the attention in Africa, there are also good sorcerers, who are seldom discussed. That is, wherever bad sorcerers harm, good sorcerers are needed to undo the harm, as Rosy (1992) points out. Good healers are necessarily good sorcerers, because they have to be powerful to combat evil. Occasionally, a healer gains international recognition as a sorcerer-fighter. One such person is priestess-healer Aman Afala of Côte d'Ivoire, West Africa (Seri, 1997). Known throughout sub-Saharan Africa for her success in treating illnesses and fighting sorcery, people as far away as Europe consult her for various unrelenting problems.

## ❖ IMPLICATIONS FOR COUNSELING AND PSYCHOTHERAPY

As the basic cosmology of the sub-Saharan African people, animism influences the nature of healing in ethnic cultures of the region. The conception of an illness, its etiology, who should treat it, and how to treat it are all related to animism. People in each group establish their own expectations of healers. The most effective therapeutic agents are those who embody the culture of their clients. In a sense, the client's culture is the healing instrument (NGOMA, 2003).

Healing practices are by-products of a worldview. Over time, each population develops its own weltanschauung. It is consciously and unconsciously passed from one generation to the next. The perception of health and illness is a significant part of it. Each group's cosmology is unique. It is produced by years of accumulated and reinforced experiences. Members of each culture share a common heritage. They are each endowed with a unifying cultural intuition and mutual empathy. Although most people are unable to articulate the imperceptible sense of unity, they immediately "feel" the common heritage and unity when they encounter one of their cultural confreres in a strange land.

In spite of the increased interest in traditional healing and cross-cultural communication, the lack of a shared reality is one of the reasons why most attempts at cross-cultural therapy have been ineffective (Vontress, 2001). Occidental therapists often are frustrated when counseling African immigrants. To relieve the frustration, host-country counselors need to find a way to be therapeutic without imposing their psychotherapeutic "science" on people socialized in spiritually oriented societies (Torrey, 1986). Nathan (1993, 1994) has been searching for a compromise for several years. He and his colleagues in Paris integrate traditional and modern healing methodologies to obtain deep and lasting results with immigrant clients. Without trying to understand African cosmology in its totality, they adopt some of the techniques used successfully by traditional healers when counseling African-born clients in France.

At first blush, it appears that traditional and modern healers are dissimilar. In reality, the techniques of therapy used everywhere in the world have a lot in common, as Torrey (1986) pointed out. People in a given culture favor certain types of therapies because the methods are compatible with their cultural values and expectations. Culture is largely unconscious. Most of it is out of sight and out of mind. Therefore, it is doubtful that counselors can learn cognitively the culture of another people, such that they can "feel" what the native-born know intuitively. However, they can imitate, when necessary, some of the techniques used by traditional healers in order to help African-born clients. However, they always should be authentic to their own culture and not pretend be a product of the age-old African cosmology.

## ❖ CONCLUSION

During the last 25 years, Western medical professionals have demonstrated increased interest in learning about traditional healing in Africa, a continent where 80% of the population consults indigenous doctors for all problems. Although Western physicians and traditional healers now respect and aid each other, counselors and psychologists are still in the process of determining how they can ally themselves with folk healers. Their difficulty seems to derive from the fact that traditional healers are holistic. They do not segment a client into physical, psychological, social, and spiritual parts in order to treat each separately. The Western therapist who treats only the psychological concerns of African-born clients may thereby neglect the most important therapeutic consideration—the spiritual. In spite of what is a real cultural challenge, Western therapists can still help African clients, especially those with problems related to adjusting to the host country. They will probably need to do a great deal of homework to intervene effectively on behalf of clients presenting spiritually based problems.

Many African American therapists express fascination with traditional healing in Africa. The attraction is so strong that some of them would like to use at least parts of traditional healing in counseling American-born clients, especially blacks. In general, they seem to be motivated more by historical frustration with the American society than by a real consideration of the practicality of using aspects of an ethnomedical model in counseling clients socialized in a biomedical culture. Furthermore, there is not just one culture in sub-Saharan Africa. There are hundreds of ethnic cultures, many of which have little in common with each other, except that they are joined historically by animism.

## ❖ REFERENCES

Alarcón, R. D., Foulks, E. F., & Vakkur, M. (1998). *Personality disorders and culture: Clinical and conceptual interactions.* New York: John Wiley & Son.

Asia, W.-V. (1996, July 10). La pratique du fétiche dans le football ivoirien [The practice of fetishism in soccer in Côte d'Ivoire]. *Douze,* pp. 4–5.

Blackburn, S. (1994). *The Oxford dictionary of philosophy.* Oxford, UK: Oxford University Press.

Bon, D. (1998). *L'animisme: L'âme du monde et le culte des esprits* [Animism: The universal soul and spiritual cults]. Paris: Éditions de Vecchi S. A.

Bricklin, M. (Ed.). (1983). *The practical encyclopedia of natural healing* (Rev. ed.). Emmaus, PA: Rodale.

Castellan, Y. (1987). *Le spiritualisme* [Spiritualism] (7th ed.). Paris: Presses Universitaires de France.

Christoph, H., & Oberländer, H. (1996). *Voodoo: Secret power in Africa.* New York: Taschen.

Cisse, A. (1999). Healers to the rescue. *UNESCO Courier, 52*(10), 1–26.

Diallo, Y., & Hall, M. (1989). *The healing drum: African wisdom teachings.* Rochester, VT: Destiny Books.

Dickinson, G. (1999). Traditional healers face off with science. *CMAJ: Canadian Medical Association Journal, 160,* 629.

Donceel, J. F. (1961). *Philosophical psychology* (2nd ed.). New York: Sheed & Ward.

Ehrenwald, J. (Ed.). (1976). *The history of psychotherapy: From healing magic to encounter.* New York: Jason Aronson.

Ezembe, F. (1997). Les thérapies africaines revisitées [African therapies revisited]. *Le Journal de Psychologues, 147,* 46–48.

Green, M. (2002). Africa unlocks herbal secrets to fight AIDS. *Biodiversity & Human Health.* Retrieved November 12, 2003, from http://ecology.org/biod/value/AfricanHerbs.html

Guiley, R. E. (1999). *The encyclopedia of witches and witchcraft* (2nd ed.). New York: Checkmark Books.

Hahn, R. A. (1995). *Sickness and healing: An anthropological perspective.* New Haven, CT: Yale University Press.

Hammond-Tooke, D. (1989). *Rituals and medicines: Indigenous healing in South Africa.* Johannesburg, South Africa: A. D. Donker.

Handwerk, B. (2002, October 21). Voodoo, a legitimate religion, anthropologist says. *National Geographic News.* Retrieved November 17, 2003, from http://news.national geographic.com/news/2002/10/1021_021021_taboo-voodoo.htm

Hayes, S. (1995). Christian responses to witchcraft and sorcery. *Missionalia, 23,* 339–354. Retrieved November 20, 2003, from http:www.geocities.com/Athens/7734/witch1.htm

Hebga, M. P. (1979). *Sorcellerie: Chimère dangereuse?* [Sorcery: Dangerous myth?]. Abidjan, Côte d'Ivoire: Inades Éditions.

Hefner, A. G., & Guimaraes, V. (2003). *Animism.* Retrieved October 27, 2003, from http://www.themystica.com/mystica/articles/a/animism.html

*The human soul or spirit.* (2003). Retrieved November 6, 2003, from http://www.the-absolute-enormous-unity.com/26-soul-or-spirit.html

Kubukeli, P. S. (1999). Traditional healing practices using medicinal herbs. *Lancet, 354* (Suppl. 4), 24.

*Langues et religions* [Languages and religions]. (2003). Retrieved November 15, 2003, from http://www.afcam.org/Doc_illustration/AfriqueReligion.htm

*Les marabouts* [Marabouts]. (2003). Retrieved November 15, 2003, from http://members .lycos.fr/talibes/marabouts.htm

Levy, D. (1967). Macrocosm and microcosm. In P. Edwards (Ed.), *The encyclopedia of philosophy* (Vol. 5, pp. 121–125). New York: Macmillan.

Lightman, A. (1999). In God's place. *New York Times Magazine.* Retrieved November 22, 2003, from http://www.montgomerycollege.edu/faculty/~dfox/public_html/ingod-splace.htm

Mazrui, A. A. (1975). Black Africa and the Arabs. *Foreign Affairs.* Retrieved November 14, 2003, from http://www.foreignaffairs.org/19750701faessay10155/ali-a-mazrui/black-africa-and-the-arabs.html

Mbiti, J. S. (1988). *African religions and philosophy.* London: Heinemann.

Nathan, T. (1993). Ethnopsy 93 [Ethnopsychiatry 93]. *Nouvelle Revue d'Ethnopsychiatrie, 20,* 7–14.

Nathan, T. (1994). *L'influence qui guérit* [Healing influence]. Paris: Éditions Odile Jacob.

NGOMA. (2003). *Indigenous healing in South Africa: An overview.* Retrieved November 12, 2003, from http://www.wits.ac.za/izangoma/part1.asp

Rosy, E. (1992). *L'afrique des guérisons* [Traditional healing in Africa]. Paris: Éditions Karthala.

Rouget, G. (1985). *Music and trance: A theory of the relations between music and possession.* Chicago: University of Chicago Press.

Seri, J.-P. (1997, April 12–13). *Dans l'univers de la guérisseuse d'Aby: Sur les traces de la tueuse de sorciers* [In the world of the woman healer of Aby: In search of the lady-killer of sorcerers]. *Soir Info,* p. 9.

Somé, M. P. (1999). *The healing wisdom of Africa.* New York: Jeremy P. Tarcher/Putnam.

Stoller, P. (1989). *Fusion of the worlds: An ethnography of possession among the Songhay of Niger.* Chicago: University of Chicago Press.

Stoller, P., & Olkes, C. (1987). *In sorcery's shadow: A memoir of apprenticeship among the Songhay of Niger.* Chicago: University of Chicago Press.

Stone, M. H. (1997). *Healing the mind: A history of psychiatry from antiquity to the present.* New York: Norton.

Sylla, Y. (1988, June 21). *Santé: Á Dabakala, les guérisseurs ont pignon sur rue* [Health: At Dabakala, healers have a well-established business]. *Fraternité Matin,* p. 4.

Tchetche, G. D. (1998). *Psychiatrie en Afrique noire et contexte socio-culturel* [Psychiatry in black Africa in a sociocultural context]. Paris: L'Harmattan.

Torrey, E. F. (1986). *Witchdoctors and psychiatrists: The common roots of psychotherapy and its future.* New York: Harper and Row.

Tucker, N. (1999, July 26). In parts of Africa, witches are to blame. *Detroit Free Press.* Retrieved November 21, 2003, from http://www.freep.com/news/nw/qwitch26.htm

Twitchell, P. (1982). *Les plantes: Guérisseuses magiques* [Plants: Magical healers]. Menlo Park, CA: IWP Publishing.

Vontress, C. E. (1991). Traditional healing in Africa: Implications for cross-cultural counseling. *Journal of Counseling and Development, 70,* 242–249.

Vontress, C. E. (1999). Interview with a traditional African healer. *Journal of Mental Health Counseling, 21,* 326–336.

Vontress, C. E. (2001). Cross-cultural counseling in the 21st century. *International Journal for the Advancement of Counseling, 23*(2), 83–97.

*Voodoo zombies.* (2003). Retrieved November 17, 2003, from http://zombies.monstrous .com/voodoo_zombies.htm

Wheelwright, P. (1959). *Heraclitus.* Oxford, UK: Oxford University Press.

Wolff, R. P. (1976). *About philosophy.* Englewood Cliffs, NJ: Prentice Hall.

# 12

# Hindu Spirituality and Healing Practices

*Pittu Laungani*

One of the great "levellers" of humanity is the fact that regardless of the culture we belong to, we all experience illness—both physical and mental—pain, distress, loss, sorrow, and bereavement. Suffering, as the Buddha remarked, is part of the human condition. No culture has ever been successful in eliminating such conditions permanently. Each culture also acquires its own traditions that enable it to formulate its own conceptual systems that explain health and illness in all their forms. Western countries, by and large, subscribe to a scientific model of mental illness, which asserts a materialist, disease-based framework. Even in the absence of any clearly identifiable neurophysiological, biological, or genetic correlates, there is an assumption that such factors, although undiscovered and unspecified, are at work.

Scientific models of mental illness do not hold the same degree of acceptance in Eastern cultures, for such cultures are strongly embedded in their religious and spiritual philosophies, which have been part of their cultural inheritance from ancient times. Easterners in general tend to see the vicissitudes of life in religious and cosmic terms (Herman, 1976; Kakar, 1982).

Materialistic, rationalistic, and empirical models of science do not have a vital role to play in healing practices in Eastern cultures. Healing in Eastern cultures, to a large extent, is embedded in spiritual and religious beliefs and practices. Despite the variations within and between different religions—Hinduism, Islam, Buddhism, Sikhism, Judaism, Christianity, and others—there are parallels and similarities in healing strategies across religions. In this chapter, we shall consider notions of spirituality in Hinduism and examine the influence of Hinduism on the range and types of healing practices in India.

## ❖ HINDUISM AND HINDU SPIRITUALITY

Hinduism as a religion is integral to the construction of Hindu society. Indian society, not unlike other Eastern societies, is a family-based and community-centered society (Flood, 1996; Kakar, 1981; Klostermaier, 1998; Lannoy, 1976; Laungani, 1997, 1999, 2000, 2004; Lipner, 1994; Mandelbaum, 1972; Sharma, 2000; Zaehner, 1966). It is not clear what the fundamental features of Hinduism are and how they all cohere together. For a detailed and scholarly account of Hinduism, there are numerous works available for the interested reader (e.g., Bhattacharya, 1975; Brockington, 1981; de Riencourt, 1960; Flood; Klostermaier; Lipner; Madan, 1987; O'Flaherty, 1976, 1980; Pandey, 1969; Prasad, 1989; Radhakrishnan, 1929/1989; Reichenbach, 1990; Sharma; Zimmer, 1969/1989).

Hinduism is more a way of life, which embraces all aspects of culture. Because of its all-inclusive, pervasive nature, Hinduism does not separate the sacred from the secular and provides a religious interpretation to the whole of life (Klostermaier, 1998). Even the most fundamental of all questions, that is, the origin of Hinduism, is not easy to answer. At the simplest level, many scholars have argued that Hinduism, like Christianity, Islam, and Judaism, is a *revealed* religion. Others argue that Hinduism, like many other religions, has evolved over the centuries. Hinduism and Indian philosophy are so inextricably linked that one cannot study one without studying the other.

Most Hindus, however, place their trust in the Vedas, which are considered by the orthodox Hindus to be the holiest of holy books. They consist of hymns, verses, and poems and are concerned primarily with Vedic ritual, prayers, sacrifices, the chanting of secret mantras, and patterns of worship offered to the pantheon of Vedic gods. The word *Veda* is derived from the root *vid*, "to know." The Vedas, of which there are four—Rig-Veda, Sama Veda, Yajur Veda, and the Atharva Veda—are seen by many scholars as a form of personal communication from God to his chosen seers and other holy men.

In addition to the Vedas, there are a large number of books, including the Upanishads and the Dharmashastra, which are considered to be authoritative and sacred to most Hindus. Most of these books are concerned with rites, rituals, prayers, ablutions, sacrifices related to rites of passage, birth, marriage, death, and other day-to-day activities of Hindus. They are also concerned with describing the creation of the world; the origin of the four castes; the transmigration of the soul; the notions of birth, death, and rebirth, embodied in the law of karma; the nature of dharma; one's duty toward oneself, one's family, and one's society; and other matters of practical and social significance in the daily lives of Hindus. From among the vast number of books comprising Hindu scriptures, the most popular and the most revered within Hindu culture are the Ramayana, the Mahabharata, and the Bhagavad Gita, which makes up an important part of the Mahabharata. Stories from the Ramayana and the Mahabharata have become part of Hindu folklore, and during religious festivals they are enacted all over the country in villages, towns, and large cities—such is the impact of religion on the minds, actions, and lives of people in India. Virtuous and noble deeds of valor, sacrifice, and duty by the characters in the two epics are normally held up as archetypal examples for the socialization of children. The stories are told and retold in order to inculcate specific moral and spiritual values and behaviors in one's sons, daughters, daughters-in-law, friends, relatives, and others. Notwithstanding the low levels of literacy in certain parts of India, the lessons from these literary works are taken to heart and internalized into people's psyches from infancy. The lines between the sacred and the secular are blurred within the Hindu psyche. Most Hindus prefer to explain the vicissitudes of life not in medical, socioeconomic, and political terms, but in religious and supernatural language and in terms of their karma. Let us now turn to the next section of the chapter, in which we shall discuss Hindu religious and spiritual practices that allow us to explain their approach to illness, health, and other psychological disorders.

## ❖ HINDU RELIGIOUS AND SPIRITUAL PRACTICES

The following concepts and practices are of especial importance to therapists seeking to understand the Hindu approach to health and illness:

1. Caste contamination

2. Pollution and purification

3. Rituals

4. Law of karma

5. Astrology and planetary perturbations

6. Demonic spirits

Let us discuss each of them briefly.

## Caste Contamination

The most unique and distinguishing feature of Hindu society lies in its caste system. No other Eastern society has a social structure analogous to the Indian caste system. One is born into a given caste and is destined to stay in it until death. It is virtually impossible to move from one caste into another, particularly from the lower caste into the higher caste. It is, however, possible to move downward and fall from a higher caste into a lower caste. The term *varna* refers to caste, and *jati* is a subcaste of a given caste. There are four castes in all. Within each caste, there exist several hundred *jatis,* or subcastes. The castes are arranged in a hierarchical order as follows:

- Brahmins: the learned; the guardians of the Vedas, the priests
- Kshatriyas: the noble warriors; defenders of the realm
- Vaishyas: the traders, businessmen, farmers, and moneylenders
- Sudras: those who serve the needs of the upper three castes

Members of the upper three castes are known as "twice born," because their male members have undergone an initiation, a rite of passage, that transforms them into high-caste Hindus (Flood, 1996; Pandey, 1969). The ceremony that marks their "second birth" is the rite of the sacred thread ceremony, after the completion of which they are allowed to read and learn from the Vedas and participate in all religious ceremonies. This rite separates the three highest castes from the Sudras, who are not permitted such an initiation. Sudras, formerly known as "untouchables," are now referred to as *dailts,* "the oppressed ones." Sudras are subdivided into touchable and untouchable—both words in their literal meanings. All Sudras are "destined" to engage in occupations that are considered by the upper three castes to be demeaning and polluting, such as barber, tanner, cleaner, masseur, water carrier, and so forth. Untouchable Sudras, on the other hand, are obliged to engage in occupations that deal with human and animal waste and refuse, such as slaughtering animals and working in tanneries, abattoirs, and crematoriums. However, government legislation and reforms have led to some positive changes as regards these inequities.

Caste contamination can occur in a variety of ways: through marriage between the higher and lower castes, through illicit sexual relations, and through any activity that "transcends" the rigidly defined boundaries separating the three upper castes from the lowest. Among orthodox Hindus, even physical contact with an untouchable leads to the pollution of a member of any of the three upper castes.

## Pollution and Purification

Among Hindus, pollution and purification need to be understood within a spiritual context and not in terms of hygiene and biology (Chaudhuri, 1979; Fuller, 1992). The spiritual "status" of a person in India is determined by the degree of contact with the polluting agent. Certain occupations, such as those mentioned above, are permanently polluting. Such a form of pollution is collective, in that the entire family remains polluted, and it is also hereditary.

Pollution ranges from mild and temporary, through severe and temporary, to severe and permanent. One is in a state of pollution upon waking up in the morning, prior to performing one's morning ablutions, when one has eaten food touched by others, and when one has not prayed. Pollution also occurs after a sexual act; during menstruation; after one has had a haircut, pared one's nails, and so on. Such mild forms of pollution can be overcome by appropriate actions—baths, prayers, wearing clean and washed clothes, and engaging in appropriate cleansing and purification rituals. Severe pollution comes about when a high-caste Hindu comes into physical or social contact with persons of the lowest caste, the Sudras, or when a high-caste Hindu eats meat (particularly beef). No high-caste Hindu is expected to offer or accept cooked food from a low-caste Hindu. In some instances, the entire family may become polluted and may be obliged to perform a series of appropriate purification rites, rituals, and religious ceremonies under the guidance of their family priest or guru.

The most severe forms of pollution are collective, hereditary, and therefore permanent. Permanent pollution occurs when a Hindu belonging to the highest caste (Brahmin) marries a person from the lowest caste, thereby breaking the principle of endogamy (marrying within one's own caste and subcaste), which has always been regarded as one of the cementing factors that has held the caste system together. This form of pollution is extremely serious; there is the ever-present fear of untold misfortunes befalling the polluted individual and the family if the purification rites are not performed. The person in such a state of pollution may be ostracized by family members and may even be forced to become an outcast.

## Rituals

Because the majority of rituals performed either privately or collectively have a religious connotation, it is clear that ritual activity is addressed to sacred beings, such as gods or ancestors. Ninian Smart (1998) refers to such rituals as "focused rituals," where the focus is on worship. Rituals therefore are forms of personal communication with gods. Communication itself may serve different purposes: worship, giving thanks, asking for favors, expiation, and atonement. Smart adds that a variant of the religious ritual is the yogic ritual, where the performance of yogic exercises is seen as a means by which a person seeks to attain a higher state of consciousness. Although there are varying numbers of rituals recorded in different texts, the rituals appear to be organized in a sequence, which expresses the Hindu social order, or dharma. Flood (1996) points out that ritual action is what anchors people in a sense of deeper identity and belonging. The meticulous and precise performance of rites and rituals is seen as being desirable for Hindus. It binds and preserves the caste system, which in turn provides a sense of continuity and belonging. Rites and rituals legitimize social order and uphold social institutions. Rituals also enable Hindus to earn merit, which leads to their own spiritual development. The efficacy of rituals is believed to rest on their repetition; their meticulous performance provides a source of comfort to those practicing them.

The most important rituals are those related to birth, the initiation ceremony, marriage (which signals the beginning of the householder's life), and the final funeral rites and after-death rites.

Failure to perform rituals with faith and zeal leads to a form of spiritual pollution, which can "lead to" a variety of mental and physical disorders. Despite the fact that through the centuries, many ancient rituals have lost their functional value and are interpreted in different ways by Hindus in different regions, they have not been abandoned. The question that arises here is this: Why do Hindus cling to the performance of rituals with such tenacity? In what ways do ritualistic actions lead to one's spiritual development? Let us turn to the law of karma for a tentative answer.

## The Law of Karma

The law of karma, in its simplest form, states that all human actions lead to consequences. Right actions produce good consequences, and wrong actions produce bad consequences. The law of karma is not concerned with consequences in general, but with consequences that affect the individual—the doer of the action. Second, the law of karma applies specifically to the moral sphere. It is therefore not concerned with the general relation between actions and their consequences but "rather with the moral quality of the actions and their consequences" (Reichenbach, 1990, p. 1). It is argued that because all actions lead to consequences, there is absolute justice that falls to our lot, in the sense that good actions lead to happiness and bad actions to unhappiness (Hirayana, 1949). The law of karma offers explanations not only for pain, suffering, and misfortune but also for pleasure, happiness, and good fortune. Each of us receives the results of our own actions and not another's. The doer not only deserves the consequences of his or her actions but is unable to avoid experiencing them (Prasad, 1989). The actions of the doer may have occurred in his or her present life or in a past life. Similarly, the consequences of the doer's actions may occur during the person's present life or in a future life. It is impossible to avoid the consequences of one's actions.

The law of karma stands out as the most unique and significant feature of Hinduism. It has shaped the Indian view of life for centuries. One might even go to the extent of saying that the Hindu psyche is built around the notion of karma (O'Flaherty, 1976, 1980; Reichenbach, 1990; Sharma, 2000; Sinari, 1984; Zaehner, 1966). The deterministic belief that one's present life is shaped by one's actions in one's past life (or lives) engenders within the Hindu psyche a spirit of passive acceptance of misfortunes, ranging from sudden deaths within the family, glaring inequalities of caste and status, disease and illness, poverty and destitution, to exploitation and prejudice.

However, many Hindus are also guided by the belief that by performing acts of piety, they are likely to be born into a "better" family and into a higher caste in their next birth. There is also a belief that one can invoke the gods and seek their beneficent interventions. It is under those conditions that guidance is sought from priests, gurus, and other healers who may initiate a variety of propitiating and healing ceremonies, including elaborate purification rites, the feeding of mendicants, sexual abstinence, regular visits to temples, pilgrimages to the holy cities, participation in prayers, fasts, refuge in a hermitage or an ashram, yogic exercises, and so forth.

### Astrology and Planetary Perturbations

Beliefs in astrology and the malevolent (and benevolent) influences of planets on one's life are strongly ingrained in the Indian psyche. It is quite customary to have a child's horoscope cast at the time of the child's birth. The heavenly configuration of planets at the moment of birth is seen as a determinant of life chances. A carefully cast horoscope reveals a person's fate, which is written on a person's forehead (Fuller, 1992). Horoscopes are consulted prior to traveling to a foreign country, starting a new business venture, birth of a child, and the naming ceremony of children, and these horoscopes are seen as determining the chances of recovery from financial hardships, serious illnesses, depressions, and other traumas and of course the chances of finding suitable marital partners for their children. Some of the most enduring and lifelong decisions are taken on the basis of what the stars foretell.

There is also the fear that misfortunes may occur as a result of the malevolent influence of the planets, particularly Saturn, or *shani*. Shrines containing images of Saturn and other planets are found in all parts of India. On the day when Saturn moves from one house to another, people all over India offer prayers. Some express relief at having survived the last 30 months, whereas others are fearful and anxious as they hope to get through the next 30 months without calamitous misfortunes (Fuller, 1992). Others may decide to undertake arduous religious ceremonies to propitiate the evil influences of the planets.

### Demonic Spirits

In Vedic Hindu philosophy, demons are as real as gods. Each group is in eternal conflict with the other. The gods represent the good, the demons, evil. The gods fear and oppose the demons, and the demons fear and oppose the gods (Herman, 1976; O'Flaherty, 1976). Each group undertakes measures to overthrow the other and to establish its own superiority. The battles of gods against the demons can be found in the several sacred texts, including the two well-known epics, the Ramayana and the Mahabharata. Most Hindus are familiar with the stories from the epics. Plays depicting scenes from the Ramayana and other ancient texts are played out all over the country during festive seasons. Stories from the Ramayana and the Mahabharata featuring acts of bravery, valor, self-discipline, obedience, performance of austerities, prayer, bravery, revenge, and forgiveness form the basis of socialization of children.

As O'Flaherty (1976) points out, "by nature gods and demons are alike; by functions however, they are as different as night and day" (p. 58). At an intellectual, abstract level, it would seem appropriate to construe gods and demons as metaphors for human situations. But such is the strength of beliefs among Hindus that metaphors are transformed into "facts." The problem of gods and demons remains real: Hindus blame the demons and evil spirits that represent the powers of darkness for creating evil and for the pain, distress, and torment they experience as a result.

### ❖ CONCLUSION

There are variations in styles and techniques of treatment. The main object is to "cure" a person of any serious psychological or psychotic disorder, the underlying basis of which may be "possession" by a devil—a malevolent, demonic spirit. Why a demonic spirit should take possession of one individual and not another is attributed to a variety of factors, such as the person's karma; the envy of neighbors at the visible affluence, success, and good health of the afflicted person; serious quarrels among family members; disputes over wealth and inheritance among family members; sexual misdemeanors; alcoholism and drug addiction; impotence; and even physical illnesses, such as rashes, raging temperatures, and smallpox.

Certain forms of deviations may be construed as forms of mental aberrations, and once identified, these are dealt with in culturally appropriate ways. The variety of strategies include confinement, medication, exorcism, ayurvedic practices, yogic exercises, visits to shrines and temples, pilgrimages, or withdrawal to a hermitage or ashram, where the "patient" is expected to "sit at the feet" of the guru, participate in the required rituals, and imbibe the lessons and sermons imparted. Whereas the Western worldview is based on value systems that extol the virtues of individualism, empiricism, scientific objectivity, materialism, secularism, and humanism, the Eastern worldview emphasizes communalism, spiritualism, religiosity, determinism, intuition, inner reflection, and spiritual transcendence. It is clear that the different constructions of mental disorders reflect the distinct value orientations of each culture.

The multiplicity of healing strategies should not be seen as a disadvantage. In fact, they provide different cultures with exciting opportunities to learn valuable lessons from one another. It is hoped that such a course of action will not only lead to a better understanding of different healing strategies, but may also bring cultures together.

❖  REFERENCES

Bhattacharya, N. N. (1975). *Ancient Indian rituals and their social contents*. Delhi, India: Manohar Book Service.

Brockington, J. L. (1981). *The sacred thread: Hinduism in its continuity and diversity.* Edinburgh, Scotland: Edinburgh University Press.

Chaudhuri, N. (1979). *Hinduism*. Oxford, UK: Oxford University Press.

Flood, G. (1996). *An introduction to Hinduism*. Cambridge, UK: Cambridge University Press.

Fuller, C. J. (1992). *The camphor flame: Popular Hinduism and society in India*. Princeton, NJ: Princeton University Press.

Herman, A. (1976). *The problem of evil and Indian thought*. New Delhi, India: Motilal Banarsidass.

Hirayana, M. (1949). *The essentials of Indian philosophy.* London: George Allen & Unwin.

Kakar, S. (1981). *The inner world—A psychoanalytic study of children and society in India.* Delhi, India: Oxford University Press.

Kakar, S. (1982). *Shamans, mystics and doctors.* London: Unwin Paperbacks.

Klostermaier, K. K. (1998). *A short introduction to Hinduism.* Oxford, UK: One World.

Lannoy, R. (1976). *The speaking tree.* Oxford, UK: Oxford University Press.

Laungani, P. (1997). Death in a Hindu family. In C. M. Parkes, P. Laungani, & B. Young (Eds.), *Death and bereavement across cultures* (pp. 52–72). London: Routledge.

Laungani, P. (1999). Culture and identity: Implications for counselling. In S. Palmer & P. Laungani (Eds.), *Counselling in a multicultural society* (pp. 35–70). London: Sage.

Laungani, P. (2000). Why have a funeral? Hindu funerals in England: Past, present, and future. In J. D. Morgan (Ed.), *Meeting the needs of our clients creatively: The impact of art and culture on caregiving* (pp. 231–242). Amityville, NY: Baywood.

Laungani, P. (2004). *Asian perspectives in counselling and psychotherapy.* London: Brunner-Routledge.

Lipner, J. (1994). *Hindus: Their religious beliefs and practices.* London: Routledge.

Madan, T. N. (1987). *Non-renunciation: Themes and interpretations of Hindu culture.* Delhi, India: Oxford University Press.

Mandelbaum, D. G. (1972). *Society in India* (Vol. 2). Berkeley: University of California Press.

O'Flaherty, W. D. (1976). *The origins of evil in Hindu mythology.* Berkeley: University of California Press.

O'Flaherty, W. D. (1980). *Karma and rebirth in classical Indian traditions.* Berkeley: University of California Press.

Pandey, R. (1969). *Hindu samskaras: Socio-religious study of the Hindu sacraments.* Delhi, India: Motilal Banarasidass.

Prasad, R. (1989). *Karma causation and retributive morality: Conceptual essays in ethics and metaethics* (Indian Council of Philosophical Research). New Delhi, India: Munshiram Manoharlal.

Radhakrishnan, S. (1989). *Indian philosophy* (Vol. 2, centenary edition). Delhi, India: Oxford University Press. (Original work published 1929)

Reichenbach, B. R. (1990). *The law of karma: A philosophical study.* Honolulu: University of Hawaii Press.

Riencourt, A. de (1960). *The soul of India.* Bath, UK: U.K. Honeyglen.

Sharma, A. (2000). *Classical Hindu thought: An introduction.* New Delhi, India: Oxford University Press.

Sinari, R. A. (1984). *The structure of Indian thought.* Delhi, India: Oxford University Press.

Smart, N. (1998). *The world's religions* (2nd ed.). Cambridge, UK: Cambridge University Press.

Zaehner, R. C. (1966). *Hinduism.* New York: Oxford University Press.

Zimmer, H. (1989). *Philosophies of India* (Bollingen Series 26). Princeton, NJ: Princeton University Press. (Original work published 1969)

# 13

# Inner Healing Prayer in "Spirit-Filled" Christianity

*Fernando L. Garzon*

Within the past 100 years, "Spirit-filled" Christianity has grown from an embryonic revival meeting in Azusa Street, in Los Angeles, California, into an estimated half billion "believers" worldwide (Synan, 2001). The Spirit-filled movement emphasizes encountering God through the Holy Spirit in a personal and often dramatic way. These encounters frequently lead to self-reports of healings, glossolalia (speaking in tongues), prophecy, and miracles. Such "gifts of the Spirit" can happen in individual and corporate settings.

"Spirit-filled" Christianity encompasses several coevolving forms of Christianity (Miller, 1997). The early revivals (such as Azusa Street, mentioned above) led to numerous denominations (e.g., Assemblies of God, Pentecostal, Church of God, Church of God in Christ), which remain today. The 1960s and 1970s "charismatic movement" introduced Spirit-filled experiences into mainline Protestant, Roman Catholic, and Eastern Orthodox churches. "Third Wave" adherents are currently establishing independent churches and quasi-institutional structures. Syncretistic groups found in developing nations are blending this form of Christianity with their culture (Hollenweger, 1997).

Poloma (2003) notes that what connects this apparent diversity is "not a single leader, institution, or doctrine, but rather its worldview" (pp. 20–21). The mix of theologies and cultural traditions embraces an experientially centered "core spirituality," as described in Albrecht (1999):

> In asserting an underlying spirituality, I understand that each "species" of Pentecostalism has a particular type of Pentecostal spirituality. However, I do believe that amidst the many Pentecostal spiritualities there is a core spirituality, an experience in and of the Spirit that unifies the vast variety. The core ... mixes with many theologies, traditions, and cultures to produce a wide range of types of Pent/Char spirituality. (pp. 28–29)

Thus, although identifying common characteristics of all Spirit-filled constituents is a dubious endeavor, a shared transcendent worldview can be noted that "is a curious blend of premodern miracles, modern technology, and postmodern mysticism in which the natural merges with the supernatural" (Poloma, 2003, p. 22). A tendency toward fundamentalist dogmatism can be observed, but "the belief in and experience of a creative Spirit who is with the Word [the Bible] appears even stronger" (Poloma, 2003, p. 22). This chapter introduces the reader to Christian inner healing prayer (CIHP), an outgrowth of the Spirit-filled movement.

## ❖ THE DEVELOPMENT OF INNER HEALING PRAYER IN SPIRIT-FILLED CHRISTIANITY

The curious blend of premodern, modern, and postmodern elements in the Spirit-filled worldview has led to a holistic perspective on healing. Healing involves a deepening of one's relationship with God, out of which flows the secondary benefits of improved physical and emotional health (Csordas, 1988). Repentance and receiving God's forgiveness begin this spiritual perspective on healing, and extending forgiveness toward others deepens the process, permitting a greater outflow of spiritual reality into the physical and emotional realms.

A major aspect of CIHP is to facilitate Christ's presence as restorer and healer in the forgiveness process, especially when someone has experienced deep emotional wounds (J. L. Sandford & M. Sandford, 1992). Although much more scholarly work has explored the sometimes dramatic Spirit-filled deliverance-type interventions that "battle the demonic," little has been written on CIHP as the predominantly quiet alternative to such demonstrative healing strategies.

CIHP focuses on loving a needy soul to health through attentive listening, comfort, a supportive relationship, and petitioning the Divine to enter into the sufferer's pain. Hurding (1995) defines CIHP more specifically as "a range of 'journey back' methodologies that seek under the Holy Spirit's leading to uncover personal, familial, and ancestral experiences that are thought to contribute to the troubled present" (p. 297). Some forms of CIHP focus more specifically on childhood or traumatic memories and are sometimes interchangeably referred to as "healing of memory prayers." These CIHP types are "designed to facilitate the client's ability to process affectively painful memories through vividly recalling these memories and asking for the presence of Christ (or God) to minister in the midst of this pain" (Garzon & Burkett, 2002, p. 43).

CIHP can lead to a variety of client sense experiences. When effective, many clients experience powerful visual imagery; others sense a deep peace or the presence of Christ where pain once dwelled; and still others may hear the "still, small voice of the Spirit" speaking to them about their troubles.

## ❖ HISTORICAL BACKGROUND

In addition to its birth in the current Spirit-filled Christian movement, one might conceptualize CIHP as a recent seed planted in 2,000 years of contemplative Christian meditative prayer soil. Yet CIHP has clear differences that make it distinctive from the Christian contemplative tradition. CIHP considers current psychological findings regarding the effects of trauma, environmental deprivation, and neglect as much as the traditional concepts of sin, the fallen nature, and the demonic as precursors to soul distress. Indeed, contemporary understandings and traditional church teachings are interwoven into a conceptual framework that is acceptable to many in the Spirit-filled community (Poloma, 2003).

## ❖ THE MODERN HISTORY OF CIHP

The seed of CIHP sprouted in the 1950s through the ministry and writings of a Spirit-filled Episcopalian woman named Agnes Sanford. Sanford (1947/1972) theorized that just as natural laws regulate the physical world, spiritual laws regulate the realm of prayer. One might do experimentation to learn the spiritual laws governing prayer just as one might do experimentation to learn natural laws governing the physical world. Her experiments led to an appreciation for the roles of love and forgiveness as components of healing. Sometimes, she found that having the distressed person engage in imagery or visualization during prayer was helpful in deepening the prayer's impact.

Sanford's (1947/1972) writings began influencing pastors and caregivers from a variety of Christian traditions. Many apprenticed under her ministry and were eventually labeled as "inner healers." Ministers such as Francis MacNutt (1977/1999), Ruth Carter Stapleton (1976), and John and Paula Sandford (1982; see also J. L. Sandford & M. Sandford, 1992) crafted their own systems of CIHP from principles found in Agnes Sanford's writings. Other leaders have emerged as a third generation in the ongoing development of CIHP. These include pastoral counselors (e.g., Payne, 1991, 1995; Seamands, 1985), clinical psychologists (Tan, 1996), and most recently Ed Smith's (2002) theophostic prayer ministry (TPM).

## ❖ A SAMPLE INNER HEALING PRAYER FORM: THEOPHOSTIC PRAYER MINISTRY

Smith combined two Greek words, *theos* for "God" and *phos* for "light," in order to create a unique name for his approach. TPM, according to Smith (2002), helps God to "shine his light" into the wounds of those who are hurting. He has developed extensive training materials, which include a basic training manual with its accompanying audio/video course, a manual written to prepare clients to receive TPM, an advanced training seminar, and two weeklong "internships" of apprenticeship training.

TPM's particular approach conceptualizes a client's emotional distress as arising from maladaptive core beliefs ("lies") developed from painful experiences in childhood. The approach theorizes that for healing to occur, the original source of the pain must be discovered; the lies developed there must be identified; and Jesus must reveal His truth to the client in that place of pain, thereby dispelling the lies developed there. In some ways, TPM resembles adaptations of cognitive therapy for trauma-based or personality-disordered conditions (see, e.g., Young, Klosko, & Weishaar's 2003 experiential strategies for cognitive restructuring); however, TPM diverges greatly from such treatments in how the actual cognitive restructuring takes place (Garzon & Burkett, 2002). Therapist and client do not collaborate to restructure the lie (cognition) in the memory; rather, petition is made for Jesus to come and do this.

To begin the typical prayer ministry, a client is normally oriented to the approach through verbal preparation during the first session, listening to an introductory audiotape, and reviewing a written client manual for homework. The TPM practitioner invites the client to discuss current difficulties and aspects of his or her personal background. Probes and reflections explore client affect, and the practitioner attends to emotionally laden key words or phrases that may indicate the presence of lies. When the timing appears right, an affect bridge technique ensues in which the client is asked to drift to the place where the salient emotions originated. The initiation of this drift might take the form of a prayer, such as, "Lord Jesus, would You take Jane to the source and origin of this pain?"

One or more memories usually surface at this point. For simplicity in this brief description, let us assume that one memory has surfaced. The lies in this memory are carefully identified, and as the "lies assessment" ends, an exposure protocol of sorts ensues. In this "protocol," the client is requested to repeat mentally the lies identified, not resisting them but rather experiencing the full affective effects of their presence. When the client appears to be doing this, the practitioner asks Jesus to come and reveal truth to the client in whatever way He chooses. This petition is made in as nondirective a fashion as possible, so that any imagery or other sense experiences that surface have not been suggested or directed by the practitioner (Smith, 2000a, 2002).

Within a few minutes, the client often perceives Christ's healing presence. This sometimes occurs through visual imagery, a deep sense of peace, hearing Jesus's voice, or in other ways. The client then reevaluates the believability of the previously held lies. If the client reports a sense of peace and calm, the prayer is considered complete. Lack of peace may indicate the presence of other memories linked to the cognition or previously unidentified lies present in the current memory.

What happens if a perception of Christ's healing does not occur right away? In these instances, a search for potential obstacles begins. True to the CIHP application of both traditional church and contemporary psychological constructs, Smith (2000a) notes an ancient and contemporary mixture of such obstacles, including the presence of strong anger, unconfessed sin, dissociation, demonic interference, intellectualizing defenses, and "guardian lies," which are defensive rationalizations that impede the identification of core affects and beliefs.

Concerning demonic interference as a hindrance, Smith (2000a) does not get into dramatic "power encounters" typical of some deliverance interventions. Rather, the goal, like that of most CIHP strategies, is to quiet any disturbance appearing as demonic. TPM then focuses on any lie-based avenues that have opened the door to such "manifestations." As noted above, Smith is aware of dissociative disorders. It should also be noted that Smith (2000a) does assert that one does not have to believe in the demonic to apply his method successfully in most cases. After any obstacles are addressed, Christ is again petitioned to reveal His truth. Following a sense of peace, prayer for the Lord's blessing and affirmation of the client are made.

## ❖  SAMPLE CASE OF CIHP USING TPM

A large exploratory survey (Garzon & Poloma, 2003) and 16 outcomes-based case studies (Garzon, in press) suggest the merits of a randomized controlled group trial of TPM on appropriately religious clients. Accordingly, therefore, the sample CIHP case will use this approach. The deidentified case took place in a Spirit-filled North American church's lay ministry setting. The lay ministers were a married couple supervised by a licensed mental health professional. They have received basic and advanced training in TPM and have well over 100 hours of TPM experience.

Evelyn is a 40-year-old white woman who came for ministry seeking alleviation of sexual intercourse difficulties with her husband of 5 years. These problems surfaced within a few months of getting married. During intercourse, she would sexually shut down secondary to flashbacks of childhood sexual abuse and anxiety. To cope, Evelyn has tried combining prayer with self-talk (e.g., "I know that this is my husband so this is OK . . . I am pure in Your [God's] sight so it is OK . . . please help me, Lord."). These coping strategies made physical intimacy tolerable for the first couple of years, but eventually they no longer assisted her. The subsequent stress and marital difficulties have led to recent threats of divorce, which overwhelmed Evelyn. Diagnostically, she might be diagnosed with post-traumatic stress disorder, latent onset, resulting in sexual difficulties.

Evelyn was the youngest of three children, with a sister 2 years older and a brother 4 years older. During her childhood, her parents (still currently married after 45 years) were "always arguing." She viewed her mother as loving, nurturing, and supportive but saw her father as "controlling and very critical." She did, however, have other men in her life (uncles) whom she perceived as more supportive.

Sadly, however, one uncle was not trustworthy. When Evelyn was in the fifth grade, this uncle sexually abused her four times. The first three incidents involved fondling and petting, and the last incident led to more full genital contact.

Evelyn was "saved" at age 12, but she retrospectively reports feeling "too dirty" for God. In the sixth grade, she started "rebelling," perhaps in response to her father's criticisms and her abuse experiences. As she got into junior and senior high school, arguments with her father were frequent. She eventually began using drugs, drinking, and having sex with her boyfriends. She managed to keep her grades up, which enabled her to hide these behaviors until she could find a way to leave the home. She moved out in her junior year and began working at a restaurant as a waitress.

When Evelyn was 28, her sister-in-law shared the Gospel with her, and she recommitted her life to Christ. She started attending a Spirit-filled nondenominational church and stopped drinking and doing recreational drugs. She continued growing in her renewed faith and eventually met her future husband in the church environment. After a 6-month dating period, they got married. Although her husband was aware of her past sexual abuse experiences, Evelyn did not share with him about the flashback and anxiety symptoms. As noted, the flashbacks became noticeably worse about 2 years into the marriage. Evelyn's husband's lack of understanding about her sexual difficulties caused her to feel revictimized.

Prior to the first session, the lay ministers did an intake interview and discussed the information with the licensed mental health professional who supervises their work. Evelyn was given a tape describing TPM as well as a manual (Smith, 2000b) designed to help orient persons considering this prayer ministry.

To permit a comfortable reading of Evelyn's treatment, the first session will be described in detail below, with the first-person *we* representing the lay ministry couple. The narrative elements were reconstructed on the basis of an interview done with the lay ministers, an examination of their notes, and a discussion with Evelyn. A more detailed account of Evelyn's treatment experience can be found in Garzon (in press). The material presented in this chapter has been used with permission.

During the first prayer session, Evelyn tearfully shared about the abuse and her current marital anguish. We empathized with her experience and built a solid "therapeutic alliance." We then asked the Lord to take Evelyn where He wanted her to go in her heart that connected with her pain.

Evelyn immediately drifted to the first abuse incident with her uncle. Fear and confusion enveloped the memory picture. She vividly described the scene of being an 11-year-old playing alone in the living room when her Uncle John sat down beside her and eventually began fondling her. She verbalized confusion, shame, and embarrassment, wondering also if he was going to stop. We explored the lies she believed around these feelings, which were, "I did something to provoke this. It is my fault. . . . It is my fault because it continued and it had to be kept a secret—I should have told [my parents] anyway."

"Lord Jesus, would you reveal your truth about these beliefs, or take Evelyn wherever else you want her to go?" we prayed. Evelyn drifted to the final abuse experience, when her uncle asked her parents if she could go up north with him and his wife to his cabin.

"What are you feeling, Evelyn?"

"Fear and dread."

"Help us understand the thoughts that go with this fear and dread."

"I'm angry at my parents for sending me up here. I'm angry at me, too, for not telling them what was going on." As we continued processing these feelings, she drifted without prompting to a visual image of bedtime at the cabin. Tears streamed down her face as she recounted the sexual violation. Our hearts wept for her as we periodically let her know of our presence and quietly prayed, waiting for the right time to invite the Lord's presence.

At this time, Evelyn asked a profound question that sometimes surfaces in ministry to sexual abuse victims. "Why didn't Jesus stop this? Why did He let it go on?" Knowing better than to naively try to answer such an agonizing question, we lifted it up to the Lord instead.

"Lord Jesus, why didn't You stop it?"

"Evelyn," we cautioned, "don't try to 'figure out' an answer, just listen with your heart and see if you get a sense of a response. If nothing happens, that's okay; we'll deal with that, too."

"Jesus is trying to tell me that He cared, He was there. It was not my fault. Man is fallen and sinful, what he [the uncle] did was wrong. I did not know the right thing to do. It was not my fault." Evelyn paused, "I see Jesus wrapping His arms around me [as a little girl]. He's stroking my hair and telling me 'It's OK, you are not dirty.'" Evelyn remained "in Jesus's presence" for several minutes while we silently prayed and gave thanks to God for what He was doing. At the session's end, Evelyn felt much more peaceful and felt as though there was much "revelation truth" revealed in this CIHP session.

Evelyn later reported that after she left the first session, she went home and told her mother about what had happened. The prayer, she noted, had given her the strength to do this. Her mother responded in a supportive manner, and the poisonous family secret was no more. The uncle who had committed this crime had later divorced Evelyn's aunt, so direct family confrontation of him did not take place, but much healing occurred in her parents' petition of her forgiveness for inadvertently allowing the abuse to take place in the first place.

Three more 2-hour prayer sessions were done with Evelyn. In these, further prayer processing of her abuse experiences occurred, as well as receiving "the Lord's truth" regarding painful memories of her dad's hypercriticalness. After her second session, she reported having intercourse with her husband without experiencing any flashbacks or anxiety. She stated that she was actually enjoying the experience now.

❖  FOLLOW-UP AND CASE COMMENTARY

At the time of this chapter's writing, it has been a year and a half since Evelyn received CIHP in the form of TPM. She continues to report a normal, enjoyable marital sex life and attributes this outcome to the healing she received through TPM. Her husband likewise confirms these results.

Consistent with the transcendent worldview of Spirit-filled Christianity, Evelyn attributes her healing of sexual dysfunction and posttraumatic stress symptoms to the "now," living, personal "revelation truths" that she received from Jesus. Her experience highlights the experiential encounter with the Divine that forms the core spirituality linking subtypes of Spirit-filled Christianity and their ministry strategies. Evelyn's spirituality was deepened through these intensely personal encounters, which she believed were from Christ, so emotional healing was a "natural supernatural" consequence of these experiences.

## ❖ IMPLICATIONS FOR PSYCHOTHERAPISTS

The explosive growth of Spirit-filled Christianity makes it likely that clinicians will at some time encounter these adherents as patients. Understanding the Spirit-filled worldview and "divine encounter" healing strategies these patients frequently pursue can enhance the ability to establish a working therapeutic alliance. Often, these clients will assume that the therapist takes a secularized, pathologizing stance toward religious phenomena the client regards as deeply meaningful. Accordingly, the patient will be very reluctant to share these experiences unless genuine openness, acceptance, and desire to hear about the spiritual part of their life are expressly conveyed (Richards & Bergin, 1997). Taking this religiously sensitive stance will greatly enhance the therapeutic alliance with this population.

Should the client have experienced CIHP, assessment should be made as to whether this was a positive or negative experience. Evelyn's case above highlights how profound a positive experience can be; however, negative experiences can have opposite consequences. For example, patients who did not experience a meaningful encounter with Jesus might be left with the question of "Why didn't God speak to me?" (Langberg, 1997). Understanding the CIHP outcome for a patient can inform the sensitive development of a treatment plan that incorporates awareness of this religious coping resource or sensitive explorations of disappointments in this area as well.

CIHP's explicitly spiritual focus may make it an appropriate adjunctive intervention to consider for some Spirit-filled Christian clients. Of course, thorough religious assessment, therapist competency, familiarity with the Spirit-filled Christian population, and informed consent would be needed before making such a decision (see Richards & Bergin, 1997, for an excellent discussion of how to apply these general ethical principles to spiritual interventions in psychotherapeutic treatment). Some are optimistic about the possibilities of using CIHP in a clinically and ethically sensitive manner, such as Tan (1996), whereas others are more pessimistic (e.g., Entwistle, 2004). Tan (1996) notes, "Inner healing prayer is particularly relevant in situations where the client has suffered . . . childhood traumas . . . sexual and physical abuse, rejection, abandonment [and other injuries] . . . that are still unresolved and very painful emotionally" (p. 371). Similar to the CIHP form used in the case example (TPM), Tan (1996) recommends a nondirective manner in which the therapist does not emphasize guiding any imagery that surfaces or "scripting" the patient's interaction with God. This nondirective manner may also provide a safeguard against iatrogenic injury or false memory syndrome. Richards and Bergin (1997) note diagnostic concerns for general spiritual interventions that are appropriate for those considering using CIHP. Delusional or psychotically disordered clients are not good candidates for such interventions. CIHP has been applied to patients with dissociative conditions (Garzon & Poloma, 2003); however, thorough training both in clinical treatment and CIHP are strongly recommended when considering such a strategy. Some CIHP forms offer specialized training for incorporating this resource with such complex conditions.

Should the patient indicate that he or she has begun to see a lay minister or pastor for inner healing prayer during treatment, periodically checking to see how the experience is being assimilated will be very useful. Sometimes church lay ministers collaborate with Christian mental health professionals so as to prevent the lay ministers from working with people whose problems are above their training level (Tan, 1991); however, this ideal is not always attained. Obtaining client consent to communicate with the lay minister or pastor will maximize the clinician's ability to assess the benefit to the client of adding this adjunctive treatment.

Whatever a clinician's stance regarding the potential place of CIHP in psychological treatment, knowledge of its increasing practice among Spirit-filled Christians can aid in treating this population. Empathic understanding of these patients' worldview can enhance the therapeutic alliance, facilitate assessment, and open the door to considering valuable religious coping resources that may otherwise have been missed in psychological treatment. Let us seek to learn from these clients who seek transforming healing encounters with God.

## ❖ REFERENCES

Albrecht, D. (1999). *Rites in the spirit: A ritual approach to Pentecostal/charismatic spirituality.* Sheffield, UK: Sheffield Academic Press.

Csordas, T. (1988). Elements of charismatic persuasion and healing. *Medical Anthropology Quarterly, 2,* 121–142.

Entwistle, D. (2004). Shedding light on theophostic ministry: 2. Ethical and legal issues. *Journal of Psychology and Theology, 32,* 35–42.

Garzon, F. (in press). *Spiritual healing? Cases exploring theophostic prayer ministry.* Pasadena, CA: Shepherds House.

Garzon, F., & Burkett, L. (2002). Healing of memories: Models, research, future directions. *Journal of Psychology and Christianity, 21,* 42–49.

Garzon, F., & Poloma, M. (2003, October). *The usage of inner healing prayer in the conservative Christian population: An exploratory survey.* Paper presented at the international conference for the Society for the Scientific Study of Religion, Norfolk, VA.

Hollenweger, W. (1997). *Pentecostalism: Origins and developments worldwide.* Peabody, MA: Hendrickson.

Hurding, R. F. (1995). Pathways to wholeness: Christian journeying in a postmodern age. *Journal of Psychology and Christianity, 14,* 293–305.

Langberg, D. (1997). *Counseling survivors of childhood sexual abuse.* Forest, VA: American Association of Christian Counseling.

MacNutt, F. (1999). *Healing*. Notre Dame, IN: Ave Maria Press. (Original work published 1977)

Miller, D. (1997). *Reinventing American Protestantism*. Berkeley: University of California Press.

Payne, L. (1991). *Restoring the Christian soul: Overcoming barriers to completion in Christ through healing prayer*. Grand Rapids, MI: Baker Books.

Payne, L. (1995). *The healing presence: Curing the soul through union with Christ*. Grand Rapids, MI: Baker Books.

Poloma, M. (2003). *Main Street mystics: The Toronto blessings and reviving Pentecostalism*. New York: AltaMira.

Richards, P., & Bergin, A. (1997). *A spiritual strategy for counseling and psychotherapy*. Washington, DC: American Psychological Association.

Sandford, J. L., & Sandford, M. (1992). *A comprehensive guide to deliverance and inner healing*. Grand Rapids, MI: Chosen Books.

Sandford, J. L., & Sandford, P. (1982). *The transformation of the inner man*. Tulsa, OK: Victory House.

Sanford, A. (1972). *The healing light*. New York: Ballantine Books. (Original work published 1947)

Seamands, D. (1985). *Healing of memories*. Wheaton, IL: Victor Books.

Smith, E. (2000a). *Beyond tolerable recovery*. Campbellsville, KY: Family Care Publishing.

Smith, E. (2000b). *Genuine recovery: The client orientation manual*. Campbellsville, KY: Family Care Publishing.

Smith, E. (2002). *Healing life's deepest hurts*. Ann Arbor, MI: Vine Books; New Creation.

Stapleton, R. C. (1976). *The gift of inner healing*. Waco, TX: Word Books.

Synan, V. (2001). *The century of the Holy Spirit: 100 years of Pentecostal and charismatic renewal, 1901–2001*. Nashville, TN: Thomas Nelson.

Tan, S. Y. (1991). *Lay counseling*. Grand Rapids, MI: Zondervan Press.

Tan, S. Y. (1996). Religion in clinical practice: Implicit and explicit integration. In E. Shafranske (Ed.), *Religion and the clinical practice of psychology* (pp. 365–387). Washington, DC: American Psychological Association.

Young, J., Klosko, J., & Weishaar, M. (2003). *Schema therapy: A practitioner's guide*. New York: Guilford Press.

# 14

# Islam, Divinity, and Spiritual Healing

*Qulsoom Inayat*

The belief that there is a spiritual aspect to human personality is shared by most of the world's religions. This commonly held notion, however, has been understood and expressed in a variety of ways by the different traditions. Such differences may reflect substantial differences in meanings between sets of concepts, problems of translation, as well as historical changes in the meanings of words. Religion and spirituality are key to understanding the notion of healing in Islam. Islamic spiritual healers inherited the methods that God's messengers were using, and from one generation to another they have practiced these methods up to the present time. In the Islamic tradition, healers use both medicinal remedies and spiritual means. The spiritual techniques follow principles that utilize the patient's latent energy and power contained in devotions, supplications, and meditations of the prophets, messengers, and wise men of God.

According to Witmer and Sweeney (1992), spirituality is the core unifying process that provides direction and meaning in life, whereas religion, argues Wong (1998), is one manifestation of spirituality, and as a cultural phenomenon it also includes societal institutions, shared beliefs, symbols, and rituals. More recently, Richards and Bergin (2002) have addressed this issue by developing a theistic spiritual strategy that incorporates many basic precepts common to the major religious texts. At the same time, the authors emphasize the need for specific religious and spiritual innovations that may be appropriate for specific clients. This chapter considers healing from the Islamic perspective.

In Islam the term *spirituality* is inseparable from the awareness of the One, of Allah, and a life lived according to His will. This suggests a principle of Oneness (*tawheed*), which Allah has manifested within the "soul of man." In other words, He has "breathed into man" His own spirit. The word Muslims use for spirituality is *ruhaniyyah. Ruh*, which means "spirit," is mentioned in the Quran: "The spirit is from the command of my Lord" (Quran 17:85 [Ali, 1975]). This means that Allah can treat *maradhun* (the sickness of the mind). Therefore, faith is the epitome of "psychotherapeutic treatment."

From the Islamic point of view, a spiritual approach to psychotherapy is an aspect of behavior modification that is based on the relationship between Man and his Creator (Allah). This entails an operational paradigm in which faith (*iman*) in Allah is the focal point. *Iman* is both a cognitive and an ethical construct, which incorporates the consciousness of Allah's existence and the conviction in service that serves to remove *maradhun* in people. This process involves purification of the body and soul by means of devotion.

The essence of purification of the *ruh* (spirit/soul), *qalb* (essential heart), and *nafs* (ego/self) is to bring one's *nafs* under control. The Quran states, "Successful is the one who keeps it pure and ruined is the one who corrupts it" (Quran 91:9–10 [Ali, 1975]). Study on religious experience indicates that belief, or faith, engages the body as much as it does the mind (Csordas, 1994; Mahmood, 2001; Proudfoot, 1985). It is this synergy that links Islamic spirituality to health and well-being.

### ❖ ISLAM AND HEALTH

Muslims generally hold that faith protects against ill health as well as helping manage health problems when they occur. The fact that Islam plays a major role in the Muslim's understanding, experience, and expression in mental distress is well documented (Ansari, 1992; Badri, 2000; Hussain, 1999). Among Muslims, there is a strong tendency to conceptualize illness as occurring by the will of Allah, who is understood to be a higher power that cannot be perceived by the senses. The Islamic strategy for promoting health and well-being requires the recognition of the defective nature of human beings. Constant striving to overcome this nature leads to spiritual progress, health, and Allah's pleasure (Husain, 1998).

In Islamic psychology three essential elements of the human psyche, *ruh, nafs,* and *qalb,* are considered to reside in the region of the physical heart, which is commonly indicated to be the location of emotional pain. Somatic symptoms hold a significant place in the Muslim cultural system, because psychological and spiritual development is considered to take place in the *qalb* (Sheikh & Gatrad, 2000). Here, the perception is one of connections between "psyche" and "soma," the multiple ways in which physical and psychological problems interact.[1] Therefore, the distressed person primarily notices and reports somatic symptoms. Mental unrest is thought to be a manifestation of an incongruent heart—an unstable soul—that is lost and so has become distant from its Creator. In this sense, a stable or sound state of mental health is a "well," "true," "clear," or "guided" heart that is calm and so is within the sanctions of Islamic teachings. A "rusted" or "hard" heart is a symptom of chronic ill feelings and ultimately Allah's displeasure. This state is described mainly as an aching heart, a trembling heart, or pressure in the heart. Although the head is the vital and animating principle, the heart is the locus of thought, feeling, memory, and awareness. Thus, "illness" is the illness of the heart or body. This mode of articulation is not to say that thinking in the heart is emotional illiteracy (an inability to communicate emotions adequately); rather, such thinking is metaphoric and closely connected to feelings. This feature of expression is rooted in the Quran: "In their hearts is a disease" (Quran 2:10 [Ali, 1975]).

Because mental distress in the practicing Muslim community is generally understood in terms of moral transgression or the result of Divine Will, religious intervention or methods are frequently resorted to for healing. *Sawm* (fasting), *taubah* (repentance), and regular recitation of the Quran are common features of the treatment and healing process. Thus, the belief in the treatment is closely tied to the belief about illness. Underlying this belief is the idea of regaining connection and intimacy with Allah and in the process enabling one to gain a cognitive grasp of the situation. This is expected to reduce motivation for sin and relief from distress, which leads to better health. This understanding is reinforced in the following verse of the Quran: "Surely in the remembrance of Allah do hearts find rest" (Quran 13:28 [Ali, 1975]).

## ❖ HEALING FROM THE QURAN

The teachings of Muhammad (peace be upon him) form the basis of the faith (*iman*) and practice (*din*) of Islam. Islamic philosophy can be described under three headings:

1. *Iman,* or articles of faith: The belief that there is only one God (Allah) who is the Creator and Cherisher of the universe. Muhammad (peace be upon him) is a Prophet.

2. *Ihsan,* or right conduct: The way of perfecting the character. *Al-Akhlaq* is the plural term for *Khuluq,* which means "nature" or "attribute." *Al-Khuluq* is an inner characteristic that is manifested outwardly as conduct or behavior.

3. *Ibadat,* or religious duty: Faith and right conduct were set forth in the Quran. *Ibadat* was defined by reference to *hadith* (the sayings) and *sunnah* (actions) of the Prophet Muhammad (peace be upon him).
   a. *Articles of Faith*

      *Tawhid:* the unity of God

      Right conduct

   b. *Religious Duty—Five Pillars*

      *Shahada* (repetition of the creed)

      Prayer: *salat, zikr, dua* (acts of worship)

      Zakat: almsgiving

      Fasting during the month of Ramadan

      Hajj (pilgrimage)

The Quran is not a textbook of medicine; rather, it contains rules of guidance that will promote good health and healing. That is why the Quran calls itself a book of healing[2]: "O mankind, there has come unto you a guidance from your Lord and a healing for the diseases in your hearts, and for those who believe a guidance and mercy" (Quran 10:57 [Ali, 1975]).

Verses of the Quran are often used by Islamic healers to cure their patients. Certain sections are considered to have *baraka,* or "spiritual powers." These verses can be written down on a piece of paper and put in a small leather or plastic bag, which is then used as a charm to keep away bad spirits. However, some imams (Islamic spiritual leaders) regard this practice as folklore and say it has no place in their religion. This conflict may have arisen because incantation was used in pre-Islamic times for various purposes, both constructive and destructive. The Prophet (peace be upon him) stopped the use of these incantations and substituted prayers and supplications from the Quran. The effect of this conflict is that some Muslims may consider spiritual healing to be associated with magic and thus shun its use and discussion.

### Prayer and Healing

Three practices embrace the Islamic concept of worship. *Salat* is the ritual prayer for which both patterns and times are fixed. *Zikr* and *dua* represent individual attempts to draw near to God in a more personal relationship. *Salat* is a specific practice combining body movements, recitation of Quranic verses, and supplications that must be performed five times a day. Although the true purpose of *salat* is to reach God's proximity, it can also give spiritual nourishment and harmonize the mental, emotional, and spiritual aspects of the devotee (Al-Ghazali, 2000). *Salat* is preceded by an act of ablution by which Muslims purify themselves in order to appear before God in a state of purity. Where running water is available, the body is washed. Where water is not available, sand or stone is used for a symbolic cleansing of the body. The act of ablution links water as the symbol of purity to the idea of prayer as the means of purification of the soul. The ritual of cleansing is an integral part of the ritual of prayer. Ablution provides outer purity, and prayer provides inner purity. Islamic prayer, thus, is designed to cleanse body, mind, and soul. *Zikr* is also practiced as a method to cure mental or physical illness. It is performed by repeating Quranic verses or God's attributes (the 99 names of Allah), either individually or in a group, usually under supervision of a Sufi teacher.

In the next section, I will discuss two case studies, Mohammed and Mina, who were patients in therapy with me.

## Client: Mohammed

Mohammed was seen as an inpatient on a psychiatric ward because he was experiencing suicidal ideation, low mood, poor sleep, loss of appetite, feelings of hopelessness, and anxiety. Mohammed was given antidepressant medication by the medical staff. Mohammed was a 66-year-old male Pakistani Muslim who had worked, until a year ago, as a general practitioner. Mohammed reported a happy childhood and was successful at school. He went to medical college in Pakistan, after which he married his first cousin in a semi-arranged marriage. Mohammed came to England in order to advance his career and had been highly successful. Mohammed had four children, three sons and one daughter. Mohammed's marriage broke up 18 years ago, and his wife died of breast cancer 11 years ago. Mohammed's eldest son died of AIDS 12 years ago. Mohammed had been closely involved with his local mosque for many years and considered Islam to be the mainstay of his life.

In the previous year, Mohammed was alleged to have been involved in the unlawful supply of dexamphetamines in the 5 years previous to the allegation. Mohammed was seen for 12 sessions. The treatment evolved from an early phase of supportive treatment, in which a therapeutic relationship was established, to an exploratory form of Islamic counseling that seeks to explore life events within the framework of Islamic spiritual and moral progression.

Initially, Mohammed rejected any notion that he was responsible for his actions with regard to the allegation. However, the principle of prayer was used to enable him to connect more deeply with Allah. The opening verse of prayers asks Allah to guide us on the "straight path" that leads to his pleasure. Mohammed noted that the purpose of life is to take responsibility for one's actions and to behave in a way that increases Allah's pleasure.

An examination of Mohammed's connection to Allah through prayer (Al-Ghazali, 2000) allowed for the emergence of the guilt Mohammed felt regarding his son's homosexuality. Because homosexuality is forbidden in Islam, Mohammed had rejected his son harshly. Mohammed realized that providing unlawful drugs to his patients had been his way of "helping" people rejected by those who loved them. Gradually, Mohammed was able to forgive his son for what he perceived as his defective nature.

Mohammed's faith provided emotional and spiritual support throughout therapy. In the final phase Mohammed was able to repent sincerely and know that he was forgiven for his harsh treatment of his son. Mohammed was discharged from the hospital after his 10th session. He started to attend a group for learning about the Quran in greater depth. The members of this group provided Mohammed with an essential social support network. At this time, Mohammed admitted liability for the allegation. His circumstances and psychological health were taken into account, and Mohammed felt that he was given a just sentence.

Because Mohammed and I were of the same faith, we were able to establish a rapport that included our understanding of Islam as a vehicle for understanding Mohammed's current dilemma. The spiritual interventions that I utilized enabled Mohammed to connect with his guilt. Mohammed's sincere repentance allowed him to feel Allah's forgiveness and mercy. This was mirrored by society in the diminished punishment that he received.

### Client: Mina

Mina was a 53-year-old African woman who had been converted to Islam at the age of 19. Mina had married a Muslim Pakistani man who had died of cancer 5 years previously. Mina had one 11-year-old son who was experiencing difficulties at school.

Mina had been referred by her general practitioner to a local counseling service that dealt with the needs of ethnic-minority groups. Individual therapy was provided free of charge for up to 30 sessions. Mina was seen for 28 sessions. Initially, Mina presented with depression and anxiety associated with her son's continuing difficulties. Mina was constantly in fear of the telephone ringing during weekdays, because her son's school generally telephoned to report some misdemeanor on the part of her son at least once a day. Mina had lost all pleasure in life and wished that she could just "end the pain."

Initial therapy consisted of a supportive environment in which we built a therapeutic relationship. This evolved into an exploratory form of Islamic counseling to explore current concerns using the Islamic framework. Mina's desire to end her pain was used to explore Islam's injunction regarding suicide. Mina was clear that she would not harm herself because such behavior transgresses the principle that life is a gift from Allah. Within this exploration, Mina asked for a *ruqya* (healing) to be done with her. Together we recited the opening verse of the Quran, which is purported to have healing properties (Imam Ibn Al-Jauziyah, 1999). Each session of counseling was prefaced with this *ruqya* for 20 minutes.

As therapy progressed, Mina was able to recognize that the root of her problem lay in her relationship with her son. Mina resented the fact that her son had taken up so much of her time while her husband was ill and dying. She felt that she had been unable to do everything that she could for her husband. The Divine name of *Ya Gafoor* (The All-Forgiving) was used to enable Mina to connect with this quality of Allah. In the final phase of therapy, Mina was able to forgive herself for any deficiencies in her care of her husband. At the same time, Mina was able to realize that her son was a blessing from Allah, one that provided a constant and growing link to her husband.

## ❖ ISLAM, DIVINITY, AND HEALING

In Islam the body represents the earthly origins and the spirit the divine origins of humans, and life is one of the stages of the journey to God. The body is the vehicle for this journey. In its progression through life, the physical body passes through stages from infancy to youth, adulthood, and old age. Similarly, the soul passes through specific evolutionary stages or stations (Chisti, 1991). The purpose of healing is to facilitate this evolution (see Table 14.1).

In Islamic spiritual terminology the nonphysical body is *nasma*. This exists within each physical body as a subtle vapor created by the chemical output of the physical body. *Nasma* is present in human beings just as rose water is present in the rose or as the fire in burning coals. When the flow of spiritual energy is disturbed or insufficient, the health of the patient is adversely affected, leading to pain, disease, and distress.

Spiritual healers symbolize the flowing of the driving force in the body and in the universe as vortices of energy made up of a number of smaller spiral cones of energy. These are known in Islamic terminology as *lataif,* meaning subtle manifestations or layers. The *lataif* (singular, *lateefa*) are points of maximum energy

**Table 14.1**    Stages of Spiritual Progression in Islam

| Stage of Evolution | Attribute | Expression |
| --- | --- | --- |
| Maqam an-Nafs | Egotism | Preoccupation with need for physical satisfaction. Reason and judgment not yet developed. Everyone starts at this station, and children are immune from divine judgment and punishment. |
| Maqam al-Qalb | Heart | Feels good about oneself and the world. |
| Maqam ar-Ruh | Pure spirit | Mercy, compassion, and self-discipline. |
| Maqam as-Sirr | Divine secrets | Clairaudience; conversation with angels. |
| Maqam al-Qurb | Proximity to Allah | Able to straddle this world and the next. |
| Maqam al-Wisal | Union with Allah | Divine unity. |

intake and are important focal points of balance within the energy system. Disease and illness occur if a *lateefa* is unbalanced (see Table 14.2).

*Lataif* in adults have a protective screen over them. In a healthy system, these *lataif* spin in synchronized rhythm with the others, drawing energy from the universal energy field into their center for use by the body. Each one of them is tuned to a specific frequency that helps the body to remain healthy. However, in a diseased system the vortices are not synchronized. The energy of the *lataif* that make up these vortices may be fast or slow, jerky or lopsided. Sometimes breaks in the entire energy pattern can be observed in which *lataif* may be fully or partially collapsed or inverted. These disturbances are related to dysfunction or pathology of the physical body in that area. The healer prescribes that the patient repeat different holy names of Allah in a special format for the duration of the treatment. These holy names are like energy sparks that ignite more flow from the universal energy source. The ignition also activates the focal points of the *lataif*, causing rebalancing in the body of the patient. One doctrine of *lataif* was formulated by the 13th- and 14th-century Persian Sufi Alaoddawleh Semnani. Linking the seven prophets of the Quran with the mystical physiology of seven *lataif*, Semnani referred to seven grades of being that constitute the ascent of the soul to the Godhead.

Semnani's *lataif* have a double meaning: They refer both to psychic centers (chakras) and to a succession of subtle bodies (Sanskrit *kosha*, Greek *okhema*) or levels of self. It is interesting that modern clairvoyant and theosophical writers unfamiliar with Sufi teaching also match up the seven chakras with seven bodies or levels of self (Brennan, 1988).

**Table 14.2**    The Islamic System of Subtle Energy Centers

| Lataif | Color | Prophetic Symbol |
|---|---|---|
| Qalibiyya<br>(the mold or etheric body) | Black/dark gray | Adam |
| Nafsiyya<br>(vital senses and animal soul) | Blue | Noah |
| Qalbiyya<br>(spiritual heart) | Red | Abraham |
| Sirriyya<br>(the Secret, the edge of<br>super-consciousness and<br>stage of spiritual monologues) | White | Moses |
| Ruhiyya<br>(the Spirit, the vice-regent of God) | Yellow | David |
| Khafiya<br>(organ of spiritual inspiration) | Luminous black | Jesus |
| Haqiqa<br>(divine center) | Emerald green | Mohammad<br>(peace be upon him) |

The profound experiences that compose tacit knowledge of a spiritual body in Islam connect faith and religious practice to feelings of well-being through the heart, which is seen as an organ and symbol that links spiritual, emotional, and physical experience. Ordinarily thought, memory, and imagination allow the mind to travel from the space and time of the physical body to the point at which it fades from awareness. The phenomenon of the spiritual body, however, unifies awareness of mind and body as embodied presence in the world. This phenomenon has been described as "a shiver running down the back" (d'Acquili & Laughlin, as cited in Turner & Bruner, 1986), a "bubbling up" (Durkheim, 1912/1995), or feelings of harmony in ritual (Laderman, 1991). Because the experience is both pleasurable and meaningful, individuals often engage in these behaviors in order to reproduce it.

## ❖ CONCLUSION

Muslim communities may have healing conventions that help them sustain realistic ambivalence in the context of polarizing discourses of modernity. Within a health care system premised on individualism, rights, and responsibilities, health care providers have difficulty in recognizing and engaging with these conventions. The person who turns to a healer or psychotherapist seeks not just rights but recognition.

The prevailing concepts of human unity and the fundamental equality of all persons are supported by various ideological, scientific, and religious interpretations of reality and of the human species. Muslims believe that Allah created all human beings. The Prophet Muhammad (peace be upon him) urged us to consider ourselves as human first.

## ❖ NOTES

1. The Quran does not subscribe to mind-body, soul-body, or spirit-matter dualisms. Muslims do not see human life and well-being or death and illness only in their material and physical forms. Rather, a human being is a complex unity, an organism that includes all aspects of soul, spirit, mind, heart, psyche, and body.

2. Healing from the Quran is of three types (Imam Ibn Al-Jauziyah, 1999):
   (a) Legislative: This includes faith in God not only as the Creator but as the Sustainer and Protector. This also includes the medical benefits of obligatory prayers, fasting, charity, and pilgrimage: "And we sent down in the Quran such things that have healing and mercy for the believers" (Quran 17:82 [Ali, 1975]).
   (b) Health guidelines: This includes health-promoting items from the Quran and the *sunnah* including the use of honey, olives, fruit, and lean meat; the avoidance of excessive eating; and the prohibition of alcohol, pork, sexual promiscuity, and sex during menstruation: "There issues from within the bodies of the bee a drink of varying colours wherein is healing for mankind" (Quran 16:69 [Ali, 1975]).
   (c) The direct healing effect of the Quran: This refers to recitation of the Quran by the patient or for the patient (*ruqya*): "And God shall heal the breast of the believers" (Quran 9:14 [Ali, 1975]).

## ❖ REFERENCES

Al-Ghazali, A. H. M. (2000). *Inner dimensions of Islamic worship* (H. M. Leicester, Trans.). Leicester, UK: Islamic Foundation.

Ali, A. Y. (1975). *The holy Quran: Text, translation and commentary.* Leicester, UK: Islamic Foundation.

Ansari, Z. (1992). *Quranic concepts of human psyche.* Lahore, Pakistan: Islamic Research Institute.

Badri, M. (2000). *Contemplation: An Islamic psychospiritual study* (The International Institute of Islamic Thought). Cambridge, UK: Cambridge University Press.

Brennan, B. A. (1988). *Hands of light.* London: Bantam Books.

Chisti, Sheikh H. M. (1991). *The book of Sufi healing.* Rochester, VT: Inner Traditions International.

Csordas, T. (1994). *The sacred self: A cultural phenomenology of charismatic healing.* Berkeley: University of California Press.

Durkheim, E. (1995). *The elementary forms of the religious life.* New York: Free Press. (Original work published 1912)

Husain, S. A. (1998). Religion and mental health from the Muslim perspective. In H. G. Koenig (Ed.), *Handbook of religion and mental health* (pp. 279–290). London: Academic Press.

Hussain, A. (1999). *An exploration into the importance of understanding cultural issues in the presentation of mental distress in Bangladesh.* Unpublished manuscript, University of East London.

Imam Ibn Al-Jauziyah, Q. (1999). *Healing with the medicine of the Prophet* (J. AbualRub, Trans.). Riyadh, Saudi Arabia: Darussalam.

Laderman, C. (1991). *Taming the wind of desire: Psychology, medicine and aesthetics in Malay shamanistic performance.* Berkeley: University of California Press.

Mahmood, S. (2001). Rehearsed spontaneity and the conventional of ritual: Disciplines of Salat. *American Ethnologist, 28,* 827–853.

Proudfoot, W. (1985). Religious experience. In B. Wittine (Ed.), *Beyond ego* (pp. 56–74). Berkeley: University of California Press.

Richards, P. S., & Bergin, A. E. (2002). *A spiritual strategy for counseling and psychotherapy.* Washington, DC: American Psychological Association.

Sheikh, A., & Gatrad, A. R. (2000). *Caring for Muslim patients.* London: Radcliffe Medical Press.

Turner, V. W., & Bruner, E. (Eds.). (1986). *The anthropology of experience.* Chicago: University of Illinois Press.

Witmer, J. M., & Sweeney, T. J. (1992). A holistic model for wellness and prevention over the lifespan. In M. T. Burke & J. G. Miranti (Eds.), *Counseling: The spiritual dimension* (pp. 251–263). Alexandria, VA: American Counseling Association.

Wong, P. T. P. (1998). Spirituality, meaning, and successful aging. In P. T. P. Wong & P. S. Fry (Eds.), *The human quest for meaning: A handbook of psychological research and clinical application* (pp. 359–394). Mahwah, NJ: Lawrence Erlbaum.

# 15

# Jewish Healing, Spirituality, and Modern Psychology

*Laura J. Praglin*

Themes relating to spiritual, physical, and mental healing abound in Jewish texts, oral traditions, folk customs, and ritual practices. To this day, Jews recite special healing prayers during Sabbath services and consider visiting the sick to be an important charitable act. Yet other Jewish folk practices, such as wearing protective charms to ward off illness, visiting tombs of famous healers, or consulting holy men for advice or blessings, have been largely abandoned as superstitious in the modern era. Because they are contrary to Jewish desires for "respectability" and assimilation into non-Jewish culture after the Enlightenment, such practices are rarely encountered today, except among small groups of Hasidic Jews or within those Jewish circles still remaining in Eastern Europe, Israel, and North Africa.

A recent wish to reinvigorate ancient Jewish healing rituals, as well as to create new expressions of mental and spiritual healing, has reemerged over the past several decades. This desire largely parallels trends in non-Jewish healing movements within North American and European culture and has resulted in healing services; study circles; and conferences for clergy, mental health professionals, and laypersons alike. Nevertheless, Jews as a group continue to be highly respectful of modern medicine and psychotherapy, and in fact are overrepresented as clients and practitioners. How, then, do we account for this newfound hunger professed by contemporary Jews for healing rituals and the sustaining wisdom behind them?

Several factors may account for this resurgent interest. First, the Jewish healing movement does not view its practices as posing a challenge to modern medicine. Healing practitioners make an important distinction between curing, which is left to physicians, and healing, which is viewed as adjunctive to medical intervention. Second, despite this respect for medicine, Jews have begun to acknowledge the increasing impersonality of modern health care treatment and to recognize the importance of humanizing this experience in times of crisis. Healing rituals often furnish such holistic and communal correctives. Third, many Jews have become increasingly estranged from institutional synagogue life or have grown up in secular homes. Yet some experience hunger for a Jewish community in periods of distress, including psychological or physical illness, death, or bereavement. Informal communal gatherings and healing circles again provide a needed sense of communal structure and identity to Jews in need.

## ❖ JEWISH HEALING IN BIBLICAL AND RABBINIC SOURCES

Throughout Jewish biblical sources and the later rabbinical interpretations of those sources, we find frequent references to physical, mental, and spiritual healing and curing. Israel interpreted its divine covenantal relationship to mean that God alone restored and delivered, and thus God was the sole source of individual and communal health and wholeness. In the Bible, God healed Abimelech and Miriam (Genesis 20:17; Deuteronomy 24:8–9[1]) and promised to keep Israel healthy if Israel kept the commandments (Exodus 15:26; Deuteronomy 32:39; Numbers 12). The historical books, prophets, and the psalms continue these themes (Ezekiel 34:4; 1 Kings 17:17–24; 2 Kings 2:20–22, 4:19–37, 20; Isaiah 38:1–6; 2 Samuel 12:16–23).

Yet the Hebrew Bible did not generally revere the physician, for it linked healing with magic and idolatry (Exodus 22:18; Leviticus 19:26 and 31, 20:6, 27; Deuteronomy 18:9–14; Jeremiah 8:22–9:6, 27:9–10; Ezekiel 13:17–20). This wariness, in addition to biblical laws against contact with blood or corpses, at first restricted Jewish engagement with medicine ("Medicine in Israel," 1978). Israelite priests and prophets were more likely to be consulted in cases of illness, for they understood connections between disease, impurity, and healing rituals involving sacrifice, prayer, and repentance (1 Kings 12, 13; Feldman, 1986). Later esteem for physicians may be traced to the Hellenistic era, when Stoic natural law and Greek nonmagical, "scientific" medicine removed Jewish suspicions about healing acts (Abusch, 1985; Dorff, 1986; Rosner, 1977).

Following the destruction of the Second Temple in Jerusalem in 70 CE, Judaism witnessed a decline of the institutionalized priesthood and an increase in healing remedies by prophetic magicians. These practices were later condemned after the rise of rabbinical academies and codification of the oral law (the Mishnah) starting in the third century CE (Kaufmann, 1960, p. 109) (M. Sanhedrin 7:11; B. Sanhedrin 68a; 14 B. Berakhot 34a$^2$). Although stories of healing magicians were downplayed, they nevertheless endured in the rabbinic literature (Crossan, 1991) (B. Bava Batra 16b; B. Berakhot 5b).

Beginning in the fourth century CE, normative sources for Jewish attitudes and laws regarding medicine and healing were collected in the Talmud and its commentaries. The Talmud, in fact, prohibited Jews from living in a city without a physician (B. Sanhedrin 17b). Rabbis also discerned divine instructions to heal in Leviticus 19 and 18 ("Nor shall you stand by the blood of your fellow" and "You shall love your neighbor as yourself"). Rabbis taught that God created the human body as good and as a source of intricate wonder. Unlike adherents of many Greek philosophies, rabbis did not believe that the soul was trapped in the body or that the body was a source of sin. Legitimate physical pleasures were to be enjoyed rather than withheld. Rabbinic law dictated legal as well as practical duties regarding diet, exercise, hygiene, sex, and sleep.

Rabbis also tried to clarify important links between behavior, values, and overall psychological welfare, given the integral connection between body and soul. Mental health was as significant as physical health. A threat to mental health was considered "a threat to one's physical life" (Feldman, 1986, p. 49) (B. Yoma 82), requiring the physician to call upon all known powers of cure.

## ❖ HEALING IN MEDIEVAL TIMES

Practices of Jewish healing from the 10th to the 18th centuries relied upon rabbinic sources as well as codes, such as Moses Maimonides' *Mishneh Torah* and Joseph Karo's *Shulhan Arukh*. The *Shulhan Arukh* declared that withholding treatment by a physician was analogous to shedding blood (Dorff, 1986). The mandate to heal extended to gentiles, based partly on Leviticus 25:35, which insists upon fair treatment of foreigners, and partly on pragmatic grounds, to promote good relations with Christian or Arab neighbors. Physicians treated many non-Jews who sought them out, despite church condemnation of Jewish doctors as sorcerers or murderers (Dorff). The rabbi-physician Maimonides viewed illness less as a decree of divine judgment than an opportunity to exercise human healing powers (Maimonides, 1949, *Mishneh Torah*, Hilchot Deot: 4). He also wrote about insanity and its relation to legal and moral responsibility, because those judged insane were excused from most religious obligations. Another respected physician-scholar, Nachmanides, believed that saving a soul amounted to saving a person's life (Chavel, 1978).

The obligation to heal and to visit the sick extended to the entire Jewish community. God was the ultimate healer, however, and recovery occurred only through God's will. Petitionary healing prayers became part of the daily and Sabbath liturgies (Hertz, 1948). European Jews also formed brotherhoods to visit the infirm, established inns for the sick, and helped establish hospitals in many European cities (Marcus, 1947).

The Hasidic tradition, arising in Eastern Europe in the 17th and 18th centuries, led to intense interest in spiritual and physical healing (Scholem, 1973). The movement's founder, the Ba'al Shem Tov, believed that healing involved reestablishing a proper relationship with God through prayer and charitable acts. Rabbis of the later Hasidic tradition were also regarded as great healers (Dorff, 1986). In addition to Hasidism, other movements focused on mental healing. The 19th-century Jewish movement Musar, for instance, stressed the connection between morality and behavior in the quest for a mentally balanced life (Rachlis, 1974; Ury, 1970).

## ❖ JEWISH HEALING IN THE MODERN PERIOD

The European Enlightenment's espousal of universal rights and liberal individualism brought about dramatic changes in self-perception among many Jews starting in the late 18th century. Released from medieval forms of ghetto life, they often made substantial changes in dress, customs, worship, and profession within less than one generation (Mendes-Flohr, 1991). Yet once the initial enthusiasm of modernization waned, many of these Jews faced the dilemma that they were denuded of the psychic richness and close-knit character of traditional Judaism but could not easily return to it. By the late 19th century, many Jews found themselves suffering not only from Western *anomie* (Durkheim, 1891/1997) but from resurgent anti-Semitism as well (Klein, 1985). Although many achieved professional success, owing to a heritage of scholarship and achievement (as well as light-colored skin), many Western Jews continued to remain conflicted about their national and religious identities. This ambivalence intensified for many with increasing intolerance and anti-Semitism, resulting in the destruction of vital centers of European Jewry after the Nazi Holocaust. Many Jews to this day discover themselves living between two worlds. Even without being traditionally observant, they continue to identify as Jews, given deep and distinctive ethnic ties; common psychosocial realities; and a shared, collective history of oppression (Diller, 2004).

## ❖ THE RABBI: A BRIDGE FIGURE
## BETWEEN HEALING AND COUNSELING

Always regarded as a teacher, the rabbi has also acted as the bridge between traditional healer and modern psychotherapist in the modern era. In efforts to address the widespread psychic hunger of assimilated Jews beginning in the early 20th century, some rabbis explored the new discipline of psychology, with its awareness of mental healing and the inner self. The "scientific" claims of psychology (Berger, 1965; Rieff, 1966), moreover, lent a new respectability to mental healing, and some liberal rabbis thus embraced it eagerly in counseling congregants. Psychology also encouraged reflection upon links between Judaism, healing, and curing. Such evaluations helped illuminate and revitalize healing aspects of Jewish spiritual life largely lost in the wake of modernization (Praglin, 1999).

To what extent Judaism and psychology clashed in their essential goals, and how independent of psychological models rabbinical counselors should remain in their counseling work, formed one of the most engaging struggles of the past century. Some feared that psychologically minded rabbis might find themselves involved in therapeutic issues that pitted the individual against family and tradition. Instead, they insisted, rabbis should offer advice and solace, focusing upon the individual's soul and conscience, but with the aim of reintegration into the community. Jewish literature, many claimed, spelled out the rabbinic role, as well as definitions of physical and spiritual health. Why, then, turn to psychology for answers, when the Jewish tradition had provided such direction for hundreds of generations?

Rabbinic responses to these challenges varied widely. Some found any attempt at "soul healing" a Christian practice, despite precedents for spiritual healing and counseling in Jewish sources throughout the ages. Some perceived a fundamental incompatibility between Judaism and psychological views of religion, morality, tradition, and human nature. Freud's cultural critique of religion certainly created a significant barrier. Some, however, rose above these challenges to welcome Freud's pioneering clinical understandings of the unconscious, psychic development, and psychopathology (Praglin, 1998).

The 1960s legacy of social upheaval, challenges to institutional authority, and searches for meaningful alternative lifestyles created new challenges for rabbis as well. Some encouraged explorations of mystical elements of personal spirituality and other nontraditional forms of religious expression, often spurred by defections to cults or Eastern religions. Charismatic rabbis used meditation and healing rituals to revitalize Jewish worship and helped plant seeds of the Jewish renewal movement (Schachter, 1968). The formation of small, experimental study and worship alternatives provided a sense of belonging and meaning, often unavailable in larger synagogues. Pararabbinic family empowerment programs, as well as paraprofessional counseling centers, helped Jews find solace, support, and guidance from each other, rather than from the rabbi alone (Schulweis, 1973).

A 1967 survey indicated that whereas most rabbis saw themselves as healers and counselors as well as scholars, Reform rabbis were more attuned to counseling, spent more time at it, and had undergone some specialized training. Their congregations, moreover, expected this of them. They were also more inclined to refer congregants to psychiatric professionals (Gilbreath & Hoenig, 1967). By the mid-20th century, most rabbis had heeded the warning of their rabbinical teachers and had come to realize that, without sufficient training, the rabbi could do more harm than good to counselees. By the mid-1960s, more rabbis also became chaplains or independent psychotherapist-rabbis, setting up practices away from traditional synagogue settings (Klausner, 1964).

Until the 1980s, psychiatrist Mortimer Ostow of the Jewish Theological Seminary in New York was unequivocal in emphasizing that

> our position at the Seminary is that rabbis must not see themselves as psychiatrists, nor even primarily as counselors. Their counseling function is to be performed in the course of normal congregational service and on suitable occasions. The treatment of illness, however, is not the duty of the rabbi. (Ostow, 1969, p. 4)

Later, psychiatrists at the seminary introduced new clinical issues to rabbis-in-training, such as adolescent suicide and battered woman syndrome (Klagsbrun, 1989). No doubt some of the impetus for such courses was the admittance of women as rabbinical students for the first time in the 1970s (Reform and Reconstructionist movements) and in the 1990s (Conservative movement).

A few dissenting pulpit rabbis questioned the limited counseling role prescribed for rabbis. Rabbi Steven Jacobs recalled that while enrolled in a crisis counseling course at Hebrew Union College in the early 1970s, one seminarian was heavily criticized "for having 'therapeutic ambitions.'" Many congregants, Jacobs recalled, relayed their dissatisfaction with rabbis "quick to offer advice and solutions, but little in the way of guidance and counseling." "It is precisely *because* we relate to our congregants in a wide variety of contexts and settings," Jacobs countered, "that we become most valuable to them in a counseling situation"

(Jacobs, 1977, p. 70). Like his professors, he agreed that long-term counseling was outside the domain of the congregational rabbi and that the counseling relationship must not interfere with regular interactions with congregants. Yet he did not see himself only as "advice-giver or problem-solver," but more as a "reflector, mirror, sounding board," who helped clarify problems and suggest various options, such as referral. He lived out Jewish values "as priest, counselor, educator, spiritual guide and friend," rather than only the roles of Jewish spokesman and judge, and in so doing, he restored worth and self-esteem to congregants (Jacobs, 1977).

Following Jacobs's lead, many rabbis requested greater training in counseling from their rabbinical bodies. They asked for practical clinical skills training in interviewing, diagnosis, referral, and crisis intervention, and for more prolonged case consultation and supervision. In addition, many argued that training should be offered at different levels of expertise, encompassing marriage, divorce, parent-child relations, alcoholism, old age, illness, and bereavement (Central Conference of American Rabbis, 1970, 1976). By the last decades of the 20th century, seminaries and the Jewish community at large also began to explore issues of substance abuse, battered women and children, and homosexuality in depth (Olitzky, 1993).

A consideration of the effects of the Holocaust on survivors and their children (Kanter, 1976; Kellermann, n.d.) has also remained central to rabbinical thought, healing, and counseling in recent years. This examination has engaged theological and psychological questions concerning long-term consequences of trauma, as well as moral responsibility, innocence, survivor guilt, and theodicy (Kushner, 1981; Schulweis, 1983).

Recent writings of Jewish scholars who are also mental health professionals have contributed richly to the dialogue between Jewish healing and psychotherapy as well (Meier, 1988; Schimmel, 1997; Twerski, 1993, 1997). Stuart Linke (1999), part of Britain's Jewish renewal movement, engaged Jewish practice from the standpoint of a practicing clinical psychologist. Why, he asked, do many Jews still adhere to long-established practices (including healing rituals) when they no longer ascribe to their theological underpinnings? Linke answered through the lens of mysticism and transpersonal psychology, focusing on the inner, "psychological utility" of ancient rituals to facilitate key points of growth in our lives.

Moshe H. Spero, also a practicing psychologist, declared the compatibility between *halakhah* (Jewish law) and scientific assumptions of the psychologies (Spero, 1980). In a similar vein, he later engaged Judaism and object relations theory (Spero, 1992). Spero considered the increasing number of people who seek out psychotherapy not so much to cure illness as to find an existentially meaningful existence. This search, he believed, is beyond the diagnostic and treatment capacities of psychology. Spero, however, was not averse to helping patients consider such transcendent concerns once clinical issues had been addressed (Spero, 1980).

To treat religious patients, Spero (1980) argued that clinicians need to consider many psychological theories and perspectives. Psychodynamic views might explain bereavement rituals. Cognitive approaches could appreciate the importance of intention in carrying out the law, whereas behaviorists could elucidate the drive toward sin and its repetition. Humanistic and existential therapies might assist more generally in questions of life, death, and suffering (Spero, 1980). Psychotherapy itself might be viewed as a form of confession or atonement necessary for spiritual growth (Spero, 1977). In this view, the release of repressed thoughts and feelings permit resolution of guilt while allowing for behavior modification.

According to Spero, the therapist's orientation to the world is also critical. He or she must subscribe to *halakhically* approved therapeutic theories and procedures. Furthermore, the clinician needs to be educated in the distinctive historical personal experiences of the orthodox Jew. A culturally knowledgeable therapist could assist an orthodox person to actually become "more Jewish," that is, to discern neurotic uses of religion while helping promote properly motivated behavior, creative growth, and insight. "Perhaps it is only the unconsciously troubled or guilty religionists," he mused, "who need fear psychotherapists possibly uncovering their defensive psychic infrastructure" (Spero, 1976, p. 19). In Spero's view, true healing and growth bring about *tikkun*, or reparation, between self and world. Persons move beyond self-realization toward "restoration of freedom to be holy, to become sanctified, to sacrifice." Without such a model, "the goals of 'self-knowledge' and 'insight' have often proven to be insufficient," Spero believed, and at times have even promoted self-deception (Spero, 1980, p. 25).

## ❖ CHARACTERISTICS OF HEALING SERVICES

Despite great respect for modern medicine, Jews have thus begun to find solace in healing services, which humanize the often-alienating and isolating experience of physical or psychological illness (Cohen, 1995; Holmes, 1995). Healing rituals employ meditation, instrumental music, song, prayer, reflection upon Jewish texts, and guided imagery to help attendees "develop strength; courage; a positive, non-sick identity; a sense of meaning; and a sense of belonging" ("Americans support modern science," n.d.).

Jewish healing services are best known for their small, communal, nonhierarchical, and holistic styles. They may be sponsored by synagogues, healing centers, or, increasingly, by social service agencies dealing with ill or elderly clients.

The healer-practitioner is often a woman who, in egalitarian fashion, "describes herself as part of the fellowship of those in need of healing" (Sered, 2002). This serves as a great contrast to premodern Jewish healing services, in which a revered holy man, believed to be imbued with special healing powers, blessed all those in need.

The Jewish healing movement has also provided solace to secular Jews and to Jews estranged from institutional synagogue life. During periods of great personal or family distress, some Jews nevertheless yearn for a Jewish communal connection, although they may be reluctant to visit a rabbi or a synagogue service. Informal alternatives such as healing circles often impart a needed sense of communal structure and identity, "the feeling of belonging both to an ancient tradition and to an active local community" (Sered, 2002).

The Jewish healing movement makes an important distinction between curing and healing. Healing practices are viewed as complementary to modern medical intervention. The goal of a healing service, writes Rabbi Richard Hirsh, is to "respond to the need of healing body and/or soul in a sensitive and meaningful way" while resisting "faith healing with promises of miraculous cure or recovery, especially when mediated through the personality of a charismatic spiritualist." Healing, Hirsh wrote, should not to be equated with cure, but at the same time signifies more than simply a caring presence. Healing transcends illness, whether of body or spirit, "through the affirmative response to the blessing of life . . . the worked-for and worked-through path from despair to affirmation, and from denial to acceptance" (Hirsh, 1999).

## ❖ JEWISH HEALING AND MODERN PSYCHOTHERAPY: CONCLUDING THOUGHTS

We have explored here the recent interest in reinvigorating ancient Jewish healing traditions as well as in creating new rituals to address physical, spiritual, and psychological affliction. Jews continue, however, to greatly respect modern medicine and psychology. Many reconcile this potential paradox by distinguishing curing from healing, where healing complements, rather than challenges, modern medical intervention. Yet the Jewish healing movement acknowledges the increasing impersonality of modern health care settings and the ensuing social isolation of many patients. Healing services—informal, communal, and egalitarian—often furnish holistic and communal correctives to this impersonality via meditation, healing touch, or guided imagery. For those yearning for a Jewish community in periods of crisis, healing circles also provide a needed sense of community and identity, leading to rich connections between mind, body, and spirit (Chicago Jewish Community Online, n.d.).

With some exceptions, however, we find modern counselors or psychotherapists reluctant to acknowledge these recent healing trends, whether Jewish, gentile, or New Age. Such hesitancy generally concerns professional reputation and the desire to avoid potential quackery. Rigorous training in scientific or social scientific disciplines, moreover, prevents many psychiatrists, psychologists, social workers, and counselors from engaging in techniques that cannot be verified by empirical means or measurable outcomes. Some mental health practitioners, used to one-on-one psychotherapy, may also find themselves uneasy with the communal focus of healing services, because Jewish healing presupposes that one cannot heal in isolation from the community.

Practitioners who have best integrated traditional healing with modern psychotherapy have not been the psychotherapists, but the rabbis. Whether traditional or liberal, many rabbis in the 20th century integrated the wisdom of ancient Jewish traditions concerning human nature with the modern, scientific claims of psychology. In fact, rabbis often embraced psychology, which lent a new respectability to their attempts at "soul healing" and pastoral counseling. Although this generation may never witness full integration of traditional healing practices with modern psychotherapeutic techniques, it is likely that we shall observe more in-depth conversations between the two endeavors over time. This in turn will lead to more humanizing connections between mind, body, and spirit, thus further enabling those in need to partake of our best efforts at both healing and curing.

## ❖ NOTES

1. References here cite the chapters and verses within particular books in the Hebrew Scriptures (also known as the Old Testament). References are to the edition of Berlin and Brettler (2004).

2. References in this section refer to various rabbinical writings, including the Mishnah (the codification of the oral law) and various commentaries upon it, which combine to form the Talmud. For more information on these sources, see Steinsaltz (1976).

## ❖ REFERENCES

Abusch, I. T. (1985). Physicians. In P. J. Achtemier (Ed.), *Harper's Bible dictionary* (p. 796). New York: Harper & Row.

*Americans support modern science, but "healing" makes a return.* (n.d.). Retrieved December 12, 2003, from http://www.myjewishlearning.com

Berger, P. (1965). Towards a sociological understanding of psychoanalysis. *Social Research, 32,* 26–41.

Berlin, A., & Brettler, M. Z. (Eds.). (2004). *Jewish study Bible.* New York: Oxford.

Central Conference of American Rabbis. (1970). *Yearbook.* New York: Author.

Central Conference of American Rabbis. (1976). *Yearbook.* New York: Author.

Chavel, C. B. (Ed. & Trans.). (1978). *The writings of Nachmanides* (Vol. 2). New York: Shilo.

Chicago Jewish Community Online. (n.d). *Jewish Healing Network of Chicago.* Retrieved November 17, 2003, from http://www.juf.org/services_resources/directory.asp?id=0038

Cohen, D. N. (1995). Jewish spiritual healing moves into the mainstream. *Jewish Bulletin of Northern California.* Retrieved November 11, 2003, from http://www.jewishsf.com/bk951117/usheal.htm

Crossan, J. D. (1991). *The historical Jesus.* San Francisco: Harper Collins.

Diller, J. V. (2004). *Cultural diversity: A primer for the human services* (2nd ed.). Toronto, Ontario, Canada: Brooks/Cole.

Dorff, E. N. (1986). The Jewish tradition. In R. L. Numbers & D. W. Amundsen (Eds.), *Caring and curing: Health and medicine in the Western religious traditions* (pp. 5–39). New York: Macmillan.

Durkheim, E. (1997). *Suicide: A study in sociology* (J. Spaulding & G. Simpson, Trans.). Glencoe, IL: Free Press. (Original work published 1891)

Feldman, D. M. (1986). *Health and medicine in the Jewish tradition.* New York: Crossroad.

Gilbreath, S., & Hoenig, M. (1967). Rabbis and pastoral counseling. *Review of Religious Research, 5,* 28–33.

Hertz, J. (Ed.). (1948). *Authorized daily prayer book.* New York: Bloch.

Hirsh, R. (1999). Reflections on "healing" in contemporary liberal Judaism. *Reconstructionist, 63*(2). Retrieved December 28, 2004, from http://www.rrc.edu/journal/recon63_2/hirsh.htm

Holmes, K. (1995, June 19). Jewish healing services embrace old and new. *Philadelphia Inquirer,* pp. B01, B02.

Jacobs, S. L. (1977). The rabbi as counselor: Reflections of a neophyte. *CCAR Journal,* 70–72.

Kanter, I. (1976). Social psychiatry and the Holocaust. *Journal of Psychiatry and Judaism, 1*(1), 55–66.

Kaufmann, Y. (1960). *The religion of Israel* (M. Greenberg, Trans.). New York: Schocken.

Kellermann, P. F. N. (Ed.). (n.d.). *Resources for children of holocaust survivors: Psychological/psychiatric studies.* Retrieved November 17, 2003, from http://www.judymeschel.com/coshpsych.htm

Klagsbrun, S. C. (Ed.). (1989). *Preventive psychiatry.* Philadelphia: Charles.

Klausner, S. Z. (1964). The religio-psychiatric movement. *Review of Religious Research, 5,* 63–74.

Klein, D. (1985). *Jewish origins of the psychoanalytic movement.* Chicago: University of Chicago Press.

Kushner, H. (1981). *When bad things happen to good people.* New York: Schocken.

Linke, S. (1999). *Psychological perspectives on traditional Jewish practices.* Northvale, NJ: J. Aronson.

Maimonides, M. (1949). *Mishneh Torah* (Yale Judaica Series). New Haven, CT: Yale University Press.

Marcus, J. R. (1947). *Communal sick-care in the German ghetto.* Cincinnati, OH: Hebrew Union College Press.

Medicine in Israel. (1978). In M. S. Miller & J. L. Miller (Eds.), *Harper's encyclopedia of Bible life* (p. 69). New York: Harper & Row.

Meier, L. (Ed.). (1988). *Jewish values in psychotherapy.* New York: University Press of America.

Mendes-Flohr, P. (1991). *Divided passions: Jewish intellectuals and the experience of modernity.* Detroit, MI: Wayne State University Press.

Olitzky, K. M. (1993). *100 blessings every day.* Woodstock, VT: Jewish Lights.

Ostow, M. (1969). Pastoral psychiatry. *Conservative Judaism, 23,* 4–7.

Praglin, L. J. (1998). *The rabbinate after Freud: American rabbinical responses to psychological thought and practice, 1912–1980.* Unpublished doctoral dissertation, University of Chicago.

Praglin, L. J. (1999). The Jewish healing tradition in historic perspective. *Reconstructionist, 63*(2). Retrieved December 28, 2004, from http://www.rrc.edu/journal/recon63_2/praglin.htm

Rachlis, A. (1974). The Musar movement and psychotherapy. *Judaism, 23,* 337–345.

Rieff, P. (1966). *The triumph of the therapeutic: Uses of faith after Freud.* New York: Harper.

Rosner, F. (1977). *Medicine in the Bible and the Talmud.* New York: Ktav.

Schachter, Z. (1968). *The encounter: A study of counseling in Hasidism.* Unpublished doctoral dissertation, Hebrew Union College, Cincinnati, OH.

Schimmel, S. (1997). *The seven deadly sins: Jewish, Christian, and classical reflections on human psychology.* New York: Oxford.

Scholem, G. (1973). *Shabbatai Zevi: Mystical messiah* (Z. Werblowsky, Trans.). Princeton, NJ: Princeton University Press.

Schulweis, H. (1973). Restructuring the synagogue. *Conservative Judaism, 4,* 19–23.

Schulweis, H. (1983). *Evil and the morality of God.* Cincinnati, OH: Hebrew Union College Press.

Sered, S. S. (2002). Healing and religion: A Jewish perspective. *Yale Journal for Humanities in Medicine.* Retrieved October 30, 2003, from http://info.med.yale.edu/intmed/hummed/yjhm/spirit/healing/ssered.htm

Spero, M. H. (1976). On the relationship between psychotherapy and Judaism. *Journal of Psychology and Judaism, 1*(1), 15–33.

Spero, M. H. (1977). Anxiety and religious growth. *Journal of Religion and Health, 16,* 52–57.

Spero, M. H. (1980). *Judaism and psychology: Halakhic perspectives.* New York: KTAV.

Spero, M. H. (1992). *Religious objects as psychological structures.* Chicago: University of Chicago Press.

Steinsaltz, A. (1976). *The essential Talmud.* New York: Basic Books.

Twerski, A. J. (1993). *I am I: A Jewish perspective from the case files of an eminent psychiatrist.* Brooklyn, NY: Shaar.

Twerski, A. J. (1997). *Do unto others.* Kansas City, MO: Andrews McMeel.

Ury, Z. (1970). *The Musar movement.* New York: Yeshiva University Press.

# 16

# Buddhist Moments in Psychotherapy

*Roshni Daya*

Much is written about the need to understand the diverse cultural and ethnic backgrounds of the many individuals encountered in day-to-day life and counseling practice. Equally important is the common thread of suffering experienced by all humans regardless of individuals' diverse backgrounds. Suffering is one's discomfort or pain experienced as physical, emotional, and psychic. The pain most relevant to psychology and counseling practice is emotional or psychic, that which embodies the struggles of the human spirit.

For decades, European and North American philosophies have created systems of healing designed to understand and alleviate the shared experience of human suffering. It has not been until the last 50 years that the ancient Buddhist system of alleviating suffering has been rediscovered and integrated into the Western world. Buddhism was established as a unique and separate religious system when Siddhartha Gautama, prince of the Sakya clan in India, sat under the bodhi tree to resolve his human situation of suffering. That Buddhism became established as a religious system is ironic, because Buddha never claimed to be a prophet or god. He emphasized that his teachings are a theory that should be analyzed and explored, not blindly accepted (Michalon, 2001). Buddhism, like other theories of psychology, is the codification of one person's insights about psychology developed in the course of that person's self-investigations (Rubin, 1996).

Recent literature has done a great deal to introduce Buddhist philosophy into Western thought generally and into European and North American traditions of psychology more specifically (Epstein, 1995; Molino, 1998; Rubin, 1996; Suler, 1993). Such dialogue between East and West has been primarily philosophical, comparing abstract ideas between psychoanalysis and Buddhist psychology. The literature linking Buddhist meditative techniques to psychotherapeutic practice has proven more practically helpful than the abstract discussions. Aside from suggestions on implementing meditation, clinicians are often left wondering what the integration of East and West means at a practical level.

This chapter will provide a summary of the theory of Buddhist psychology, an understanding of the Buddhist explanation of self, followed by a discussion of the application of Buddhist principles to psychotherapy. Finally, specific ideas for the integration of the Buddhist principles to therapeutic work will be explored.

## ❖ BUDDHIST PSYCHOLOGY

### The Four Noble Truths

The central principles of Buddhist psychology lie in the four Noble Truths. The symptoms, diagnosis, prognosis, and treatment plan for human suffering are addressed in these Noble Truths (Ramaswami & Sheikh, 1989).

*The First Noble Truth*

The first principle is that life consists of *dukkha,* or suffering. Buddha was speaking of the basic human condition and of the dissatisfactions present in human existence. Suffering has a shared human process, though the source of the suffering may be specific to each individual. The individuals' own likes cause suffering by creating the experience of *craving*—desiring that which one cannot have. Craving creates a struggle within the individual as he or she experiences a sense of both longing and disappointment. Being stuck with what one does not want is also a source of suffering through the experience of *aversion.* At the source of suffering is *delusion,* which obscures the mind from ascertaining reality as it is.

*The Second Noble Truth*

The cause of suffering and dissatisfaction is addressed by the second principle, the doctrine of dependent origination. Generally, an individual divides an experience into small pieces and interprets those pieces as evidence supporting or denying the presence of a concept. The evidence becomes circular in that an implicit decision has been made that the concept has its own existence before a true discussion of it occurs. Simply put, each phenomenon depends upon another to exist, and nothing can exist in isolation (Bowman & Baylen, 1994).

The core of the second principle is that suffering is caused by the individual's belief in a persistent, unchanging self. Just as other concepts or constructs in the world do not hold a permanent identity, the individual, too, is impermanent. Dis-ease arises when the individual clings to ideas, things, people, and the idea of a single constant self as permanent (Rubin, 1996). At a personal level, giving attributes to the self reifies the existence of a stable, unchanging self.

## The Third Noble Truth

The third Noble Truth is that release from the second type of suffering and serenity in the face of the first type is a real possibility (Claxton, 1986). It is seeing things as they really are or seeing "reality as it is" that releases one from dis-ease (Kawamura, 1990). Seeing "reality as it is" requires that the person see the divisions or boundaries placed around people, things, and ideas as being just that: placed there, versus belonging to those people, things, and ideas. What is important about the process of deconstructing boundaries is that in truly doing so, the individual neither judges, evaluates, nor concretizes the perceptual process or the object of perception as holding a particular existence (Kawamura, 1990).

## The Fourth Noble Truth

The fourth Noble Truth is the path through which one can alleviate pervasive feelings of dissatisfaction, or dis-ease. This essentially occurs by giving up one's clinging to ideas and concepts as realities of experience. According to Buddha, it requires the alignment of eight specific factors: understanding, thought, speech, action, livelihood, effort, mindfulness, and concentration (Epstein, 1995). These factors comprise the eightfold path to enlightenment. Much like the idea of self-actualization discussed by some Western schools of psychology, the process of enlightenment is the developing of one's potentials.

At the root of the eightfold path is mindfulness. *Mindfulness* is awareness without judgment, attachment, or aversion to what is happening in the present moment (Rubin, 1996). It is necessary to become mindful and aware in the moment when one hears a sound, sees an image, or interacts in any way with an object. By remaining mindful, one interacts with the object by seeing, touching, hearing it as it is and not with added judgments toward the object (e.g., a *nice* sound, an *awful* sound, a *pretty* dress). When objects are encountered and experienced as they are, the mind remains calm (Goleman, 2003).

The development of mindfulness is to happen in four areas: (a) bodily phenomena, such as physical sensations; (b) feelings, which are not emotions but rather reactions to things, which we classify as "pleasant," "unpleasant," or "neutral"; (c) mental phenomena; and (d) observations of whether the mental state is wholesome or unwholesome (Khema, 1987; Rubin, 1993). The development of mindfulness requires the individual to fully experience the present and to begin to be free of illusions. It is clear and single-minded awareness of what actually happens to and in the individual at successive moments of perception. It requires the individual to attend without selection or judgment to the experience of whatever mental or physical phenomenon (e.g., thoughts, feelings, sensations, or fantasies) is predominant in his or her field of awareness (Rubin, 1996). Central to the practice of mindfulness is an understanding of the Buddhist view of self.

## ❖ BUDDHIST VIEW OF THE SELF

One of the most profound differences between Western and Buddhist psychologies has been in the treatment of the concept of self (Michalon, 2001). In the West, the self is perceived as an enduring entity, and a strong sense of self is seen as a key to success. On the contrary, Buddhist theory states that a separate, permanent, and distinct self does not exist. It is the illusion of a sense of self that gives rise to suffering (Parry & Jones, 1986).

Buddhist psychology asserts that mental states are only thoughts, emotions, memories, sensations, and perceptions (Ramaswami & Sheikh, 1989). There is no self or "I" behind them, and without them there is no sense of self or sense of "I." The relationship between mental states and the sense of self is where the illusion begins. The self regards mental states as objects that belong to it, thereby giving rise to the sense of a permanent and stable sense of self, with only the mental states being considered transient (Ramaswami & Sheikh). Once the illusion of self is created, the individual begins to identify with this illusion. The basic difficulty is that insofar as the self feels separate, or autonomous, it also feels uncomfortable, because of the insecurity of an illusory separateness (Epstein, 1989). Ironically, the sense of self becomes preoccupied with trying to make itself self-existing. It follows that if the ego is a construct leading to suffering, it should be deconstructed and replaced with the notion of "no self" (Michalon, 2001). It is through the development of mindfulness that the individual experiences the transient nature of self, understands the interconnectedness of life experiences, and deconstructs the ego (Claxton, 1987). Mindfulness training assists the individual in developing awareness of the hindrances (hatred, attachment, ignorance, pride, and jealousy) that prevent the mind from experiencing reality as it is (Goleman, 2003; Kawamura, 1990).

## ❖ APPLICATION TO PSYCHOTHERAPY

The goal of theories of psychology is to explain how the human mind functions. Theories are most helpful to clinicians when abstract ways of understanding people are brought to a concrete and practical level. Thus, it is important for each theory of psychotherapy to discuss applications to the practice of psychotherapy.

### Buddhism and Meditation

Meditation is the careful, detailed, and nonjudgmental observation of proximate dimensions of consciousness (Rubin, 1985, 1993). The purpose of meditation is the acquisition of self-knowledge, which can be accomplished only by direct self-study of the mind (Suzuki, 1960). Meditation yields self-knowledge by focusing one's attention on the immediacy of experience. The meditator is instructed to notice whatever is experienced at each moment.

Through the process of noticing, the meditator begins to develop the awareness that the mind is not still but is rather in a constant state of activity. Until the individual stops to observe the mind, there is a lack of awareness of its incessant activity. Many psychologists have provided examples of successfully using meditation practices with clients (Epstein, 1995; Odajnyk, 1998; Sweet & Johnson, 1990; West, 1987).

Although meditation is central to Buddhist practices, meditative approaches do not fit every therapist or every client (Deikman, 1982; Kelly, 1996). In addition to meditation, the process focus of Buddhist psychology holds promise for its contribution to psychotherapy.

## ❖ PROCESS FOCUS OF BUDDHIST PSYCHOLOGY

Buddhist psychology is essentially a philosophy emphasizing impermanence, transience, or *process*. Just as the concept of self is central to Buddhist psychology, so is the impermanent, transient nature of the self. Because the self is constantly changing, Buddhism emphasizes not the structure of the self but that the self is constantly in process. From a therapeutic perspective, emphasis on process allows one to move away from content and toward understanding and wielding the process of changing oneself. The Buddhist discussion of process may be one of its most useful contributions to therapeutic systems. An extensive review of the literature on Buddhist psychology has led to the identification and naming of six core *process* principles of Buddhist psychology (discussed in the following sections) that may be applied in psychotherapy (Daya, 2000, 2001). It may be helpful to think of the Buddhist principles of change in terms of universal and distinct principles of change. Universal principles of change are those principles that are present across different theoretical orientations within psychotherapy. Distinct principles of change are those change processes that are specific to Buddhist psychology. Both are helpful when applied appropriately.

## Flexibility of Self

Western psychologies emphasize the need for a strong sense of self, whereas Buddhist psychology emphasizes the goal of attaining "no self." The two approaches may be integrated and their complementarity perceived by recognizing that there are stages in the development of the self (Michalon, 2001). It may be that Western traditions have mapped out the early stages of the development of self, and Buddhism has identified later stages. The notion of having a flexible sense of self assists one in moving into a later stage of development. From a therapeutic perspective, the concept of flexibility of self allows the therapist to conceptualize the client as other than the way that he or she presents. The therapist can assist the client in becoming aware of the client's rigid notions of self and the expression thereof. Such awareness assists the client in noticing his or her role in the creation of self-suffering. The therapist can then facilitate the client in loosening his or her grasp on qualities and characteristics. One's qualities are encouraged to be held loosely, as if resting on an open palm instead of squeezed in a tight fist. This loosening is a freeing experience, because it enables the client to begin to experience him- or herself as in process and with unlimited potentials.

The idea of flexibility of self may be a unique change process that is not found in Western therapeutic systems.

## Openness in the Present Moment

Very often we spend our time outside of the present moment with strong attachment to thoughts of the past or future. Thoughts about the past are often regrets or memories of positive times for which we long. By focusing on the past, one creates aversion (for regrets) or craving (for positive memories) and thereby fills his or her present with suffering. Thoughts about the future are often worries or hopes and desires, again creating aversion and craving and thereby suffering.

The present moment, free from association with the past or future, holds only potential. It is a matter of opening oneself to it. Buddhist philosophy emphasizes opening oneself to all aspects of one's experience, both internal and external. Openness in the present moment is comprised of two components: noninterfering openness and being in the present.

The role of the therapist is to facilitate the client to open to the immediate experience of the present moment without putting boundaries between the acceptable and unacceptable parts of the experience. The therapist can do this by bringing the client back to the here and now. In assisting the client to develop such openness within the context of the session, the client experientially learns the skills to remain present and open outside of the therapeutic encounter.

Openness in the present moment is similar to person-centered, gestalt, and existential-humanistic ideas of moment-by-moment living, here-and-now experiencing, and presence. All four perspectives emphasize the importance of being aware and participating as fully as one can in the moment.

### Experiencing Without Evaluation

People have developed the habit of continuously evaluating things as good, bad, and neutral. This is done in regard to emotions, body sensations, interpersonal interactions, events, and all other incidents in life. Such evaluation often occurs at a habitual level. By continually evaluating experiences, the individual creates attachment and aversion. The creation of such tendencies is the foundation of suffering, as noted in the first Noble Truth. Often the individual engages in intellectualizing as part of the process of evaluation. According to the principles of Buddhist psychology, movement away from intellectualizing is very important, because by focusing on an intellectual understanding, one distances him- or herself from experience.

Therapeutically, the goal is to move the client away from intellectualizing, because this process is considered to be a defense that serves to distance oneself from the experience. Clients will often ask the question "why?" According to Buddhist psychology, it is not necessary to ask oneself why something has occurred but rather to accept the experience without judgment and evaluation. Experiencing in this context encompasses thoughts, emotions, senses, and physiology. The therapist encourages the client to stay present with his or her experience at the level at which it occurs without judging or evaluating it. This kind of approach to life events is quite foreign to Western ways of interacting with one's life experiences, making it a unique change process.

### Compassion

This is a state of being that is nonviolent, nonharming, and nonaggressive. Compassion can be likened to the acceptance, warmth, and tenderness a mother would feel toward her newborn child. Compassion, associated with warmth, acceptance, humility, tenderness, and kindness, is a way of "suffering-with," thereby closing the distance between self and other. Compassion can be firm and confrontational at times, but it maintains the quality of joining with the other.

It is not to be confused with pity or sympathy, which serves to amplify space and distance between the giver and receiver.

Therapeutically, compassion has a role at two levels. The therapist is to treat the client with compassion, and the therapist is to facilitate the development of compassion within the client in terms of the way the client deals with him- or herself. This is particularly important for clients who have the tendency to be very negative and self-derogatory. Compassion can be considered as a way to counter such delusion and allow the client to develop a clearer mind to see self and others as they are without the element of judgment that is so often involved. The development of compassion within the individual will allow him or her to achieve and maintain a more clear and peaceful relationship with self and others. The therapist serves as an important model to the client in the way the therapist interacts with the client through compassion.

Compassion has some components that are similar to Rogers's (1980) "unconditional positive regard," as espoused by person-centered psychotherapies. Unconditional positive regard has also been called "acceptance," "respect," "liking," or "prizing." Like unconditional positive regard, compassion may sometimes be firm and confrontational. Compassion involves unconditional acceptance, espoused by Rogers as being intrinsically therapeutic. He wrote, "To be with another in this way means that for the time being, you lay aside your own views and values in order to enter another's world without prejudice. In some sense it means to lay aside your self" (Rogers, p. 143).

### Interconnectedness

Buddhist psychology places emphasis on the interconnectedness of all things. Individuals do not live in isolation from one another, nor do the components of one's life exist in isolation from one another. According to Buddhist psychology, developing an understanding and appreciation for the connectedness of all living beings is both humbling and empowering. It is a necessary component of individual growth and development to realize that all individuals are connected and that the treatment of oneself affects all other beings because of the kind tendencies that one is developing. It is necessary to accept that all components of one's life are interconnected in order to give each component the respect that is necessary.

Therapeutically, the client is encouraged to experience and examine his or her life as a whole and make changes at all levels. The therapeutic forum may expand as the therapist moves away from a problem-oriented, solution-focused paradigm. The therapist is encouraged to assist the client in gaining awareness of the common themes and connections between different components of the client's life as well as between self and other. It seems logical that such an intervention would facilitate the client's becoming aware of the possibility of change. Through the process of examining the relationships between people, things, events, and other components of life, clients may become aware of their own role in change or become aware of something that had gone unnoticed earlier. Interconnectedness is a unique change mechanism.

### Sitting With Suffering

Suffering is considered to be all uncomfortable feelings and states, ranging from emotional pain such as anger, fear, anxiety, and sadness to any kind of physical pain (Trungpa, 1973). From the Buddhist perspective, working through a problem means remaining present with one's suffering without trying to flee from it. Through being present with one's suffering, the individual grows and gains peace as he or she experientially learns that pain, too, is transient. The common practice of avoiding uncomfortable feelings and mental states through problem solving, thought stopping, intellectualizing, and so on serves only to distance the person from the present.

The therapist is encouraged to assist the client in sitting with and remaining present to the experience of suffering. The therapist is discouraged from quickly moving the client out of the discomfort. The goal is the realization that suffering is simply a component of existence, not something bad that must be changed immediately. It is necessary that the therapist be able to demonstrate comfort with the client's suffering by remaining present with it.

The last Buddhist principle, sitting with suffering, is very different from most Western perspectives of psychotherapy. An examination of most major Western theories of psychotherapy found that none spoke of the idea of sitting with one's suffering. Gurman and Messer (1995) edited a text on the various theories of psychotherapy. The expert authors were required to include a section entitled "curative factors or mechanism of change." Traditional psychoanalysis relayed insight and the relationship as the mechanisms of change (Wolitzky, 1995). Person-centered approaches emphasized the therapist's expertise with process, creativity, and relationship (Bohart, 1995). Behavior therapists emphasized operant conditioning and verbal control (Hayes, W. C. Follette, & V. M. Follette, 1995). Cognitive therapy focused on correcting cognitive distortions and their underlying schemata (Freeman & Reinecke, 1995). Existential-humanistic psychotherapy emphasized being in the present and changes in perception through insight (Bugenthal & Sterling, 1995). Finally, gestalt therapy focused on contact, being in the present, and the therapist-client relationship (Yontef, 1995). Sitting with suffering appears to be more foreign than unhelpful.

## ❖ CONCLUSION

Buddhism is a deep psychological tradition that has roots in India. The foundation of this theory can be found in the four Noble Truths, which capture the suffering of the human condition. The four Noble Truths are concerned with how the individual causes his or her own suffering through creation and identification with illusion, and the way to begin to dissolve such illusions. The basic tenets of Buddhist psychology have been outlined with a discussion of the Buddhist view of self, health, emotions, and wellness. The philosophy has been concretized with the six Buddhist principles of change so that the practitioner can understand how the theory may be applied in psychotherapeutic work. Finally, the six principles of change—identified as flexibility of self, compassion, openness in the present moment, experiencing without evaluation, interconnectedness, and sitting with suffering—have been discussed as universal and distinct change processes.

## ❖ REFERENCES

Bohart, A. C. (1995). The person-centered psychotherapies. In A. S. Gurman & S. B. Messer (Eds.), *Essential psychotherapies: Theory and practice* (pp. 85–127). New York: Guilford Press.

Bowman, R. L., & Baylen, D. (1994). Buddhism and second-order change. *International Journal for the Advancement of Counselling, 17,* 101–108.

Bugenthal, J. F. T., & Sterling, M. M. (1995). Existential–humanistic psychotherapy: New perspectives. In A. S. Gurman & S. B. Messer (Eds.), *Essential psychotherapies: Theory and practice* (pp. 226–260). New York: Guilford Press.

Claxton, G. (1986). The light's on but there's nobody home: The psychology of no self. In G. Claxton (Ed.), *Beyond therapy: The impact of Eastern religions on psychological theory and practices* (pp. 49–70). London: Wisdom.

Claxton, G. (1987). Meditation in Buddhist psychology. In M. A. West (Ed.), *The psychology of meditation* (pp. 23–38). New York: Oxford University Press.

Daya, R. (2000). Buddhist psychology, a theory of change processes: Implications for counsellor. *International Journal for the Advancement of Counselling, 22,* 257–271.

Daya, R. (2001). *Buddhist moments in psychotherapy.* Unpublished doctoral dissertation, University of Calgary, Calgary, Alberta, Canada.

Deikman, A. (1982). *The observing self: Mysticism and psychotherapy.* Boston: Beacon Press.

Epstein, M. (1989). Forms of emptiness: Psychodynamic, meditative, and clinical perspectives. *Journal of Transpersonal Psychology, 21,* 61–71.

Epstein, M. (1995). *Thoughts without a thinker.* New York: Harper Collins.

Freeman, A., & Reinecke, M. A. (1995). Cognitive therapy. In A. S. Gurman & S. B. Messer (Eds.), *Essential psychotherapies: Theory and practice* (pp. 182–225). New York: Guilford Press.

Goleman, D. (2003). *Destructive emotions: How can we overcome them?* New York: Bantam Dell.

Gurman, A. S., & Messer, S. B. (Eds.). (1995). *Essential psychotherapies: Theory and practice.* New York: Guilford Press.

Hayes, S. C., Follette, W. C., & Follette, V. M. (1995). Behavior therapy: A contextual approach. In A. S. Gurman & S. B. Messer (Eds.), *Essential psychotherapies: Theory and practice* (pp. 128–181). New York: Guilford Press.

Kawamura, L. S. (1990). Principles of Buddhism. *Zygon: Journal of Religion and Science, 25*(1), 59–72.

Kelly, G. F. (1996). Using meditative techniques in psychotherapy. *Journal of Humanistic Psychology, 36*(3), 49–66.

Khema, A. (1987). *Being nobody, going nowhere: Meditations on the Buddhist path.* London: Wisdom.

Michalon, M. (2001). "Selflessness" in the service of the ego: Contributions, limitations, and dangers of Buddhist psychology for Western psychotherapies. *American Journal of Psychotherapy, 55,* 202–219.

Molino, A. (Ed.). (1998). *The couch and the tree: Dialogues in psychoanalysis and Buddhism.* New York: North Point Press.

Odajnyk, V. W. (1998). Zen meditation as a way of individuation and healing. In A. Molino (Ed.), *The couch and the tree: Dialogues in psychoanalysis and Buddhism* (pp. 131–144). New York: North Point Press.

Parry, S. J., & Jones, R. G. A. (1986). Beyond illusion in the psychotherapeutic enterprise. In G. Claxton (Ed.), *Beyond therapy: The impact of Eastern religions on psychological theory and practice* (pp. 173–192). London: Wisdom.

Ramaswami, S., & Sheikh, A. A. (1989). Buddhist psychology: Implications for healing. In A. A. Sheikh & K. S. Sheikh (Eds.), *Eastern and Western approaches to healing: Ancient wisdom and modern knowledge* (pp. 91–123). New York: John Wiley & Sons.

Rogers, C. R. (1980). *A way of being.* Boston: Houghton Mifflin.

Rubin, J. B. (1985). Meditation and psychoanalytic listening. *Psychoanalytic Review, 72,* 599–613.

Rubin, J. B. (1993). Psychoanalysis and Buddhism: Toward an integration. In G. Stricker & J. Gold (Eds.), *Comprehensive handbook of psychotherapy integration* (pp. 249–266). New York: Plenum Press.

Rubin, J. B. (1996). *Psychotherapy and Buddhism: Toward an integration.* New York: Plenum Press.

Suler, J. R. (1993). *Contemporary psychoanalysis and Eastern thought.* New York: Plenum Press.

Suzuki, D. T. (1960). Lectures on Zen Buddhism. In D. T. Suzuki, E. Fromm, & D. Martino (Eds.), *Zen Buddhism and psychoanalysis* (pp. 1–76). New York: Harper & Row.

Sweet, M. J., & Johnson, C. G. (1990). Enhancing empathy: Interpersonal implications of a Buddhist meditation technique. *Psychotherapy, 27*(1), 19–29.

Trungpa, C. (1973). *Cutting through spiritual materialism.* Berkeley, CA: Shambala.

West, M. A. (Ed.). (1987). *The psychology of meditation.* Oxford, UK: Oxford University Press.

Wolitzky, D. L. (1995). The theory and practice of traditional psychoanalytic psychotherapy. In A. S. Gurman & S. B. Messer (Eds.), *Essential psychotherapies: Theory and practice* (pp. 12–54). New York: Guilford Press.

Yontef, G. M. (1995). Gestalt therapy. In A. S. Gurman & S. B. Messer (Eds.), *Essential psychotherapies: Theory and practice* (pp. 261–303). New York: Guilford Press.

# PART IV

## Traditional Healing and Its Contemporary Formulations

# 17

# The Sweat Lodge as Psychotherapy

*Congruence Between*
*Traditional and Modern Healing*

*David Paul Smith*

Traditional, religiomagical healing persists in the modern world even among the scientifically trained. Recent research in psychotherapy indicates that many psychotherapists draw on a wide range of belief systems, both scientific and religious, in their work. (Bilgrave & Deluty, 2003; Smith, 2003; Smith & Orlinsky, 2003). This chapter discusses a healing method that has been in use for thousands of years, the sweat lodge or steam bath, and presents an ethnography of an Ojibwa sweat lodge ceremony. The sweat lodge and many traditional systems of healing share much in common with modern psychotherapy (J. D. Frank & J. B. Frank, 1991). The sweat lodge can heal by creating meaning for groups and individuals. Ritual narrative is fundamental to the construction of cultural identity and to social cohesion. Therefore, it may build culturally congruent meaning in ways that modern psychotherapy does not (E. Duran & B. Duran, 1995; Gone, 2000). The sweat lodge is already used in medical settings and modern therapeutic contexts, such as counseling centers, hospitals, and prisons (Harrison, 2000; Norrell, 2005; Okiciyapi Wellness Center, 2003).

Considering the prevalence of its use, it is surprising that relatively little research has been done on the use and effectiveness of this ancient therapeutic technique. This chapter focuses on the Native American sweat lodge and attempts to elucidate the practice in terms of modern psychotherapeutic theory. Understanding the sweat lodge in modern psychological terms can help clarify its fit and function in the context of medical settings and psychotherapeutic practice.

## ❖ HISTORY OF THE SWEAT LODGE

The practice of the sweat lodge or sweat bath dates back to prehistoric times and can be found in many guises in a multitude of cultures around the world. It is common to Scythians, Slavs, and Finns. Herodotus wrote of the sweat bath as early as 425 BC (Krickeberg, 1939). Furthermore, the sweat lodge or steam bath is one of the most widespread healing rites in the indigenous cultures of North and South America (Driver, 1970; Lopatin, 1960). Ethnohistorical accounts of the sweat lodge in North America date back to the 17th century and were described in the accounts of fur traders and missionaries.

The sweat lodge was seen as a cure to many illnesses, from constipation to nervous disorder or paralysis. Also, among Native people it was one of the most important forms of ritual purification. It was conducted before religious ceremonies, hunts, and war parties and trips and was used to treat the sick (Bruchac, 1993; Bucko, 1998; Grim, 1983; Krickeberg, 1939).

The Ojibwa used the sweat lodge for a variety of purposes. The process of purification was called for in many circumstances, and the sweat lodge was used frequently. For example, Vecsey (1983) writes that the Ojibwas used the sweat bath (a low lodge in which a person bathed in steam created by pouring cold water over hot stones) in all important ceremonies and undertakings. The bath purified and strengthened a human before entering into contact with the *manitos* (spirits), before consulting a healer, before an important decision, or simply by itself as a curing rite (Vecsey, 1983).

Today, the sweat lodge continues as a common practice among Native American communities and elsewhere. During the late 1960s, the sweat lodge became an important spiritual practice to promote political awareness (Bruchac, 1993). Presently, more than half of U.S. Indian Health Service facilities use the sweat lodge as a complement to their other forms of treatment. It is a common practice for individuals or groups to prepare for counseling or medical interventions (Cohen, 2003).

## ❖  THE PHILOSOPHY OF THE SWEAT LODGE

The purpose of the sweat lodge in the contemporary context, as it was explained by my informant, coincides with the traditional use of the sweat lodge. The sweat provides a context that facilitates spiritual and psychological balance. During the ceremony, a person reorients himself or herself to feel emotionally grounded in a greater source of meaning. My informant described it as "a way of getting people in touch with something greater than their selves."

The sweat lodge is seen as an opportunity for spiritual and physical healing. Generally, among Native American cultures throughout North and South America, fire and water or a combination of both are used for purification. Furthermore, an element of sacrifice is incorporated into the ceremony. There is a giving up of the old and a birth of the new. Individuals can "bath[e] in the breath of the Great Spirit and they are reborn" (Cohen, 2003, p. 255).

During the sweat lodge, the leader is sensitive toward a wide framework of environmental factors that impinge upon the healing process. The leader is sensitive to his or her own subjective experience, which is affected by interactions with the participants as well as the land, the weather, the lodge, and every aspect of the environment. E. Duran and B. Duran (1995) state that "the Native American worldview is one in which the individual is a part of all creation, living life as one system and not in separate units that are objectively relating with each other" (p. 15). This close alliance with nature and dependence on "all relations" (ancestors, friends and relatives, plants and animals) is distinct from much of Western science and psychology (Vogel, 1970).

## ❖  THE HEALERS

The person who directed this ritual is a medicine man named Don Beaucage. He performs traditional healing work and makes a living as a counselor with youth and adults. At times, he integrates traditional beliefs into his practice as a counselor and has used traditional rituals in his work. However, he typically does his traditional healing work with people who call on him for help outside the context of his paid profession (see Grim, 1983). At the same time, he feels that his traditional perspective offers an approach to healing that incorporates values beneficial to healing but not always part of modern therapy.

Don Beaucage was about 40 years of age at the time this sweat lodge was conducted. He is of Ojibwa (Anishinabe) descent, a member of the First Nation Nipissing Band. His grandmother and grandfather were well-known medicine people. Although his grandmother encouraged his training, he did not fully commit to this vocation until a fortuitous meeting with an important Elder, the medicine man Dan Pine.

During the course of his training, starting in his teenage years, Don studied Ojibwa medicine and religious practices with most of the prominent medicine people in Canada. During this time, he also completed a bachelor's degree at a Canadian university. He moved to the southwest part of the United States when he was in his mid-30s and worked as a counselor and therapist with children in psychiatric settings. He continues to work in the field of mental health in New Mexico.

Don's introduction to Ojibwa medicine and his training were congruent with historical patterns of legitimization in practice. Traditionally, Native people were chosen for indoctrination into the medicine path either because of family lineage or because of an aptitude with the spirits and with healing. Then, an established medicine man or woman would take them as an apprentice. A third option, among the Ojibwa, allowed a person to pay to join the *Midewiwin*.[1]

Today, the process is more complex. Because of the breakup of Native communities, the history of genocide, and forced relocation of families, the continuities of culture and religious teaching have been strained. There are few healers available, and the role has become disentangled from the fabric of the community. Many Native American healers work hard to keep their heritage and traditional beliefs alive. The importance of this effort was related to me on many occasions during the time I spent with Don.

Don's motivation to teach others is reflected in the following story, which was told to him by his teacher, Dan Pine:

> The Indian peoples had the teaching of the drum many years ago although other people in the world had lost this teaching. When the Europeans came to North America, knowledge among the Native people was lost and the teachings were hanging by a thread. We are in the time of the eighth fire. A few coals are left with which this fire will ignite and our children will be the builders of this fire. In this night the coals must be kept alive; this is important. The truth must be shared so the teachings will not be lost forever.

### ❖ METHODS OF HEALING

The basic components of the sweat lodge are similar throughout the world. For example, they include a small space, heated stones, no smoke hole, a method for generating steam by throwing water onto heated stones, and fragrant herbs. All sweat lodge rituals have both therapeutic and social characteristics (Lopatin, 1960).

Among the Ojibwa (Anishinabe) people, the sweat was often customary before a meeting of the *Midewiwin*. Heated stones, a basin of water, and grass are used. The lodge consists of a framework of bent poles closely covered with blankets, and no air is allowed to enter (see Figure 17.1). Stones are heated in a large fire in front of the lodge and then brought in through the entrance. Then the entrance is closed. During the ceremony, water and grass are sprinkled on the hot stones. The ceremony involves drumming and chanting, songs and prayer. The participants pray for health and long life. The round is completed by opening the entrance (Densmore, 1979).

The following case study presents a description of the sweat lodge ritual that culminated after a week of preparation that involved building the lodge, collecting the rocks used in the ceremony, and preparing the participants. This ritual is presented in the form of a classic ethnography, or "thick description" (Geertz, 1974).

Ethnographic presentation is a common technique for describing and analyzing cultural practices, thus deriving meaningful interpretations. Participating in a ritual, taking careful notes, and interpreting the process is referred to as participant observation. It is an approach to understanding that is consistent with psychodynamic tradition. Harry Stack Sullivan described both therapy and ethnography as participant observation (Sullivan, 1964). This method offers an "experience near" description of the ritual, a useful approach for gaining insight into the meaning of the healing process (Lee & Martin, 1991).


## ❖ ETHNOGRAPHY (CASE STUDY)

*Prior to the ceremony, each participant was smudged as he or she came to the lodge. Sweetgrass was lit from a burning coal shoveled from the fire, and the smoke was waved over each person for purification. It was very difficult to get too close to the central conflagration because the heat was more than formidable. Later, all the people participating were smudged, that is, bathed in smoke from braided sweetgrass with prayer for the purpose of purification. The tools used in the ceremony, such as shovels, pitchfork, shakers, bucket and ladle, were also smudged. These were set next to the entrance of the lodge (see Figure 17.2).*

*Don smudged the lodge and hung an eagle feather from the center of the dome over the central pit where the rocks would be set. Wood stacked for the fire sat away from the lodge and fire pit, just to the south. The fire that heated the rocks burned for over an hour before the ceremony. The atmosphere that was building in the group was grave and sober. There was no room for frivolity or small talk.*

**Figure 17.1**    Diagram of the Sweat Lodge—Representation

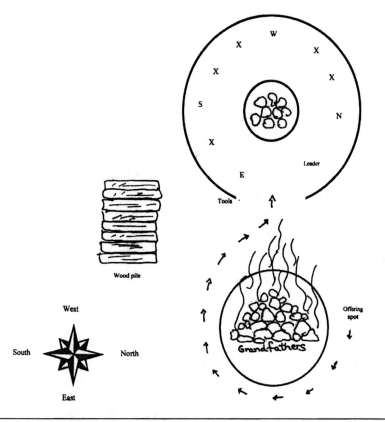

**Figure 17.2**    Diagram of the Sweat Lodge—Above View

**The Ceremony**

*Another man and I were given the responsibility to tend the fire. He whispered to me that everyone seemed nervous. He went on to say that the fear would make a big shift in the lodge, and the tension would break during the sweat. The leader entered the lodge alone.*

*When people were told to enter, they came to the north corner of the fire pit (see Figure 17.2, offering spot). There, a fire tender held a bowl with tobacco and told each person to take some tobacco, make a prayer, and offer the tobacco to the grandfather fire. Then each participant walked around the fire clockwise and crawled into the lodge (see arrows, Figure 17.2). Once inside the lodge, each person crawled around the pit clockwise to the respective positions (the positions are signified by an x and directions in Figure 17.2). The leader sat to the right of the entrance and told people where to sit as they entered the lodge.*

*The two fire tenders were to shovel the coals back behind the rocks, to the back slope of the pit (east side of the "grandfathers," Figure 17.2). It was so hot that both men could not get at the rocks without jumping back from the fire in pain. I was pulled aside and told that if I listened closely, the whole process would be easier. It was important to take my time, because the approach was everything. In this case, if enough time was put into getting the coals out of the way, the rocks would be easier to access.*

*My partner and I were reminded to work together. I shoveled a rock onto the pitchfork, and excess coals were shaken off so that the smoke inside the lodge would be minimized. It was important not to drop the rocks, because these were the "grandfathers." It helped to build a rhythm and not move too fast. We had a hard time concentrating on our efforts as we persevered against the burning heat and the sweat dripping in our eyes. It was difficult to be very controlled, because every step forward caused one to retreat.*

*Seven grandfathers were passed through the entrance. Each one was greeted with a resounding "Boozhoo!" (meaning "welcome"). Then the round was ready to commence.*

**Round 1**

*After handing in the grandfathers, we entered the lodge. The other fire tender sat near the door, the "eastern doorway." A young woman who was not participating in this sweat was given the task of "door watcher"; she stayed outside to help lift the door at the end of the round. I sat in the "western doorway" (signified by the W in Figure 17.2). The leader's wife did not participate in this round. All other people were inside, 10 in all plus the leader of the ceremony.*

*A chant was started, and we all prayed to the grandfather spirits. This first round directed our attention to ask for help and healing. The song was sung in the native Ojibwa language, and others joined in even if they did not know the words. People soon participated once they had grasped the articulation and rhythm of the chant. The shaking of rattles accompanied the chanting, and out of the darkness came the periodic piercing sound of the whistle. At different points during the song, the leader ladled water onto the rocks from a bucket of water next to him. The rate and volume of the chanting increased with each offering of water to the Grandfather Spirit.*

*This song went on for quite some time, possibly 15 to 20 minutes. It reached an intensity that corresponded to the increasing heat. The water turned to steam with each ladle given to the rocks, and the air became thick with moisture. The rhythm and intensity of participation in the chanting corresponded to the attempt to brace ourselves from the strain of the burning; the thick steam in the air; the singeing inhalations; and the cramping, painful claustrophobia. As the sweat became more intense, the group chanted harder and harder. Eventually, the song slowed down and came to an end. No more water was given to the rocks. At the end of the song the group was led in yelling out, "Ho!" four successive times, which was a signal for the door keeper to open up the lodge.*

*The general nature of problems addressed in the sweat lodge ritual involved matters of acceptance, rejection, anger, and forgiveness. Requests were made for guidance and direction, help with allaying the anxiety associated with indecision, and fear of the unknown. People prayed for health and the health of others. Also, prayers were made for support and perseverance during the round.*

## Round 2

*Four more rocks were brought in. People asked for water, but the leader said we had to offer water to the grandfathers first. The bottle was passed around, and everyone was told to offer some but not drink any. He spilt some on the ground. Then each person took the bottle and offered some water to the pit, sizzling on the grandfathers. The bottle went around two times, and people had to wait. In fact, nobody was allowed to drink until after the round was finished.*

*The door was closed, and the grandmother spirit was called in. A woman who had come specifically to be healed of an ailment (she had offered tobacco to Don at the beginning of the week to request help) was sitting to the right of the leader.*

*We were led in a song of healing. After a while, out of the hot darkness there was a break in rhythm. The leader's chanting was interrupted by a surge of nausea. He vomited into the pit and then struggled an imperative that everyone had to sing harder. He tried to continue singing but continued to throw up several times.*

*Everybody attempted to persevere, and the leader encouraged all to "pray hard." He continued to sing although he was viscerally convulsing, and later I found out that the woman with a chronic illness who was the focus of this sweat was having a hard time staying upright and had her head on his shoulder. He had run up against the wall that he was expecting earlier in the week.*

*The song went on, and the total process became more intense, more straining, and more anxious. When the door was finally opened, the cool night air and light from the fire were a welcome relief.*

### Round 3

*More rocks were introduced, and the director of the sweat lodge called his wife for the third round. She ran this round, and Don took a break to recuperate and think things over. He later told me that he left the lodge to "try and get in touch with what was going on," that is, to reassess the process.*

*Don's wife sat in the leader's position next to the door. The person in the western doorway was given the raven shaker and told to pray to all the spirits that went before us. The door was shut.*

*The leader prayed and asked each person in turn to pray silently. Starting on her left and working clockwise, the leader prayed for each individual. Her prayers were quite insightful. They reflected what she perceived to be each person's strengths and weaknesses. For instance, when she came to me, I was encouraged in my academic and vocational endeavors. Yet she said that it was important to take care of myself. Effort must be given to maintain health and treat my body well. Not only was her suggestion pertinent, but also it was in fact something that I had had on my mind that week. The prayers were intuitive and, as she explained to me later, inspired by the Spirit. They were spontaneous and seemed to generate from a deeper sense of the group process and her surroundings.*

*Following this segment of the round, we chanted while more prayers were made and steam was periodically added to the pit. Finally, the door was opened.*

### Round 4

*Before this round began, the two fire tenders and the medicine person directing the sweat left the lodge and joined the door watcher outside. Don's wife ran this round.*

*I talked to Don, and he explained that the round had hit him hard. He said that there was a lot of resistance in the healing process. The person who had come for healing was stubborn and did not want to let up. This of course was not a conscious thing, yet her character was determined, and she was holding onto her illness. He felt that after the vomiting and his psycho/physical struggle during the ritual, the "ice was broken," that is, the healing process was put into motion. The patient's resistance was broken, and the process was slowly starting to move forward.*

Two more rounds completed the lodge, atypical in length but not uncommon for Don during that time. Following the sweat, the towels and mats were taken out. The time of day was around 11:50 p.m., and we had started at around 7:00 p.m. Overall, we averaged 40 minutes a round.

## ❖ PSYCHOTHERAPEUTIC ASPECTS OF THE SWEAT LODGE

The relation between the leader and the participants, and everyone's relationship to the ritual context and therapeutic space, played an important role in the healing process. Rapport and proper frame are important in the sweat lodge ritual as well as in modern psychotherapy. The leader of the ritual conveys a serious mannerism and sensitivity. Examples of these values can be found in psychotherapeutic theory. For example, in "The Problem of Responsibility in Psychotherapy," Helmut Kaiser argued that a therapist should behave in such a way as to promote in the patient a feeling of responsibility for his or her words and deeds (cited in Fierman, 1965).

Furthermore, Don emphasized the importance of building the proper relationship with the people involved in a healing ceremony. In psychotherapeutic literature, the importance of building the proper alliance with the patient is generally considered significant in therapeutic outcome. Without a proper alliance, the prognosis for therapy is generally poor (Greenson, 1967). Also, in preparation and practice of a sweat lodge ceremony, Don exhibits something analogous to an evenly suspended or raised attention. This type of attention is an important aspect of psychoanalytic technique.

The sweat lodge ritual emphasizes respect and dependence on others. The Ojibwa teach responsibility toward relations seven generations prior and seven generations in the future. The past and future converge in the presence of potentially flesh-singeing rock and steam. The sense of spatial boundaries is obliterated in the darkness. Prayers offered in the lodge are directed to the dead, the living, and the yet to be born. The physically and mentally challenging nature of the ritual stresses the individual and encourages each individual to invest in the support of the group, human and otherwise.

Stress and frustration are produced from the structure of the lodge itself. Transference issues are exacerbated under the stress of the ritual. Although people struggle through physical and mental exasperation, they are reminded that they have the power to persevere. It is at these points, when the end of a round is nearing, that people rely on whatever resources are necessary to complete the round. The various functions performed by the leader and members of the group provide the emotional support, the behavioral modeling, or the symbolic framework that a person can use to maintain a sense of balance or cohesion. When a round comes to a close, the entrance is opened, and this is accompanied by the relief of cool air and a sense of accomplishment. After the self undergoes what can be considered a fragmentation, each person grapples with mental supports to emotionally survive the round. Each time, participants are relieved. Surviving each small ordeal, they are confirmed in their beliefs, anxiety proceeds to satisfaction, and each person is born anew. As the leader has directed in other sweats that I have attended, "Pray to come out of the lodge like a brand-new baby."

## ❖ INTEGRATION OF THE SWEAT LODGE IN COUNSELING AND PSYCHOTHERAPY

As stated earlier, the sweat lodge is used in more than half of the U.S. Indian Health Service facilities as a complement to other forms of treatment (Cohen, 2003). However, there is little scientific or empirical research on the effectiveness of traditional healing systems in general. Nevertheless, there are important reasons to include traditional methods of healing in modern practice. The sweat lodge has always functioned as a precursor to counseling and other types of doctoring. Also, as argued above, the sweat lodge is an effective therapeutic method in its own right, particularly for Native populations. It is arguably therapeutic on two fronts.

First, the sweat lodge likely has physiological benefits, as suggested by some research on the medical benefits of hyperthermia (Bruchac, 1993; Hooper, 1999). Clearly, the therapeutic benefits of the sweat lodge can be supported and elaborated by further scientific research.

Second, the sweat lodge is psychotherapeutic. Traditional healing methods provide a basis for the construction of cultural identity and support social cohesion. The sweat lodge helps provide meaning to experience, promotes self-esteem, and promotes solidarity in the group. In general, traditional healing can renew moral strength and help individuals to come to terms with trauma in a manner consistent with their sense of self and community (E. Duran & B. Duran, 1995; Gone, 2000). The sweat lodge can help create a cohesive sense of self, particularly in terms of Native American heritage.

The sweat lodge provides a context for symbolic healing. Anthropologists have acknowledged the importance of symbols in the healing process cross-culturally. Symbolic reconstitution of the self is an important topic in the studies of religious healing and shamanic practice (Dow, 1986; Levi-Strauss, 1963). Recently, research has shown how symbolic construction is specifically involved in affect regulation. Important works in philosophy of mind, child development, and psychoanalytic theory have elucidated the process of how a cohesive sense of reality emerges from physical and emotional challenges (Fonagy, 2003; Gendlin, 2000; Zachar, 2000). Symbolic organization and regulation of affect are at the heart of early developmental adaptation. This process is arguably the essence of the psychotherapeutic process. This new research is consistent with Kohut's concept of transmuting internalizations (Zachar, 2000). If mentalization and the symbolic organization of physical and emotional deregulation are at the heart of therapy, it becomes clearer why the sweat lodge has persisted over thousands of years.

As stated earlier, the sweat lodge is already in prominent use in conjunction with counseling and psychotherapy. It is growing in use in Native communities in hospital settings, outpatient treatment centers, retreat centers, and prisons (Cohen, 2003; Kirmayer, Brass, & Tait, 2000). Therefore, formal attention to the proper integration of the sweat lodge ritual with counseling and psychotherapy is a pressing issue.

Formal integration and attention to the therapeutic use of the sweat lodge can provide several advantages. First, the integration into established medical systems can help promote a standard of care and proper practice of the ceremony. A standard of care could be established with Native authorities and medical professionals.

Second, support and regulation by medical systems with the participation of Native authorities can help maintain ethical standards that are shared by medical and psychotherapeutic institutions. This is important, because the traditional supervision and regulation of traditional medicine have suffered in the wake of the breakdown of traditional Native systems. Native people continue to struggle for legitimacy and recognition. There is concern with inauthentic and arguably unethical practice. Rituals are often performed by non-Native people with questionable training and no authentic claim to a traditional role (Bruchac, 1993; Kirmayer et al., 2000; Wallis, 2003).

Finally, the formal integration of the sweat lodge and traditional medicine into systems of counseling and psychotherapy can provide government and financial support that can contribute to the legitimacy and support of traditional medicine. Overall, the sweat lodge is already an important technique that is incorporated into modern counseling and psychotherapy. It continues to function as a traditional healing ritual inside and outside of medical contexts. However, further research is needed to elucidate its therapeutic value and to maximize its therapeutic efficacy in conjunction with modern approaches in behavioral and medical practice.

## ❖ NOTE

1. The establishment of the *Midewiwin* or grand Medicine Society of the Anishinabe is itself, arguably, a response to European Jesuit contact and an attempt to maintain a cohesive religious tradition in the 17th century (Grim, 1983).

## ❖ REFERENCES

Bilgrave, D., & Deluty, R. (2003). Religious beliefs and political ideologies as predictors of psychotherapeutic orientations of clinical and counseling psychologists. *Journal for the Scientific Study of Religion, 37,* 329–349.

Bruchac, J. (1993). *The Native American sweat lodge: History and legends.* Freedom, CA: Crossing Press.

Bucko, R. A. (1998). *The Lakota ritual of the sweat lodge: History and contemporary practice.* Lincoln: University of Nebraska Press.

Cohen, K. (2003). *Honoring the medicine: The essential guide to Native American healing.* New York: Ballantine Books.

Densmore, F. (1979). *Chippewa customs.* St. Paul: Minnesota Historical Society Press.

Dow, J. (1986). Universal aspects of symbolic healing: A theoretical synthesis. *American Anthropologist, 88*(1), 56–69.

Driver, H. E. (1970). *Indians of North America.* Chicago: University of Chicago Press.

Duran, E., & Duran, B. (1995). *Native American postcolonial psychology.* Albany: State University of New York Press.

Fierman, L. B. (Ed.). (1965). *Effective psychotherapy: The contribution of Hellmuthy Kaiser.* New York: Free Press.

Fonagy, P. (2003). The development of psychopathology from infancy to adulthood: The mysterious unfolding of disturbance in time. *Infant Mental Health Journal, 24,* 212–239.

Frank, J. D., & Frank, J. B. (1991). *Persuasion and healing: A comparative study of psychotherapy.* New York: Schocken Books.

Geertz, C. (1974). Thick description: Toward an interpretative theory of culture. In *The interpretation of cultures: Selected essays by Clifford Geertz* (pp. 3–30). New York: Basic Books.

Gendlin, E. T. (2000). The "mind"/"body" problem and first-person process. In R. D. Ellis & N. Newton (Eds.), *Advances in Consciousness Research Series: Vol. 16. The caldron of consciousness: Motivation, affect and self-organization—An anthology* (pp. 109–118). Philadelphia: John Benjamins.

Gone, J. (2000). "We were through as keepers of it": The "missing pipe narrative" and Gros Ventre cultural identity. *Ethos, 27,* 415–440.

Greenson, R. (1967). *The technique and practice of psychoanalysis* (Vol. 1). New York: International Universities Press.

Grim, J. A. (1983). *The shaman: Patterns of religious healing among the Ojibwa Indians.* Norman: University of Oklahoma Press.

Harrison, J. (2000). Overview of program, Na'Nizhoozhi Center. Retrieved December 31, 2004, from http://www.wellbriety-nci.org

Hooper, P. L. (1999). Hot-tub therapy for type 2 diabetes mellitus. *New England Journal of Medicine, 341,* 924–925.

Kirmayer, L. J., Brass, G. M., & Tait, C. L. (2000). The mental health of aboriginal peoples: Transformations of identity and community. *Canadian Journal of Psychiatry, 45,* 607–616.

Krickeberg, W. (1939). The Indian sweat bath. *Coba Symposia, 1*(1), 19–25.

Lee, R. R., & Martin, J. C. (1991). *Psychotherapy after Kohut: A textbook of self psychology.* Hillsdale, NJ: Analytic Press.

Levi-Strauss, C. (1963). The effectiveness of symbols. In W. A. Lessa & E. Z. Vogt (Eds.), *Readings in comparative religion: An anthropological approach* (4th ed., pp. 318–327). New York: Harper & Row.

Lopatin, I. A. (1960). Origin of the Native American steam bath. *American Anthropologist, 62,* 977–993.

Norrell, B. (2005, January). Federal prisons increase restrictions. *Indian Country Today.* Retrieved January 5, 2005, from http://www.indiancountry.com

Okiciyapi Wellness Center. (2003). *Regional behavioral health program, Sioux Xan Hospital.* Retrieved December 31, 2003, from http://www.his.gov/facilitiesservices/areaoffices/aberdeen/rapidcitysu/mentalhealth.asp

Smith, D. (2003, July). *Secular or religious: The experience and meaning of psychotherapist's spirituality.* Paper presented at the International Conference for Client Centered and Experiential Therapy, Eggmond an Zee, The Netherlands.

Smith, D. & Orlinsky, D. (2003, June). *The psychotherapist and culture of secularism: Reflections in the light of recent evidence.* Paper presented at the International Conference for the Society for Psychotherapy Research, Weimar, Germany.

Sullivan, H. S. (1964). *The collected works of Harry Stack Sullivan, M.D.: Vol. 1. The psychiatric interview* (H. S. Perry, M. L. Gawel, & M. Gibbon, Eds.). New York: Norton.

Vecsey, C. (1983). *Traditional Ojibwa religion and its historical change.* Philadelphia: American Philosophical Press.

Vogel, V. J. (1970). *American Indian medicine.* Norman: University of Oklahoma Press.

Wallis, R. J. (2003). *Shamans/neo-shamans: Ecstasy, alternative archaeologies and contemporary Pagans.* New York: Routledge.

Zachar, P. (2000). Child development and the regulation of affect and cognition in consciousness: A view from object relations theory. In R. D. Ellis & N. Newton (Eds.), *Advances in Consciousness Research Series: Vol. 16. The caldron of consciousness: Motivation, affect and self-organization—An anthology* (pp. 205–222). Philadelphia: John Benjamins.

# 18

# *Maat*

## An African-Centered Paradigm for Psychological and Spiritual Healing

*Mekada Graham*

B lack, Asian, and other minority communities often receive a service that fails
to address their mental health needs (Leong, Wagner, & Tata, 1995; Raleigh,
2000). Conventional therapeutic systems, which seek to nurture and heal, can
nevertheless be oppressive toward black individuals and families.[1] These perspectives are drawn from psychological theories that have their origins in
Eurocentric understandings of human behavior and well-being. Contemporane-
ously, there is a history of racism in psychology that spans several centuries, and
this legacy continues to challenge the discipline's theories and practice in contemporary society. Given the history of deep-seated racism and exclusion experienced by black people, it is testament to the human spirit that they have
transcended these assaults to not only function effectively in hostile environ-
ments but also to lead successful and fulfilling lives. These factors draw attention
to the urgent need for new approaches and innovative service developments that
can respond effectively and offer new pathways toward healing and well-being.
New approaches require new ways of thinking about mental health across a

multidimensional sphere that includes engaging with black communities and their traditional healing practices as the focus for change.

Black scholars have engaged in recovering African philosophies as a way of reconnecting with cultural antecedents as a source for therapeutic ideas in the helping process (Graham, 2002a). Black communities have applied these ideas and frameworks of knowledge to everyday living to cope and manage with stressful circumstances and to offer new pathways toward healing individuals and promoting community well-being. This chapter is divided into two broad sections. First, I outline the psychocultural perspectives that emerge from black communities as a paradigm for nurturing and healing. The power and symbolism of time-honored traditions, religions, customs, and mythologies throughout the African diaspora provide a framework for a holistic approach to well-being in which the complex linkages to the spiritual and psychosocial are explored. Second, I introduce the concept of *Maat* as a philosophical and spiritual knowledge system that is derived from ancient Kemetic religious precepts. Throughout the past decades, black scholars have been engaged in recovering ancient classical African texts as a way of reconnecting with cultural antecedents to assist in community regeneration and cultural renewal. The key features of Maat (a conceptual framework that articulates social and cultural values) have been translated into the language of modern moral discourse in order to uncover cultural connections with an ancestral past (Karenga, 1994). Maat and Nguzo Saba (a value system based on seven principles) assist individuals, families, and communities in obtaining wisdom about self and connection to the spiritual and material realms of being (Graham, 2002b). These cultural elements offer a unique approach to restoring and nurturing psychological well-being through seeking balance and harmony in the dynamic process of energy fields and forces of life to bring about a unified whole and optimal health. This framework provides the context for the second section, which considers the place of spirituality and cultural knowing in counseling relationships and draws briefly upon a case history to illustrate the healing potential in black communities.

### ❖ RACISM IN PSYCHOLOGY AND PSYCHOTHERAPY

The history of racism in psychology has been well documented by several researchers and psychologists (Howitt & Owusu-Bempah, 1990; Richards, 1997). The new science of psychology emerged within the context of European expansion and imperialism during a historical period when differences between human beings were categorized and became a legitimate area of scientific inquiry. As a result of this process, it is clear that psychology as a discipline developed and reflected the ideological and social context of white superiority and domination. The legacy of racism in psychology persists through its insistence upon psychological universalism and some cultural arrogance about traditional healing practices.

Many black people have perceived psychology as a tool of oppression and social control that compounds cultural and racial stereotypes held by the wider society. Under these circumstances, many black psychologists and other professionals sought to develop theoretical frameworks that explore black subjectivities as a reference point for culturally relevant and appropriate practice. These ways of healing and offering support are sometimes ridiculed as primitive superstition or "magic" (Fernando, 2002). It is largely the case that traditional healing practices do not command respect and are perceived as unscientific—a kind of "mumbo jumbo" in comparison to Western "scientific" psychiatry. These circumstances highlight power relationships that can marginalize and negate the interpretative frameworks of black communities to explain human behavior. It appears that psychotherapy and mental health services have generally failed to consider the diverse pathways of understanding human experience.

Conventional models of counseling and psychotherapy continue to be challenged for their failure to address racism, cultural identities, and the socioeconomic context of the individual, including the strengths of black people as an integral part of practice. These concerns have focused on the lack of knowledge and understanding of black people within their cultural context and social world. These understandings provide the conceptual tools to engage in thinking about the particularity and complexity of black people's experiences and to connect these elements to the realities of practice. It is within this perspective that conventional models of counseling and psychotherapy have infused cultural sensitivity as a way of addressing cultural diversity. As a consequence of this process, there has been some commitment to opening up new knowledge and skills.

## ❖ AFRICAN-CENTERED WORLDVIEWS

African-centered worldviews, view of self, and notions of consciousness begin with a holistic understanding of the human condition and can be articulated across three principal areas:

- The spiritual nature of human beings
- The interconnectedness of all things
- Oneness of mind, body, and spirit

Spirituality forms the central plank of African-centered worldviews and frames knowledge and understanding of human behavior and life worlds. There are several definitions of spirituality in current usage. *Spirituality* here is defined as the creative life force, the very essence of all things that connects all human beings to each other. Spirituality connects all elements of the universe—people, animals, and inanimate objects are viewed as interconnected. Because they are dependent upon each other, they are in essence considered as one (Mbiti, 1990). The concept of interconnectedness of all things posits no separation between the material and the spiritual; "reality is at one and inseparably spiritual and material as all reality [the universe] begins from a single principle" (Myers, 1988, p. 24). Human beings are perceived as an integral part of nature, and living in harmony with the environment helps them become at one with all reality.

Grills (2002) uses the term *spiritness* to describe a real and symbolic meaning that characterizes African social thought. The human being is an embodied subject so that spirit is the energy force and the basis of existence. The central place of spirituality within this cultural paradigm carries the precept that every social problem or concern has a spiritual dimension (J. Martin & M. Martin, 2002).

Spirituality holds a central place and reflects the human need to connect to the life force, and tapping into these knowledge forms "gives power and strength in physical communication as a means of connecting the inner strengths and character to the outer existence and collective identity" (Dei, 1999, p. 6). The spiritual aspect of human beings is translated socially, so that the human being is never an isolated individual but always the person in the community. The community defines the person—I am because we are, and because we are, therefore I am. The individual becomes a person through interaction with others. In this way, the individual comes to know self through others. Spiritual knowing entails the individual sharing experiences of the universal meaning of human existence through relationships with others. This interrelated understanding of self is expressed in the words *umuntu ngumuntu ngabantu,* that is, "a person is person through other persons" (Holdstock, 2000). These philosophical assumptions transmit to the psyche a sense of connection with others and to a higher being. This is because mutuality and individuality are inextricably linked in the concept of self. These assumptions help people conceptualize and tap into sources to enhance human achievement (Schiele, 2000).

In this context, the individual's moral growth and development facilitates the growth of others. The development of self is characterized as an act of becoming. The act of becoming is a process of attainment and incorporation into a community, which negates the idea that personhood is achieved simply by existence. The process of the life journey is marked by a series of passages, and in this way a person is afforded challenges to grow, change, and develop in order to attain moral growth within the context of community. The life journey is not a linear process that results in decline as a result of the aging process. Life follows the same path as the cosmos—a zigzag spiral path of Maat. As Oba T'Shaka (1995) writes,

> The progression of consciousness . . . occurs because, as we go through the cycles of life, as we learn the lessons of Maat, the lessons of the cosmos. As we internalize these lessons, we transform our thoughts, words and actions to conform to Maat. We ascend the spiral ladder of transformation through the cycles of life, rising to the level of perfection where the body becomes one with the soul. (p. 19)

The process of becoming is set within the context of a spiritual matrix where the connection with others provides the basis for healing, transformation, and spiritual renewal. The idea of the interconnectedness of all things means there is no separation between the material and the spiritual, because all reality begins from a single principle. Human beings are perceived as an integral part of nature and as living in harmony with the environment. This existence supports and facilitates a person's becoming one with all reality. The concept of oneness relates to those not yet born and those who have died, so that all human beings are linked together across time and space.

African-centered worldviews consider the mind, body, and spirit as one. Each is given equal value, and they are believed to be interrelated. The knowledge of self is the key to optimal health in order to seek divinity through Maat (truth, justice, righteousness, harmony, balance, order, propriety, compassion, and reciprocity). These concepts and ideas are translated into maintaining balance and peace in the face of adverse external social forces. It is when this inner peace is compromised that the psychological, social, and physical well-being of a person is threatened, leading to personal anxieties and fears.

These ways of understanding human behavior and life are closely associated with ideas of wellness. Optimal health provides the frame for physical, intellectual, emotional, and spiritual well-being. This means that the complex interplay between mind, body, spirit, relationships, and environment is the focal point to restore harmony and balance.

## ❖ MAAT: A GUIDE FOR LIVING

The philosophical, spiritual, and cultural system of Maat is a central feature of African worldviews that is reflected in principles for living "to support and facilitate the full expressions of one's spiritual essence [sense of self]" (Parham, 2002, p. 41). These cultural forms that frame spirituality provide the lens through which experiences of reality continue to inform the ethos of black communities. These cultural forms are expressed and articulated through sayings and dialogue in everyday life and have been revitalized as the living past that informs the present and the future. The ancient goddess of Maat represents the heart and balance in all things. People sometimes speak about their feelings in terms of "heaviness of the heart" when they are troubled by anxieties or problems of living. The heart is perceived as being in harmony with Maat through behavior and moral conduct. The principle of Maat holds a multiplicity of meanings, including the virtues of truth, balance, harmony, propriety, reciprocity, and order. Maat incorporates the scales of justice and truth. These principles are perceived as essential human qualities and represent the benchmark for human conduct (Arewa, 1998). They are, in effect, a guide for living the good life.

Maat also represents the orderly movement and flow of all things—seasons, cosmos, society, family, and relationships. Maat is conceived as a symbolic entity that defines and perceives realities through "divine energy in the universe that sustains and maintains the relationship between unseen cosmic forces and physical realities" (Beatty, 1997, p. 220). The sense of interrelatedness, interdependence, and interconnectedness is critical to this philosophical concept, because Maat regulates the "I" mentality to restore the "we." This is because harmony and balance through relationships and coexistence support the continuation of Maat. Maat is expressed through seven cardinal virtues, which have been translated into the Nguzo Saba (Karenga, 1997). The Nguzo Saba translates an important aspect of Maat, that is, the need to understand one's humanness. This is expressed in the human potential for transformation and the need to strive toward human betterment and personal excellence. This is a lifelong process, because the path to personhood, that is, to become the divine within you, is achieved through equilibrium and optimal health. The nature of human beings is goodness, and everyone needs to experience harmony and balance. Harmony and balance in everyday living represent inner peace, and these are personified through alignment with natural forces. The lessons of living Maat are often expressed in the form of sayings, proverbs, and through dialogue. Maat is not an object in the sense that it can be isolated or separated into distinct parts. It accommodates elasticity in its meanings, which allows for creative thought about new and ongoing challenges to black communities in the African diaspora. The reality of Maat is expressed in personal and social practice. These social concerns are found in the quality of relationships and reciprocal unity. From this perspective, Maat has been restored as a living past with cultural elements and products that can be translated into a way of being, transformation, and healing. The integration of knowledge and cultural substance can be empowering to black communities in reaffirming purpose and meaning in life (Graham, 2004). This is one of the major challenges for psychotherapy and counseling. Can conventional therapies work together alongside traditional healing practices as equal partners to provide a holistic and relevant service for black communities?

The next section uses a case vignette to draw together some of the ideas and practices described in this chapter.

## ❖ CASE VIGNETTE: RICHARD'S STORY

Richard (a pseudonym) is a 48-year-old man who has been separated from his wife for several years. He lives alone and works for a local company as a plumber. Richard has been feeling depressed and anxious for some time now but has been able to manage his job reasonably well. However, recently Richard has become increasingly isolated from friends and from some members of his family. He has a friend who visits regularly, and during their discussions, Richard tells Joe about his worries, the racism he experiences at work, and the stresses of living in general. Joe suggests he should talk to someone in the community that he has heard about. Apparently there is a meditation and health class on a Saturday afternoon that is run by a group of black women and men, and individual counseling sessions are available. Most referrals to traditional healers and counseling services happen through word of mouth, and references to the good intentions of healers and counselors are a key aspect of referral. This is an important aspect of traditional healing, because there are risks involved in approaching a healer who is unknown within a community. Richard seeks out the recommended counselor-healer for consultation. The therapeutic relationship begins with Richard telling his story and establishing a rapport that includes cultural reference points that engage Richard and assist in establishing trust with his counselor-healer. The traditional healer explores all aspects of Richard's being. This process begins with exploring his physical health. This is because if the body is run down, with little life force or vitality, this will affect an individual's response to emotional traumas and will lead to difficulties in managing life problems and experiences.

The focus upon physical health is important, because this will enable Richard to be an active participant in his recovery and well-being. He will be advised about diet and the ways in which some foods affect emotions, feelings, and anxieties. The next area of exploration relates to the individual's psychological well-being. Richard talks about his anxieties and worries, and the healer-counselor explores these anxieties and worries through readings/oracles as a way of identifying and connecting with energies that govern his situation. These readings/oracles are based upon identifying the particular spheres that are dominant in the makeup of Richard's personality and way of being. This information will enable the healer to identify the combination of cosmic energies that assist in alignment to universal principles toward healing. These factors assist in framing the focus of healing potentials and practices.

This holistic approach addresses all aspects of the human condition to bring about harmony with the universal principles governing the spirit. In this way, the healer engages Richard in working with meditation practices that include visual imagery to enable him to have a sense of power to change his life and circumstances. This is because the frame of therapeutic intervention perceives a person as encompassing an infinite potential for transformation. The individual is in essence a spiritual being whose nature is one of inner peace. This inner peace has been compromised through the process of programming of human experiences and socialization in society.

In order to return to a state of inner peace, the spirit through the mind requires slowing down. In Richard's case, this is enacted through chanting, sacred words, and relaxation so that his mind can be receptive and open to receive energies and alignment with the different principles that govern his situation (which have been identified by the healer). This is based upon the assumption that everything in the universe vibrates, and alignment with these energy fields can assist in recovery and return to inner peace. Therapy engages in restoring intellectual health through the telling of stories and the problems of living that preoccupy the client as well as letting go of anxieties and worries. This cognitive process, a kind of mind massaging, is reinforced and driven through a spiritual component that brings the individual back into interaction with others.

The relationship between client and therapist is a partnership where the therapist explores the meanings of existence and is able to steer and provide a sense of direction. This relationship acknowledges the right of the individual to recognize, appreciate, and understand his or her own selfhood rather than subject the individual to preconceived notions of what a person is or should be. For example, the concept of giving and receiving is an important part of the healing process and alignment with Maat as a universal principle—the idea here is reciprocity. This means that the process of healing is centered on the active participation of the client in recovery and treatment, which expresses the energy of giving and receiving. Richard also attended the weekly meetings and meditation classes. He learned techniques of meditation and took part in food preparation with other members of the group. This group experience provided support from others who had similar cultural values and understandings, and it became an important resource in his recovery.

This supportive environment becomes a field of positive energy that nourishes giving and receiving, seeking nothing in return, as an important principle of Maat. Richard's contributions to the group process over time enhanced the field of positive energy, enabling the group to develop and grow in all aspects of life. Richard made considerable progress throughout the year. He became gregarious in the group setting and interacted with others, taking on various responsibilities. These experiences within the group setting, together with increased knowledge about his health and well-being, provided the foundation of increased confidence in interaction with others and in dealing with life's problems and life choices.

❖ CONCLUSION

This chapter has drawn attention to the critical need to engage black communities' own interpretations and understandings of human behavior to assist in the recovery and general maintenance of well-being. Despite the reluctance of established counseling services to connect and associate with traditional healing practices, some black people seek these services instead of or as well as conventional therapies. New ways of thinking and approaches are required to deal with and manage the stresses of modern life, which are compounded through experiences of racism and oppression. The untapped resources and healing potential within black communities are often neglected and perceived as irrelevant by institutions and established counseling and psychotherapy services. Resources within the black community include various kinds of practices including religious healing; meditation; homeopathy; spiritual healing and mentoring; learning about self; and the power of energy, spirit, and life force to offer a more holistic approach steeped in cultural and spiritual knowledge and understanding. These considerations raise important issues about the need for culture-specific psychotherapies to move beyond multicultural approaches, which seek to adapt existing models to be more culturally sensitive. Culturally specific psychotherapies use a spiritual frame of interconnectedness drawing upon cultural antecedents as a source for healing practices. These forms of knowledge can be a powerful and creative resource in the helping processes for individuals.

❖ NOTE

1. I recognize and acknowledge the cultural diversity and shifting identities of people of African descent. This means there are different ways of being "black" located in the life worlds and experiences in the African diaspora.

## Acknowledgments

I would like to thank Dr. Showa Omabegho, Tau Napata, and Dr. Gillian Berry for their support, encouragement, and useful comments in the preparation of this work.

## ❖ REFERENCES

Arewa, C. (1998). *Opening to spirit.* London: Thorsons.

Beatty, M. (1997). Maat: The cultural and intellectual allegiance of a concept. In J. Carruthers & L. Harris (Eds.), *African world history project* (pp. 211–240). Los Angeles: Association for the Study of Classical African Civilizations.

Dei, G. S. (1999). *Rethinking the role of indigenous knowledges in the academy.* Public lecture presented to the Department of Sociology and Equity Studies, University of Toronto, Toronto, Ontario, Canada.

Fernando, S. (2002). *Mental health, race and culture.* Basingstoke, UK: Palgrave.

Graham, M. (2002a). Creating spaces: Exploring the role of cultural knowledge as a source of empowerment in models of social welfare in black communities. *British Journal of Social Work, 32,* 35–49.

Graham, M. (2002b). *Social work and African centered worldviews.* Birmingham, UK: Venture Press.

Graham, M. (2004). Empowerment revisited—Social work, resistance and agency in black communities. *European Journal of Social Work, 7,* 43–56.

Grills, C. (2002). African-centered psychology. In T. Parham (Ed.), *Counseling persons of African descent* (pp. 10–24). Thousand Oaks, CA: Sage.

Holdstock, L. (2000). *Re-examining psychology: Critical perspectives and African insights.* London: Routledge.

Howitt, D., & Owusu-Bempah, J. (1990). *The racism of psychology: Time for change.* Hemel Hempstead, UK: Harvester Wheatsheaf.

Karenga, M. (1994). *Maat: The moral ideal in ancient Egypt: A study of classical African ethics* (Vol. 1). Unpublished doctoral dissertation, University of Southern California, Los Angeles.

Karenga, M. (1997). *Kwanzaa, a celebration of family, community and culture.* Los Angeles: University of Sankore Press.

Leong, F. T. L., Wagner, N. S., & Tata, S. P. (1995). Racial and ethnic variations in help-seeking attitudes. In J. G. Ponterotto, J. M. Casas, L. A. Suzuki, & C. M. Alexander (Eds.), *Handbook of multicultural counseling* (pp. 415–438). Thousand Oaks, CA: Sage.

Martin, J., & Martin, M. (2002). *Spirituality and the black helping tradition in social work.* Washington, DC: National Association of Social Workers.

Mbiti, J. S. (1990). *African religions and philosophy* (2nd ed.). Oxford, UK: Heinemann Educational.

Myers, L. J. (1988). *Understanding the Afrocentric worldview: Introduction to an optimal psychology.* Dubuque, IA: Kendall/Hunt.

T'Shaka, O. (1995). *Return to the African mother principle of male and female equality.* Oakland, CA: Pan Afrikan.

Parham, T. (Ed.). (2002). *Counseling persons of African descent.* Thousand Oaks, CA: Sage.

Raleigh, V. S. (2000). Mental health in black and ethnic minorities. In C. Kaye & T. Lingiah (Eds.), *Race, culture and ethnicity in secure psychiatric practice* (pp. 1–20). London: Jessica Kingsley.

Richards, G. (1997). *Race, racism and psychology: Towards a reflective history.* London: Routledge.

Schiele, J. (2000). *Human services and the Afrocentric paradigm.* New York: Haworth Press.

# 19

# Morita Therapy

## A Philosophy of Yin/Yang Coexistence

*Charles P. Chen*

Morita therapy is a Japanese psychotherapy established by psychiatrist Shoma Morita in the late 1910s and early 1920s (Morita, 1928/1974). Rooted in the Eastern philosophy of maintaining a balanced lifestyle, Morita therapy was originally developed for the treatment of clients with the general symptom of nervousness and social anxiety (*shinkeishitsu* in Japanese) (Kitanishi, 1992; Kora, 1991). The therapy is one of the very few Eastern or Asian therapeutic models that has received considerable attention in the Western helping professions for the last several decades, especially since the 1970s. There has been much interest in exploring the clinical value of Morita therapy through both research and practice (Alden & Ishiyama, 1997; Ishiyama, 2003; Reynolds, 1976, 1984, 1989; Walsh, 2000; Watanabe, 1992). This chapter intends to provide a very brief overview of Morita therapy and to address the therapeutic value of some of the core Morita theoretical principles in current counseling and psychotherapy practice in general, and in treating social anxiety in particular. It illustrates that, by viewing basic human functioning differently from the views that have formed many traditional therapeutic orientations in the Western world, Morita therapy can provide a viable alternative approach to help clients deal with anxiety-related issues in their personal and social domains.

### ❖ MORITA THERAPY: BACKGROUND AND THEORETICAL FRAME

Morita therapy was named after its founder, Dr. Shoma Morita (1874–1938), a Japanese psychiatrist and a professor of neuropsychiatry at a medical school in Tokyo. Based on his 20 years of treatment experience with patients with neurosis, Dr. Morita formed this therapeutic approach around 1919. Like most of the contemporary mental health professionals at his time, Morita was initially influenced by the dominant psychoanalytical theory and studied and practiced psychoanalytical therapy. But he eventually came to the conclusion that a new therapeutic approach was needed in order to work more effectively with patients who suffered from nervousness, or what is now called social anxiety disorder. This conclusion grew out of his clinical observations and interventions with his patients over the course of many years. It was also partly influenced by his personal experience with and interest in searching for a better cure for the neurosis disorder. Morita had suffered from neurotic symptoms such as heavy and anxious feelings in his own life since his teenage years, and the symptoms were not cured by any psychotherapy treatment at the time. In developing this therapy, Morita first experimented with it with several neurotic patients at his home, conducting the therapy as a residential treatment trial. This residential treatment method later became a standard clinical intervention format of Morita therapy in other institutional settings such as hospitals, therapeutic residences, and treatment centers (Fujita, 1986; Goto, 1988; Morita, 1928/1974; Reynolds, 1976, 1984; Smith, 1981).

The therapy gained much attention in Japan and became one of the most dominant psychotherapeutic approaches in the country. Many Japanese scholars and practitioners continued their efforts to utilize Morita therapy in their clinical practice. They studied and expanded on the original Morita model, making the therapy a much more flexible intervention that can be applied to a variety of clinical settings and situations, including various nonresidential treatment interventions (Tamai & Takeichi, 1991; Tashiro & Tamai, 1993) in individual and group counseling. Of note, Morita therapy was first introduced to North America in the late 1940s. Its influence in the Western psychotherapeutic world grew steadily during the 1950s and 1960s. It has generated even more interest during the 1970s and 1980s, becoming one of the very few well-recognized, well-respected, and influential Eastern psychotherapeutic models in the realm of counseling and psychotherapy in the Western world in general, and in North America in particular

(Reynolds, 1976, 1984; Smith, 1981; T. Suzuki & Kataoka, 1982; T. Suzuki & R. Suzuki, 1977). Because of the accumulated contributions made by many scholars and practitioners to the continuing development of the therapy, the current Morita therapy represents an enriched and more complex therapeutic system that is much broader and more integrated than its original model (Chen, 1996, 1998, 2003; Ishiyama, 1986, 1988a, 1988b, 1991, 2003; LeVine, 1993).

The theoretical foundation of Morita therapy was strongly influenced by Zen Buddhist ideology and other Eastern ways of thinking (Kondo, 1992; Matesz, 1990). Essential to the theoretical formation of the therapy was the Chinese philosophy of yin and yang, that is, the idea that the essence of maintaining a healthy mental state rests on one's right attitude and capacity to practice harmony in life (Chen, 1998). The next section illustrates how this theoretical principle guides the therapy via an action-oriented intervention process.

## ❖ THE TRADITIONAL TREATMENT PROCESS OF MORITA THERAPY

### Theoretical Principles

The original Morita therapy adopts a behavioral intervention in the treatment of neurotic disposition and social anxiety symptoms. According to Morita philosophy, what aggravates the client's symptoms of anxiety is his or her contradictory thoughts and obsession with excessive self-attention. When one is obsessed with unnecessary inward-looking behavior and characteristics, he or she becomes trapped into an overly self-centered and self-focused psychic interaction, generating and intensifying the arousal of social anxiety. By training the client to be engaged in focused behavioral practice, the therapeutic intervention aims to break down the contradictory thoughts and anxious feelings in a gradual and natural way. As the client learns to adopt an obedient attitude toward his or her natural living environment with various human experiences including anxious feelings and other inconvenient thoughts, he or she becomes more adaptable to personal experiences in the daily routine, which is never anxiety free. This process will gradually break down the vicious circle of exorbitant attention to self and its associated nervous sensation (Miura & Usa, 1970; Morita, 1928/1974).

Morita therapy is primarily a treatment approach guided by the Eastern philosophy of following a natural life path and practicing one's natural life functioning. It teaches the client to obey his or her own nature, that is, to adopt an accepting attitude toward life experiences as they are (Aldous, 1994; Chen, 1997, 1998). Thus, the therapist does not play the role of an active teacher or adviser who provides the client with persuasion and didactic suggestions for solutions. Neither does the intervention attempt to focus on tracing the sources or causes of the conflicting thoughts and feelings. The central task of the therapist is to provide the client with necessary didactic guidance through critiques on the client's activity records (such as diaries) and lectures on the client's life-coping experiences. As a central feature of treatment intervention, these criticisms and teaching are intended to direct the client to become more immersed in his or her actions and life experiences. The therapy does not draw the client's attention to attitudinal and emotional symptoms. Rather, it helps clients focus on practicing normal activities without being consciously concerned with their current state of mind (Ishiyama, 1987, 1990).

As the client mobilizes to act and to experience, his or her anxious symptoms become less dominant in life, and the negative influences from these symptoms will naturally decrease. A key purpose of the therapeutic intervention is to let the client avoid being consciously concerned with the intellectualized thoughts and emotions, because it is these attitudinal and emotional elements that trigger the anxiety arousal in the first place. The therapy, therefore, helps the client let go of some of the anxious feelings through a gradual, normal, and natural process. Such a process of therapeutic change will occur if the client is able to practice and obtain more effective behavior via his or her involvement in actions and activities at the four stages of the treatment. Of note, this four-stage therapeutic process follows the framework of a residential treatment model—a traditional intervention paradigm that requires clients to stay in a hospital or treatment center for 4 to 6 weeks (Morita, 1928/1974). Although this inpatient service format still exists in current Morita therapy practice (especially in Japan), the Morita therapy practice is now widely adopted in other forms of outpatient services such as individual counseling and psychotherapy sessions, group work, and other diverse psychoeducational interventions (Brown, 1989; Chen, 1996, 1998; Ishiyama, 1987, 1990, 1991, 2003; Watanabe, 1992). Also, it must be noted that Morita therapy is highly selective regarding its clientele. In other words, this therapy is not for clients in all kinds of psychological difficulties. Rather, Morita therapy considers as its target client population only those clients who suffer from social anxiety and nervous symptoms and their related problems. Thus, only those clients who seek help in dealing with social anxiety and its closely associated personal issues will be accepted for treatment (Morita, 1928/1974).

## Stage 1: Absolute Bed Rest

This is the beginning period of therapy; it usually lasts from 4 to 7 days, depending on the needs and situation of each client. As the client enters the treatment, he or she is isolated from any social contacts and activities. The client is asked to stay in bed all the time except for basic living activities such as having meals and going to the washroom. The therapist asks the client to encounter rather than avoid the psychological agony. The underlying rationale for intervention at this first stage is to minimize the span of contradictory thinking and negative feelings that have been intensified in the client's mind. This will lead to reducing the client's inner conflicts to a simpler form of psychic interaction. The intense bed rest aims to help the client recover from exhaustion caused by the inner psychic conflicts, inducing the client's spontaneous desire for action.

## Stage 2: Light Work

After the completion of the absolute bed rest, the client is instructed to carry on some light work assignments related to the daily routine. This period will last between 3 and 7 days, depending on each client's situation. As well, the client is not permitted to socialize or associate with other people. Sleeping time is substantially reduced—limited to 7 or 8 hours every night. The client must stay outdoors during the day to be involved in any actions that will require the use of muscles such as looking at the sky, climbing stairs, and any other physical exercises. The therapist provides lectures three times a week to the client. The main focus of the lectures is on explaining the process of recovery in reference to the client's diary. It helps the client become aware of the relationship between desires and facts. The primary function of this second stage is to initiate a transition from absolute rest to spontaneous activity. This reflects an essential rationale of Morita therapy— drawing attention to action. In focusing on unrelated and simple activities, the client is given an opportunity to break away from contradictory thoughts and anxious feelings. This helps the client gain insight into the dynamics of the paradox. The amount of work at this stage is critical, because it forms the foundation for stimulating further spontaneous action at the next stage.

## Stage 3: Chores

The chores period can be between 7 and 20 days. A variety of daily tasks, such as washing things, kitchen work, and cleaning rooms, is given to each client according to his or her state of health. The therapist can let the client work on whatever he or she can do. A client who wishes to may now also choose these tasks based on his or her own interest. Through work, he or she develops a sense of patience with the task at hand while gradually gaining a sense of happiness and satisfaction in discovering his or her own courage and capacity for being involved in working activities. As an extension of the second stage of the intervention, the guiding principle of the third stage is to expand the scope and increase the workload in action taking and action implementation. The more time and effort spent in these living tasks, the more confident the client feels about his or her ability and potential to live a productive life. Because needs and progress vary from one client to another, the timeline for intervention at the third stage also varies more substantially for each individual client than in the previous stages.

### Stage 4: Complicated Practical Life Experience

This last stage of Morita therapy usually lasts for about 10 days. It is a therapeutic period that expands on what has already been achieved through the previous stages. Moreover, it is a vital transition period that helps the client go back to a normal and integral life experience in the real world. The intervention attempts to encourage the client's patience through continued application of steady effort in daily work experiences. The client must now take on diverse tasks he or she encounters, regardless of personal interest or desires. As the final stage of the therapeutic intervention, stage 4 aims to prepare the client to go back to his or her actual and real life with a new and positive mental state—the ultimate goal of Morita therapy. By taking away all the restrictions on most aspects of one's personal and social life, especially those restrictions on interpersonal communication and relationships, the client is encouraged to reexperience a complex, dynamic, and multifaceted personal and social life reality. The therapy is not concerned with generating a treatment strategy to cure or reduce symptoms of psychopathological character or related disorders. Instead, Morita therapy focuses on bringing about conditions under which the client can let his or her inner character and awareness come into play freely. He or she will then utilize the character and awareness as resources for a gradual and positive change. This change directs the client to resume a normal and healthy functioning in life.

### ❖ MORITA THERAPY IN CURRENT PRACTICE

As has been illustrated, Morita therapy is a very unique behavioral therapeutic intervention with deep philosophical roots in the Eastern worldview. To utilize this therapeutic intervention in current practice of counseling and psychotherapy, it is of vital importance to note the main limitations of this therapeutic approach. First, although the traditional treatment process as described in the previous section still exists, it is not a very viable treatment modality for the majority of the counseling and psychotherapy contexts in the Western world in general, and in North America in particular. The residential intervention format does not make much sense financially, nor is it applicable to the pace of life in current Western society. Second, the traditional therapeutic modality is quite confined by its excessive focus on behavioral modification. There is much room for integration of cognitive and emotive considerations to strengthen the effectiveness of the therapeutic intervention. Third, Morita therapy is mainly a treatment for dealing with symptoms related to social anxiety, and its applications to other psychological problems beyond this spectrum still remain to be developed. This very limited scope means that Morita therapy may not pertain to many clients who have other psychological problems, and it is relevant only to a highly selective group of clients.

Notwithstanding these limitations, some key theoretical tenets and techniques from Morita therapy can be adapted to various intervention contexts such as regular individual counseling and psychotherapy, group counseling, and short-term solution-focused therapeutic interventions (Watanabe, 1992). This section of the discussion demonstrates how some of Morita therapy's key concepts and principles (Donahue, 1988; Fujita, 1986; Goto, 1988; Morita, 1928/1974; Reynolds, 1976, 1984, 1989) can be incorporated into the helping process for clients experiencing social anxiety difficulties.

## ❖ OBEDIENCE TO NATURE

A central premise of Morita therapy is its harmonious view about the relationship between humans and nature. The physical environment and the psychological world we encounter are natural phenomena that always accompany our lives. Living a life means to embrace these natural experiences. Thus, attempts to artificially control or resist natural phenomena are counterproductive. The Morita principle of obedience to nature points to the importance of our respect for, and acceptance of, living experiences in our daily routine. With such an attitude, we humans integrate ourselves into nature, that is, we become truly a part of the whole ecological system and function with the flow of the natural world.

To utilize this concept in counseling, the counselor helps the client put anxious feelings into perspective. Like other human emotions, social anxiety reflects a natural phenomenon that is part of one's living experiences. Obeying nature here does not mean a passive stance to give up one's efforts at problem solving, awaiting a miracle that would eliminate the emotional roadblock one is facing. Rather, one externalizes the psychological difficulty in a constructive manner. That is, the client comes to realize that he or she does not need to be burdened too much by anxious emotions or inconvenient feelings. While recognizing the negative nature of such feelings, one is still capable of taking productive actions to acquire positive living experiences. The main function of these productive actions is to make the coping endeavor a natural process to coexist with life experiences such as anxious feelings in one's life. The more comfortable and confident the client feels about his or her coexistence with anxious emotions, the less anxious he or she will feel in life situations. The negative impact of social anxiety on the person will gradually decline. As such, inconvenient emotions such as social anxiety will not become a significant hindrance to the client's healthy functioning, even though the anxiety feeling, as a natural phenomenon, will never totally disappear from one's life experiences.

Because the emotional self is considered a natural part of the total flow of human life, one's feelings, whether positive or negative, should be accepted as the way they function. Instead of making efforts to fight against and eliminate the anxiety symptoms, the valuable time and energy can be better used to pursue more productive activities. Counseling and psychotherapy teach the client to make peace with anxiety, normalizing the perceived negative feelings. When the client realizes that inconvenient feelings are a normal part of his or her emotional reaction to life events, the negative impression and connotations regarding anxiety will gradually disperse. The client feels less bothered by the anxiety while taking proactive actions and living a more fulfilling life. In other words, rather than being "anxiety free," the client accepts the emotional self as a companion in life and learns to make friends with inconvenient feelings. The attention fixation and action-focused therapeutic intervention strategies aim to help the client draw attention to his or her energy and potential to achieve optimal outcomes with the existence of anxiety emotions. As one comes to realize that he or she can live a productive life without eliminating emotional disturbances, he or she will be minimally affected by the negative impact of the inconvenient feelings (Chen, 1996, 1998).

## ❖ BILATERALITY AND TWO-SIDEDNESS

Drawn from the ancient Chinese philosophy of the coexistence of yin and yang, the Morita philosophy views human life as a whole entity that is composed of, and maintained by, a balance between these two basic sources of energy. Similar to the two sides of the same coin, these two aspects always coexist in the universe as well as in human life experiences. Following this bilateral worldview, there is no absolute definition or perfect solution for a living experience. This is because seeming opposites, such as positive-negative, good-bad, peaceful-violent, optimal-dissatisfactory, sufficient-inadequate, and active-passive, always coexist in life, even though one variable in this coexisting ecology may be perceived as more influential than the other at certain times and under certain circumstances. However, the balance between the two variables can change if other contexts surrounding them alter.

This bilateral perspective can be applied as a very effective helping methodology to guide the client in dealing with anxiety arousal. The client is very often overwhelmed by the magnitude of the inconvenient feelings he or she is experiencing at the moment. This makes him or her more obsessed with the sense of negativity. As a result, the client has a very difficult time seeing through to what the situation means "on the other side of the same coin," that is, issues and points that may be implied or reflected in a not-so-obvious manner with the very same experience he or she is encountering. The main task of the counselor, therefore, is to help the client to broaden the horizon so that he or she can become more aware of the two-sidedness in a life experience. The goal is for the client to feel more comfortable and competent in perceiving life experiences with a flexible, dynamic, multifaceted, and—most of all—comprehensive manner. As the client is given the opportunity to take a look at his or her personal life experiences, he or she comes to realize that the intermingled yin-yang coexistence is actually a common phenomenon in everyday life.

Of essential importance in coping with anxious emotions is one's mindfulness of the often hidden aspects at the other side of the same experience. For example, one's fear of not preparing well enough for an academic examination or a job interview actually reflects his or her desire to succeed in these situations. Also, feeling anxious could certainly hinder one's effective use of his or her capacity and energy. Yet, it is the experience of social anxiety that urges the person to face the problem and find ways to cope with the problem. Insights gained through these examples could become transferable to other situations in life, leading to a bilateral perspective in one's coping efforts. Such an effort can facilitate and empower contextual meaning making. This means that the client is encouraged to learn to adopt different perspectives in dealing not only with issues in the emotional self, but with other aspects of life as well. Meanings of events can be interpreted and reinterpreted by making a balance between the two sides of each emerging episode and experience in one's life journey (Ishiyama, 1991).

## ❖ CONCLUSION

A Japanese psychotherapy approach based on the Eastern worldview, Morita therapy provides a heuristic alternative for helping clients deal with social anxiety-related psychological difficulties. The meaningfulness of drawing attention to this therapeutic approach lies with the possibility of adopting its key theoretical tenets in counseling and psychotherapy in Western society. These theoretical concepts and principles have brought and will bring a very different perspective to the therapeutic intervention for social anxiety and other related issues in human emotion. Although Morita therapy has been one of the very few most recognizable non-Western therapeutic models in the realm of counseling and psychotherapy, its greater applicability and potential for therapeutic intervention remain to be explored. With a strong focus on constructive human action, the centrality of Morita therapy rests on the premise that humans are capable of living a quality life along with the presence of emotional arousal. Humans will experience positive changes if they are able to learn to live positively with anxious feelings and other inconvenient emotions. As such, Morita therapy can certainly contribute to the addition of a more balanced and holistic helping model in counseling and psychotherapy.

## ❖ REFERENCES

Alden, L., & Ishiyama, F. I. (1997). Shyness and social phobia: Japanese and Western views. *Canadian Clinical Psychologist, 7*(3), 4–7.

Aldous, J. L. (1994). Cross-cultural counselling and cross-cultural meanings: An exploration of Morita psychotherapy. *Canadian Journal of Counselling, 28,* 238–249.

Brown, M. J. (1989). Unobtrusive uses of Morita therapy in an adult education setting. *International Bulletin of Morita Therapy, 2*(1), 24–28.

Chen, C. P. (1996). Positive living with anxiety: A Morita perspective of human agency. *Counselling Psychology Quarterly, 9,* 5–14.

Chen, C. P. (1997). Using Morita principles in career counselling. *Cognica, 29*(2), 14–15.

Chen, C. P. (1998). A holistic approach to worklife dynamics: Morita-philosophy–based career counselling. *Counselling Psychology Quarterly, 11,* 239–256.

Chen, C. P. (2003, March). *Morita therapy intervention for work-related anxiety.* Paper presented at the American Psychological Association's Fifth Interdisciplinary Conference on Occupational Stress & Health, Work Stress and Health: New Challenges in a Changing Workplace, Toronto, Ontario, Canada.

Donahue, P. A. (1988). Practical application of basic Morita concepts in fostering productive living: A trainee's account. *International Bulletin of Morita Therapy, 1*(1), 26–30.

Fujita, C. (1986). *Morita therapy: A psychotherapeutic system for neurosis.* New York: Igaku-Shoin.

Goto, K. (1988). Shinkeishitsu treatment by Morita therapy in its original form. *International Bulletin of Morita Therapy, 1*(2), 37–42.

Ishiyama, F. I. (1986). Morita therapy: Its basic features and cognitive intervention for anxiety treatment. *Psychotherapy, 23,* 375–381.

Ishiyama, F. I. (1987). Use of Morita therapy in shyness counseling in the West: Promoting clients' self-acceptance and action taking. *Journal of Counseling & Development, 65,* 547–551.

Ishiyama, F. I. (1988a). Current status of Morita therapy research: An overview of research methods, instruments, and results. *International Bulletin of Morita Therapy, 1*(2), 58–84.

Ishiyama, F. I. (1988b). Morita therapy: A treatment of dogmatic self-containment in anxious and nervous clients. *Psychotherapy Patient, 4,* 243–262.

Ishiyama, F. I. (1990). A Japanese perspective on client inaction: Removing attitudinal blocks through Morita therapy. *Journal of Counseling & Development, 68,* 566–570.

Ishiyama, F. I. (1991). A Japanese reframing technique for brief social anxiety treatment: An exploratory study of cognitive and therapeutic effects of Morita therapy. *Journal of Cognitive Psychotherapy, 5,* 55–70.

Ishiyama, F. I. (2003). A bending willow tree: A Japanese (Morita therapy) model of human nature and client change. *Canadian Journal of Counselling, 37,* 216–231.

Kitanishi, K. (1992). Morita therapy: Its theory and practice in Japan. *International Bulletin of Morita Therapy, 5*(1–2), 3–9.

Kondo, A. (1992). A Zen perspective on the concept of self and human nature. *International Bulletin of Morita Therapy, 5*(1–2), 46–49.

Kora, T. (1991). An overview of the theory and practice of Morita therapy: IV. Understanding and treating shinkeishitsu symptoms in Morita therapy. *International Bulletin of Morita Therapy, 4*(1–2), 42–46.

LeVine, P. (1993). Morita therapy and its divergence from existential psychotherapy: A proposal for adopting a Morita-based philosophy for use in counseling and psychotherapy. *International Bulletin of Morita Therapy, 6*(1–2), 47–58.

Matesz, D. (1990). Morita and Buddhism: On the nature of suffering. *International Bulletin of Morita Therapy, 3*(1), 14–25.

Miura, M., & Usa, S. (1970). A psychotherapy of neurosis: Morita therapy. *Psychologia, 13,* 18–34.

Morita, S. (1974). Shinkeishitsu-no Hontai-to ryoho [Nature and treatment of nervosity]. In S. Aizawa & M. Maruyama (Eds.), *Shoma Morita collected works* (pp. 279–442). Tokyo: Hakuyosha. (Original work published 1928)

Reynolds, D. K. (1976). *Morita psychotherapy.* Berkeley: University of California Press.

Reynolds, D. K. (1984). *Playing ball on running water: The Japanese way to building a better life.* New York: Quill.

Reynolds, D. K. (1989). *Flowing bridges, quiet waters: Japanese psychotherapies, Morita and Naikan.* Albany: State University of New York Press.

Smith, K. (1981). Observations on Morita therapy and culture-specific interpretations. *Journal of Transpersonal Psychology, 13*(1), 59–69.

Suzuki, T., & Kataoka, H. (1982). On the long-term development of shinkeishitsu-neurotics treated by Morita therapy: A statistical quantitative analysis. *Psychiatria Clinica, 15,* 145–152.

Suzuki, T., & Suzuki, R. (1977). Morita therapy. In E. D. Wittkower & H. Warner (Eds.), *Psychosomatic medicine: Its clinical applications* (pp. 264–288). New York: Harper & Row.

Tamai, K., & Takeichi, M. (1991). Morita therapy for treating borderline personality disorder: The utility of treatment structuredness and limit-setting. *International Bulletin of Morita Therapy, 4*(1–2), 32–41.

Tashiro, N., & Tamai, K. (1993). A theoretical view of modified Morita therapy for neurotic patients. *International Bulletin of Morita Therapy, 6*(1–2), 18–29.

Walsh, R. (2000). Asian psychotherapies. In R. Corsini & D. Wedding (Eds.), *Current psychotherapies* (6th ed., pp. 407–444). Itasca, IL: F. E. Peacock.

Watanabe, N. (1992). The expansion of Morita therapy. *International Bulletin of Morita Therapy, 5*(1–2), 50–55.

# 20

# Pagan Approaches
to Healing

*Estelle Seymour*

W ith the influence of the transpersonal in psychology and the growth of
respect for indigenous traditions in the helping professions, a need for the
inclusion of a spiritual dimension in therapy is now accepted in many quarters.
Much of the literature on the role of spirituality and healing in therapy is based
in a Christian context; some draw from the Native American and shamanic traditions, as well as the Eastern influences of Zen Buddhism, Sufism, and Taoism.
In terms of Paganism, there appears to be very little current counseling and therapy literature available to counter the misinformation published during the early
1990s, which linked witchcraft, magic, and the occult with satanism and ritual
child abuse.

It has been suggested that from the 1970s onward, the United States has
been "the world centre of modern paganism . . . probably containing the greatest
number of its adherents" (Hutton, 1999, p. 340). Paganism is also said to be one
of the fastest growing religions in the United Kingdom and is, arguably, the
indigenous belief system of the British Isles.[1] Given the popular misconceptions
and religious freedom issues encountered by Pagans (Cookson, 1997), it is a valid
assumption that potential clients who identify themselves as Pagan might be

wary about disclosing this aspect of their lives in therapy. This chapter explores the contribution of Paganism to the healing process and the implications for counselors and therapists.

## ❖  HISTORY AND PHILOSOPHY OF PAGANISM

### The Development of Modern Paganism[2]

Modern Paganism, initially manifesting as Gardnerian witchcraft, grew in popularity in the United Kingdom during the 1950s and 1960s after the repeal of the Witchcraft Act in 1951.[3] Initially a conservative, hierarchical, initiatory mystery religion, it migrated to the United States in the 1970s, where it became an inspiration for the radical feminist movement. Although the Gardnerian tradition still exists, modern Paganism has grown substantially in definition and scope.

The interpretation of Pagan witchcraft in the United States contrasted with the essentially conservative English approach, where the genders were balanced in creative polarity. Hutton (1999) suggests that the tension was resolved through the work of Starhawk, a Gardnerian witch who, along with other feminist witches, forged a link between Gardner's Wicca and American social reform ideas that were set into motion in the 1960s (Orion, 1995). Starhawk "reinterpreted magic in the terms of human psychology, as a set of techniques for self-discovery, self-fulfilment, and the realization of true individual human potential" (Hutton, 1999, p. 346). Starhawk's popularization of the concepts of shared power, immanence, and creating community through ritual have become well established within the modern Pagan philosophy.

### Philosophies Informing Modern Paganism

Hutton (1996) suggests that modern Paganism

was neither the descendant of a continuous sectarian witch cult, nor born fully-fledged from the imagination of one man (Gerald Gardner) in the 1940s. It is, on the contrary, a particular and extreme incarnation of some of the broadest and deepest cultural impulses of the nineteenth and twentieth century British world. (p. 13)

In examining these "cultural impulses," Hutton (1996) identifies four direct lines of historical connection. First, there is the influence of high ritual magic, which involves the summoning and control of supernatural forces by the use of invocations and sacred equipment. The roots of the Western occult tradition may be traced back to Gnostic Hermeticism, "Egyptian" religion, the Renaissance, and the magic of Giordano Bruno (Orion, 1995). More recent influences also include Freemasonry and Theosophy (Hutton, 1999). Second, there is the influence of "hedge" witchcraft, the popular magic of the local wise woman and cunning man, which was learned from Eastern European shamans as they migrated across Europe. This involved the use of herbs, cures, and spells. Third is the influence of the art and literature of the ancient world. With industrialization came an "almost hysterical celebration of rural England" (Hutton, 1996, p. 9), which drew on the ancient images with a poetic vision of the great goddess as Gaia or Mother Earth and Pan as the horned god. Finally, Hutton (1996) identifies the influence of folk customs and rituals. Industrialization inspired interest in "old" religions, fertility cults, and nature spirits, which were attributed to the Druids in the 18th and 19th centuries.

## ❖ DEFINING PAGANISM

*Paganism* is an umbrella term that embraces a number of paths; Paganism can be distinguished from other world religions by its "extreme polymorphism" (York, 2003). Common factors of Paganism include respect for individual spiritual experience, reverence for Nature, recognition of many divinities, and insistence on the importance of the Goddess as well as the God. Other elements include beliefs in the immanence of divinity (i.e., the idea that God is present throughout the material universe), pantheism (i.e., God and the universe are identical), and animism (i.e., the idea that souls are quasi-physical and can exist outside the body, can be transferred from one body to another, and persist after the death of the body).

*Paganism* may thus be defined as "an affirmation of interactive and polymorphic sacred relationship by [the] individual or community with the tangible, sentient and nonempirical" (York, 2003, p. 157).

## ❖ PAGANISM AND ITS RELATIONSHIP TO MAGIC(K)[4]

"Not all Magicians are Pagans, but a significant number are. Not all Pagans engage in magic, but a significant number do" (Harvey, 1997, p. 87). Although the majority of Pagans will use ritual for magic and rites of passage, there are magicians who would not class themselves as Pagan. Such magicians tend to be

Christian in orientation, but Aleister Crowley's magical orders did invoke Pagan deities, and his writings exerted an important early influence on Gardnerian witchcraft (Adler, 1986; Hutton, 1999). *Magic(k)* has been defined as "the science and art of causing change to occur in conformity with will" (Aleister Crowley, as cited in Symonds & Grant, 1973, p. 131) and as "the art of causing changes to occur in consciousness" (Dion Fortune, as cited in Richardson, 1987, p. 13). By *will,* Crowley refers to an inner wisdom that has been accessed through self-knowledge after a period of magical training. It is similar to the functioning of Carl Rogers's organismic self.

The purpose of magic, then, is growth and spiritual development, which parallels the Jungian concept of individuation. Western magic can be seen primarily as a means of personal growth and self-expression bearing considerable similarities to other contemporary quests for self-understanding and growth (Harvey, 1997). Similarly, the Wiccan "Charge of the Goddess" teaches the wisdom of looking within for self-discovery and development. There are obvious parallels here with therapy.

## ❖ CONCEPTS OF PAGAN HEALING

The dimensions of healing, specifically in Wicca, include healing the self, others, and the environment. For the purposes of this chapter, the focus will be on psychological methods of healing. Healing the self may be accomplished first through embracing and developing the persona of the healer, whether as witch, shaman, priest, or priestess. Second, one attunes to the natural universe, especially solar and lunar rhythms. Third, one works in harmony with these to perform natural and sympathetic magic, often after communion with the spirit world.

Western psychological healing is limited and fraught with difficulty for Pagans whose animistic beliefs accept supernatural causes for some illnesses. The beliefs of indigenous cultures resonate strongly with many Pagans.

Murdock (cited in Orion, 1995) classified supernatural causes of illness across cultures into three groups: mystical, animistic, and magical. Mystical causes, such as fate, may be disregarded for Pagans, who generally believe that there is a logic and purpose behind everything and subscribe to the idea of mystical retribution as the "threefold law" or karma.[5]

Animistic causes of illness include "soul loss" (caused by human repression of unacceptable aspects of the self, rather than supernatural causes) and spirit aggression, where protection is needed against disembodied spirits seeking physicality. Whether these exist in "reality" or are a function of our own psychic energy is debatable, depending on how "psychological" the outlook.

Finally, magic itself may be believed to be the cause of illness. Fear of harmful magic can outweigh the "reality" of its existence and may lead to paranoia if the person perceiving a "magical attack" does not have a strong enough ego.

## ❖ THE PRACTICE OF PAGAN HEALING

In common with many spiritual paths and mystery religions, both Pagans and magicians use ritual. Sacred space is created through ritual to delineate the boundaries between the mundane world and the realms of the otherworld.[6] Within the sacred space, rituals may be performed to celebrate the changing seasons or as rites of passage. Magical rituals may be used to contact deeper powers of consciousness for specific purposes, such as healing.

### Healing the Self: Embracing and Developing the Persona of the Healer

For many women (and men), involvement with Wicca/witchcraft can be a healing experience. Women brought up in a patriarchal environment may have low self-esteem and feel powerless. A religion that venerates the feminine principle may help redress this imbalance.

Greenwood (2000) suggests that

> Feminist witchcraft offers the clearest and most distinct form of magical healing from what is described as an alienating patriarchy, and its rituals are largely those of rebellion against the dominant culture.... The politics of reclaiming the self are seen as central to its practice ... healing from patriarchy involves a politics seeking to effect deep internal and external change. Healing is primarily based on erotic energy, relationships and democratic community expressed through ritual. (p. 128)

### Performing Natural and Sympathetic Magic

For Pagans, just as for members of indigenous cultures, psychological conditions are particularly responsive to magic, because these involve movement of energy and change of consciousness (Orion, 1995). Within the sacred space, rituals, which may be enacted as psychodramas to connect with mythological and archetypal images, can put a "depth charge" into the unconscious and cause material to surface. Techniques used in ritual may include active imagination or "pathworking," imagery from the tarot, kabbalah or astrology, devotion, and the invocation of specific god-forms. The idea of the God/Goddess as immanent can help raise consciousness and lead to mystical experiences. The aftereffects of ritual may cause a period of emotional or physical instability while material is processed and integrated into everyday life.

Rituals for healing other people may involve raising and directing energy to that person as a form of absent healing. In cases where the best outcome is not clear (e.g., when someone is critically ill), the spirit world or Goddess may be asked to intervene as they or she sees fit (similar to "not my will but thy will be done"). For women who have been abused or raped or have miscarried, there is a "reconsecrating the womb" ritual (Ashcroft-Nowicki, 1993). There will often be tangible, energetically charged objects used to aid the healing process. These may be something that belongs to or symbolizes the person being healed, bundles of significant objects to effect healing (talismans), or pieces of paper on which significant symbols are written that may be kept or burned (sigils). Healing the earth is a primary focus for many Pagans, who will raise and transform energy in order to effect tangible change based on the principle of "think globally, act locally." Since the early 1980s, drumming and chanting have featured in these mass rituals (V. Crowley, 2000).[7]

Many Pagans become attuned to the natural rhythms of the universe by celebrating the changing seasons marked by the eight Celtic festivals. These mark the journey of the sun; its effects on the land; and the cycles of birth, death, and rebirth. Honoring these festivals keeps the recurring themes of transition, change, and loss in mind. In addition, developing an awareness of lunar cycles, particularly for women, and the wider astrological influences can offer a sense of tuning into the tides of change and influence.

❖   RELATIONSHIP TO CONTEMPORARY THERAPIES

The Pagan concept and practice of healing have much in common with contemporary therapies. Both share the ideas that healing involves integration and empowerment and that crises offer opportunities for growth. Both address imbalances and blocks in the mind, body, and spirit to different degrees and acknowledge their interrelationship. For both Pagans and counseling clients, healing takes place in a ritual space. Both utilize ritualized behavior in the creation of boundaried space created for the purpose of facilitated healing activities. Pagan therapists may choose to protect, charge, and cleanse the energy of both themselves and the therapy room before and after sessions. For diagnosis and assessment, Pagans will tend to choose from a wide, nonempirical range of tools (such as tarot) in order to reach a wider understanding of the issue. It could be argued that therapists use intuition and "gut feeling" alongside more formal "scientific" tools. Both offer methods for effecting change. A range of Pagan magical techniques (spells) may be better understood as applications of cognitive-behavioral theory. Both take heed of that which is "out of awareness," or the unconscious. Therapists are bound by a professional code of ethics. For the most part, Pagan ethics are simple: "And it harm ye none, do what thou wilt," often within the context of the threefold law. Both offer some latitude for individual interpretation.

## ❖ INTEGRATING PAGAN APPROACHES INTO COUNSELING AND PSYCHOTHERAPY

Ideally, religious (or any other) orientation should have no bearing on the therapist's ability to enter into the client's world. This may not work in practice, because it is impossible to be totally value free. Therapists, informed by their own cultural values and theoretical approach, have a map of the healing process, and the client's experience is viewed from within this framework. Difficulties may ensue when therapists are unfamiliar with the world inhabited by some of their clients, particularly when those clients are seen as members of "deviant" minority groups.

It has been suggested that because people "suspect . . . that admission of magical beliefs might be an open indicator of pathology, most people are reluctant to admit to any reliance on magical thinking" (Spiegel, 1993, p. 173). Although this relates to psychoanalysis, there are parallels to be drawn with other therapeutic approaches. Allman, de-la-Rocha, Elkins, and Weathers (1992) found that psychodynamic and behavioral therapists attributed significantly more pathology to clients who reported mystical experiences than did humanistic/existential therapists. More recent research with counseling psychologists suggests a positive relationship between a cognitive-behaviorist orientation and conservative Christian beliefs and a negative relationship between a psychodynamic orientation and Eastern and mystical beliefs (Bilgrave & Deluty, 2002). Despite these findings, there is some evidence to suggest that therapists who follow a spiritual path are able to offer greater acceptance and empathy to clients on spiritual journeys, particularly in cases that may manifest as psychic phenomena (Walters, 1998).

Issues regarding the preference of black and gay clients for similar therapists have been discussed elsewhere. The advantages of matching (enhanced empathy, positive role model, and no need for the client to educate the therapist), and the disadvantages as well (potential collusion and lack of objectivity), can be applied to Pagan clients. The argument for gay-affirmative therapy and application of the Coleman model of "coming out" (Davies & Neal, 1996) are also applicable to the Pagan context.

Some Pagan clients have suggested that another dimension could be added to the therapeutic relationship by the counselor's having a Pagan perspective. Practitioners may not be sympathetic with this desire, and careful consideration needs to be given to the merits and demerits of self-disclosure (Audet & Everall, 2003).

> There have been many times I would have given my eye-teeth (so to speak) to have the opportunity of accessing a pagan counsellor . . . since "coming out" as a pagan, I have made a point of saying so and found the response to be supportive—but there was an obvious lack of empathy or frame of common reference. (Seymour, 1998, p. 52)

Non-Pagans may find it difficult to understand the reluctance many Pagans have to be open about their chosen path. References have already been made to difficulties some Pagans have experienced with religious freedom (Cookson, 1997) and possible lack of validation of their worldview. In addition, Pagans struggling with their new identity may experience disapproval from family, friends, and work colleagues.

## ❖ RAISING SPIRITUAL ISSUES IN THERAPY

There are ethical and practical considerations to the integration of religious themes and rituals into traditional therapy models (Miller, 2003). The balance between being client led and therapist directed may constantly shift as both work toward empowerment of the client.

Perlstein (2001) suggests that it may be useful to offer the spiritual dimension when themes of anomie, disconnectedness, emptiness, isolation, or somatic symptoms frequently recur. It may be noted that these symptoms may also be understood as representing "soul loss." Perlstein and other therapists describe utilizing therapeutic techniques that are familiar to Pagans, such as the cocreation of rituals to provide continuity and to bolster ego strength and stability. In Perlstein's view, the sharing of ceremonial events can bring deeper meaning, closeness, and connection. Clients can learn empowering ways to support clinical issues they are working on while learning to honor the sacred in themselves and others.

A model for ritual used in therapy based on the healing principles of centering, assessment, gathering and directing energy, gratitude, and closure has been found to be useful (Cole, 2003).

It has been suggested that therapeutic healing with women clients can be enhanced through the use of ancient healing techniques such as oracles, astrology, shamanism, and collective ritual (Noble, 2001) and goddess myths (Mijares, 2003) and that underworld myths may offer a helpful archetype for women in recovery programs (O'Hare-Lavin, 2000). J. Bermudez and S. Bermudez (2002) describe the uses of making altars in family therapy, particularly with Latino and Hispanic clients or clients familiar with Catholicism or folk healing beliefs. It is suggested that altar making can help people explore spiritual themes, cope with bereavement and grief, and help strengthen families and couples.

There is a need for therapists to be able to distinguish between episodes of psychosis, which are retrogressive, and the progressive episodes of spiritual awakening (which also have retrogressive aspects) (S. Grof & C. Grof, 1989, 1991; Watson, 1994). Rowan (1990) contributes a useful perspective on ego inflation and psychosis connected with spiritual awakening, and an example of a progressive psychotic episode is offered by Thorne (1998).[8]

## ❖ TRAINING AND FUTURE RESEARCH

Including spirituality in training courses is not widespread, although there are references for the need for spirituality to be included in counselor training programs (Everts & Agee, 1994). Rowan (1990) suggests four aspects: intellectual, emotional, spiritual, and practical. Other suggestions for including spirituality in counselor education and personal development training are made by Pate and Bondi (1992), Grimm (1994), Fukuama and Sevig (1997), Ingersoll (1997), West (2000), and Souza (2002).

In counselor training courses in which facilitators wish to explore issues of spirituality and its place in the counseling relationship, students could initially be encouraged to examine their own beliefs, values, and attitudes toward spirituality. It is important to distinguish between spirituality and religion. The concept of spirituality can embrace any experience that offers a sense of a universal force or the divine. Once students have shared their own frameworks (and, ideally, extended them), they will be in a position to draw boundaries and establish their levels of comfort in the area of spirituality. Theoretical inputs could include an overview of the historical development of the relationship with counseling, maps and models of consciousness, an introduction to a range of forms of spirituality in different cultures, and healthy versus unhealthy expressions of spirituality. Students would need to explore the relevance of spirituality in their own counseling relationships, how and when it might be relevant to address it with clients, and what tools might be helpful. Students who follow a spiritual path would need to be clear about the boundary between being a counselor and a spiritual adviser. Trainers may choose to offer experimental workshops that include techniques for connecting with intuitive faculties.

Existing modules on "working with difference" could focus on the social context of minority groups, including religious and cultural issues, mental health constructs, and "deviance." This would form the basis for a grounding in working with a range of clients. It is assumed that the Pagan worldview would only need to be added to an existing scheme of work.

## ❖ CONCLUSION

Paganism has developed as a modern religion over the past 50 years but has yet to be fully acknowledged and understood. There are many resonances with other traditional and indigenous belief systems of which healing is an integral aspect. Although there are ethical issues in introducing a Pagan (or any other) worldview into therapeutic relationships, being informed by that worldview could make a substantial difference to the relationship. Pagans may be understood as creative individuals (Orion, 1995) who push boundaries and are deeply concerned with the environment. For those who identify as Pagan, much healing and support are contained within the community. There are also isolated individuals who may disclose experiences of disquieting psychic phenomena, seeking reassurance that they are not mad. In these cases, the skill of the therapist is in exploring the boundaries of spiritual awakening and the borders of psychosis and knowing when to refer. This awareness on the part of therapists, coupled with further research into Pagan healing, perhaps beginning with counseling trainers' attitudes toward Pagan spirituality, will support the development of an inclusive practice in therapy.

## ❖ NOTES

1. Hutton (1999) suggests that "Pagan witchcraft is the only religion which England has ever given the world" and estimates that there are between 90,000 and 120,000 Pagans in Britain.

2. It is beyond the scope of this chapter to document the history and development of modern Paganism in detail. See Orion (1995) for a history of modern Pagan witchcraft in the United States and Hutton (1999) for the development in England.

3. The Act was repealed 3 years after the Roman Catholic Church proclaimed as infallible the doctrine of the Assumption of the Virgin Mary, suggesting an acknowledgment of the feminine in spiritual matters.

4. *Magick* is "spelt with a *k* to distinguish it from the ordinary, lesser magic, or *mere conjuring*" (Aleister Crowley, as cited in Symonds & Grant, 1973).

5. The threefold law posits that whatever is sent out will return threefold.

6. Rituals are commonly held in the sacred space of a circle with the elements and directions corresponding to Jung's typology of psychological types: north/earth/sensation; east/air/thinking; south/fire/intuition; west/water/feeling.

7. The healing properties of drumming have been documented elsewhere (see Diallo & Hall, 1989; Friedman, 2000).

8. As a result of the proposal from transpersonal therapists working with spiritual emergencies, the *Diagnostic and Statistical Manual of Mental Disorders*, 4th edition (American Psychiatric Association, 1994) now includes a diagnostic category referring to spiritual or religious problems (Lukoff, Lu, & Turner, 1998). The spiritual emergency movement grew out of this need as a way of offering support (Bragdon, 1990; S. Grof & C. Grof, 1989, 1991; Porter, 1995; Watson, 1994).

## ❖ REFERENCES

Adler, M. (1986). *Drawing down the moon* (2nd ed.). Boston: Beacon.

Allman, L. S., de-la-Rocha, O., Elkins, D. N., & Weathers, R. S. (1992). Psychotherapists' attitudes toward clients reporting mystical experiences. *Psychotherapy, 29,* 564–569.

American Psychiatric Association. (1994). *Diagnostic and statistical manual of mental disorders* (4th ed.). Washington, DC: Author.

Ashcroft-Nowicki, D. (1993). *Daughters of Eve.* London: Aquarian.

Audet, C., & Everall, R. D. (2003). Counsellor self-disclosure: Client informed implications for practice. *Counselling and Psychotherapy Research, 3,* 223–231.

Bermudez, J., & Bermudez, S. (2002). Altar-making with Latino families: A narrative therapy perspective. *Journal of Family Therapy, 13,* 329–347.

Bilgrave, D. P., & Deluty, R. H. (2002). Religious beliefs and political ideologies as predictors of psychotherapeutic orientations of clinical and counselling psychologists. *Psychotherapy: Theory, Research, Practice, Training, 39,* 245–260.

Bragdon, E. (1990). *The call of spiritual emergency: From personal crisis to personal transformation.* San Francisco: Harper & Row.

Cole, V. L. (2003). Healing principles: A model for the use of ritual in psychotherapy. *Counseling and Values, 47,* 184–194.

Cookson, C. (1997). Reports from the trenches: A case study of religious freedom issues faced by Wiccans practicing in the United States. *Journal of Church and State, 39,* 723–748.

Crowley, V. (2000). Healing in Wicca. In W. Griffin (Ed.), *Daughters of the Goddess* (pp. 151–165). Walnut Creek, CA: AltaMira.

Davies, D., & Neal, C. (1996). *Pink therapy.* Buckingham, UK: Open University Press.

Diallo, Y., & Hall, M. (1989). *The healing drum: African wisdom teachings.* Rochester, VT: Destiny.

Everts, J. F., & Agee, M. N. (1994). Including spirituality in counsellor education: Issues for consideration, with illustrative reference to a New Zealand example. *International Journal for the Advancement of Counselling, 17,* 291–302.

Friedman, L. (2000). *The healing power of the drum.* Reno, NV: White Cliffs Media.

Fukuama, M. A., & Sevig, T. D. (1997). Spiritual issues in counseling: A new course. *Counselor Education and Supervision, 36,* 233–244.

Greenwood, S. (2000). The magical will: Gender and power in magical practices. In G. Harvey & C. Hardman (Eds.), *Pagan pathways* (pp. 191–203). London: Thorsons.

Grimm, D. W. (1994). Therapist spiritual and religious values in psychotherapy. *Counseling and Values, 38,* 154–164.

Grof, S., & Grof, C. (Eds.). (1989). *Spiritual emergency.* Los Angeles: Tarcher.

Grof, S., & Grof, C. (1991). *The stormy search for the self.* Los Angeles: Tarcher.

Harvey, G. (1997). *Listening people speaking Earth: Contemporary Paganism.* London: Hurst.

Hutton, R. (1996). The roots of modern Paganism. In G. Harvey & C. Hardman (Eds.), *Pagan pathways* (pp. 3–15). London: Thorsons.

Hutton, R. (1999). *The triumph of the moon: A history of modern Pagan witchcraft.* Oxford, UK: Open University Press.

Ingersoll, R. E. (1997). Teaching a course on counseling and spirituality. *Counselor Education and Supervision, 36,* 224–232.

Lukoff, D., Lu, F., & Turner, R. (1998). From spiritual emergency to spiritual problem: The transpersonal roots of the new DSM-IV category. *Journal of Humanistic Psychology, 38,* 21–50.

Mijares, S. G. (2003). Tales of the Goddess: Healing metaphors for women. In S. G. Mijares (Ed.), *Modern psychology and ancient wisdom: Psychological healing practices from the world's religious traditions* (pp. 71–95). New York: Haworth Press.

Miller, G. (2003). *Incorporating spirituality in counseling and psychotherapy: Theory and technique.* New York: Wiley.

Noble, V. (2001). Letting nature take its course. *Women and Therapy, 24,* 193–208.

O'Hare-Lavin, M. E. (2000). Finding a "lower," deeper power" for women in recovery. *Counseling and Values, 44,* 198–212.

Orion, L. (1995). *Never again the burning times.* Prospect Heights, IL: Waveland.

Pate, R. H., & Bondi, A. M. (1992). Religious beliefs and practice: An integral aspect of multicultural awareness. *Counselor Education and Supervision, 32,* 108–115.

Perlstein, M. (2001). A spiritual coming out: The use of ritual in a psychology practice. *Women and Therapy, 24,* 175–192.

Porter, G. (1995). Exploring the meaning of spirituality and its implications for counselors. *Counseling and Values, 40,* 69–79.

Richardson, A. (1987). *Priestess: The life and magic of Dion Fortune.* Northampton, UK: Aquarian.

Rowan, J. (1990). Spiritual experiences in counselling. *British Journal of Guidance and Counselling, 18,* 233–249.

Seymour, E. (1998). *Towards a Pagan/magickal approach to counselling?* Unpublished dissertation, University of Bristol, UK.

Souza, K. Z. (2002). Spirituality in counseling: What do counseling students think about it? *Counseling and Values, 46,* 213–215.

Spiegel, S. (1993). The utilization and investigation of "luck" in psychotherapy. *Contemporary Psychoanalysis, 29,* 173–180.

Symonds, J., & Grant, K. (Eds.). (1973). *Aleister Crowley: Magick.* London: RKP.

Thorne, B. (1998). *Person centred counselling and Christian spirituality.* London: Whurr.

Walters, P. (1998). *Counselling and Paganism—Uneasy bedfellows?* Unpublished dissertation, University of Bristol, UK.

Watson, K. W. (1994). Spiritual emergency: Concepts and implications for psychotherapy. *Journal of Humanistic Psychology, 34,* 22–45.

West, W. (2000). *Psychotherapy and spirituality.* London: Sage.

York, M. (2003). *Pagan theology: Paganism as a world religion.* New York: New York University Press.

# 21

# Yoga and Its Practice in Psychological Healing

*Josna Pankhania*

I n this chapter, I will endeavor to outline the historical background of yoga, identify the main sources of yoga, and offer an introduction to yoga and meditation. Yoga covers a vast field of philosophy, psychology, and practice, and in the section on the limbs and branches of yoga, I will outline Patanjali's eight limbs or steps of yoga and the main branches of yoga. Millions of people throughout the world currently practice yoga on a regular basis. This vigorous growth and blossoming of yoga across the globe raises the question, "What are people who practice yoga seeking through yoga?" The section on research into yoga will explore this question. Modern psychology has emerged as a distinct science in the last hundred years, whereas the systematic study of psychology in India has been evolving over a few thousand years. Yoga psychotherapy is more ancient than any other form of psychotherapy. In the section on yoga psychology, the yogic principles of psychotherapy will be explored within the context of yogic meaning and purpose of life. This leads to the central question of this chapter, that is, to what extent can Western-trained psychotherapists really utilize yogic principles and practice for their work with people who are seeking psychological healing?

## ❖ HISTORICAL BACKGROUND

*Yoga* refers to the enormous wealth of philosophical, psychological, and spiritual knowledge that has developed in India for at least five millennia and that has been regarded as the very foundation of the ancient Indian civilization. Yoga is a spectacularly multifaceted phenomenon, and as such, it is very difficult to define. The Sanskrit word *yoga* is most frequently interpreted as referring to the "union" of the individual self with the supreme self. Yoga is the process of uniting our finite, microcosmic, individual self with the infinite, macrocosmic, pure consciousness. Kumari (2003) writes, "Yoga is the tuning up of the chords of one's being so that it chimes in harmony with the music of the cosmos" (p. v).

The desire to transcend the human condition, to go beyond our ordinary consciousness and personality, is a deeply rooted impulse that is as old as humanity's self-awareness. Feuerstein (1998) asserts, "Nowhere on Earth has the impulse towards transcendence found more consistent and creative expression than on the Indian peninsula. The civilization of India has spawned an almost overwhelming variety of spiritual beliefs, practices and approaches" (p. xxv). And Eliade (1958) writes, "Yoga constitutes a specific dimension of the Indian spirit to such a degree that wherever Indian culture and religion have penetrated, one finds also a more or less pure form of yoga" (p. 101).

For thousands of years within the philosophical traditions of the various historical periods of India—the Indus Sarasvati civilization (4500–2500 BCE), the later Brahmanical (2500–1500 BCE), the Upanishadic (1500–1000 BCE), the Epic (1000–100 BCE), the Classic (100 BCE–500 CE), Tantric (500–1300 CE), Sectarian (1300–1700 CE), and Modern (1700 CE–present)—yoga has flourished, and it continues to do so today (Feuerstein, 1998). Ancient texts such as the Puranas and the Brahmanas, the Ramayana, the Mahabharata, the Bhagavad Gita, and the Yoga-Sutra of Patanjali have all contributed to the yogic tradition.

## ❖ SOURCES OF YOGA

The Bhagavad Gita is regarded in India as the greatest compendium of religious inspiration, including devotional, philosophical, ethical, and moral thought. The title of each chapter of the Bhagavad Gita is a form of yoga: the yoga of action, the yoga of knowledge, the yoga of devotion, the yoga of the royal science, and so forth. In the Bhagavad Gita, Sri Krishna explains to Arjuna that yoga is the supreme secret of life and destroyer of pain (Wood, 1959, p. 216). The Yoga-Sutra, compiled by Patanjali, represents the climax of a long development of the yogic tradition in India. Patanjali, who gave the yoga tradition its classical format, was the first to write down and codify classical yoga. The techniques of asceticism and meditation elaborated by Patanjali are certainly of great antiquity: They are not his discoveries or those of his time, and they had been put to the test many centuries before him. The Yoga-Sutra consists of four books: the first contains 51 aphorisms, or sutras, and is the section on "yogic ecstasy" (*samadhipada*); the second, containing 55 sutras, is called "realization" (*sadhanapada*); the third, which contains 55 sutras, deals with the "marvelous power" (*vibhuti*); and the fourth contains 34 sutras and is about "isolation" (*kaivalya*) (Eliade, 1958).

## ❖ YOGA PHYSIOLOGY

According to yogic physiology (Saraswati, 1993), there are five *koshas,* these being dimensions of human existence or experience or layers of consciousness. *Annamaya kosha* concerns the material existence, the physical. *Pranamaya kosha* focuses on the energy body. *Manomaya kosha* concerns the mental activity of our minds, with *mind* understood as the externalized or manifest aspect of consciousness, more subtle than the physical body. *Vijnanamaya kosha* includes the subtle level of energy and consciousness, the level of intuition and wisdom, the higher mind. *Anandamaya kosha* focuses on the dimension of perfection, the bliss layer, the transcendental. Yoga offers a pathway for harmonizing the different *koshas,* for, according to yogic philosophy, when the layers of the body, energy, and the mind are in balance, we are more open to the higher experiences associated with *vijnanamaya* and *anandamaya koshas.*

## ❖ LIMBS AND BRANCHES OF YOGA

Patanjali outlined eight limbs or steps of yoga: *yama,* abstention; *niyamas,* observances; *asana,* postures; *pranayama,* breath control of *prana* or the life force; *pratyahara,* sense withdrawal; *dharana,* concentration; *dhyana,* meditation; and *samadhi,* contemplation. These eight limbs of yoga are an integral part of all the different branches of yoga.

The many branches of yoga include hatha yoga, mantra yoga, karma yoga, bhakti yoga, raja yoga, and gyana yoga, which are explained by Swami Niranjanananda Saraswati (1993). Hatha yoga involves the purification of the body and the mind. Mantra yoga includes chanting mantras, subtle sounds, or combinations of sounds, which are used for the liberation of consciousness from the limitations of mundane awareness. Karma yoga refers to the yoga of dynamic meditation, the yoga of action performed with meditative awareness. Bhakti yoga refers to pure, intense, inner devotion or love and the channeling of the intellect, emotions, and the self toward a higher purpose, the yogic path of devotion. Raja yoga literally means the royal path of yoga and aims to enter into the realm of psychic consciousness to discover the dormant areas of the mind and the consciousness. *Gyana* means "knowledge," and gyana yoga refers to the process of meditative awareness that brings one closer to one's higher self. Through the different branches of yoga, we can see that yoga encompasses the mind, the body, and the spirit and that it is fundamentally a spiritual practice (Saraswati). The different branches of yoga offer a range of practices for a range of personalities and purposes.

## ❖ YOGA TODAY

Yoga as we know it today includes the spiritual values, attitudes, precepts, and techniques that have been developed in India for at least five millennia. Traditionally, it was believed that one could not learn yoga alone, that one required a teacher or guru (Dobia, 1999). The student of yoga, the yogi, began by renouncing the secular world of the family and society, to be guided by the guru through the initiatory structure of yoga. Today, in India and throughout the world, yoga is taught en masse in gymnasiums and sports centers, through mainstream television, and with the help of yoga kits comprising videotapes or DVDs.

Yoga offers a holistic framework for physical, mental, and spiritual health and well-being (Desikachar, 1995). It helps the whole person become balanced and integrated. Unlike allopathic medicine, it does not treat a symptom on the physical level only but sees the person as an integrated unit of body, mind, and spirit (Gharote & Lockhart, 1987). Because of a lack of such a holistic model for health care and self-development in Westernized countries, more and more people are looking to the East for alternatives such as yoga. With its spread across the globe, it appears that yoga transcends racial, cultural, and religious barriers. Yoga's deep and lasting value as a comprehensive system for personal health care and development continues to be discovered by people from every culture, in every part of the globe (Kraftsow, 1999).

Millions of people throughout the world currently practice yoga on a regular basis, and there are many reasons for this. Cope (1999), a Western-trained psychotherapist who has lived and taught yoga at one of the largest yoga centers in the United States, the Kripalu Center for Yoga and Health in Lenox, Massachusetts, argues that yoga enhances cardiovascular health as well as musculoskeletal strength and flexibility without the painful, often damaging, side effects of high-impact aerobics. It tunes up every system in the body—respiratory, digestive, reproductive, endocrine, lymphatic, and nervous. Yoga cultivates the body's capacity to relax and dramatically reduces the negative effects of stress. With regular yoga, people have found that they breathe better, sleep better, and feel better. Many people have even found that they begin to recover from chronic illness.

Some would argue that the physical benefits of yoga, which are widely reported in medical journals and the mainstream press, are only the tip of the iceberg. Regular practitioners of yoga describe a whole host of subtle transformations in their lives, changes that seem more mysterious, more difficult to quantify and even to describe. Cope (1999) has observed of his students that

> Many experience moments of sharply increased mental focus and clarity, and heightened perceptual and intuitive powers. Some describe a dramatic increase in energy and stamina, emotional evenness and equanimity. Others report a heightened feeling of connection to an inner self, ecstatic states of bliss, and profound wellbeing. And there are the not infrequent stories of truly miraculous healings—physical, emotional, spiritual. (p. xii)

Although yoga for many people, both in the East and the West, is a means for achieving physical, emotional, and mental health, yoga also offers a pathway for spiritual growth and development. Gharote and Lockhart (1987, p. 3) argue that although millions of people purport to practice yoga, its essential nature seems to have been grasped by very few. Within the context of Western European colonialism and cultural imperialism, the West's interest in yoga can be seen as a puzzle, a triumph, or a dilemma. On one hand, there are the racist ideological manifestations at the institutional, structural, and interpersonal levels from the days of the empire, which still continue today. On the other hand, there is a fascination by some Europeans with the Indian culture and religion. This fascination has been expressed in many ways, one of which has been through the undertaking of a great range of Indological studies and research (Das, 1995). This has contributed to the revival of various ancient Indian practices in India such as tantric yoga, which was previously marginalized. Thus, the West's fascination with Indian culture and religion has contributed toward the popularization of yoga, both in the West and within India.

Research into the impact of yoga tends to focus on a range of physical, psychological, and emotional benefits that can be acquired through aspects of yoga practice such as *asanas* (physical exercises), *pranayama* (breathing exercises), or *dhyana* (meditation). Research into the impact of individual aspects of yoga such as the *asanas, pranayama,* or meditation is well documented and often includes measurable areas such as the positive benefits of yoga in the management of asthma (Cooper et al., 2003; Manocha, 2003), menopausal symptoms (Adams, 2003), autonomic nervous system (Raghuraj & Telles, 2003), stress (Roth & Stanley, 2002), back pain (Hudson 1998), and autonomic cardiovascular rhythms (Bernardi et al., 2001) and in the care of infants and children with Down syndrome, cerebral palsy, and learning disabilities (Reilly, 1999).

❖ YOGA PSYCHOLOGY

According to yoga, most psychological problems are caused by ego involvement and overidentification with pain and pleasure, failure and success. Psychological problems may also arise as a result of nonacceptance of the present; false ideas about the self, others, or different situations; and reactions in the form of anger, jealousy, hatred, indifference, fear, anxiety, repulsion, and so on (Saraswati, 1993). All of this can lead to fragmentation within the person, or, as Gharote and Lockhart (1987) write,

> In yogic terms, disease is caused by lack of wholeness. Yoga helps us to rediscover how to bring about that state of wholeness within ourselves. Some people are able to do this entirely alone. Some need the help of a teacher to guide them through the techniques. Others are in such an acute state of imbalance that they need the help of a therapist to show them yogic methods to restore health and harmony that are particularly effective for them as individuals. (p. 1)

As mentioned earlier, modern psychology has developed as a distinct science only in the last hundred years, whereas in India, psychology has been studied systematically over a period of a few thousand years. Thus, yoga psychotherapy is more ancient than any other form of psychotherapy. Yoga is based on the principle that self-realization is a process of purification, the removal of impurities that obscure one's true nature as pure consciousness, in order to be free of all distress and suffering. Pollutants are found in various forms and in all aspects of our being. The body is believed to be polluted by toxins, and the mind is seen as being contaminated by thoughts that do not reflect the underlying reality. Modern psychology identifies the human being with his or her personality and thoughts and considers the person's environment to be the external surroundings. Yoga psychology considers consciousness to be the essence of a person and all else to be the environment in which consciousness is embedded. Swami Niranjanananda Saraswati (1993) writes,

In psychology we have the conscious, subconscious, unconscious, and superconscious. These same states of experience are known in yoga as jagrit, swapna, nidra, and turiya. The aim of the yogi is to reach the turiya state by going through the conscious, subconscious, and unconscious, and becoming aware of the different expressions, impressions, actions, and reactions. This awakening of the mind is known as self-realization. (p. 468)

Whereas the fundamental aim of yoga is liberation through self-realization, the aim of psychoanalysis is the harmonization of the human personality (Spiegelman & Vasavada, 1987). Nevertheless, the common ground that Western psychology shares with yoga is interesting. Certain elements of the yogic concept of karma can be seen in Freud and Jung's conceptualization of memory. According to Patanjali, karma is a memory trace recorded in the unconscious by any thought or action a person has carried out in this or previous lives. These karmic memory traces, *samskara,* remain in the unconscious as a predisposition toward carrying out the same action or thought again in the future. Sufficient repetitions of the same action or thought produce a strengthening of the predisposition. Such a karmic habit pattern, or *vasana,* can be taken as the yogic equivalent for the modern psychological notion of motivation.

Both yoga and Freud agree that memory and motivation are parts of a single psychic process that also embodies choice or selection. However, there is disagreement between yoga and Freud as to the degree that this choice process is free or determined, as well as to the extent to which the process of memory and motivation can be transcended. Both yoga and Freud agree that the bulk of this memory and motivation psychological process occurs within the unconscious. Jung, who was strongly influenced by yoga psychology during the 1920s and 1930s, took a middle path between his teacher Freud and yoga. This middle path lay between the determinism of Freud and yoga's ideal of absolute freedom once all karma is annihilated. Jung, like Freud, could not conceive of the unconscious ever becoming completely known and denied that the unconscious could ever be totally overcome or transcended. Nevertheless, Jung was influenced by the yogic notion of karma in significant ways. Jung spent time in India and studied Sanskrit and Patanjali's Yoga-Sutras, and the notion of karma sparked the formation of Jung's concepts of the archetypes, universal dispositions of the mind that, in Jung's view, are inherent in the collective unconscious of each human being. The collective unconscious is the psychobiological memory of our ancestors, our psychic heritage. The collective unconscious is the psychic heritage that is passed on to us by our animal ancestors, primitive human ancestors, ethnic group, nation, tribe, and family. Besides the collective unconscious, the content of the unconscious also consists of the personal unconscious. The personal unconscious consists of the past experiences of the individual's own lifetime that have been either forgotten or repressed. Real memory, according to Jung, involves raising to consciousness the ancestral traces or archetypes of the collective unconscious as well as the content of the personal unconscious (Coward, 2002).

Thus, the ancient yoga conception of karma can be shown to have points of significant contact with modern psychology. Freud and Jung both assert, as Patanjali did long ago, that memory and motivation are part of our unconscious psychic process, but neither believed, as Pantanjali did, that the unconscious can be known in the quest for omniscience.

Swami Ajaya (1983) asserts that modern psychotherapy, for the most part, is oriented toward the development and strengthening of the ego. He argues that this is quite appropriate for those who are struggling to free themselves from the preoccupations of the more primitive levels of consciousness. Swami Ajaya explains that yoga therapy also helps those who are functioning at those levels to develop their ego capacities, but whereas current models of psychotherapy generally neglect to help one reach beyond identification with the ego, yoga is especially beneficial in this latter phase of development.

Yoga helps the ego surrender its authority and embrace a universal nurturing center of love and wisdom. Swami Ajaya (1983) explains that by identifying with the more circumscribed ego, the center of one's interest becomes some aspect of universal consciousness and the object of one's devotion. Further detachment from the limited perspective of the ego enables one to become a neutral observer of the melodramas of life, experiencing an underlying unity of being. The ultimate aim of yoga is to pass beyond all involvement with form and realize the highest state of consciousness.

As Swami Niranjanananda Saraswati (1993) writes,

> Through yogic techniques we can develop the ability to relax in any situation under any condition. We can also develop the capacity to concentrate, to collect all our dissipated energies and focus them at one point. Then the combination of mental force and vital force becomes a very powerful tool in opening up the different dimensions of the human personality. (p. 461)

## ❖ APPLICATION OF YOGIC PRINCIPLES AND PRACTICE TO PSYCHOLOGICAL HEALING

The strengths of yoga therapy complement the weaknesses of Western psychotherapy so elegantly that many people are already turning to the holistic and spiritual path of yoga in their efforts to find healing and peace. The challenge for cross-cultural psychotherapists is to see how they might draw upon Eastern and Western psychotherapeutic wisdom in order to serve the best interests of all the people with whom they work.

An integral part of the work of cross-cultural psychotherapists is to interact with people from diverse cultural backgrounds. The question is, What ideology, philosophy, terms of reference, and frameworks do cross-cultural psychotherapists use, especially with clients from diverse cultural backgrounds? The challenge for cross-cultural psychotherapists is to see how the wisdom and knowledge of other, particularly non–Western European, traditions might be incorporated into their practice. To what extent is it possible for cross-cultural psychotherapists to incorporate non-European psychotherapeutic traditional healing systems such as yoga into their work? And what about psychotherapists who work only with people from Western European backgrounds—is it possible for them to utilize non-European psychotherapeutic traditions in order to offer their clients a broader range of choices in their healing? Many psychotherapists are already utilizing yogic techniques such as meditation and yogic breathing in their work (Fontana & Slack, 2002). The central question that remains is, To what extent can Western-trained psychotherapists really utilize yogic principles and practice for their work with people who are seeking psychological healing?

First, yogic principles cannot be learned from lectures and books (Dobia, 1989). Ideally, one would learn from a guru. One also needs to learn from one's own rigorous and disciplined practice. Without knowing yoga through experience, how can one really know or understand yogic principles? Psychotherapists who have not integrated yoga into their lifestyle can offer their clients only a limited, theoretical insight into the healing principles of yoga. Second, there is also the issue of ideology. Western counseling and psychotherapy generally do not engage with the spiritual dimension of life. Psychotherapists generally maintain a distinction between psychotherapy and religion and do not enter into the realm of spirituality. In yoga, a consideration of the spiritual dimension of life is the foundation of the therapeutic process (Ajaya, 1983).

The integration of the wisdom about healing from the East and the West is a complex process, for the East and the West both have different historical contexts. The process of transferring long-accumulated wisdom that has been developed for thousands of years within a specific cultural context to another that has a different linguistic and philosophical heritage is not easy. Wilber (2000) attempts to embrace the East and the West, ancient and modern, through "integral psychology." Wilber offers us a psychological model that includes waves of development, streams of development, states of consciousness, and the self through the pathway of the subconscious to self-consciousness to superconsciousness. Nevertheless, if mainstream psychotherapists, including integral psychologists, do not learn yoga through practice in order to have the practical experience to guide their clients along a yogic healing journey, then the time has come for them to learn about yogic healing in order to guide their clients towards properly trained yoga therapists as and when appropriate.

## ❖ CONCLUSION

With the recognition of yoga and other traditional healing systems by psychotherapists, all people attending psychotherapy will benefit. Furthermore, people from culturally and linguistically diverse backgrounds will no longer be invisible within the mainstream psychotherapy world. Their cultural heritage becomes a respectable and knowledgeable element in the search for healing, thereby moving toward equity and justice in psychotherapy. Because mainstream Western psychotherapy models do not, at present, have a systematic approach to holistic health, psychotherapy in the West could benefit from the knowledge and wisdom of many traditional practices. The inclusion of the Indian traditional healing systems of yoga within psychotherapy offers greater choice for treatment and serves to validate and honor the historical contribution of people from the East to the development of healing systems and spiritual knowledge.

### Acknowledgments

I would like to acknowledge and thank Paramahamsa Satyananda Saraswati, Paramahamsa Niranjananada Saraswati, Swami Dr. Shankardevananda Saraswati, Sannyasi Dharmadeva Saraswati, Swami Kriyatmananda Saraswati, Brenda Dobia, and John Cameron.

## ❖ REFERENCES

Adams, J. (2003). Exploring yoga to relieve menopausal symptoms. *Holistic Nursing Practice, 17,* 166–167.

Ajaya, Swami. (1983). *Psychotherapy East and West: A unifying paradigm.* Honesdale, PA: Himalayan International Institute of Yoga Science and Philosophy.

Bernardi, L., Sleight, P., Bandinelli, G., Cencetti, S., Fattorini, L., Wdowczyc-Szulc, J., et al. (2001). Effect of rosary prayer and yoga mantras on autonomic cardiovascular rhythms: Comparative study. *British Medical Journal, 323,* 1446–1449.

Cooper, S., Oborne, J., Newton, S., Harrison, V., Thompson Coon, J., Lewis, S., et al. (2003). Effect of two breathing exercises (buteyko and pranayama) in asthma: A randomized controlled trial. *Thorax, 58,* 674–679.

Cope, S. (1999). *Yoga and the quest for the true self.* New York: Bantam Books.

Coward, H. (2002). *Yoga and psychology: Language, memory, and mysticism.* Albany: State University of New York Press.

Das, V. (1995). *Critical events: An anthropological perspective on contemporary India.* Delhi, India: Open University Press.

Desikachar, T. K. V. (1995). *The heart of yoga, developing a personal practice.* Rochester, VT: Inner Traditions International.

Dobia, B. (1989). Yoga therapy. In R. Hetzel (Ed.), *The healing arts* (pp. 137–146). Melbourne, Australia: Houghton Mifflin.

Dobia, B. (1999). Light comes to darkness: An interview with T. K. V. Desikachar. *Yoga International, 47,* 28–33.

Eliade, M. (1958). *Yoga: Immortality and freedom.* London: Penguin.

Feuerstein, G. (1998). *The yoga tradition: Its history, literature, philosophy and practice.* Prescott, AZ: Hohm Press.

Fontana, D., & Slack, I. (2002). *Teaching meditation to children: Simple steps to relaxation and well-being.* London: Thorson.

Gharote, M. L., & Lockhart, M. (Eds.). (1987). *The art of survival: A guide to yoga therapy.* London: Unwin.

Hudson, S. (1998). Yoga aids in back pain. *Australian Nursing Journal, 5*(9), 27.

Kraftsow, G. (1999). *Healing with the timeless teachings of Viniyoga: Yoga for wellness.* New York: Penguin.

Kumari, M. L. (2003). *What yoga is? Yoga: The science of holistic living* (4th ed.). Chennai, India: Vivekananda Kendra Prakashan Trust.

Manocha, R. (2003). Sahaja yoga in asthma. *Thorax, 58,* 825–826.

Raghuraj, P., & Telles, S. (2003). Effect of yoga-based and forced uninostril breathing on the autonomic nervous system. *Perceptual Motor Skills, 96,* 79–80.

Reilly, L. (1999). Yoga for the special child: A therapeutic approach for infants and children with Down syndrome, cerebral palsy, and learning disabilities. *Teaching Exceptional Children, 31*(3), 83.

Roth, B., & Stanley, T. W. (2002). Mindfulness-based stress reduction and healthcare utilization in the inner city: Preliminary findings. *Alternative Therapies in Health and Medicine, 8*(1), 60–62, 64–66.

Saraswati, Swami N. (1993). *Yoga Darshan: Vision of the yoga Upanishads.* Munger, Bihar, India: Yoga Publications Trust.

Spiegelman, J. M., & Vasavada, A. U. (1987). *Hinduism and Jungian psychology.* Phoenix, AZ: Falcon Press.

Wilber, K. (2000). *Integral psychology consciousness: Spirit, psychology, therapy.* Boston: Shambhala.

Wood, E. (1959). *Yoga.* Harmondsworth, UK: Penguin Books.

# 22

# Holistic Healing, Paradigm Shift, and the New Age

*Patricia A. Poulin and William West*

I t seems that by the end of the second millennium, close to half of the American population was using one form or another of complementary and alternative medicine (Kessler et al., 2001; see also Eisenberg et al., 1998) for a wide range of concerns, including those manifesting primarily at the mental and emotional levels (Simon et al., 2004). The increasing use of complementary and alternative medicine reflects changing internal beliefs about health and illnesses in the West (Astin, 1998). More people are now embracing a holistic philosophy of health, recognizing, among other principles, the indivisibility of mind, body, heart, and spirit and the importance of considering all of these levels in healing (e.g., Cunningham, 2001; Northrup, 1998; Shannon, 2002; Weil, 1997; Wilber, 2000).

The New Age movement, characterized by recognizing the depth of our interconnectedness, valuing multiple ways of knowing and healing, and seeking to transform our social institutions toward more equitable and loving practices (Taylor, 1999), has created a space for holistic healing to become more accepted and sought after.

Although the roots of the New Age movement are quite old (Williams, 2002), this psychospiritual revolution has started gaining increasing momentum in the

West since the counterculture of the 1960s. This occurred as a large segment of the population started rejecting institutionalized religions; questioning science; and reacting to the impact of materialism, corporate capitalism, human rights abuse, wars, and the destruction of the environment. Simultaneously, the revival of Pagan practices, exploration of altered states of consciousness, the birth of humanistic and transpersonal psychology, and access to teachings from the world's great wisdom traditions, including Aboriginal knowledge, supported people's exploration of alternative forms of spiritual and transformative practices.

Writings by physicists focusing on the implications of some of the research findings in the field of quantum physics also strengthened the movement (e.g., Bohm, 1983; Capra, 1983; Zohar, 1990) and called for a paradigm shift from fragmentary, reductionistic, and positivistic methods in our inquiries and practices toward approaches that are more holistic, participatory, and reverential (see also Tarnas, 1991).

For many people touched by this psychospiritual revolution, the boundaries between spirituality, healing, growth, and transformation are fluid. At the core of New Age spirituality is a focus on the importance of finding one's own path and trusting one's experience. In this sense, New Age spirituality shares commonality with humanistic and transpersonal psychology (West, 2000). In finding this path, New Age people may integrate aspects of traditional spiritual paths such as Buddhism, Hinduism, Taoism, Christianity, Paganism, Aboriginal spirituality, and shamanism, as well as esoteric teachings. Some people are also drawn to work that offer a synthesis of the great wisdom traditions, such as *The Spectrum of Consciousness* (Wilber, 1993), or to channeled text, such as *A Course in Miracles* (Foundation for Inner Peace, 1975). In addition, the use of divination practices for guidance, such as the I Ching, is not uncommon.

In the next section, we briefly present a number of important influences that have shaped the New Age movement, its associated spiritual practice, and the holistic healing modalities that are increasingly sought after now.

Before we proceed, however, it is important to acknowledge that "holistic healing" represents an eclectic mix of therapeutic modalities, including traditional medical systems that are grounded in knowledge that has been accumulating over thousands of years (e.g., traditional Chinese medicine, *qigong*, naturopathy, and ayurveda) and other comprehensive modalities that have been formulated more recently (e.g., network chiropractics; see Epstein, 2002).

At the core of most holistic healing modalities is a trust in the inner wisdom and self-healing potential of the body and mind (Shannon, 2002). The focus is on supporting the person in establishing the ground for the healing process to unfold. Many people are already integrating various forms of holistic healing into their practice (see West, 2004). It is not uncommon to find nurses who practice therapeutic touch; physicians who practice acupuncture; and therapists incorporating or working in concert with practitioners of spiritual healing, homeopathy, naturopathy, chiropractic, craniosacral therapy, and bodywork.

Psychology has yet to formally address the integration of holistic healing in practice, education, and research. As a result, the students and therapists who share an integrative approach to healing are left at the margin and find themselves grappling with important issues around scope of practice and supervision (see West, Chapter 4 in this volume).

## ❖ SOURCES OF INFLUENCES

### Meditation: Eastern Contemplative Traditions

The practices and teachings from various lineages of Buddhism and Hinduism have influenced a large segment of the population in the West over the last four decades (Williams, 2002). Currently, mindfulness meditation is gaining increasing attention in psychology and behavioral medicine. The popular mindfulness-based stress reduction training (Kabat-Zinn, 1982, 1990), a structured 8-week intensive training in mindfulness meditation, has helped thousands of individuals experiencing chronic pain (e.g., Weissbecker et al., 2002), cancer (e.g., Carlson, Speca, Kamala, & Goodey, 2003; Speca, Carlson, Goodey, & Angen, 2000), disordered eating (Kristeller & Hallet, 1999), and anxiety (e.g., Miller, Fletcher, & Kabat-Zinn, 1995). A similar program adapted to group cognitive therapy (Segal, Williams, & Teasdale, 2002; Teasdale et al., 2000) seems to be an effective intervention to prevent relapse among people who have had multiple depressive episodes (Ha & Teasdale, 2004). Mindfulness has also been integrated into a number of psychological interventions such as dialectical behavior therapy (Linehan, 2000), Hakomi (Kurt, 1990), and sensorimotor psychotherapy (Ogden & Minton, 2000).

The research supporting the clinical use of mindfulness is quite compelling (Baer, 2003). Meditation is a good example of the possibility of successfully integrating holistic healing approaches within more conventional therapeutic frameworks.

### Esoteric Teachings

Esoteric teachings from various schools have also been an important source of influence on the New Age movement and associated healing practices

(Levin & Coreil, 1986). In the treatise *Esoteric Healing,* Bailey (1953) delineates the various energetic bodies (e.g., etheric and astral) and energetic centers of our constitution (chakras)—also found in the Indian yogic literature—and their functions. These subtle energetic bodies constitute what is often called the human aura.

Illnesses, disease, or imbalances can manifest at various overlapping levels of our constitution. Energetic distortions in the etheric body or astral body, which can be caused by trauma as well as other factors, are perceptible to sensitive practitioners. Healing can be supported by modalities that can clear and support the vitalization of the energetic bodies, such as shiatsu (Endo, 1995; Jarmey & Mojay, 1991), acupuncture (Kaptchuk, 1983), homeopathy (Bassman, 1998), *qigong,* and other forms of energy healing (e.g., Brennan, 1988).

The handbook *Vibrational Medicine* (Gerber, 2001) offers an overview of the human energetic constitution, tables of the neurophysiological and endocrine functions theoretically associated with the chakras, as well as a synthesis of various forms of subtle energy healing modalities.

### Transformative and Therapeutic Use of Altered States of Consciousness

From the early experimentation with psychedelic drugs in the 1960s (e.g., Dass, 1971), the transformative and therapeutic use of altered states of consciousness (ASC) has been refined (Grof, 2000). Transpersonal psychology, the fourth wave of therapeutic development, is a growing field of research and practice that seeks to better understand these states, their prophylactic potential, and their ability to support personal growth.

In addition to occasionally allowing mystical experiences, techniques such as drumming, chanting, and holotropic breathwork (e.g., Moss, 1986) can elicit a state of absorption that supports the resolution of traumatic experiences. Hence, it is not surprising that many psychotherapeutic modalities rely on ASC.

In primal integration (see, e.g., Marquez, 2000; Rowan, 1988a, 1988b, 1988c), deep emotional processing therapy (Berger, 2000), Reichian therapy (see West, 1994a, 1994b), and sensorimotor psychotherapy (Ogden & Minton, 2000), an altered state is reached by tracking feeling states and bodily sensations. This allows unresolved experiences to come into awareness and be worked through by allowing the body to express through movement and sound the impact of these experiences. These may include trauma that occurred during the prenatal period (e.g., abortion attempts, accidents) or the birth experience (e.g., use of forceps, being separated from one's mother and mishandled) or childhood emotional and physical abuse or neglect (see Feindeisen, 1993; Noble, 1993). Once these experiences are fully worked through at the physical and emotional levels, their implications can be discussed to support life-affirming changes. Often from this work emerges an increased ability to be present to oneself and others and to perceive reality as it presents itself (see, e.g., Turton, 2000).

Interestingly, in many holistic healing modalities, there is an understanding that people commonly spontaneously enter an ASC and experience this type of relieving in session, leading to insight into the roots of their physical pain, patterns of emotional reactivity and beliefs, as well as considerable relief.

## ❖ INTEGRATING HOLISTIC HEALING APPROACHES

In this section, we present a brief description of holistic healing modalities that can work in concert with or be integrated into counseling and psychotherapeutic practice, provided appropriate training is undertaken.

Given that the body is often forgotten about in mainstream practice (Ogden & Minton, 2000), we selected to focus on body-centered and energetic healing approaches. It is important to highlight that although we describe what these modalities look like to an observer, the techniques of each modality form a sort of language that allows for the communication of understanding, empathy, and positive regard between the practitioner and the receiver. As is the case in counseling and psychotherapy, presence (Rogers, 1980) and responsive attunement facilitate the unfolding of the healing process. Here, however, the dialogue is occurring beyond words, and the parts of experience that cannot be expressed through language or sound are "heard" through other channels. And as is the case with spiritual healing (West, 2004), there is a reverence for the process and an understanding that forces beyond the grasp of practitioners are at work in healing moments.

## ❖ NETWORK CHIROPRACTICS AND CRANIOSACRAL THERAPY

Epstein (2002), as others have articulated before (e.g., Lowen, 1976; West, 1994a, 1994b), highlights that there is a relationship between posture or the spinal structure and a person's mental and physical health. When a person does not fully recover from an event (e.g., the loss of a loved one), the spine and nervous system reflect this in restricted movement and breath, tension, and pain. Patterns of tensions are often associated with trauma or unresolved experiences connected together by a certain emotional charge or theme. Release of the tension can support the integration and working through of these events.

Network spinal analysis (Epstein, 2002) is a gentle form of chiropractic that focuses on improving spinal flexibility and responsiveness through sequential spinal adjustments. Treatment involves applying light pressure to various points on the spine, which invites increased awareness of that region and dissipation of tension through breathing and gentle movement. This supports the body's ability to self-correct spinal subluxations.

Whereas network chiropractics focuses on the spine, craniosacral therapy focuses on the connective tissue and the movement of fluids within connective tissue and cavities to support the self-correction of structural imbalances resulting from traumatic experience (Sills, 2004). Treatment involves attunement of the practitioner to the subtle movement and tension patterns of the body followed by very gentle manipulations and holding of various parts of the body, often involving the cranial bones, the rib cage, and the pelvis.

Once there is sufficient trust, it is not uncommon during a network or craniosacral session for someone to reassume the postures that are associated with a traumatic experience, to make movements and sound, as well as to express emotions associated with that experience. This can lead into insight about one's present-day difficulties. Through counseling, these insights can be further integrated and discussed so as to maximize the possibility for change and growth to occur.

Among the clinical vignettes he presents in his book, Epstein (2002) relates the story of a man who had not been able to experience and express grief and who cried for the first time in years during a network session that he attended to address his back pain. As the session was ending, the man spontaneously commented that he had almost cried, which is something that he never did. Upon saying this, he started to cry and reported afterward a sense of religious peace. His natural ability to experience and express emotions was being restored, which supported his recovery.

### Shiatsu

Shiatsu is a form of energy/bodywork rooted in traditional Chinese medicine and *ampuku* (therapeutic massage of the abdomen). There are various forms of shiatsu, but all involve using pressure to various parts of the body to facilitate healing (Jarmey & Mojay, 1991). In Zen shiatsu (i.e., meridian shiatsu; Masanuga & Wataru, 1977), the treatment focuses on applying pressure on various points located along the meridians of the body in order to support the self-correction of energetic (*qi*) imbalances and stimulate circulation. These imbalances may be due to factors such as prenatal history, emotions, trauma, lifestyle, and climate.

Although this has not been reported frequently, shiatsu can work in concert with psychotherapy (Z. Bergman, Witzum, & T. Bergman, 1991). Currently, shiatsu is offered in some nursing homes, where it is found to decrease wandering and challenging behaviors (Sutherland, Reakes, & Bridges, 2000) and improve the quality of sleep of elderly people (Chen, L. C. Lin, Wu, & J. G. Lin, 1999).

As a shiatsu practitioner, the first author was called to work on a 26-year-old woman who was working through fears and phobias through primal integration. During the session preceding the shiatsu treatment, she had traced some of her present-day feelings to a cluster of related events of her childhood and birth in a country affected by wars, with fear and grief as dominant emotions. She had chosen to consciously revisit these experiences, and she felt good about the psychotherapeutic work she had done. However, she described herself as feeling not quite "integrated."

The first few minutes of the session focused on establishing a grounding contact to support reintegration. Her breathing became noticeably deeper, and simultaneously the first author experienced a deepening sense of stillness (see also Adams, 2002, for similar comments). The woman spontaneously reported that she was feeling energy move down in her legs, right into her feet, and that she was feeling better. The rest of the session focused on providing a nurturing and calming space for her to recuperate from her psychotherapy session and strengthening the most depleted organs through selecting a series of particular points to treat. The points were selected taking into account the dominant emotions being worked through and their organ correspondence (e.g., fear: kidney; grief: lung and large intestine). After a few months of primal integration work and occasional shiatsu sessions as a support, the young woman in question reported feeling an increased sense of connectedness with herself, others, and nature; greater ability to process her emotions in a healthy way; and increased creativity and ability to be active in the world.

### Reiki, Therapeutic Touch, and Energy Healing

Reiki, therapeutic touch, and energy healing are rooted in several ancient healing practices such as the laying on of hands. They consist of a practitioner's becoming a "conduit" for energy to be absorbed by the receiver. Some energy healing systems (e.g., "hands of light" healing; Brennan, 1988) work with the knowledge of the human energetic constitution described previously.

Practitioners will typically start by centering themselves fully into the present moment (this is the case also of the other modalities mentioned above) and will then scan the body with their hands, about 2 to 6 inches from the skin, "listening" for cues (e.g., variation in temperature) that an area of the body requires some attention. A treatment can involve long sweeping movements a few inches above the body (i.e., clearing), holding areas of the body to mobilize or direct energy, and finally, supporting the balancing of the energy field and evaluating the session with the receiver.

Many well-documented clinical vignettes have demonstrated the versatility of therapeutic touch. The most robust finding in the research literature is that therapeutic touch is an effective way to alleviate anxiety (see Banadonna, 2002).

## ❖ IMPLICATIONS AND CONCLUSION

The increasing appreciation for holistic approaches to healing that is currently expressed by a large segment of the population has implications for psychological practice, research, and education. Shannon (2002) articulates common response patterns of practitioners vis-à-vis holistic healing: Some are interested only in being able to discuss holistic healing when the people they work with ask about it; others are in the process of clarifying their personal philosophy about healing and its implication for their practices; and others have views of healing that are broader and more inclusive and are struggling with dominant psychological theories.

West (Chapter 4 in this volume) reports that there is a process by which therapist-healers come to integrate various ways of healing in their practice. Although more research is needed to develop a better appreciation of their indication and effectiveness, counselors and psychotherapists will benefit from being well acquainted with holistic healing practices. How do we create a space for the sharing of experience and knowledge about various ways of healing in our curriculums and institutions? How do we negotiate some of the ethical considerations that guide psychological practice and that may require attention when counseling and holistic healing intersect in the counseling space in the interest of the person seeking support? These are questions that are left to teachers, students, counselors, healers, psychotherapists, and practitioners to ponder in the journey toward developing more integrative psychologies.

### Acknowledgments

We would like to acknowledge and thank the following people for their help in the preparation of this chapter: Sam Turton, Maja Zilih, Karuna O'Donnell, Jane Lewis, Carol Holmes, Evelyn McMullen, Cie Simmuro, Leny Carbone, Marg Schneider, and Corey Mackenzie.

## ❖ REFERENCES

Adams, G. (2002). Shiatsu in Britain and Japan: Personhood, holism and embodied aesthetics. *Anthropology Medicine, 9*, 245–265.

Astin, J. A. (1998). Why patients use alternative medicine: Results of a national study. *Journal of the American Medical Association, 279,* 1548–1553.

Baer, R. A. (2003). Mindfulness training as a clinical intervention: A conceptual and empirical review. *Clinical Psychology, Science and Practice, 10,* 125–143.

Bailey, A. A. (1953). *Esoteric healing.* New York: Lucis.

Banadonna, J. R. (2002). Therapeutic touch. In S. Shannon (Ed.), *Complementary and alternative therapies in mental health* (pp. 231–248). San Diego, CA: Academic Press.

Bassman, L. (Ed.). (1998). *The whole mind: The definitive guide to complementary treatments for mind, mood, and emotion.* Novato, CA: New World Library.

Berger, J. (2000). *Emotional fitness: Discovering our natural healing power.* Toronto, Ontario, Canada: Prentice Hall.

Bergman, Z., Witzum, E., & Bergman, T. (1991). When words lose their power: Shiatsu as a strategic tool in psychotherapy. *Journal of Contemporary Psychotherapy, 21,* 5–23.

Bohm, D. (1983). *Wholeness of the implicate order.* London: Ark Paperback.

Brennan, B. A. (1988). *Hands of light: A guide to healing through the human energy field.* New York: Bantam Books.

Capra, F. (1983). *The turning point: Science, society and the raising culture.* Toronto, Ontario, Canada: Bantam Books.

Carlson, L. E., Speca, M., Kamala, D., & Goodey, E. (2003). Mindfulness-based stress reduction in relation to quality of life, mood, symptoms of stress, and immune parameters in breast and prostate cancer outpatients. *Psychosomatic Medicine, 65,* 571–581.

Chen, M. L., Lin, L. C., Wu, S. C., & Lin, J. G. (1999). The effectiveness of acupressure in improving the quality of sleep in institutionalized residents. *Journal of Gerontology, 54,* 289–394.

Cunningham, A. (2001). Healing through the mind: Extending our theories, research, and clinical practice. *Advances in Mind-Body Medicine, 17,* 214–227.

Dass, R. (1971). *Remember: Be here now.* Boulder, CO: Hanuman Foundation.

Eisenberg, D. M., Davis, R. B., Ettner, S. L., Appel, S., Wilkey, S., Rompay, M., et al. (1998). Trends in alternative medicine use in the United States, 1990–1997: Results of a follow-up survey. *Journal of the American Medical Association, 280,* 1569–1575.

Endo, R. (1995). *Tao shiatsu: Life medicine for the twenty-first century.* Tokyo: Japan Publications.

Epstein, D. M. (2002). *12 stages of healing: A network approach to wholeness.* Novato, CA: Amber Allen.

Feindeisen, B. (1993). Rescripting destructive birth patterns. In W. B. Lucas (Ed.), *Regression therapy: A handbook for professionals* (pp. 64–76). Crest Park, CA: Deep Forest Press.

Foundation for Inner Peace. (1975). *A course in miracles.* Tiburon, CA: Author.

Gerber, R. (2001). *Vibrational medicine: The #1 handbook of subtle energy therapies.* Rochester, VT: Bear & Company.

Grof, S. (2000). *Psychology of the future: Lessons from modern consciousness research.* Albany: State University of New York Press.

Ha, H., & Teasdale, J. D. (2004). Mindfulness-based cognitive therapy for depression: Replication and exploration of differential relapse prevention effects. *Journal of Consulting and Clinical Psychology, 72,* 31–40.

Jarmey, C., & Mojay, G. (1991). *Shiatsu: The complete guide.* London: Thorsons.

Kabat-Zinn, J. (1982). An out-patient program in behavioral medicine for chronic pain patients based on the practice of mindfulness meditation. *General Hospital Psychiatry, 4,* 33–47.

Kabat-Zinn, J. (1990). *Full catastrophe living: Using the wisdom of your body and mind to face stress, pain and illness.* New York: Dell.

Kaptchuk, T. (1983). *The web that has no weaver: Understanding Chinese medicine.* New York: Congdon & Weed.

Kessler, R. C., Davis, R. B., Foster, D. F., Van Rompay, M. I., Walters, E. E., Wilkey, S. A., et al. (2001). Long-term trends in the use of complementary and alternative medical therapies in the United States. *Annals of Internal Medicine, 135,* 262–268.

Kristeller, J. L., & Hallet, C. B. (1999). An exploratory study of a meditation-based intervention for binge eating disorder. *Journal of Health Psychology, 4,* 357–363.

Kurt, R. (1990). *Body-centered psychotherapy: The hakomi method.* Mendocino, CA: Life Rhythm.

Levin, J. S., & Coreil, J. (1986). "New age" healing in the U.S. *Social Sciences in Medicine, 23,* 889–897.

Linehan, M. (2000). The empirical basis of dialectical behavior therapy: Development of new treatment versus evaluation of existing treatments. *Clinical Psychology: Science and Practice, 7,* 113–119.

Lowen, A. (1976). *Bioenergetics.* New York: Arkana.

Marquez, A. (2000). Healing through prenatal and perinatal memory recall: A phenomenological investigation. *Journal of Prenatal and Perinatal Psychology and Health, 15,* 146–172.

Masanuga, S., & Wataru, O. (1977). *Zen shiatsu: How to harmonize yin and yang for better health.* Tokyo: Japan Publications.

Miller, J. J., Fletcher, K., & Kabat-Zinn, J. (1995). Three-year follow-up and clinical implications of a mindfulness meditation–based stress reduction intervention in the treatment of anxiety disorders. *General Hospital Psychiatry, 17,* 192–200.

Moss, R. (1986). *The black butterfly: An invitation to radical aliveness.* Carmarthenshire, Wales, UK: Cygnus Books.

Noble, E. (1993). *Primal connection.* New York: Fireside.

Northrup, C. (1998). *Women's bodies, women's wisdom: Creating physical and emotional health and healing.* New York: Bantam Books.

Ogden, P., & Minton, K. (2000). Sensorimotor psychotherapy: One method for processing traumatic memory. *Traumatology, 6*(3). Retrieved January 1, 2005, from http://www.sensorimotorpsychotherapy.org/articles.html

Rogers, C. (1980). *A way of being.* Boston: Houghton Mifflin.

Rowan, J. (1988a). Primal integration. In J. Rowan & W. Dryden (Eds.), *Innovative therapy in Britain* (pp. 12–38). Philadelphia: Open University Press.

Rowan, J. (1988b). *Primal integration: Practice.* Retrieved January 1, 2005, from http://www.primals.org/articles/rowan02.html

Rowan, J. (1988c). *Primal integration: The change process in therapy.* Retrieved January 1, 2005, from http://www.primals.org/articles/rowan03.html

Segal, Z. V., Williams, J. M. G., & Teasdale, J. D. (2002). *Mindfulness-based cognitive therapy for depression.* New York: Guilford Press.

Shannon, S. (2002). The emerging paradigm. In S. Shannon (Ed.), *Complementary and alternative therapies in mental health* (pp. 3–20). San Diego, CA: Academic Press.

Sills, F. (2004). *Craniosacral biodynamics.* Berkeley, CA: North Atlantic Books.

Simon, G. E., Cherkin, D. C., Sherman, K. J., Eisenberg, D. M., Devo, R. A., & Davis, R. B. (2004). Mental health visits to complementary and alternative medicine providers. *General Hospital Psychiatry, 26,* 171–177.

Speca, M., Carlson, L. E., Goodey, E., & Angen, M. (2000). A randomized, wait-list controlled clinical trial: The effect of a mindfulness meditation–based stress reduction program on mood and symptoms of stress in cancer outpatients. *Psychosomatic Medicine, 62,* 613–622.

Sutherland, J. A., Reakes, J., & Bridges, C. (2000). Foot acupressure and massage for patients with Alzheimer's disease and related dementia. *Image: Journal of Nursing Scholarship, 31,* 347–348.

Tarnas, R. (1991). *The passion of the Western mind: Understanding the ideas that have shaped our world view.* New York: Harmony Books.

Taylor, E. (1999). *Shadow culture: Psychology and spirituality in America from the Great Awakening to the New Age.* Washington, DC: Counterpoint.

Teasdale, J. D., Segal, Z. V., Williams, J. M., Ridgeway, V. A., Soulsby, J. M., & Lau, M. A. (2000). Prevention of relapse/recurrence in major depression by mindfulness-based cognitive therapy. *Journal of Consulting and Clinical Psychology, 68,* 615–623.

Turton, S. (2000). *Primal Zen.* Retrieved January 1, 2005, from http://www.primals.org/articles/turton01.html

Weil, A. (1997). *Roots of healing: The new medicine.* Carlsbad, CA: Hay House.

Weissbecker, I., Salmon, P., Studts, J. L., Floyd, A. R., Dedert, E. A., & Sephton, S. E. (2002). Mindfulness-based stress reduction and sense of coherence among women with fibromyalgia. *Journal of Clinical Psychology in Medical Settings, 9,* 297–307.

West, W. (1994a). Clients' experience of bodywork psychotherapy. *Counseling Psychology Quarterly, 7,* 287–303.

West, W. (1994b). Post Reichian therapy. In D. Jones (Ed.), *Innovative psychotherapy: A handbook* (pp. 131–145). Buckingham, UK: Open University Press.

West, W. (2000). *Psychotherapy and spirituality: Crossing the line between therapy and religion.* London: Sage.

West, W. (2004). *Spiritual issues in therapy: Relating experience to practice.* New York: Palgrave Macmillan.

Wilber, K. (1993). *The spectrum of consciousness.* Wheaton, IL: Theosophical Publishing House.

Wilber, K. (2000). *Integral psychology: Consciousness, sprit, psychology, therapy.* Boston: Shambala.

Williams, P. W. (2002). *America's religions: From their origins to the twenty-first century.* Urbana: University of Illinois Press.

Zohar, D. (1990). *The quantum self: Human nature and consciousness defined by the new physics.* New York: Morrow.

# PART V

## Finding the Link Between Traditional Healing and Therapy

# 23

# Spiritual and Healing Approaches in Psychotherapeutic Practice[1]

*Robert N. Sollod*

C opernican, Newtonian, and Freudian conceptual revolutions have led to the notion of human beings as purposeless, determined organisms acted upon by physical and biological laws. A range of spiritual and healing traditions, however, emphasizes the central importance of the connection of all life to spiritual or cosmic realities. In these views, healing is usually seen as restoring a condition of wholeness or harmony (Carlson & Shield, 1989). Beyond any specific techniques, contemporary psychotherapy has much to gain from the worldviews and practices of healing that reconnect human beings with one another and with universal and spiritual purposes (Miller, 2003; Richards & Bergin, 1997; Sollod, 1993).

This chapter will indicate some links between traditional healing and psychotherapy. It then will focus on some common factors, techniques, approaches, and concepts found in many spiritual healing traditions that might be relevant for the contemporary practice of psychotherapy. It will also present guidelines and approaches to the possible psychotherapeutic integration of spiritual healing traditions.

## ❖ LINKS BETWEEN HEALING AND PSYCHOTHERAPY

Spiritual traditions and associated healing techniques have long been a major but largely hidden and poorly acknowledged source of psychotherapeutic innovation. A large portion of current psychotherapeutic practice appears either to have been derived from spiritual traditions and teachings or to consist of approaches and practices similar to those found in spiritual healing traditions.

From the development of psychotherapeutic uses for dreams to hypnosis, biofeedback, and relaxation techniques, Western psychotherapeutic innovators have drawn upon antecedent traditional approaches. Rogers (1980) has indicated that Taoism was an influence on his development of client-centered therapy; secularized aspects of Protestantism also are present in his therapeutic approach (Sollod, 1978). Gnostic elements were prominent in aspects of Freudian psychotherapeutic techniques (Sollod, 1982). Freud traced his emphasis on the importance of dreams to biblical writings, and the idea of the subconscious mind was known to kabbalistic mystics (Fodor, 1971).

Even when contemporary schools of thought may not have their origins in spiritual and healing traditions, surprising parallels and similarities are often present. For example, Adler's (1959) view of the individual as an active creator may be considered an exoteric version of kabbalistic thinking. Skinner's model of individual behavior as completely conditioned and shaped by the environment was antedated by Uspenskii (1929), a Russian mystic and student of Gurdjieff (King, 1927/1996). Albert Ellis (1970) has cited the insights of Epictetus, the ancient Greek spiritual master, to support the validity of his rational-emotive approach. A major tenet of rational-emotive therapy—that an individual's thought shapes experience—although presumably based upon empirical scientific considerations, is consistent with Stoicism as well as with some Christian, Buddhist, and kabbalistic teachings.

Another type of clinical antecedent is the fact that healers in a variety of traditions have not restricted themselves to physical illnesses but have also typically addressed problems and concerns that are now commonly considered the exclusive province of psychotherapeutic intervention (Berthold, 1989). Traditional cultural and spiritual teachings have developed approaches to a variety of conditions that also could be described within the framework of psychiatric and psychological diagnosis (Buhrmann, 1984; Wilson, 1989). The integration of traditional healing approaches with more conventional practice has also been noted or suggested (Gordon, 1990; H. Rappaport & M. Rappaport, 1981).

Frank (1973) indicated that contemporary psychotherapies have many features in common with traditional healing approaches. The underlying structure of psychotherapy itself, that is, of a person seeking help (the "healee") by going to a specifically trained or qualified individual (healer) for the purpose of seeking some type of solace or remediation of a problem, appears to be derived either from healing traditions themselves or from aspects of human nature appreciated both by healing traditions and by contemporary practice. Traditional spiritual forms of healing do consist, in part, of suggestion and placebo, but upon further examination it becomes apparent that active therapeutic ingredients also must be present (Colijn & Sollod, 1990). Many such active ingredients that contribute to demonstrable changes in thinking, feeling, and behavior have been identified and utilized within various healing traditions during the millennia in which spiritual healing approaches have developed. In addition, the significance of motives associated with the archetype of healer in the psychotherapist is an important factor that suggests the value of the integration of spiritual healing approaches and methods within psychotherapy. Many therapists appear to be motivated by an inner directionality similar to that experienced by healers in traditional societies (Wilmer, 1987). Such an archetype involves service and the development of the power to change the lives of others as a result of specific training and experiences; privileged access to the often hidden experiential world of others and awareness of one's own problems (the "wounded healer") also are aspects of this archetypal pattern.

Some therapeutic training programs, most clearly psychoanalytic institutes, have already incorporated elements of initiatory schools. From the standpoint of spiritual traditions, such programs represent pseudo-Gnostic initiations (Sollod, 1982); nonetheless, they engage the archetypal energies of would-be psychoanalysts. A more direct acknowledgment of the connection between the roles of psychotherapist and healer in the training of psychotherapists generally could foster their development.

## ❖ COMMON ELEMENTS OF HEALING

The appraisal of frequent practices within spiritual healing approaches leads to the possibility of their integration within psychotherapeutic practice (Sollod, 1988). Some elements commonly found in spiritual healing may serve to reinforce or highlight aspects of current psychotherapeutic practice. Other elements suggest that innovative techniques and approaches may be beneficial.

A sampling of current healing methods in a variety of traditions reveals major aspects of spiritual healing practices (Bloomfield, 1984; Carlson & Shield, 1989; Markides, 1985, 1988). Principles and approaches considered important in many of these healing traditions include the following:

1. There is an alteration of the healer's state of consciousness. The healer has expertise in entering a variety of states of consciousness that differ from ordinary waking consciousness.

2. The healer's view or manner of perceiving and conceptualizing the person seeking help is an important factor in spiritual healing.

3. The healer accesses and uses intuitive understanding.

4. There is no clear separation between the processes of the healer and those of the person seeking healing. In some cases, a sense of fusion between the healer and the person seeking healing constitutes a basic element of the healing process.

5. Healing may involve the healer's successful resolution of certain personal issues that arise because of contact with the healee (cf. counter-transference).

6. There may be considerable use of visualization by the therapist and the client.

7. Reestablishing a conscious relationship with spiritual life and developing an appreciation of divine or universal laws are often seen as resulting in the restoration of health.

8. Prayer and meditation are frequent therapeutic activities.

## ❖ TWO CONTRASTING HEALING APPROACHES

Although it is not feasible to illustrate the entire range of healing approaches here, space does allow a brief summary of the contrasting approaches of two healers—Joel Goldsmith and Stylianos Atteshlis. These examples illustrate many of the principles indicated above.

Joel Goldsmith (1963) was an American healer who led meditation, healing, and spiritual development circles throughout the world. Writing within a Judeo-Christian framework, Goldsmith emphasized the importance of the state of consciousness of the healer. He stressed that in healing, it was important to enter a different state of consciousness in which one felt an inner wholeness or oneness with God. Goldsmith considered it unnecessary and even detrimental to focus on the type of illness or problem of the healee. The healing approach seemed to involve an effort to achieve "at-one-ment," and the healing was thus caused by spiritual forces beyond the activity of the ego. The healer's activity involved a suspension of normal ego functioning and an attempt to reach an inner stillness. Healing was said to take place within that stillness. Goldsmith did not do hands-on healing and indicated that healing could be done either in the presence of the healee or at a distance.

Stylianos Atteshlis was a native of Cyprus who engaged in spiritual healing and teaching for much of his life. He was commonly referred to as "Daskalos," which is the Greek word for teacher. His activities have been the focus of two books by the sociologist Kyriacos Markides (1985, 1988), and he also contributed his own teachings and writings about spirituality and healing (Atteshlis, 1990a, 1990b, 1991). Working within an esoteric Christian framework, Daskalos also emphasized the importance of the healer's state of consciousness. Unlike Goldsmith, he believed that the healer might try to affect the condition of the client through conscious control of the healer's own thoughts and feelings. He taught that the healer could intentionally direct energy, often through imagery, in such a way as to enhance the well-being of the healee.

Daskalos devoted considerable attention to the art of psychotherapy (S. Atteshlis, personal communication, February 1988; Markides, 1985, 1988). He stated that conventional psychotherapy does not get to the root causes of psychological problems. He viewed such root causes as the thought-desire forms, or "elementals," that a person has developed and energized over the years. Daskalos taught that the process of psychotherapy should include helping a person to develop more benign patterns of thought and feeling and to depotentiate destructive and negative patterns. This process may be aided, in Daskalos's view, through the creation of therapeutic elementals as well as by example and persuasion.

LeShan (1974), who has developed conceptual models of alternate states of consciousness and meditation, also presented a typology of healing approaches (Goodrich, 1978). In type I healing, the healer enters an altered state of consciousness characterized by experiential fusion with the healee and a state of deep, caring love. Type I healing may be done in the presence of the client or at a distance. In type II healing, there is an attempt to direct the healing process. Therapeutic touch or the "laying on of hands" characterizes this approach. Applying this typology, it appears that the type I approach best describes Goldsmith's approach to healing, whereas Daskalos's activities include both type I and type II processes, as well as other aspects that do not fit into either pattern.

## ❖ INTEGRATING THESE APPROACHES INTO PSYCHOTHERAPY

In a psychotherapeutic approach incorporating the principles of spiritual healing, there must be major emphasis on the inner activities of the therapist. The therapist in such an approach is ideally able to move into altered, often transcendent, states of consciousness that may be beneficial for the therapeutic process. Some such states may be similar to—though deeper than—the empathic and objective, almost meditative awareness of the therapist in various approaches of psychotherapy. Other states of receptivity, awareness, and nonordinary altered states of consciousness also may be accessed. Such states may involve a deep feeling of unselfish love, enhanced sensitivity to the other, contact with inner resources of compassion and understanding, and perception of the client as whole or potentially whole.

Conventional approaches to therapy also focus to a certain extent on the level of consciousness utilized by the therapist. Psychoanalysts, for example, are trained to develop a certain type of hovering attention. Therapists with a client-centered orientation evidence a special type of empathic awareness. Experiential psychotherapists access their embodied feeling states as an essential part of the therapeutic process (Mahrer, 1989). Conventional therapeutic approaches also emphasize the importance of therapists' specific thoughts and feelings, although in a different way for the most part than do spiritual traditions.

The therapist, because of training and experience, should be able to enter a variety of distinct states of consciousness. An ideal primary state is called self-observation, self-remembering, or witness-consciousness (Tart, 1987). In this state, the therapist is able both to attend to the communications of the client and to monitor his or her own reactions as they occur. This process goes beyond intellectual appreciation of one's own reactions and consists of a conscious, nonjudgmental awareness of thoughts and emotions as they occur. This state may be accompanied by an associated emotional state that consists of access to deeply loving and compassionate feelings toward the client. For some therapists, self-remembering may be accessed only temporarily; for others, it can become a more pervasive or central state.

The psychotherapist should be able to utilize several additional states of consciousness. One is a state in which he or she accesses intuitive knowledge; another is a state of empathic fusion with the client. The specific contents of the therapist's consciousness are also of particular relevance to a psychotherapeutic form integrating insights from healing traditions. Wilbur (1980, 1981) has written extensively about consciousness and has compared consciousness to a building. The levels of consciousness constitute a type of deep structure and are analogous to the different floors. Specific contents of consciousness are compared to the floor plans and the furniture.

These contents of consciousness, although more superficial than the deep structure of levels of consciousness, are nonetheless significant. Specifically, as in the healing traditions, seeing the client as deficient, defective, and diseased is viewed as detrimental, whereas seeing the client as potentially empowered, happy, healthy, and whole is beneficial. In such a psychotherapeutic approach, the diagnostic process is approached with caution. The therapist may utilize diagnostic constructs to assist in describing a case, but only if he or she realizes that the current pathological condition is not supported by the deepest level of reality of the client or of the cosmos. Such an insight should be conveyed to the client. As Daskalos (S. Atteshlis, personal communication, 1988) has said, "Help them [people seeking help] to see that their problems in time and space are just illusions." It is vital for the therapist not to become caught up in a sense of the client's limitations, because it is precisely the therapist who is responsible for helping the client to relinquish views and activities that are causing difficulties.

Some techniques that emerge from these considerations emphasize pleasant, life-enhancing activities. This approach is very similar to that developed by LeShan (1990) for psychotherapy with cancer patients. He has indicated that another useful beginning point is to ask the client what he or she would most like to do with the gift of a year of life that could be shaped in any manner the client desired. LeShan has also provided many additional techniques that can be used. The client also may be encouraged to undertake more helpful, altruistic activities in daily life. Such participation in new, life-enhancing activities should be deeply grounded in the therapist's belief that people have the power to change, that they are capable of rational choice, and that they are fundamentally responsible for the quality of their experiences and for the quality of their relationships with others.

Techniques that may be used to facilitate the building of new patterns of thought, feeling, and behavior, in addition to those commonly used by cognitive therapists, are affirmations, prayers, and visualization techniques. In spiritual healing traditions, such techniques are thought to potentiate specific contents of thoughts and feelings. Thus, autosuggestion and suggestion are considered as potentially therapeutic processes. Both utilize the mind's ability to shape experience and even to affect physiological responses. Suggestion, in this approach, is not viewed as a placebo. It is an active ingredient of therapy (Barber, 1978).

An additional technique that may be incorporated into psychotherapy is hands-on healing. Therapeutic touch (Kepner, 1987) and a variety of other healing traditions employ a technique of touch or near-touch in which healing energy is assumed to pass from the healer to the healee (Brennan, 1987). This hands-on approach may be used to help a client to become relaxed, to feel more energized, or even to resolve specific problems that might have a somatic representation. Empirical research has documented the impact of therapeutic touch and related approaches (Krippner, 1980; Wirth, 1989). However, within current ethical and professional guidelines for many helping professions, the use of therapeutic touch is, in itself, still a "touchy" issue. The practitioner should be careful to work within the professional and ethical guidelines of his or her discipline and also should consider the possible threatening aspects of such an approach for some clients.

Meditation and prayer also may be used in a variety of ways to facilitate therapeutic change. Meditation, for example, has been found to result in greater relaxation, disidentification, alertness, awareness, empathy, sensitivity, and openness to change (Carrington, 1977; LeShan, 1974; Shafii, 1985). Both therapist and client may benefit from meditative practice. Meditation may be practiced both within and outside the therapist's office. Different types of prayer have been vital to many spiritual traditions (Bloom, 1980; Laubach, 1946). Prayer also may be part of spiritually oriented psychotherapy. The therapist may pray for or with the client, as a significant minority of therapists do (Nix, 1978). The client's prayer life also may be supported in therapy.

Alongside the more conventional appreciation of the possible effects of such techniques, Jamesian parapsychic (Fuller, 1986) and transpersonal explanations also may be considered. A tenet of transpersonal psychology, consistent with spiritual healing traditions, is that the directed inner activities of a person may affect others. In addition to praying for the client, the therapist may direct visualizations or thoughts to facilitate beneficial changes in the client. Imagery that presumably results in changes in another person is termed *transpersonal imagery* (Braud & Schlitz, 1989; Samuels, 1990).

Some empirical support exists for the assertion of transpersonal influence. More than 35 studies have indicated that prayers and meditations can be beneficial even for individuals at a distance (Byrd, 1988). The results of hundreds of studies have strongly suggested the possible influence of attention on electronic functioning as well as on living organisms. Changes in electroencephalogram patterns were recorded when persons tried to communicate with others at a distance (Orne-Johnson, Dilbeck, Wallace, & Landrith, 1982). Braud and Schlitz (1989) conducted a study in which transpersonal visualization was used to alter the autonomic nervous system activities of others remotely. It appears that adequate methodological procedures were utilized in many of these studies.

Another therapeutic activity that integrates spiritual healing techniques into psychotherapy is the reliance of the therapist on an intuitive process to guide therapeutic activities. Intuition—"listening with the third ear"—involves the ability to access thoughts and feelings that reflect an inner knowing or understanding (Agor, 1984). In a psychotherapeutic approach connected with healing traditions, a close connection between the client and the therapist exists. At times, a sense of therapist-client experiential fusion is an important ingredient that facilitates therapeutic change. In addition, the therapist seeks to find an underlying meaning for the therapeutic encounter and to understand what he or she is to learn through working with a specific client. Contact with a client may challenge the therapist to reexamine certain preconceptions, to learn to be more accepting of various aspects of experience, and to change his or her approach to life. Sometimes, this "work on oneself" is necessary for the therapist to be able to provide a truly therapeutic relationship.

## ❖ CONCLUSION

It is possible that techniques and approaches indicated here will be increasingly incorporated into psychotherapeutic practice during the coming years. This would represent the continuation of a process that began with the earliest stages of verbal psychotherapy—the borrowing and integration of techniques and insights from traditional spiritual and healing approaches.

Many questions remain concerning how such integration might occur (Sollod, in press). One area of concern is whether such methods would be subject to adequate empirical testing and outcome research before they become widely used. Some empirical research has already been conducted regarding the therapeutic impact of imagery (A. A. Sheikh, Kunzendorf, & K. S. Sheikh, 1989), hypnosis (Bertrand & Spanos, 1989), and meditation (Shafii, 1985). The effects of prayer and hands-on healing, although studied outside of psychotherapy, have to date been the focus of very little investigation within psychotherapeutic practice.

Another area of concern is the training of therapists in such techniques. Is it possible for therapists to learn such techniques through courses alone? Perhaps extensive workshops might be necessary to teach meditation or visualization skills. Alternatively, it might even be beneficial for therapists to participate in spiritual disciplines that involve extensive commitment to learning about such skills and approaches. Another question about the integration of such approaches and techniques into psychotherapy is to what extent the integration could occur on the level of technique alone, leaving the underlying view of the model of personality and of psychopathology unaffected. It is possible that some techniques could lose their effectiveness when separated from a spiritual tradition of which they were an integral part (Sollod, in press). However, perhaps they would prove as effective even when practiced as part of a technically eclectic approach.

It is possible that the continuing integration of spiritually based healing techniques into psychotherapy will lead to a questioning and redefinition of the deepest levels of the psychotherapeutic enterprise. It is also possible that empirically validated, spiritually oriented integrative psychotherapeutic forms containing elements of traditional healing practices may emerge further within a contemporary Western framework.

## ❖ NOTE

1. This chapter is adapted from the *Comprehensive Handbook of Psychotherapy Integration*, "Spiritual and Healing Approaches in Psychotherapeutic Practice," edited by George Stricker and Jerold R. Gold. Copyright 1993. Reprinted with kind permission of Springer Science and Business Media.

## ❖ REFERENCES

Adler, A. (1959). *The practice and history of individual psychology.* Totowa, NJ: Littlefield-Adams.

Agor, W. H. (1984). *The intuitive manager.* Englewood Cliffs, NJ: Prentice Hall.

Atteshlis, S. (1990a). *Esoteric teachings* (R. Browning & A. Browning, Trans.). Nicosia, Cyprus: Imprinta. (Available from P.O. Box 4105, Nicosia, Cyprus)

Atteshlis, S. (1990b). *Lectures.* Presented in Strovolos, Cyprus.

Atteshlis, S. (1991). *The parables and other stories.* Nicosia, Cyprus: Imprinta. (Available from P.O. Box 4105, Nicosia, Cyprus)

Barber, T. X. (1978). "Hypnosis," suggestions, and psychosomatic phenomena: A new look from the standpoint of recent experimental studies. In J. L. Fosshage (Ed.), *Healing: Implications for psychotherapy* (pp. 269–298). New York: Human Sciences Press.

Berthold, S. (1989). Spiritism as a form of psychotherapy: Implications for social work practice. *Social Casework, 70,* 502–509.

Bertrand, L. D., & Spanos, N. E. (1989). Hypnosis: Historical and social psychological aspects. In A. A. Sheikh & K. S. Sheikh (Eds.), *Eastern and Western approaches to healing: Ancient wisdom and modern knowledge* (pp. 237–263). New York: John Wiley & Sons.

Bloom, A. (1980). *School for prayer.* London: Dartort, Longman & Todd.

Bloomfield, R. (1984). *The mystique of healing.* Edinburgh, Scotland: Charles Skilton.

Braud, W., & Schlitz, M. (1989). A methodology for the objective study of transpersonal imagery. *Journal of Scientific Exploration, 3,* 43–63.

Brennan, B. A. (1987). *Hands of light: A guide to healing through the human energy field.* New York: Bantam.

Buhrmann, M. V. (1984). *Living in two worlds: Communication between a white healer and her black counterparts.* Cape Town, South Africa: Human & Rousseau.

Byrd, R. C. (1988). Positive therapeutic effects of intercessory prayer in a coronary care unit population. *Southern Medical Journal, 81,* 826–829.

Carlson, R., & Shield, B. (1989). *Healers on healing.* Los Angeles: Tarcher.

Carrington, P. (1977). *Freedom in meditation.* Garden City, NY: Anchor Press/Doubleday.

Colijn, S., & Sollod, R. (1990, April). *The relevance of traditional healing for psychotherapy: Content and/or context.* Paper presented at the Sixth Annual Convention of the Society for the Exploration of Psychotherapy Integration, Philadelphia.

Ellis, A. (1970). *Reason and emotion in psychotherapy.* New York: Lyle Stuart.

Fodor, N. (1971). *Freud, Jung and occultism.* New Hyde Park, NY: University Books.

Frank, J. D. (1973). *Persuasion and healing* (2nd ed.). Baltimore: Johns Hopkins University Press.

Fuller, R. C. (1986). *Americans and the unconscious.* New York: Oxford University Press.

Goldsmith, J. S. (1963). *Parenthesis in eternity.* New York: Harper & Row.

Goodrich, J. (1978). The psychic healing training and research project. In J. L. Fosshage (Ed.), *Healing: Implications for psychotherapy* (pp. 84–110). New York: Human Sciences Press.

Gordon, J. S. (1990). Holistic medicine and mental health practice: Toward a new synthesis. *American Journal of Orthopsychiatry, 60,* 357–370.

Kepner, J. I. (1987). *Body process: A gestalt approach to working with the body in psychotherapy.* New York: Gardner Press.

King, C. D. (1996). *The butterfly: Symbol of conscious evolution.* New York: Bridge Press. (Original work published in 1927 as *Beyond behaviorism*)

Krippner, S. (1980). Psychic healing. In A. Hastings, J. Fadiman, & J. S. Gordon (Eds.), *Healing for the whole person* (pp. 169–177). Boulder, CO: Westview Press.

Laubach, E. (1946). *Prayer: The mightiest force in the world.* Westwood, NJ: Fleming Revell.

LeShan, L. (1974). *How to meditate.* Boston: Little, Brown.

LeShan, L. (1990). *Cancer as a turning point: A handbook for people with cancer, their families, and health professionals.* New York: Flume.

Mahrer, A. R. (1989). *Experiencing: A humanistic theory of psychology and psychiatry.* Ottawa, Ontario, Canada: University of Ottawa Press.

Markides, K. (1985). *The magus of Strovolos: The extraordinary world of a spiritual healer.* Boston: Routledge & Kegan Paul.

Markides, K. (1988). *Homage to the sun: The wisdom of the magus of Strovolos.* Boston: Routledge & Kegan Paul.

Miller, G. (2003). *Incorporating spirituality in counseling and psychotherapy: Theory and technique.* New York: Wiley.

Nix, V. (1978). *A study of the religious values of psychotherapists.* Unpublished doctoral dissertation, New York University.

Orne-Johnson, D., Dilbeck, M. C., Wallace, R. D., & Landrith, G. S., III. (1982). Intersubject EEG coherence: Is consciousness a field? *International Journal of Neuroscience, 16,* 203–209.

Rappaport, H., & Rappaport, M. (1981). The integration of scientific and traditional medicine: A proposed model. *American Psychologist, 36,* 774–781.

Richards, P. S., & Bergin, A. E. (1997). *A spiritual strategy for counseling and psychotherapy.* Washington, DC: American Psychological Association.

Rogers, C. (1980). *Personal correspondence: Sollod papers* (Archives of the History of American Psychology). Akron, OH: University of Akron.

Samuels, N. (1990). *Healing with the mind's eye: A guide for using imagery and visions for personal growth and healing.* New York: Summit Books.

Shafii, M. (1985). *Freedom from the self: Sufism, meditation and psychotherapy.* New York: Human Sciences Press.

Sheikh, A. A., Kunzendorf, R. G., & Sheikh, K. S. (1989). Healing images: From ancient wisdom to modern science. In A. A. Sheikh & K. S. Sheikh (Eds.), *Eastern and Western approaches to healing: Ancient wisdom and modern knowledge* (pp. 470–515). New York: John Wiley & Sons.

Sollod, R. (1978). Carl Rogers and the origins of client-centered therapy. *Professional Psychology, 9,* 93–104.

Sollod, R. (1982). Non-scientific sources of psychotherapeutic approaches. In E. Sharkey (Ed.), *Philosophy, religion and psychotherapy* (pp. 41–56). Washington, DC: University Press of America.

Sollod, R. (1988, August). *The relevance of healing techniques for the helping relationship.* Paper presented at the annual convention of the American Psychological Association, Atlanta, GA.

Sollod, R. (1993). Integrating spiritual healing approaches and techniques into psychotherapy. In G. Stricker & J. Gold (Eds.), *The comprehensive handbook of psychotherapy integration* (pp. 237–248). New York: Plenum.

Sollod, R. (in press). Integrating spirituality with psychotherapy. In J. Norcross & M. Goldfried (Eds.), *Handbook of integrative psychotherapy.* New York: Guilford Press.

Tart, C. (1987). *Waking up: Overcoming the obstacles to human potential.* Boston: Shambala.

Uspenskii, E. D. (1929). *Tertium organum: The third organ of thought: A key to the enigmas of the world* (N. Bessarsboff & C. Bragdon, Trans., 2nd ed.). New York: Knopf.

Wilbur, K. (1980). *The Atman Project: A transpersonal view of human development.* Wheaton, IL: Theosophical Publishing House.

Wilbur, K. (1981). *Up from Eden: A transpersonal view of human evolution.* New York: Doubleday.

Wilmer, H. A. (1987). *Practical Jung: Nuts and bolts of Jungian psychotherapy.* Wilmette, IL: Chiron.

Wilson, J. P. (1989). Culture and trauma: The sacred pipe revisited. In I. E. Wilson (Ed.), *Trauma, transformation and healing: An integrative approach to theory, research and post-traumatic therapy* (pp. 38–71). New York: Brunner/Mazel.

Wirth, D. E. (1989). Unorthodox healing: The effect of non-contact therapeutic touch on the healing rate of full-thickness dermal wounds. In *Proceedings of Presented Papers: 32nd Annual Parapsychological Association Convention* (pp. 251–268). Durham, NC: Parapsychological Association.

# 24

# Psychotherapy as Ritual

## Connecting the Concrete With the Symbolic

*Michael Anderson*

I n this chapter, I will explore psychotherapy as a form of ritual that seeks to satisfy a social need, albeit in an ostensibly individualistic way. Although the content of a psychotherapeutic session is highly specific and unique to the people who constitute it, the form is standard and can be conceptualized in the same way as traditional ritual forms have been. This article is informed by my research (Anderson, 2002) that looked at the cultural role of psychotherapy.[1]

Counseling and psychotherapy have generally become taken-for-granted aspects of Western culture. When social artifacts become so seamlessly sutured to the rest of society it suggests that they have become such integral parts of that society that they cease to be seen, even less examined. McLeod (2001) maintains, "Counseling is not just something that happens between two people. It is also a social institution which is embedded in the culture of modern industrialized societies" (p. 2).

Contemporary psychotherapy offers a means of solving real or potential problems related to the reconciliation of self and society and a ritual dramatization of the tensions between our key cultural concerns. With this in mind, I would like to provide a perspective on psychotherapy not as a psychotherapist might but as a social anthropologist might—as a cultural event, a ritual, rather than as a means of individual psychological "cure."

## ❖ RITUAL AS A CONCEPT

Rituals have been practiced for as long as humans have populated the planet. People have sought in many places and for many ages to link spheres of existence to their land, the cosmos, and to each other. Generally, the form this has taken has been what we commonly describe as ritual. It is difficult and perhaps even unnecessary to define *ritual* explicitly. Gluckman (1962), for example, characterized it as expressive of human relationships but with reference to mystical or religious notions. Leach (1954) argued that ritual was an aspect of social behavior that was related to its symbolic value rather than to its practical utility or the ends it was intended to achieve.

More recent, Turner's (1967) work among the Ndembu has proved more enduring in helping researchers understand the symbolic aspects of rituals. He argued that each symbolic object in the ritual possesses a broad range of social, psychological, and physiological meanings. Based on this idea, the meaning of a ritual is complex, because it can have many levels of meaning for different people. Turner maintained that ritual ultimately serves to connect fundamental abstract principles of a culture and its sociological relations to physiological and psychological realities. Drawing on the work of Arnold van Gennep (1909/1960), whom I will be returning to in greater detail later, Turner also revitalized the formal structure of van Gennep's universal model of ritual and introduced new ways of developing theory around the concept of *liminality*—the central phase of a ritual process in which the critical themes, relationships, and concepts are brought to the fore.

## ❖ PSYCHOTHERAPY AS RITUAL

How can the activity of psychotherapy be described as "ritual"? The answer is, as Anthony Cohen (1985) comments, because "ritual transforms experience" (p. 91). Ritual provides a stage upon which, and exacts a process in which, transition (individual or social) can take place. There are many opinions within social anthropology on what ritual is and does. The anthropologist Mary Douglas (1966), although she has not focused her career on ritual, nevertheless has made apposite and concise comments regarding this particular point: "Ritual 'frames' action in such a way as to enable us to experience what might otherwise not be disclosed to us. [Ritual] . . . can permit knowledge of what would otherwise not be known at all" (Douglas, 1966, p. 64). In other words, it takes ritual for change to be effected. It is difficult to conceive of a marriage (secular or religious) taking place or the prosecution of a criminal without some sort of ritual process occurring (through a wedding or court trial, respectively). To witness the ritual is to witness the "fact" of marriage or prosecution. The ritual is necessary in order to create the (nonritual) reality.

In respect to issues that have psychological health as their focus, McLeod (2001) argues, "People in all societies, at all times have experienced emotional or psychological distress. . . . In each culture there have been well established ways of helping people to deal with these" (p. 13). Some kind of ritual process then is often necessary in order to bring about formal change.

Ritual provides a social and conceptual frame for the resolution of the social or personal chaos and ambiguity that emerge as problems in understanding how our worlds are organized and how we identify ourselves within those worlds. Such is the threatening incongruence between the idealized and the actual life that the relationship between them needs to be formerly and carefully managed, set apart in a domain all its own and (ideally) reconciled. Cohen (1985) comments,

It has been argued that this kind of reconciliation also lies at the heart of religious and ideological belief systems. In all these forms—and especially ritual—is the mechanism which bridges the gap. The disjunction caused by social change [emotional turmoil] might be seen as a particular instance of the disjunction between the ideal [belief] and the actual [experience]: one in which the ideal [belief] takes the place of the familiar and actuality [experience] appears as the unfamiliar and, therefore, the feared and/or resented . . . symbolic forms can massage away the tension. (p. 92)

Cohen (1985) uses ritual to highlight tension (which is the cause of the need for ritual to be enacted) as a common condition of human life that is experienced not just in between the categories of "self" and "society" but also between different aspects within the self (the different ways a self relates to society).

There is implicit support for this idea of dealing with the self/social tension in the work of Philip Cushman (1995). Commenting on the situation in the United States, he contends that new ways of thinking about the relationship between self and society may emerge but that "psychotherapy . . . has been and will continue to be instrumental in that struggle" (Cushman, p. 3). These are important ideas in relation to the ritual of psychotherapy.

## ❖ THE RITUAL STRUCTURE OF THERAPY

The idea of therapy as ritual is not new (Gellner, 1985; McLeod, 1997; Turner, 1962). Classically, Arnold van Gennep (1909/1960) conceptualized rituals in broad terms by analyzing their commonalities in his own cross-cultural ethnographic research. He theorized that ritual structures, wherever they were performed, possessed a basic universal form, a form that we can borrow to make anthropological sense of psychotherapy.

Essentially, van Gennep (1909/1960) argued that rituals are made up of three distinct but intersecting parts. These parts can be described as separation, transition, and reincorporation, and these are understood as shifting sequentially from one into another. That is, any ritual can be characterized by the symbolic separation of an individual or group of people for whom the ritual is being enacted from the rest of their society; the transitional movement of categorical change from one state or status to another; and, finally, by the individual's or group's reincorporation back into the rest of society as a reconstituted member or members of a different social category.

The three stages of a rite of passage together construct a process of movement from one social category to another. Central to van Gennep's (1909/1960) thought was the concept of *liminality*, an idea that refers to the pivotal, middle stage of the ritual process and divides the other two stages: separation (preliminal) and reincorporation (postliminal). The actual social process corresponds to the conceptual one as follows:

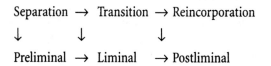

So separation is to preliminal as transition is to liminal and as reincorporation is to postliminal. In order to illustrate the idea of the psychotherapeutic event as ritual in a similar way, we can describe it in van Gennep's terms.

### Separation From Society (Preliminal)

The first, or preliminal, stage is characterized by a separation from society. For example, a candidate for christening (initiation into the Christian community) is taken with members of that community to have the candidate's membership in the community established. A couple to be married are also physically and symbolically separated from the witnesses at their wedding, a separation that confirms their status as of neither one social identity nor another and as such the focus of the ritual process. Anthropology has provided many other rich examples of ritual separation, such as those described by Audrey Richards (1956), Poole (1982), Victor Turner (1967), and Ray Raphael (1988). The commencement of therapy likewise involves the client's separation from society into a confined space, devoid of any other human presence save that of the therapist.

Seclusion in the therapeutic process is normally voluntary, but it occasionally implies the latent or very explicit danger or risk the client poses not just to him- or herself but to society as a whole, particularly if the client is psychotic or violent. A client's separation from society is a symbolic act underlining this point. It should be noted, however, that there is a modern tendency (among some therapists) to eschew the therapy room (i.e., explicit exclusion) for a walk in the park with the client or a seat by the river, which suggests the opposite of such separation. Even here, however, such locations are usually quiet and limited in their human occupation (i.e., stimulus from other human activity is kept to a minimum).

In van Gennep's (1909/1960) terms, *preliminal* refers to the start of the ritual, its preparation. So, in therapy it is here that introductions may be made between client and therapist, and the therapist makes some effort to put the client at ease. What therapists call "building rapport" is deemed to be vital to the success of the remainder of the therapeutic process (Mearns & Thorne, 1999). This is likely to be a short period of time relative to the main work of the therapy hour, which would best be described as the transitional or liminal phase.

### The Transitional Phase (Liminal)

The term *liminal* is critical in understanding the nature of social and psychological "movement" or transition. It is derived from the Latin word *limen*, which means "threshold" or "in between." The central or liminal phase of a ritual is the most critical. It is here that the main work of transition is undertaken, but it is also here that the individual is ambivalent: neither one thing nor the other. The individual is categorized as "client," which is an identification neither of what he or she was (sick, depressed, abused, etc., but not yet in therapy) nor of what he or she is yet to become (cured, healed, and no longer a client). The individual is, as Turner (1962), commenting upon van Gennep's (1909/1960) model, put it, "betwixt and between" one state and another.

As is testified to by much anthropological literature (Poole, 1982; Richards, 1956; Turner, 1962), the subject is temporarily suspended in a classificatory no-man's-land, and the liminal individual is invariably treated with great attention, caution, seriousness, and even fear. Moreover, this ambiguity may be marked by the suspension of normal rules of social interaction. In therapy, the client seeks to move (transit) from one "state" to another ("sick" to "well"). Often painful, challenging, and confusing, the "middle" work of therapy is beyond rapport building but relies on it. It is serious and precarious and involves the displacement of usual norms of one-to-one social interaction with much more formalized techniques designed to effect that transit. Formalized rules of interaction ("techniques") of the ritual specialist dominate the interaction in order to bring about precisely that movement or transition.

### Reincorporation Back Into Society (Postliminal)

The final stage of van Gennep's (1909/1960) tripartite structure is that of the *postliminal* phase, or the reincorporation of the subject back into society. It occurs when the ambiguity of the liminal stage has been satisfactorily resolved and the transition successfully completed. Its ending marks the ending of the ritual and the reincorporation of individuals back into the society or community from whence they came, but now in a new, "transformed" state. It would be overstating the case to say that a "new identity" is effected or conferred in the therapeutic process, but it would be accurate to say that individuals are changed by the process.

At the end of the session, the client leaves the therapy room, the presence of the therapist, and the engagement with the therapeutic techniques and returns to regular life once again. It would be crass to suggest that psychotherapy most commonly would achieve its aims (making the client well) in one session (though one of the ideals of "brief therapy" in particular is to achieve precisely this; Griffin & Tyrrell, 2003, pp. 257ff). Rather, the process most often takes several sessions, and perhaps many, to achieve its aims completely. In this case, it is necessary to see the ritual process as a sequential but also an intermittent one. This is not as forced as it seems, given the tendency of many therapists to talk about "beginnings," "middles," and "endings" in long therapeutic treatments (see Mearns & Thorne, 1999).

Van Gennep's (1909/1960) model provides us with a way of thinking about and describing therapy as a ritual process and makes it sociologically compatible with the notion of *therapeutic movement,* a term frequently used by therapists to denote a process of transition from one state to another. Using van Gennep's model, the end of the therapy is marked by the departure of the client from the counseling room and the client's "reincorporation" back into his or her normal routine.

### ❖ THE THERAPY ROOM AS RITUAL SITE

Ritual sites are usually carefully choreographed, with necessary articles, furniture, and other accoutrements precisely arranged. This is one way in which the therapeutic room or clinic clearly qualifies as a ritual site. For example, Jonathan's therapy room is bright and airy. It is about 15 feet by 12 feet and finished in magnolia. A large mirror above the original iron fireplace is faced on the other side by 3-foot by 2-foot prints of French Impressionist paintings. There is a vase of flowers on a large wall-mounted bookshelf that is as wide as the 12-foot wall but only about two thirds of the way up. A single window looks out onto the street below. The room is warm and comfortable, with three armchairs. There is a small coffee table in the middle of the room, which, Jonathan was keen to tell me, never "comes between the chairs" (as coffee tables in a domestic setting might)! There is a large glass bowl on the table filled with pebbles and small rocks. These are sometimes used "therapeutically," as when Jonathan has a client choose one and describe its shape, texture, and contours. "It can help them get in touch with their own feelings . . . rough edges . . . comfort zones," and so on. He continues, "Some people are more tactile and like something tangible to help them express their thoughts and feelings." He doesn't use them much but believes they are helpful with "youngsters."

"The ambience of the room has to be right," he says. Normally he would have chosen "burnt red" walls, but, feeling this might be "too much" for some clients, he opted for a "safer" color. The "safety" of the room in this sense is defined by the décor and coloring that would be least noticeable. The extremes of his own personal tastes are suppressed to permit what he sees as a potentially less noticeable environment—attention should not be drawn away from the interchange between the therapist and the client. Jonathan says of his therapy room: "You can do therapy anywhere . . . and sometimes you have to . . . but it often helps if you have somewhere appropriate where people can relax like this, somewhere the client can feel comfortable and relaxed where they can work on their issues."

Ritual space is invariably a very carefully prepared space. Separated space is only recognizable as such if it is different from other space around it. This is evident in many anthropological accounts of ritual (e.g., Kapferer, 1991; Turner, 1967). Jonathan's ritual space is deliberately arranged and prepared for the purpose. Colors, furniture, and artifacts are all configured to achieve an overall "appropriate" effect.

Generally, ritual sites are bounded both literally and symbolically. They exclude all but essential attendees, which in the case of psychotherapy means all except the therapist and the client. There are no observers, no spectators, no judges. Privacy is a contractual condition of therapeutic space and time. The private nature of the therapeutic session reflects the subjective nature of the content: The therapy room is designed to be nondistracting and unobtrusive, yet supportive and provocative—the balance is critical.

For the client, therapy and where it happens create a space and time of "backstage" (Goffman, 1969) reparation, a place for "resolution" of all those thoughts, feelings, drives, compulsions, and behaviors that are somehow and otherwise "unacceptable" in the normal fray of social life. For the therapist, on the other hand, in equally Goffmanesque terms, the space is very much his or her professional "frontstage," his or her public arena, a platform for professional performance, the place in which talent is put to the test, and where he or she may be judged. The contrast in roles is stark, but the site must support the roles of both.

## ❖ RITUAL SPECIALIST: THERAPIST AS SHAMAN

From a social anthropological perspective, the therapist equates most closely to what might be described as a "ritual specialist." This is the agent who orchestrates the social, artifactual, and rubrical dimensions of the ritual process. A ritual specialist is the central figure whose knowledge, ability, skill, and so forth permits him or her to specialize in the role of leading ritual practices and is comparable to what might also be described as a "shaman."

Shamans generally can be found in many cultural settings, including those in the West. They are most commonly consulted on matters of personal and social significance by sufferers themselves and sought out to help with any kind of psychological, social, or spiritual problem (Eliade, 1964; Halifax, 1991). But shamanic activities are not limited to curing and healing ailments. Shamans may also accompany individuals and communities that are by all accounts already healthy (Eliade; Myerhoff, 1974). However, that their role is almost invariably (in one way or another) spiritually or psychologically intended to be health promoting is unquestioned. Those shamans who are specifically sought as sources of curing for a particular ailment often encourage their clients to do battle with and defeat or befriend their spiritual curiosities and fears, or at least to render them ineffective as sources of anxiety and harm to self or others, and shamans employ a variety of means for doing this. Listening, empathizing, advising, and instructing are among the techniques shamans might use that are most comparable with those used most commonly in psychotherapy.

Definitions of shamans and their activities differ depending on the local cultural circumstances within which they live and work. But it is clear that they are given to similar social and professional activities as psychotherapists. Shamans are consulted to help others in their communities, to help understand and resolve their predicaments (in either psychological, spiritual, or social terms), and they are largely trusted individuals who appear to have clients and the common good as their core interest. For example, Amazonian shamans are commonly central actors in the political, religious, and social systems and are not only responsible for healing and the spiritual protection of their society but are also thought of as conduits for cultural and mythical knowledge (Plotkin, 1993).

Similarities between shamans and contemporary psychotherapists are supported by Krippner (1988), who maintains that psychotherapy, hypnotherapy, psychodrama, and similar therapies parallel traditional native healing methods. Conventional therapeutic approaches focus, to a large extent, on the belief systems of the clients and emphasize the importance of the clients' "frame of reference," or, conversely, the therapeutic approach can force the client into the therapist's frame of reference and make the client see a "problem" in terms of a psychological theory (e.g., psychoanalysis). Either way, each follows similar methods and approaches of one-to-one consultation, with an emphasis on understanding the client's psychological needs and trying to resolve the tension in these in a way that is keeping with a common store of values and beliefs. Also, there is clear evidence of ritual structures similar to those described in van Gennep's (1909/1960) work. That is, those who consult shamans are often in the process "set apart," for example, by being taken to a location at which only they and the shaman are present. Moreover, such consultations often have a clear liminal phase in which the shaman (or client) may be entranced and "communing" with the spirits (LaBarre, 1970), which may happen, for example, in a critical phase of the ritual.

It must be conceded, however, that there are also differences. For the most part, shamanic practices almost invariably involve some spiritual aspect, whereas psychotherapeutic practices mostly do not (Sollod, 1993), because under a pretext of attempting to be "scientific," Western therapeutic approaches largely avoid (though not entirely) spiritual or religious aspects. For example, Freud's thoughts on spirituality as "infantile neurosis" were significant (and continue to be!) in the development of modern therapy. Although what became known as the "humanistic" approach in psychotherapy to some extent reinstalled spiritual and religious aspects to psychotherapeutic philosophy, this was more an effort to affirm categories of individuality and holism in a discipline that had become predominantly a "top-down" scientism (and less a client-focused problem-resolution process) than an attempt to affirm a distinctive spiritual dimension. There is also much to indicate that altered psychological states, hysteria, and the use of hallucinogenic substances are very much a part of the paraphernalia required by many shamans to accomplish their work (Myerhoff, 1974). Not only would this not figure in the work of the psychotherapist, it would likely contravene agreed-upon ethical guidelines of most counseling and psychotherapeutic bodies.

The therapist as a shamanic figure, then, is only partially complete. Despite a number of general similarities of form and structure between some shamanic practices and some psychotherapeutic ones and between their respective positions in the societies in which they practice, the differences, where they exist, are clearly qualitative—both in the means used to effect cures and in the objects addressed as the source of that cure. It is also important to consider, if the point were not already obvious, that the breadth in types and kinds of shamanic practice (Eliade, 1964) (and for that matter in psychotherapy!) is such as to preclude easy comparison, either within the number of its self-declared practitioners or with nonshamanic healers. Without being unfairly strict or ethnocentric on what might count as a discrete shamanic activity, it is perhaps inappropriate to use shamanism in comparison with psychotherapists. Future studies of comparison or contrast would do better to compare particular, individual practitioners with each other. This of course would be limited in its general and theoretical applicability but would at least be accurate.

## ❖ CONCLUSION

The practice of psychotherapy in anthropological terms is perhaps best conceptualized as a postmodern ritual. It is ritual in that it constitutes a set period of time in a particular space, and it is separated off from the rest of social life. It has an identifiable structure arranged so as to "appropriately" manage the contents of personal change. It is postmodern in that it largely involves only the individual client in the process of change and is principally concerned with the unique worldview of that person.

The reconciliation of the social and the individual, of the self and society, is a primary human function of ritual. In general, much of the work of anthropologists on ritual has highlighted this and the role of it as attempting to reconcile and resolve the contradictions between these. The "disruptions" in personal lives caused by depression, abuse, illness, fear, anxiety, or relationship breakdown can be seen as very particular examples of such "contradictions," as well as disjunctions between the ideal life and the actual life. Psychotherapy mythologizes the resolution of this through theory and ritualizes it through its practice.

## ❖ NOTE

1. The topic has been of personal interest to me for a number of years. It has been supported in part by research grants from the Economic and Social Research Council (research grant number R000223679) and through support from the Newcastle Centre for Family Studies at the University of Newcastle, UK.

## ❖ REFERENCES

Anderson, M. (2002). *The role of counsellors in British society* (Report for the ESRC). Swindon, UK: Economic and Social Research Council.
Cohen, A. P. (1985). *The symbolic construction of community*. London: Routledge.

Cushman, P. (1995). *Constructing the self, constructing America: A cultural history of psychotherapy.* Reading, MA: Addison-Wesley.

Douglas, M. (1966). *Purity and danger: An analysis of the concepts of pollution and taboo.* London: Ark Paperbacks.

Eliade, M. (1964). *Shamanism.* New York: Princeton University Press.

Gellner, E. (1985). *The psychoanalytic movement: The cunning of unreason.* Evanston, IL: Northwestern University Press.

Gluckman, M. (Ed.). (1962). *Essays on the ritual of social relations.* Manchester, UK: Manchester University Press.

Goffman, E. (1969). *The presentation of self in everyday life* (2nd ed.). Harmondsworth, UK: Penguin Books.

Griffin, J., & Tyrrell, I. (2003). *Human givens: A new approach to emotional health and clear thinking.* Chalvingtonm UK: Human Givens Publishing.

Halifax, J. (1991). *Shamanic voices: A survey of visionary narratives.* New York: Penguin.

Kapferer, B. (1991). *A celebration of demons: Exorcism and the aesthetics of healing in Sri Lanka.* New York: Smithsonian Institution Press.

Krippner, S. (1988). Shamans: The first healers. In G. Doore (Ed.), *Shaman's path: Healing, personal growth and empowerment* (pp. 101–114). Boston: Shambala.

LaBarre, W. (1970). *The ghost dance: Origins of religion.* Garden City, NY: Doubleday.

Leach, E. (1954). *Political systems of highland Burma.* London: Bell.

McLeod, J. (1997). *Narrative and psychotherapy.* London: Sage.

McLeod, J. (2001). *An introduction to counselling.* Buckingham, UK: Open University Press.

Mearns, D., & Thorne, B. (1999). *Person-centred counselling in action.* London: Sage.

Myerhoff, B. G. (1974). *Peyote hunt: The sacred journey of the Huichol Indians.* Ithaca, NY: Cornell University Press.

Plotkin, J. (1993). *Tales of a shaman's apprentice: An ethnobotanist searches for new medicines in the Amazon rain forest.* New York: Viking.

Poole, J. F. P. (1982). The ritual forging of identity: Aspects of person and self in Bimin-Kuskusmin male initiation. In G. H. Herdt (Ed.), *Rituals of manhood: Male initiation in Papua-New Guinea* (pp. 99–154). Berkeley: University of California Press.

Raphael, R. (1988). *The men from the boys: Rites of passage in male America.* Lincoln: University of Nebraska Press.

Richards, A. (1956). *Chisungu: A girl's initiation ceremony among the Bember of northern Rhodesia.* London: Faber and Faber.

Sollod, R. (1993). Integrating spiritual healing approaches and techniques into psychotherapy. In G. Stricker & J. Gold (Eds.), *The comprehensive handbook of psychotherapy integration* (pp. 237–248). New York: Plenum.

Turner, V. W. (1962). Three symbols of passage on Ndembu circumcision ritual: An interpretation. In M. Gluckman (Ed.), *Essays on the ritual of social relations* (pp. 124–173). Manchester, UK: Manchester University Press.

Turner, V. W. (1967). *The forest of symbols: Aspects of Ndembu ritual.* Ithaca, NY: Cornell University Press.

van Gennep, A. (1960). *The rites of passage.* Chicago: University of Chicago Press. (Original work published 1909)

# 25

# The Healing Path

*What Can Counselors Learn From*
*Aboriginal People About How to Heal?*

Rod McCormick

I t is with great pleasure that I am able to share this information with the reader. As an Aboriginal psychologist who is a product of both Aboriginal and Euro-Western cultures I have had the opportunity to see the differences and similarities between these two traditions of healing. For most of the last few centuries, Aboriginal people have been seen by the majority culture as disempowered, defeated, and disabled. Early on in my career, I made the decision to focus on the tremendous strengths of Aboriginal peoples and their many rich cultures in an effort to balance the body of research that attempted to pathologize and disempower Aboriginal peoples. Aboriginal psychology and healing are considerably older and consequently more complex than Euro-Western therapies. Because of space constraints I will briefly describe just a few of the "teachings" that Aboriginal peoples can offer the profession.

This chapter will briefly examine the role of spirituality in healing, the role of nature, the role of cleansing, the role of culture in healing, the model of the circle and Medicine Wheel, the concept of balance, the role of connection, and the role of ceremony in healing. Please note that although I use the inclusive term *Aboriginal* in this text, it is interchangeable with the terms *Native, Metis, Indian,* or *First Nations* and refers to the same people. All references to Aboriginal peoples and Aboriginal healing practices in this chapter refer to the Aboriginal peoples of Canada. Canada has more than 500 "First Nations" or Aboriginal cultures, and it is not my intention to suggest that this material is representative of all Aboriginal peoples in the country. It has therefore been necessary to speak broadly about healing practices in an effort to present common themes across the cultures.

This chapter will describe some of the healing approaches that contemporary counseling and psychotherapy can learn from Aboriginal healing. Although many of the practices described are uniquely Aboriginal, they nevertheless can provide Euro-Western therapists with new insights and ideas on how to expand their practice. For most of these approaches a brief description will be provided with some references to the research literature. This will be followed by excerpts from Aboriginal people that describe how the specific approach was used in their personal healing. Because these examples represent what works for Aboriginal peoples, I will not presume to recommend that they should be used by non-Aboriginal clients or therapists. They are humbly offered to the readers, who will then take the teachings that are important to them.

## ❖ THE ROLE OF SPIRITUALITY IN HEALING

One of the major distinctions between Aboriginal healing and Euro-Western healing is the role that spirituality has in the healing process. For Aboriginal people, spirituality is central. The Creator is not separate from humans or nature but is part of all of creation. Spirituality takes on such an important role in healing that it is seen as the essence of healing for many Aboriginal people (Hammerschlag, 1988; Locust, 1988; Medicine Eagle, 1989; Torrey, 1986).

Separation of religion or spirituality and the psychological reality does not exist for Aboriginal people as it does for Westerners. Within Aboriginal traditions the healer also serves as the priest and psychotherapist and not only helps people stay in balance within the earthly context, but also helps the individual understand and stay in accord with the sacred dimension of existence (E. Duran & B. Duran, 1995, p. 46).

Examples demonstrating the important role of spirituality in healing can also be found in research conducted by the author (see, e.g., McCormick, 1995, 1996, 1997a, 1997b, 1997c, 1998, 2000). In this research spirituality encompassed prayer; attending church services; and other forms of connection and communication with the Creator, Great Spirit, God. The examples in this chapter are taken from this research to illustrate the way in which Aboriginal people in their healing journeys utilize spirituality. (Please note that these illustrative quotes are in the exact words of Aboriginal participants from the author's research.)

Examples:

> The realization that the spirits of my grandmother and grandfather and my ancestors are with me has helped me because I know that they are always there and I just have to ask them to come. Knowing that I'm not alone helped me to want to live.

> My spiritual guides have helped me with my healing. I went through a lot of prayer and meditation and this has helped me to be objective; it helps me to understand.

What Euro-Western healers can learn from Aboriginal peoples in this section is that spirituality must be considered as part of the healing process. In all of the categories presented in this chapter, the reader will find that spirituality is inextricably woven within the process. Spirituality need not be a religious endeavor but rather a way to transcend the self and connect with something greater than oneself. Through such connections Aboriginal people have obtained perspective, comfort, empowerment, and support.

## ❖ ROLE OF NATURE IN HEALING

Nature is similar in concept to the role of spirituality in Aboriginal healing. Like the spiritual realm, the natural realm forms the second component of Aboriginal cosmology. The third and final component is the human realm. It is to Mother Earth (natural realm) and Father Sky (spiritual realm) that humans turn when they need help. Among many Aboriginal people, human beings are considered frail and as requiring the guidance and assistance of the natural and spiritual worlds. Speaking of the majority culture's relationship to nature, Ross (1992) states, "We must modify our insistence of manipulation and mastery in the direction of accommodation and respect" (p. 67). In respecting nature, Aboriginal people see nature as providing a sort of blueprint of how to live a healthy life. In my own research (McCormick, 1995), I found nature to be a large part of what facilitates healing for Aboriginal people. Examples from this research include being in or with nature and using the natural world for self-healing. For many Aboriginal people, a spiritual connection exists between nature and humans in that humans are seen as part of nature. Connection with nature is sometimes seen as getting back to creation and the Creator. Examples ranged from the use of water in healing to the healing benefits of forests, mountains, rocks, the wind, the earth, and the sky. Nature helped people feel relaxed, cleansed, calmed, and stronger. Examples provided here will focus only on the ways in which water, trees, the sky, and animals have helped Aboriginal people with their healing journeys.

### Water

Something that helped me was the noise of the water. Rivers slow me down. I can sit and go the same pace as the river and enjoy it and the sound . . . The water helped to calm me inside and it gave me strength.

I would give a stone all of my bad feelings and then put the stone in running water because then it would get carried away. I would be cleansed.

### Trees

When I felt alone and couldn't cry anymore, I would walk in the woods and this let me talk to the Creator and feel the presence by the things around me like the trees. I realized I was not alone.

Find a tree that has meaning to you and tell it all of your problems because I was told that every tree has a spirit and that they are there to listen.

### Sky

Looking at the stars is spiritual and helps because it gets you to look up and notice what's around you. If you think that everything is caving in on you it really helps you to expand and put things into perspective.

On a full moon I talk to the moon and that is a good way for me to talk about my feelings because the moon is like a mother to me.

Open spaces help me to feel that the sky is open and I can feel the Creator and sense the things that the Creator has given to me and everyone else that's alive.

### Animals

I used to take a walk in the bush where it was isolated. During the time that I was depressed I would walk along the power lines behind my village. One day I was sitting in a favorite spot there thinking about what I should do about the pain that I am carrying around when just then a bear came crashing out of the bush, crossed the clearing, and went crashing back into the bush on the other side. When I walk through the bush it is really tangled and tough to walk through. Watching the bear encouraged me to go straight forward and not be afraid of sobriety. At that time everybody else was poking fun at me and saying that I must have thought I was better than them because I stopped drinking. Thinking and acting like that bear taught me that it was OK to take big steps. This helped me to feel a lot better about not using alcohol but in finding straighter paths to deal with my problem. My grandfather's guardian spirits were the wolf and the bear and I think that they are there for me now too.

### Cleansing

Most cultures have some form of emotional cleansing or emotional expression. For Aboriginal peoples, this cleansing tends to be a holistic process that symbolically involves emotional, physical, mental, and spiritual cleansing. Examples of cleansing or ritually cleaning oneself range from cleansing through sweats and ritual bathing to using cedar boughs for cleansing. Participants benefited by feeling lighter and more balanced.

I cleanse myself with water. In my culture you cleanse yourself with water, your eyes, your face, your ears, your hands. . . . You would say prayers while you are doing this as it is a thank you for all that we are given. I have done this regularly like praying and it has helped me to be strong and to heal.

Bathing helped me because it was a cleansing time. Whatever it was that I wanted removed I could cover my body with mud or sand and then go into the river and wash it away. I did this for a month. This helped because I had to put a name to what it was that I wanted to get rid of and then washed it away. The physical washing affected the emotional and spiritual by washing and cleansing them as well. I would do this bathing the first thing before the sun was up and the last thing before the sun was down. In the city I can do this by washing with just water from the tap.

### ❖ ROLE OF CULTURE IN HEALING

Many Aboriginal people believe that not maintaining one's cultural values and community respect is one of the reasons for psychological and physical problems

(Lafromboise, Trimble, & Mohatt, 1990). It is therefore thought that one of the roles of therapy for traditional Aboriginal society has been to reaffirm cultural values. Aboriginal people have recently witnessed a renaissance of traditional healing ways that are of interest not only to Aboriginal people but to all people. There are many examples of this reemergence of traditional Aboriginal medicine (Neligh, 1990; Van Uchelen, Davidson, Quressette, Demerais, & Brasfield, 1997; Waldram, Herring, & Young, 1995; Wyrostock & Paulson, 2000). McCormick (1995) conducted one of the few comprehensive studies examining the facilitation of healing for Aboriginal people in British Columbia. Although there was some mention of Western healing approaches in the results, the majority of the findings reflected the strength of traditional approaches to healing. In this research, *culture* referred to the individual's learning about and participating in Aboriginal culture and traditions. It did not include the participation in traditional ceremonies but did include all other aspects of traditional culture and knowledge. These events ranged from learning about cultural practices to speaking one's language. Many participants considered gaining knowledge of their culture to be an important step in becoming healthy. Cultural confusion and lack of connection to traditional culture and values were often identified as reasons for anxiety and pain. The following are examples of how Aboriginal people were able to utilize culture as part of their healing:

I left home and hitchhiked back to my reserve and that helped a lot with the healing because I stayed there until I learned about my Native culture. It was a learning quest and that was very healing for me. My grandparents and relatives taught me about my culture so now I feel like I can fit into both cultures.

Finding out who I was again helped me a lot. I left residential school not knowing who I was. I was like a shattered person. Reconnecting with my culture and with spirituality gave me back my identity. I knew who I was again.

❖ THE CIRCLE/MEDICINE WHEEL MODEL

*"You have noticed that everything an Indian does is in a circle, and that is because the power of the world always works in circles, and everything tries to be round. . . . Everything the power of the world does is done in a circle . . . Our tepees were round like the nests of birds, and these were always set in a circle, the nation's hoop, a nest of many nests, where the Great Spirit meant for us to hatch our children."*

—Black Elk, Oglala Sioux Holy Man (1863–1950)

One of the most prevalent symbols in the Aboriginal worldview is the circle. The circle and the Medicine Wheel can be thought of as a model of Aboriginal cosmology and as a tool to understand our relationship with creation and how to lead a healthy life. Aboriginal elders explain this symbol more effectively than I can. Lame Deer, a Sioux Elder, said,

> We see in the world around us as many symbols that teach us the meaning of life. . . . The Indian's symbol is the circle, the hoop. . . . The bodies of human being and animals have no corners. Our circle is timeless, flowing; it is new life emerging from death—life winning out over death. (quoted in Halfe, 1993, p. 27)

Throughout most Aboriginal cultures we see the symbol of the circle. One example used in healing is the talking circle.

> The Talking Circle is a form of group therapy where participants sit in a circle. The Talking Circle begins by individuals smudging themselves with sweet grass or sage. The group elder or leader opens the meeting by describing some personal experience, followed by individuals of the group doing likewise. (Abbott, 1998, p. 2623)

The following are a few examples of how Aboriginal people utilize the circle in healing:

> Talking circles helped me because I could talk and hear myself and decide whether this was a true thing or a passing state of being of how I was feeling. From time to time I could clarify this by hearing myself speaking about my feelings and by having other people witness it. I was able to evaluate the transition and see my progress from circle time to circle time as well. Seeing other people having similar problems also helped me to see that I was not alone and that was a source of comfort.

> I pick the sharing circles and ceremonies where people feel its ok to crumble because there were a lot of times when I crumbled and just let go of the pain.

A variation of the circle is the model of the Medicine Wheel. Although it is not as universally accepted as the circle, the Medicine Wheel reflects a traditional Aboriginal worldview of healing. The Medicine Wheel shows the separate entities—mental, physical, emotional, and spiritual—as being equal and as part of a larger whole. This reinforces the concept of interconnectedness and the belief that one part cannot be the center but must instead learn to work in harmony with all of the other parts. The Medicine Wheel is viewed as "movements in the cycle of human development from our birth to our unity with the whole of creation" (J. Bopp, M. Bopp, Brown, & Lane, 1984, p. 14). Another teaching of the Medicine Wheel is that of balance. Traditional Aboriginal healing incorporates the physical, social, psychological, and spiritual being. It is difficult to isolate any one aspect (Primeaux, 1977).

### Balance

Building on an important component of the Medicine Wheel is the teaching of balance. It is believed that a healthy life is one in which there is an approximation of balance between the mental, physical, emotional, and spiritual dimensions of the individual. It is believed that you get sick when you are not in balance (Medicine Eagle, 1989).

> Throughout the history of Aboriginal people—the definition of health evolved around the whole being of each person—the physical, emotional, mental and spiritual aspects of a person being in balance and harmony with each other as well as with the environment and other beings. This has clashed with the Western medical model which, until very recently, has perpetuated the concept of health as being "the absence of disease." (Favel-King, 1993, p. 125)

As mentioned earlier, traditional Aboriginal healing addresses a person's physical, social, psychological, and spiritual needs, without isolating any one aspect (Primeaux, 1977). Balance, then, is essential for the Aboriginal person, because the world itself is seen as a balance of transcendental forces, human beings, and the natural environment (Hammerschlag, 1988).

### ❖ ROLE OF CONNECTION IN HEALING

Another key factor in healing for Aboriginal people is the role of connection. Connection can mean the process of dealing with problems with the assistance of others and not by oneself. Assistance can be obtained from friends, the family, the community, and in the context of group counseling or on a social basis. In research conducted by McCormick (1995), several of the 14 categories established had a theme of connecting or interconnectedness. The extended family, friends, and members of the community were seen as a natural support for Aboriginal people and as illustrating the importance of belonging. Similarly, it was seen as desirable for many Aboriginal people to be connected to and belong with nature and spirituality and, ultimately, to be a part of and belong to all of creation.

For traditional Aboriginal people, healing is often in the form of a community-sanctioned and community-run cleansing ceremony that involves the whole community (Ross, 1992; Torrey, 1972). In his work examining Aboriginal world-view, Ross states,

> All of the outlawed and denigrated facets of traditional culture—the spirit dances, the sweat lodge and pipe ceremonies, the regular ritual offering of tobacco as a symbol of gratitude—must be seen for what they really were: tools to maintain and deepen a belief in the inter-connectedness of all things. Now that such practices are being slowly brought back, they serve a second function too, for they offer an alternative focus to that of our individualistic and materialistic value system. (p. 183)

In some Aboriginal cultures, establishing harmony within the community and improving interpersonal relationships among members of the community are seen by members of the community as the goals of therapy (Torrey, 1972). Katz and Rolde (1981) found that the goal of traditional Aboriginal healing was not to strengthen the client's ego, as in non-Aboriginal counseling, but to encourage the client to transcend the ego by considering himself or herself as embedded in and expressive of community. Like family therapy, systems therapy, and community psychiatry, Aboriginal healing promotes the idea of bringing together many forces to best utilize the powers that promote health (Hammerschlag, 1988).

❖ THE ROLE OF CEREMONY

An important contribution to healing made by Aboriginal people is the inclusion of ceremony in the healing process. Examples range from the sweat lodge ceremony to the pipe ceremony. There are many different ceremonies in Aboriginal culture, and ceremonies vary from nation to nation. Participation in ceremony is a traditional form of healing used by Aboriginal people for thousands of years and is still recognized as an important form of healing today. The sweat lodge ceremony, for example, is often considered to be a cleansing or rebirthing ceremony (see Smith, Chapter 17 in this volume). Elements of this ceremony, such as the darkness and the drumbeat, are likened to the experience of being in the womb of Mother Earth. The process of sweating can represent the intermingling of the participant's life fluids with that of Mother Earth. Ceremonies such as the spirit dances, the sweat lodge, and the pipe ceremonies are tools to maintain and deepen the individual's sense of connectedness to all things (Ross, 1992). The vision quest ceremony is said to help a person to realize the vastness of the universe and, by enabling the person to transcend him or herself, to realize ultimately his or her oneness with nature (McGaa, 1989).

> Sweats are an intense powerful healing method for me. [It's] cleansing and it opens my mind. I tend to shut off my mind but when I was in a sweat the visions that I saw and what I heard opened me up so that my whole world was wide open. I walked out a lighter person and whatever burdens I had weren't there any more or if they were there they weren't as heavy any-more. . . . The process of bringing the rocks and water into the sweat is peaceful and calming. It's also like I was the only one there, it doesn't matter how many people are actually in the sweat. I was the only one there in connection with the spirits.

## ❖ PATH TO HEALING

A final piece of wisdom derived from Aboriginal healing is in the form of a common path to healing. Although this "path" is somewhat speculative and not yet supported by research, it nevertheless can be commonly found in many Aboriginal healing stories. Research conducted by McCormick (1995) attempted to discern a path to healing common to all Aboriginal ceremonies and healing journeys. A study of the stories of the participant in this study revealed a common path in the form of four clear stages in the healing process. The four stages can be described as follows: separating from the unhealthy life, obtaining social support and resources, experiencing a healthy life, and living a healthy life.

*In the first stage,* separating from the unhealthy life, an individuals first removes himself or herself from the unhealthy way of being in order to determine, clarify, and make sense of the problem.

*In the second stage,* obtaining social support and resources, the individual seeks help and support from others and establishes social connections with others. This support takes the form of encouragement, motivation, acceptance, validation, and reassurance. The individual feels socially connected when he or she is able to get beyond his or her own world through social interaction.

*In the third stage,* experiencing a healthy life, the individual learns how to live a fuller life doing many or all of the following: participating in ceremony, learning from a role model, establishing a spiritual connection, establishing a connection with nature, and anchoring oneself in tradition. The feeling of integration with one's culture provides a strong sense of direction and belonging.

*In the final stage,* living and maintaining a healthy life, the person takes steps to ensure that he or she is able to live and maintain the new life experienced in the previous stage. Many feel optimistic and empowered by this new involvement in challenging activities and in a new sense of discipline.

## ❖ CONCLUSION

This chapter has briefly described some of the healing approaches used by Aboriginal people from which contemporary counseling and psychotherapy might learn. A strong value among Aboriginal peoples is sharing. This small glimpse into Aboriginal healing has revealed that such traditions of healing are holistic and multifaceted. Although it would not be appropriate for a non-Aboriginal therapist to attempt to run an Aboriginal healing ceremony, there are perhaps elements of the approaches presented here that an enlightened therapist may be able to incorporate into his or her practice in a respectful and culturally appropriate way.

## ❖ REFERENCES

Abbott, P. J. (1998). Traditional and Western healing practices for alcoholism. *American Indians and Alaska Natives: Substance Use Misuse, 33,* 2605–2646.

Bopp, J., Bopp, M., Brown, L., & Lane, P. (1984). *The sacred tree.* Lethbridge, Alberta, Canada: Four Worlds Development Press.

Duran, E., & Duran, B. (1995). *Native American post colonial psychology.* Albany: State University of New York Press.

Favel-King, A. (1993). The treaty right to health. In *The path to healing: Report of the National Roundtable on Aboriginal Health and Social Issues* (pp. 120–127) (Royal Commission on Aboriginal Peoples). Ottawa, Ontario: Canada Communication Group Publishing.

Halfe, L. (1993). Native healing. *Cognica, 26*(1), 21–27.

Hammerschlag, C. A. (1988). *The dancing healers: A doctor's journey of healing with Native Americans.* San Francisco: Harper & Row.

Katz, R., & Rolde, E. (1981). Community alternatives to psychotherapy. *Psychotherapy, Theory, Research and Practice, 18,* 365–374.

Lafromboise, T., Trimble, J., & Mohatt, G. (1990). Counseling intervention and American Indian tradition: An integrative approach. *Counseling Psychologist, 18,* 628–654.

Locust, C. (1988). Wounding the Spirit: Discrimination and traditional American Indian belief systems. *Harvard Educational Review, 58,* 315–330.

McCormick, R. M. (1995). The facilitation of healing for the First Nations people of British Columbia [Monograph]. *Canadian Journal of Native Education, 21,* 251–319.

McCormick, R. M. (1996). Culturally appropriate means and ends of counselling as described by the First Nations people of British Columbia. *International Journal for the Advancement of Counselling, 18,* 163–172.

McCormick, R. M. (1997a). First Nations counsellor training: Strengthening the circle. *Canadian Journal of Community Mental Health, 16*(2), 91–100.

McCormick, R. M. (1997b). Healing through interdependence: The role of connecting in First Nations healing practices. *Canadian Journal of Counselling, 31,* 172–184.

McCormick, R. M. (1997c). An integration of healing wisdom: The vision quest ceremony from an attachment theory perspective. *Guidance and Counselling, 12*(2), 18–22.

McCormick, R. M. (1998). Ethical considerations in First Nations counselling and research. *Canadian Journal of Counselling, 33,* 284–297.

McCormick, R. M. (2000). Aboriginal traditions in the treatment of substance abuse. *Canadian Journal of Counselling, 34,* 25–33.

McGaa, E. (1989). *Mother Earth spirituality: Native American paths to healing ourselves and our world.* San Francisco: Harper & Row.

Medicine Eagle, B. (1989). The circle of healing. In R. Carlson & J. Brugh (Eds.), *Healers on healing* (pp. 58–62). New York: Tarcher.

Neligh, G. (1990). Mental health programs for American Indians: Their logic, structure and function [Monograph]. *American Indian and Alaskan Native Mental Health Research, 3*(3), 1–280.

Primeaux, M. H. (1977). American Indian health care practices: A cross cultural perspective. *Nursing Clinics of North America, 12,* 55–65.

Ross, R. (1992). *Dancing with a ghost: Exploring Indian reality.* Markham, UK: Octopus.

Torrey, E. F. (1972). *The mind game: Witch doctors and psychiatrists.* New York: Emerson Hall.

Torrey, E. F. (1986). *Witchdoctors and psychiatrists: The common roots of psychotherapy and its future.* New York: Harper & Row.

Van Uchelen, C. P., Davidson, S. F., Quressette, S. V. A., Demerais, L., & Brasfield, C. R. (1997). What makes us strong: Urban Aboriginal perspectives on wellness and strength. *Canadian Journal of Community Mental Health, 16*(2), 37–50.

Waldram, J. B., Herring, D. A., & Young, T. K. (1995). *Aboriginal health in Canada: Historical, cultural, and epidemiological perspectives.* Toronto, Ontario, Canada: University of Toronto Press.

Wyrostock, N. C., & Paulson, B. L. (2000). Traditional healing practices among First Nations students. *Canadian Journal of Counselling, 34,* 14–24.

# 26

# *Herbalistas, Curandeiros,* and *Bruxas*

## Valuable Lessons From Traditional Systems of Healing

*Birdie J. Bezanson, Gary Foster, and Susan James*

In Plato's *Symposium,* when it is the physician Eryximachos's turn to speak in honor of the god Love (*Eros*), he gives us an insight into the nature of ancient Greek medicine. He compares the art of medicine to that of music, in that the goal is to bring about a harmony or concord of the loves, which in turn brings harmony to one's life and health (Plato, 1956). Such a claim about medicine strikes our modern, scientific ears as strange, and we may suspect that Eryximachos is simply the victim of a less enlightened, highly superstitious time in history. But we think that the issue goes deeper than that. If we can get beyond a surface understanding of the mythology expressed in this account of love and medicine, we come to realize a very different ontology of healing and of the relation between physical health and moral or spiritual well-being. This holistic view of health stands in stark contrast to many mainstream Western notions of healing, which tend to reduce the human body to a mechanism that needs fixing. In this chapter, we will explore this Western notion of healing and contrast it with the more holistic view of traditional Portuguese healers.

This essentially "reductionist" view of medicine and health is not found in all traditional cultures. Indeed, many cultures still see health as tied to the religious, the spiritual, or the moral. The research findings of our study of *agonias* (see James, 2002) among Portuguese immigrants help bring to light this important point. The study suggests that certain somatic experiences cannot be reduced to merely empirical or biological referents. *Agonias*, for instance, translated as "the agonies," is often understood and classified by clinicians under the broad category of "anxiety disorder." The problem with such a characterization, however, becomes apparent when one realizes the particular cultural meanings, contexts, and circumstances associated with the onset and experience of this phenomenon. Clinicians who work with Portuguese immigrants in the United States have expressed frustration regarding their attempts to treat this condition "as" a general anxiety disorder (James).

These findings are consistent with the theoretical framework for cultural psychology developed in "Narratives and Culture: 'Thickening' the Self for Psychotherapy" (James & Foster, 2003). According to this framework, one cannot fully understand or treat an individual in isolation from the context within which the individual makes sense of the world, in other words, the cultural context. This is because we are not merely biological or physical entities but are also linguistic and cultural "beings." Emotions and psychological experience involves not only physical or chemical processes, but also conceptual and cultural understanding and expression. This is not to suggest that a scientific conception of medicine is not valuable. The idea is rather that we see modern medicine as part (a very important part) of the process of healing, which may work together with other traditional or culturally informed practices. When we examine the field of psychology, and psychotherapy in particular, we can readily see the importance of such a holistic, cultural approach.

An understanding of human beings as merely physical, biological entities is insufficient when it comes to treating various psychological maladies. The primary reason for this is that we are creatures of culture and language, that is, we are "self-interpreting animals," as Charles Taylor (1985) puts it (p. 45). Not only do we inhabit a culture and a linguistic community, but our understanding of our self and the world is profoundly shaped by the conceptual network that we inherit. We cannot understand our selves or the world apart from the concepts and the framework that we inhabit. Any attempt to abandon such a framework, to reject it, will necessarily be done with the tools at our disposal, that is, those very same concepts that have shaped our experience. This does not imply that we are trapped or locked into our own limited cultural or personal spheres forever, but it does challenge the Western, individualistic concept of self that appears free to reject and step outside of this cultural sphere. In the West we tend to see culture and cultural beliefs as optional, something that the individual, autonomous self can throw off. The picture here is of two separate realms: self and society or culture. We believe that a hermeneutic understanding of this relation gives us a more accurate picture. The self, which is largely a product of culture, can certainly challenge and critically assess its own culture. To a large degree, one can even reject one's own culture. But this rejection, and the subsequent "independence," can happen only by making use of resources or concepts that are also culturally informed. This picture suggests what has been called the "hermeneutic circle." The idea here is that understanding the relation between one's self and one's culture takes the form of a circle that encompasses both self and culture. We can understand the self or the "part" only in terms of the culture or "whole," and we can fully appreciate the whole only in terms of the parts or the individuals who create, embody, and express cultural beliefs, values, and concepts.

Understanding the relation between the individual and culture hermeneutically has certain implications for psychology and psychotherapy. The most obvious is that we cannot properly understand the self apart from some understanding of the culture that informs the self. Many indigenous forms of medicine or health care take into account various beliefs and values that a member of a particular culture holds, and these may therefore provide an important ally or partner in psychological healing. In what follows, we will examine the role of multiple healers or healing systems in the context of the Portuguese immigrant community in North America. We will attempt to show that the utilization of multiple approaches to health or healing may provide better client care than a more homogeneous science-based approach, especially because of the cultural significance of traditional approaches. We will provide specific examples in the following sections of how this multiresource approach may work and be understood from the perspective of a hermeneutically informed approach to cultural psychotherapy.

❖ MENTAL HEALTH IN THE
   PORTUGUESE IMMIGRANT COMMUNITY

For the Portuguese immigrant community, the use of multiple healing systems is commensurable simply because allopathic and indigenous healers are both considered extensions of God's domain. Besides consulting a contemporary health provider, the majority of Portuguese mental health patients will also seek other methods of healing: Some pray or consult a priest, others visit a traditional healer, and some may access all three types of healers. For instance, a 56-year-old Portuguese immigrant who suffered from multiple symptoms felt like she was *faltando de ar* ("missing air"), along with experiencing dizzy spells and hot flashes. The woman's physician gave her an asthma ventilator, her psychiatrist gave her Valium, her traditional healer gave her menopause vitamins, and her priest suggested prayer. Not an exception but rather the norm, this example illustrates the multiple layers of care a Portuguese descendant might use. Within these layers, the Portuguese community can access three types of traditional healers: *herbalistas*, *curandeiros*, and *bruxas*.

## ❖ TRADITIONAL HEALING

The *herbalista* is the most sought after of the traditional healers in the immigrant community. Working from a storefront that could easily be confused with a North American health store selling vitamins and herbs, the *herbalista* is consulted for reasons that can vary from weight loss to sexual dysfunction. Unlike other traditional healers, the *herbalista* works solely with the physiological aspects of an illness and is quick to refer if necessary. For example, the *herbalista* may suggest a priest if the issue appears to be of a spiritual nature. This natural healer may seem more integrated into the local community, because the *herbalista*'s services more closely resemble those of a naturopath. Aids might be tea recipes brought from Portugal, teas from the North American market, or vitamins, all of which are considered supplements.

A saliva or urine sample is used to gather information that will indicate what the body is lacking or, alternatively, what the body has too much of. The *herbalista* will seek to reestablish the balance in the immune system. The first form of treatment is to suggest a diet more reminiscent of rural Portugal, which incorporates a healthy regime of unprocessed foods. This would be supplemented with different types of herbal teas, vitamins, exercise, or some combination of the three, depending on what the body needs in order to restore a healthy equilibrium. An *herbalista* acts less as an expert and more like an investigator, gathering information and giving suggestions from which the client can then choose. One *herbalista* very clearly defines his position within the health profession: "I am not a healer. . . . I don't act as a doctor or a healer, no, I'm just asking what are the symptoms of the person, then I give the information that is available and the person decides." Still, the same *herbalista* has very clear ideas about the origins of illness that would not fit into a more contemporary medical model: "Illness is in the organs when they are weak, cells that are sick, are weak, and need a new energy so that they can be reestablished and therefore give health to the person."

The *curandeiro* (the word comes from the verb *curar,* "to heal") is the second most popular type of healer in the Portuguese immigrant community. A person may seek a *curandeiro* either alone or with family members. Reasons to seek help can be both physical and emotional. Aids to the healing process can be in the form of oils, massage, water, salt, teas, vitamins, or herbs, but the most powerful aid is prayer, an indicator of the strong religious beliefs within the community. Although the strong ties with religion cultivate a spiritual explanation for physical or emotional ailments, *curandeiros* tend to have a medical approach to treatment. The *curandeiro* will provide a list of foods and beverages that are banned and will prescribe herbal teas. But treating the community remains a truly spiritual endeavor for the *curandeiro:* "What gives the healing is what the gift explains to me to write the herbs that are needed." Diagnosis and treatment may well rely on the medical model, but the ability to diagnosis and prescribe proper treatment is attributed to a spiritual source.

The *curandeiro* works on three levels to heal psychologically, spiritually, and physically. On a psychological level, if counsel is what is needed, a *curandeiro* will meet with a client for an hour to discuss the client's difficulties; superficially, this may resemble a North American therapist-client relationship. Simultaneously, the *curandeiro* may also be evaluating the client's aura as part of the information-gathering process. For difficulties of the spiritual realm, the *curandeiro* will often pray with clients or suggest prayers for them to perform on their own. They may also suggest things that can be done in the house to ward off evil spirits, such as hanging garlic in the doorway. For physical ailments, *curandeiros* might suggest healing teas or vitamins for their clients to take, or they may utilize body manipulation as a chiropractor would do. In this way, *curandeiros* offer a more holistic form of treatment for clients. Many *curandeiros* have an office in their home, much like a therapist's office with a waiting room. Clients do not make appointments, but rather the *curandeiro* will see people on a first-come, first-served basis. The strong religious beliefs of the *curandeiro* are evident in the many amulets of saints in the office and the waiting room. The *curandeiro's* abilities are seen as a gift from God that has been passed down from generation to generation within the family.

Quite rare in North America, the *bruxa* is the least common traditional healer to consult. When the Portuguese feel that spirits are causing their symptoms, they will consult a *bruxa.* More mysterious, a *bruxa* may be conceived of as a witch doctor or a medium by those outside the elderly Portuguese community. *Bruxas* use the spiritual realm to do good for unfortunate people or souls in purgatory. The rituals entail offering prayer, fruit, flowers, incense, or candles. One physician within the Portuguese community explains the process:

She [the *bruxa*] works as a medium and seeks help from the good spirits, usually the patient's relatives who have passed on. They then intercede for the patient and fight the bad spirits. There is usually some praying and a vigil around the house accompanied by cleansing fumes and the ingestion of special beverages.

Members of the community often report that they turn to the Divine for healing, in which case the clergy becomes an integral part of the healing system. An elderly Portuguese woman expresses her devout faith in God's abilities to heal: "I have a lot of faith in God because He is the one who helps us. . . . If God can't help us, nobody on earth can."

## ❖ ACCEPTANCE OF MULTIPLE SYSTEMS

Traditional healers usually feel that it is acceptable for people to seek help in more than one healing system, as one client's story illustrates:

I went to a *curandeiro* who said that the teas would help my asthma. He didn't tell me to stop the medications from my doctor. He said that it is not bad for me to take both the medications and the tea so I drink one of those teas every now and then.

Research by Harris and James (2002) has demonstrated that psychotherapists also support their clients' seeking treatment from traditional healing systems. As one psychotherapist indicated, a full grasp of how traditional healers work is not always necessary: "If it makes my patient feel better, I have no reason to argue, you know. Even though I cannot explain it, even though I might not totally understand it or agree with it." Other psychotherapists felt that seeking traditional healers gave the clients some control over their care, which, in the long run, would prove to be beneficial to the client. One therapist consistently asked his clients if they had attended church the previous Sunday. Attendance was a strong indication of mental wellness, whereas nonattendance might indicate distress.

Faith in the Divine or traditional healers does not negate the usefulness of modern-day medical practitioners. One physician describes how different treatments are compatible and complementary:

They feel that we have the power to help them but the ultimate outcome is dictated by God's will. If it's meant to be, they will get better. On the other hand, they also feel that doctors should be consulted and that we are not trying to take God's place. . . . If it is meant for them to get better, it's a way of getting better faster.

Research conducted by James, Navara, Haskell, and Clarke (2002) with the Portuguese immigrant population in Boston found that 42% of the participants used medical healing only; 22% used both medical and traditional healing; 14% used medical and religious healing; and 22% used medical, traditional, and religious healing together. In fact, echoing the sentiments of the physician quoted above, the respondents believed the more healing systems used the better.

## ❖ IMPLICATIONS FOR COUNSELING AND PSYCHOTHERAPY

Our research highlights the importance of mental health clinicians' understanding and eliciting the help of indigenous and religious healers within the Portuguese community. Working collaboratively and making referrals may expedite the path to health. In some cases, it may simply be appropriate, and therefore beneficial, to the therapeutic process for a therapist to suggest that a client solicit a *curandeiro's* approval before therapy commences (Araujo, 1996).

As an ongoing practice, community healers could be invited to attend consultation meetings or asked to provide workshops for mental health teams to ensure that cultural knowledge is more readily assimilated into case conceptualizations.

An assumption of the medical model is that there is no meaning in suffering. Validation of the significance of suffering within the Portuguese community is not only important, but necessary in some cases. For members of this community, suffering has complex links to their social and religious context. Suffering links them to others and the Divine, creating a mind/body/spirit holism that is not often discussed in theories of psychotherapy. Friends, traditional healers, and God are expected to listen tirelessly and compassionately to various physical complaints, and it is assumed that the therapist will do so as well. Contemporary therapists who attempt to minimize suffering, as some models of therapy dictate, may in effect be promoting more discomfort. Only when clients feel that their suffering and symptoms are taken seriously can the therapist move on to specific interventions.

Being open to alternatives allows practitioners to create networks where different mental health services can complement each other, rather than acting as parallel but unrelated treatments. One barrier is the language of the different types of healers, where we find little intersection. At a superficial level, it may seem that treatments from different types of healers are working at cross-purposes, but on a closer look we can see they are actually complementary. For example, in one discipline, *agonias,* as an emotional and somatic ailment, is a psychiatric disorder that requires medication or therapy; in another it is anxiety of sin that requires prayer; and in another discipline it is menopause and requires vitamins (James & Clarke, 2001). *Agonias* is often discussed using words such as *anxiety, depression,* or even *asthma,* depending on the therapists, when in fact these words do not capture the true experience of the disorder for the client (James, 2002). Developing a culturally sensitive therapy plan; combining it with prayer and church attendance as prescribed by the client's priest; and supporting a regime of vitamins, teas, and healthy eating habits as outlined by the *herbalista* or possibly the *curandeiro* fit well with the "more is better" worldview of this immigrant population.

Much can be learned from the *herbalista* and the *curandeiro's* holistic model of treatment, which conforms to the person rather than the diagnosis. *Herbalistas* are quick to enlist the help of other forms of healing, and *curandeiros* will remain aware of the client's aura, using their gifts and intuition to best serve the client. Speaking to the relevance of the spirit to the therapeutic process, information on auras or human energy fields (system) is becoming somewhat more visible in the psychotherapy literature (West, 2000). Twenty percent of the general population is said to have the ability to see auras (Bain, 1997), yet this ability is not often addressed in psychotherapy training, supervision, or practice. Because such phenomena are treated as taboo in practice, we are more often likely to label awareness of transcendental dimensions as intuition, which should be treated with caution rather than explored and developed. Therapists who do utilize this ability remain cognizant of their own energy fields and those of their clients as a way to support a strong empathic understanding and a more profound experience within therapy (Mintz, 1978; Mollon, 1991).

Another reason to be open to mystical experiences, such as sensing auras, is that it may reflect the lived experience of one's clients. In a survey of members of the American Psychological Association (Allman, De La Rocha, Elkins, & Weathers, 1992), practitioners reported that almost 5% of their clients disclosed having mystical experiences. Exploration of these experiences in a therapeutic environment could lead to misinterpretation if the therapist were not aware of or not willing to consider different worldviews. A client's persistent description of a transient feeling of unity and spiritual awakening could easily lead to misdiagnoses. Contemporary models of therapy suggest that our competence in providing therapy to clients of a different culture can be greatly enhanced by awareness of our racial identity. It would follow that awareness of our views around spirituality and religion would also enhance our practice. To ensure that our biases and values do not interfere with our ability to work with clients with different beliefs, we must be aware of the differences and how they affect the therapeutic process. Offering a more intuitive and holistic type of care for spiritually minded clients of any culture is the basic responsibility of therapists.

Often, as practitioners in North America, we are compelled to act according to an idealized picture of what is considered "good therapy." For example, a therapist running a highly successful women's group within the Portuguese community in the Boston area was hesitant to allow one of the authors (James) to attend one of the group sessions. On further investigation it was discovered that the therapist was allowing the participants to bring their knitting to therapy. The therapist was apprehensive that the author would not consider it "good therapy" simply because of the unorthodox appearance. The knitting reflected the culture (by incorporating a common cultural practice—the "knitting group") and allowed the therapist to facilitate the process of change for women who would not readily give up time for talk therapy. Another therapist used the technique, commonly used by a *curandeiro* or *herbalista,* of writing instructions on a prescription pad in order to make psychological remedies more concrete for his clients. The same therapist found biofeedback to be an effective way for some clients to circumvent the discomfort around dialoguing solely about their feelings. Biofeedback trains clients to use signals from their own bodies to improve their health. The success of these different ways of doing therapy highlights the importance of incorporating a holistic model of treatment.

Professional ethics codes present a challenge to any attempt to incorporate a more holistic approach to therapy. Such codes seek to avoid problematic situations that result from ambiguous relations between therapist and client. To this end, professional ethical codes require therapists to draw sharp lines in their relationship with clients in order to maintain the integrity of the profession. The aim, of course, is to keep interactions on a professional level and avoid dual relationships. These same codes address the issue of cross-cultural therapy by directing the therapist to respect cultural differences and to gain knowledge of the culture one is working with. A problem arises, however, when the particular culture one is working with operates with a different understanding of the relationship between health provider and client.

Teresa, a Portuguese immigrant woman, illustrates this point. She initially sought therapy because frequent fainting spells were inhibiting her ability to work. It became evident to the therapist that many of her symptoms were precipitated by the need to write a letter, in English, to the Immigration and Naturalization Service. The seemingly simple task had caused debilitating fear that she might be deported if she did not send the letter or—worse, although unrealistic—if she did send the letter and her language skills were lacking. The therapist was torn, faced with the choice of either finding a translator in the community that the client could hire (Teresa was very poor) or simply doing it herself, the latter being an efficient and inexpensive solution, but more ethically questionable.

This example shows that perhaps our professional ethical codes are too rigid to meet the demands of a multicultural context. Although we acknowledge the importance of such codes, perhaps more discretion should be given to the counselor for interpreting or applying them. Such flexibility allows the therapist to be more sensitive to the cultural context and more discriminating in decision making.

Finally, we would like to conclude by suggesting that by using a hermeneutic approach, therapists can find a way to link traditional healing and counseling and psychotherapy. A hermeneutically informed approach to psychotherapy attempts to combine the best of contemporary therapy and indigenous forms of healing. Hermeneutics, the science (or art) of interpretation, considers the relationship between the whole and the part. Although traditionally applied to the interpretation of texts, especially religious texts, the approach may also be applied to human activity to support the integration of contemporary psychotherapy and the use of traditional healers. Understanding or interpreting human behavior necessitates an understanding of both personal (the part) and cultural (the whole) factors.

Clinical and counseling theories would be significantly enhanced by incorporating a hermeneutic approach to cultural psychology with the complex religious and sociocultural awareness that it seeks to privilege. The framework situates the individual in his or her local world and expands the field of inquiry in the psychological and psychiatric realm to consider other levels of analysis. We are challenged to move from primarily focusing on the level of the individual to also considering the social, cultural, religious, and moral domains, presenting a more complex, integrative, and meaningful view that reflects the relationship between part and whole stressed by a hermeneutic understanding of therapy. We are further challenged to accept and even incorporate methods of healing that have a tradition of success within the immigrant Portuguese community. These methods, rather than being a hindrance to modern understandings and approaches to healing, may in fact provide what is missing: cultural context and a belief structure that gives the client confidence and trust in health providers.

## ❖ REFERENCES

Allman, L. S., De La Rocha, O., Elkins, D. N., & Weathers, R. S. (1992). Psychotherapists' attitudes towards clients reporting mystical experiences. *Psychotherapy, 29,* 654–659.

Araujo, Z. A. (1996). Portuguese families. In M. McGoldrick, J. Pearce, & J. Giordano (Eds.), *Ethnicity and family therapy* (pp. 583–594). New York: Guilford Press.

Bain, G. H. (1997). *Auras 101: A basic study of human auras and the techniques to see them.* Sedona, AZ: Light Technology.

Harris, S. G., & James, S. (2002). *Portuguese psychotherapists treating Portuguese clients: Exploring a hermeneutic approach to therapy.* Manuscript submitted for publication.

James, S. (2002). Agonias: The social and sacred suffering of Portuguese immigrants. *Culture, Medicine and Psychiatry, 26,* 87–110.

James, S., & Clarke, J. (2001). Surplus suffering: The case of Portuguese immigrant women. *Feminist Review, 68,* 167–170.

James, S., & Foster, G. (2003). Narratives and culture: "Thickening" the self for psychotherapy. *Journal of Theoretical and Philosophical Psychology, 23,* 1–25.

James, S., Navara, G. S., Haskell, S., & Clarke, J. N. (2002). *Can psychiatric categories capture immigrant illness experience?: An inquiry into the "agonies" (agonias) of Portuguese immigrants.* Manuscript submitted for publication.

Mintz, E. E. (1978). Transpersonal events in traditional psychotherapy? *Psychotherapy: Theory, Research and Practice, 15,* 90–94.

Mollon, P. (1991, November). *Psychotherapists' healing attitude.* Paper presented at the Symposium on the Critical Factors in Psychotherapy and Psychoanalysis, Manchester, UK.

Plato. (1956). Symposium. In W. H. D. Rouse (Trans.), E. H. Warmington, & P. G. Rouse (Eds.), *Great dialogues of Plato* (pp. 69–117). New York: New American Library.

Taylor, C. (1985). *Philosophical papers: 1.* Cambridge, UK: Cambridge University Press.

West, W. (2000). *Psychotherapy and spirituality: Crossing the line between therapy and religion.* London: Sage.

# 27

# Sharing Healing Secrets

## Counselors and Traditional Healers in Conversation

*Rebecca Gawile Sima and William West*

I n most African countries, before the arrival of the colonizers, the Africans had their own indigenous institutions for dealing with social, psychological, and physical problems, and these institutions used both formal and informal mechanisms. Informally, the problems were handled by relatives, particularly the Elders or trusted friends. Formally, there were a few "identified people," to whom others could turn when necessary, who handled everyone's problems (Makinde, 1984). These identified people had what Sue and Zane (1987) called "ascribed status," which refers to the role or position that others assign one person or group of persons in the society. The talents of these people were recognized from early times in their indigenous schooling (Mbilinyi, 1979).

In many African societies, healing was one of the courses offered in indigenous education, as distinct from contemporary formal education. According to Mbilinyi (1979), African societies had their own education systems relating to various kinds of production systems. In the education system, youths were taught special skills and knowledge, including those related to medicine and rituals. People whose natural talent led them to become medicine men were given special training and were given different names when it was time for them to take over the healing activity. Some were called "healers," others "diviners" or simply "peacemakers," with the name depending on the nature and severity of the problems they attended, as well as the technique used in helping the individual. The name was also affected by the specific culture within the larger African cultural heritage. In many cultures, such talented people were believed to possess knowledge, awareness, and skills that grew out of their timeless wisdom. The wisdom was elicited to help people solve their problems and make decisions (Lee & Armstrong, 1995).

In many African societies, age and gender were the most important determinants in identifying people with ascribed status. Age indicates a high level of experience and accumulation of wisdom; also, respect for Elders is a tenet of the philosophy of African communities (Ishumi & Maliyamkono, 1980). Gender was also important, because in some cultures, as much as possible, healing was rendered according to gender (Mbilinyi, 1979). Healing was in the form of authority, advice, opinion, and directives, all of which helped individuals to develop a sense of social responsibility (Biswalo, 1986).

## ❖ THE STATUS OF HEALING
PRACTICES IN THE POSTCOLONIAL ERA

When colonizers arrived in African countries, along with political colonization, they brought with them other aspects of Western culture, including education, healing practices, and religion. This new culture influenced not only social, political, and economic life but also psychological thinking, including the construction and sense of self. According to McLeod (1998), the sense of what it means to be a person varies across cultures. The new culture influenced the way people in Africa constructed the "self," especially in cities and towns and among the formally educated people, who were Christian.

African people are currently experiencing variations in their sense of self. In villages, people are still largely experiencing traditional life, and therefore the self is experienced in the sense of togetherness and collectivism. As Landrine (1992) writes, "The self is not an entity existing independently from the relationships and contexts in which it is interpreted . . . the self is created and recreated in interactions and contexts, and exists only in and through these" (p. 406).

In contrast, people in cities and towns experience a more complex self, that is, the traditional self that has been influenced and changed by foreign culture through colonialism. This complexity of self leads to what Some (1999) called "loss of identity," whereby a person feels that he or she fits nowhere.

The introduction of Western culture brought about the abandonment of many traditional practices (Ishumi & Maliyamkono, 1980), including indigenous healing. Ademuwagun, Ayoade, Harrison, and Warren (1979) contend that in the encounter between indigenous African religions and their related healing systems and the Christian and Islamic faiths, a blow was dealt to the indigenous systems. The colonial authorities officially outlawed most African religions with their healing systems. The indigenous systems were undermined by several generations of Africans' being taught by Western educational systems that the indigenous religions and healing were savage or primitive. Thus, traditional healing, which was initially integral to community life, having arisen from the richness of the culture, suffered separation, segregation, and suppression. Erny (1981) affirms that since then, most of the African sources of healing have been eroded and fallen into disuse. Furthermore, he states that this decline has been acknowledged and the necessity for alternative services recognized. The acknowledged alternative services include Western medical and health care to address physical problems and professional counseling to counter psychological, social, and personal problems. The latter is the main interest of this chapter, which concentrates on the possibility of integrating counseling with traditional healing for effective psychological, social, and personal care. However, before we suggest the possible areas for integration, we discuss the fundamental differences between counseling and traditional healing.

## ❖ POSSIBILITY OF INTEGRATING COUNSELING WITH TRADITIONAL HEALING: A TANZANIAN CASE STUDY

The discussion in this section is informed by the research that Sima conducted in Tanzania (see Sima, 2002). It focuses on the information gathered in part of the study involving a group meeting of six people (three counselors and three traditional healers). The discussion focused on the possibility of integrating traditional healing with counseling by analyzing the areas that could be addressed collaboratively by traditional healers and counselors. The social, cultural, and colonial history of Tanzania has resulted in a multicultural society where the use of both traditional and modern ways of healing is inevitable. What follows is the main ideas that were raised by practitioners who were involved in discussing the issue of integration.

### Compatibility of Counseling and Traditional Healing Practices

Through discussions, it was apparent that to a large extent, counselors were very aware of and knew about traditional healing, whereas their counterparts, the traditional healers, on the whole knew very little about counseling and psychotherapy. The counselors had some reservations about the secrecy that existed in traditional healing. They commented that they thought the time was right for traditional healers to be more open and share their secrets.

On this issue of secrecy, one of the traditional healers had this to say:

> The secret that people talk about in traditional healing actually is . . . I can say is the power itself . . . the power to heal. I am talking about spiritual healing. I understand that there is a kind of power in spiritual healing. That power is not known and that is the secret that people would always wish to understand. (Sima, 2002, p. 227)

Another of the participants, who was a spiritual healer, said,

> In spiritual healing the person does not own that power to heal but he possesses the spirits, which have the healing power. . . . [T]he person is just used as a tool through which his or her spirits pass over onto him/her the healing power. It is very difficult for a normal person to understand this. . . . As you see me here, I am not different from all of you, but anything can happen here and you see changes as soon as the spirits reveal themselves if need to. . . . Not physical change, but that kind of energy that is filled in me, you may notice it in practice when things change. . . . That is the experience . . . the experience when I am full of energy to heal . . . the power that I cannot explain, when I am directed what to do about the situation. . . . Many people do not believe in it until that time when he is helped then he/she may preach to others the wonders of spiritual healing. That is spiritual healing . . . it is not that we deceive our people as many people think. (Sima, 2002, p. 227)

One of counselors commented that the two methods were not compatible, because they approached the problems so differently.

> There are many aspects that are different. . . . First of all one is a modern psychological way of looking [at] and working on the problems as they call it "scientific way." . . . People have to go for formal schooling and later engage in intensive training to gain some knowledge and skills so that they can practice counselling. Traditional healing is a more customary approach, which is determined by the society. . . . Traditional healing is one among many traditional practices that is inherited and not every one can decide to do [it]. (Sima, 2002, p. 227)

The discussion about the two approaches was in depth and touched many issues, including the beliefs in spirituality and Christianity. It seemed that the belief in Christianity was more acceptable to both Christians and a few non-Christians than the belief in ancestral spirituality. These views seemed to concur with the findings from research interviews (details in Sima, 2002) that indicated that the approaches were indeed very different. In the final analysis, the findings seemed to suggest that total integration between counseling and traditional healing was not possible. However, there was still a possibility for some cooperation between the two approaches.

### Cooperation in Referral Services

It was strongly agreed that referral services could be one of the best areas for cooperation between counseling and traditional healing, which would strengthen the helping services in Tanzania, because more than 80% of Tanzanians live in rural areas where traditional services are dominant. However, traditional healers raised concerns as to how they could cooperate in effecting referral services if they did not know and understand how their counterparts worked. As one traditional healer stated,

> It is true that we can co-operate in the use of referral services, but we can still ask ourselves how many traditional healers know what counselling is and how it works? . . . I live in this city . . . and have been here for years. I have heard about counseling, but I ask myself few things like if we agree that we can co-operate in referrals, which problems shall I refer to counsellors? . . . I do not know. I refer many physical or clinical problems to doctors in hospitals. I refer few cases to my fellow traditional healers including mental cases like severely cursed people who become totally mentally confused and those who are severely possessed with demons, and other few spiritual cases to priests because I am also a Christian. Unfortunately I have not referred any of my clients to counsellors and I think none of my fellow traditional healers has done so . . . and because I am an expert I can categorise problems and refer people to other helpers whom I think can give better service than what we can offer. But up to now I do not know which problems of all that I have mentioned could be referred to counselors. . . . Perhaps we need to know the type of problems that counselors deal with so that we can see where we can co-operate. (Sima, 2002, p. 228)

The important message that emerged from these voices was similar to that which emerged from the individual research interviews (Sima, 2002) concerning traditional healers' knowledge about counseling. This was a big challenge for counselors, who admitted that they had not popularized counseling and that they do not provide this important service in villages. Participants emphasized that knowledge about counseling was important not only for traditional healers but also for society at large. One counselor commented,

> Counseling is still new, very new, very minute number of people seek counselling out of millions. Tanzania is a large country with population of about, er, we are talking of more than thirty million people today, I think what we have to do is to popularise counselling in the larger society including villages. Then all people will understand that we have another kind of helping service and therefore automatically people will get used to it and traditional healers will be referring clients to us as they do referrals to hospitals. (Sima, 2002, p. 229)

This counselor, who worked part-time with a nongovernmental organization's projects, told the group that their project had extended its counseling service into one of the villages in a particular area (the Arusha region). They were training a few villagers to become counselors. He told the group that the village was selected because many of its people were in high-risk groups for contracting HIV/AIDS. He emphasized that people in that village were very responsive to counseling, even though it had just started. This would be the best way to popularize counseling. From this counselor's explanation, we could see that counseling was more associated with HIV/AIDS than with any other type of problem in the country. Hence, it was suggested that the community needed to learn and understand that counseling was not there for HIV/AIDS problems only, but for many more different problems.

## Consultation Services Among Traditional Healers and Counselors

The idea that consultation could occur between counselors and traditional healers was considered. This means that practitioners would have the opportunity to consult with other helpers for problems that they could not help. As one counselor explained,

> I mean to consult each other whenever we think there is a need. I think it is important, and this service is important not only for helping practitioners to work out certain problems but also it can help us understand how practitioners from each approach work. For example, if you consult a counsellor for a certain problem, that consultation will not only help you understand

more about that problem but also to understand more about counselling itself. So, I think if we develop this habit of consulting each other we can come to a point where we can understand each approach better than what we understand now. . . . We could even understand the secret of ancestral spiritual healing [big laughter]. . . . I mean it; we need to understand these things. (Sima, 2002, p. 230)

Consultation services are a relatively new phenomenon and very rarely used in traditional practice, because of lack of trust and because of taboos that restrict them from sharing certain information. This group gave it a lot of thought, and all agreed that it could be one of the best ways to help practitioners work cooperatively and to strengthen the helping sector.

### Cooperation in Research Activities and Sharing of Information

The issue of research was discussed as another area that could be considered for cooperation. One of the traditional healers felt that research would discriminate against traditional healers. He said,

You all know that almost all traditional healers have not gone very far with formal schooling, how do you expect us to co-operate on research. Is that a way you want to discriminate us? I think you need to think of something else, which we can do together like what we have agreed initially that is, referrals and consultations, but not research. . . . By all means we will not be involved . . . you will do it because you know it and how to do . . . you are educated people and researches are always conducted by educated people . . . you see. (Sima, 2002, p. 231)

This was a very interesting aspect of the discussion, because the healer who raised this argument did not know that all people in the group were involved in the research study. To the best of this healer's knowledge, Sima (the first author of this chapter) was the only person who was doing research. Sima then briefed this healer on the ethics and processes that guided the research. She also emphasized the value and benefits all parties hoped to gain from research results.

### ❖ CASE STUDY DISCUSSION

Sima invited participants to share their views on a case study of a woman called Aikaeli. Sima had met the client at the healer's premises; the woman had consulted the healer on a problem related to bewitchment (see Sima, 2002, for further details). The following were some of the views that were expressed:

I am sure that is where the difference between counselling and traditional healing becomes obvious. I would be surprised to see a case of bewitchment coming to me because people in this society understand very well and they can clearly categorise their problems. Such cases are very common in our society. We, or let me say I have personally witnessed such cases many times. . . . People believe so much in witchcraft . . . they were brought up to believe so . . . it is no wonder many HIV/AIDS victims have lost their lives because when it started they associated it with witchcraft. As we all understand that many diseases that are not treated in hospitals are translated in traditional meanings and associated with witchcraft, so was AIDS. So, I think this kind of belief is there and that is what drove that lady to consult traditional healer and not any other helper around her. (Sima, 2002, p. 232)

The contribution from this counselor raised arguments within the group, because some participants agreed with her, and others did not. One of them said that Aikaeli already held a strong belief in the theory of bewitchment, that is, she believed that the cut piece of *kanga* was being used to bewitch her, so the traditional healer was the right choice for her, as traditional healers were believed to be able to counteract witchcraft. However, another participant held a different opinion. He argued,

I agree that people have inbuilt belief that all things that are difficult to explain are translated in that way . . . er, like associating them with witchcraft. Unfortunately such problems are not brought to counsellors where maybe we could approach them differently and it could work. Er, if that problem was brought to me I would have worked with this lady's fears and help her to get out of those fears. I believe, as that traditional healer found, that there is someone just out of jealousy who decided to create fears for this lady. (Sima, 2002, p. 232)

This again created further debate, because other participants believed that it would be easy to work with her fears only if the woman had not had any preconceived ideas about witchcraft. As one counselor said,

This lady came to the healer saying that there were all signs that someone was going to harm her. At that point if she had come to me there was nothing I could do more than referring her to traditional healer. Taking into account the strong belief that is inbuilt in people about witchcraft I think even if you worked with her fears to the best of your knowledge you would not meet her expectations. She wanted to know her enemy, she wanted protection and she wanted revenge. She would be satisfied only if all those expectations were met. I could not meet all those so the only thing I could do was to advise her to consult another helper whom she thought could help . . . and obviously she could go to a traditional healer as she did. (Sima, 2002, p. 233)

One of the traditional healers stated quite firmly that the solution for such a problem could be sought and found only from traditional healers. He emphasized that modern professionals were experts in many problem areas but that they should learn to refer culturally oriented problems to traditional healers, who are more equipped to deal with them. Nevertheless, all participants agreed that healers should not include revenge as part of the healing. They said that healers should work more on protection than identification of the enemies and revenge, both of which can create more harm. One of them said that it was difficult for people to distinguish between healers and witches, because there were times when healers could be just as destructive as witches, particularly when they engaged with issues of revenge. In the final analysis, this proved to be a very strong challenge for healers. So, they needed to work on this challenge to win acceptance from their counterparts. If they engaged only in constructive roles, they would be accepted for helping with traditional problems, which proved difficult for counselors to deal with.

## ❖ CONCLUSION

The issue of integrating counseling with traditional healing is a complex and confounding one, but there is nonetheless the potential for referral, consultation, and research. If the two approaches are there to stay, then cooperation is inevitable. The existence of traditional and cultural problems necessitates the support of traditional healers, whereas, particularly in the urban metropolitan areas, modern and postmodern stresses require the help of counselors and psychotherapists.

## ❖ REFERENCES

Ademuwagun, Z. A., Ayoade, A. A., Harrison, I. E., & Warren, D. M. (1979). *African-therapeutic systems*. Los Angeles: Crossroads Press.

Biswalo, P. (1986). *The impact and effectiveness of existing guidance and counselling services in Tanzania: A research report.* Dar es Salaam, Tanzania: Department of Education, University of Dar es Salaam.

Erny, P. (1981). *The child and his environment in Black Africa.* New York: Oxford University Press.

Ishumi, A., & Maliyamkono, T. L. (1980). *Education and social change.* Dar es Salaam, Tanzania: Black Star Urgencies.

Landrine, H. (1992). Clinical implications of cultural differences: The referential versus the index self. *Clinical Psychology Review, 12,* 401–415.

Lee, C., & Armstrong, K. (1995). Indigenous models of mental health interventions: Lesson from traditional healers. In J. Ponterotto, J. M. Casas, L. A. Suzuki, & C. M. Alexander (Eds.), *Handbook of multicultural counselling* (pp. 441–456). London: Sage.

Makinde, O. (1984). *Fundamentals of guidance and counselling.* London: Macmillan.

Mbilinyi, M. (1979). History of formal education in Tanzania. In H. Hinzen & V. H. Hundsdorfer (Eds.), *Education for liberation land development: The Tanzania experience* (pp. 121–133). Hamburg, Germany: UNESCO Institute for Education.

McLeod, J. (1998). *An introduction to counselling* (2nd ed.). Buckingham, UK: Open University Press.

Sima, R. G. (2002). *Possibilities and constraints of integrating counselling with traditional healing in Tanzania: Counsellors and traditional healers' experiences.* Unpublished doctoral thesis, Manchester University, UK.

Some, M. P. (1999). *The healing wisdom of Africa—Finding life purpose through nature, ritual and community.* New York: Tarcher/Putnam.

Sue, S., & Zane, N. (1987). The role of culture and cultural techniques in psychotherapy: A critique and reformulation. *American Psychologist, 42,* 37–45.

# Index

Pages marked with *t* are tables; pages marked with *f* are figures.

# About the Editors

**Roy Moodley**, Ph.D., is Associate Professor in Counselling Psychology at the Ontario Institute for Studies in Education at the University of Toronto. Research and publication interests include traditional and cultural healing; multicultural and diversity counseling; race, culture, and ethnicity in psychotherapy; and masculinities. He coedited (with Stephen Whitehead) *Transforming Managers: Gendering Change in the Public Sector* (UCL Press/Taylor & Francis, 1999) and (with Colin Lago and Anissa Talahite) *Carl Rogers Counsels a Black Client: Race and Culture in Person-Centred Counselling* (PCCS Books, 2004).

**William West**, Ph.D., is Senior Lecturer in Counselling Studies at the University of Manchester. He is a Fellow, an accredited practitioner, and Special Adviser on Research to the British Association for Counselling and Psychotherapy. Research and publication interests include traditional healing, spirituality, culture, supervision, and postmodern qualitative research methods. He has published two books, *Psychotherapy and Spirituality: Crossing the Line Between Therapy and Religion* (Sage, 2000) and *Spiritual Issues in Therapy: Relating Experience to Practice* (Palgrave Macmillan, 2004).

# About the Contributors

**Michael Anderson,** Ph.D., is Academic Director of Postgraduate Diploma Programmes in the Warwick Business School at the University of Warwick in the United Kingdom. He is a social anthropologist with interests in identity, the self, counseling, coaching, and organizational culture. He is also a freelance trainer and consultant in management development.

**Birdie J. Bezanson,** M.A., is a doctoral candidate at the University of British Columbia, Vancouver, Canada, in the counseling psychology department. She has developed an interdisciplinary program of research and study of the systems of healing of Portuguese traditional healers and the implications for practice in North America.

**Dinesh Bhugra,** Ph.D., is Senior Lecturer, Honorary Consultant, and Reader in Cultural Psychiatry at the Institute of Psychiatry, London, UK. He was appointed to the Chair of Mental Health and Cultural Diversity in 2002 and is Dean of the Royal College of Psychiatrists. Research and publication interests include psychosexual medicine, cross-cultural psychiatry, schizophrenia, pathways into psychiatric care, deliberate self-harm, and primary care.

**Olaniyi Bojuwoye,** Ph.D., is Professor of Educational Psychology at the University of Kwazulu Natal, Durban, South Africa. His research interests include traditional healing/mental health delivery services and cross-cultural counseling.

**Ann Charter,** M.A., is a Senior Lecturer in the Faculty of Social Work, University of Manitoba. Anne is an Aboriginal woman who is actively involved in both the traditional and contemporary communities. Her publications and research interests include traditional healing and adult education.

**Charles P. Chen,** Ph.D., is Assistant Professor of Counselling Psychology at the Ontario Institute for Studies in Education, University of Toronto, Canada. He is also a Visiting Professor in Applied Psychology at Shanghai Normal University, China. His research interests include vocational and career psychology and counseling, Morita therapy, and Morita philosophy–based career counseling.

**Lilián González Chévez,** M.D., Ph.D., is a Professor and Researcher in the Department of Anthropology at the Universidad Autónoma del Estado de Morelos, México. Her research areas are medical anthropology, ethnobotany, and migration. She is the author of several book chapters and papers, among them "Dimensión Antropológica," "Salud Pública de México," and "Agriculture and Human Values."

**Roshni Daya,** Ph.D., is a private practitioner in Calgary, Alberta, Canada. She has a strong interest in Buddhist philosophy and its application to psychotherapy. Research and publication interests include Buddhism in counseling and psychotherapy, and forensic psychology.

**Gary Foster,** Ph.D., is an Instructor in the philosophy department at Dalhousie University in Halifax, Nova Scotia, Canada. His research interests include ethics, hermeneutics, narrative and existentialism, hermeneutically informed theoretical frameworks for cultural psychotherapy practice, and the ethics of psychotherapy.

**Fernando L. Garzon,** Psy.D., is an Associate Professor in the School of Psychology and Counseling at Regent University, Virginia Beach, Virginia. His major research areas include forgiveness, inner healing prayer, and multicultural issues. He is also an Associate Pastor in an area Latino church (El Mundo Para Cristo) located in Virginia Beach. He is active in the regional Latino community.

**Mekada Graham,** Ph.D., is an Assistant Professor in the Department of Social Work Education, California State University at Fresno. Her publications include *Social Work and African Centered Worldviews* (Venture Press, 2002), and her research interests include social policy, education, and black communities; spirituality and counseling; social work philosophy; and African-centered approaches to social work.

**Qulsoom Inayat,** Ph.D., is a counselor and counseling psychologist. She was Director of the Islamic Counselling Service in London and worked for 20 years in universities teaching health psychology, counseling, and counseling psychology. Currently, she is Visiting Lecturer at Southampton University and Kings College Hospital, London. Research interests include Islamic counseling and diversity issues in psychotherapy.

**Susan James,** Ph.D., is an Assistant Professor at the University of British Columbia, Vancouver, Canada, in the counseling psychology department. Research and publication interests include cultural psychotherapy, health care of Portuguese immigrants, and the integration of anthropology and philosophy with cultural psychology.

**Manoj Kumar,** Ph.D., is a Specialist Registrar in adult psychiatry on St. Mary's rotation in London and is also an honorary Specialist Registrar at the Maudsley Hospital, London. He is interested in cross-cultural psychiatry, organizational psychology, and spirituality and psychiatric practice.

**Pittu Laungani,** Ph.D., is a Senior Research Fellow at Manchester University. Until recently he was Reader in Psychology at South Bank University, London.

Research and publications are in cross-cultural psychology, in which he has published 70 research papers and several books, including his most recent one, *Asian Perspectives in Counselling and Psychotherapy* (Brunner-Routledge, 2004).

**Ronald Marshall,** Ph.D., is a Lecturer in the Department of Behavioural Sciences, University of the West Indies, St. Augustine Campus, Trinidad. Research and publications include *Sociology of Health and Illness Behaviour; Social Organisation and Methodology, Alcoholism, Genetic Culpability or Social Irresponsibility;* and *Return to Innocence, a Study of Street Children in the Caribbean.* He is coauthor of *The Socio-economics of Health Care in the Caribbean.*

**Rod McCormick,** Ph.D., is a member of the Mohawk Nation and works as a Professor of Counseling Psychology at the University of British Columbia (UBC). He was also director of the Native Indian Teacher Education Program at UBC from 1993 to 2000. Rod has worked as a therapist, professor, and administrator in the field of First Nations health/psychology and education for the past 15 years.

**Tobie Nathan,** Ph.D., is Professor of Clinical Psychology and Psychopathology at the University of Paris 8. In 1979, he created the first ethnopsychiatry consultation in France, and in 1993 he founded the Georges Devereux Center. He is author of 25 books, 250 articles, and 4 novels. He is currently Cultural Counselor at the Embassy of France in Israel.

**Josna Pankhania,** M.Phil., is a counselor and psychotherapist in Sydney, Australia. She is a doctoral candidate researching the spiritual dimensions of yoga. Research and publication interests include antiracism and feminist politics, multicultural counseling, and postcolonial history.

**Anne Poonwassie,** M.A., is the founder and director of the Prairie Region Centre for Focussing and Complex Trauma in Winnipeg, Manitoba, Canada, which provides a variety of entry- and advanced-level programs for counselors and therapists in First Nation communities. Publications, training, and research interests include traditional healing and focusing.

**Patricia A. Poulin,** M.A., is a doctoral candidate in counseling psychology at the Ontario Institute for Studies in Education, University of Toronto. She is a shiatsu practitioner. Research interests include facilitating resolution of early trauma and the clinical application of mindfulness meditation.

**Laura J. Praglin,** Ph.D., is Assistant Professor of Social Work at the University of Northern Iowa. Research and publication interests include religion; social work and its interface with religion and spirituality; minority group relations; conflict resolution; and the history of social work.

**Estelle Seymour,** M.A., has since 1990 been a member of the student counseling service at Solihull College, Solihull, UK, where she coordinates the counselor education and skills training program. She is currently a regional coordinator for the Pagan Federation and has a passion for West African drumming, culture, and healing. She is also influenced by Taoism.

**Rebecca Gawile Sima,** Ph.D., is a Lecturer in Psychology and Counselling at the University of Dar es Salaam, Tanzania. Research and publication interests include counseling in Tanzania, reproductive health and HIV/AIDS counseling, and cultural and gender issues in counseling and educational settings.

**Jagmohan Singh,** M.D., is a Consultant Neurosurgeon in Stoke-on-Trent, United Kingdom. Research interests include the interface between faith and psychiatry and head injury and psychiatric implications.

**David Paul Smith,** M.A., Ph.D., is a licensed clinical psychologist who works in the Chicago area. He received an M.A. degree from the Master of Arts Program in the Social Sciences and a Ph.D. from the Committee of Human Development at the University of Chicago. He has completed postdoctoral training in psychopharmacology and hypnotherapy. He is an active member of the Society for Psychotherapy Research. His research involves the study of psychotherapy, cultural parameters of healing, and the psychology of religion.

**Joseph K. So,** Ph.D., is Professor of Anthropology at Trent University in Peterborough, Ontario, Canada. A biomedical anthropologist specializing in cross-cultural mental health, he has done fieldwork in China, investigating the use of traditional medicines in treating psychiatric and psychological disorders. Active in community volunteerism, he has received Volunteer Services Awards from the Ontario Ministry of Citizenship and Culture.

**Robert N. Sollod,** Ph.D., is a Professor of Psychology at Cleveland State University. He is the coauthor with the late Christopher Monte of the text *Beneath the Mask: An Introduction to Theories of Personality* (7th ed., John Wiley). In addition, his academic interests focus on the interfaces between psychology and spirituality and between psychotherapy and values.

**Anne Solomon,** M.A., is a social worker and doctoral candidate. She is a mental health professional and an indigenous traditional healer trained from adolescence in her Anishinabe traditions. She works in private practice and with Aboriginal men in prison with and through her traditional ceremonies.

**Clemmont E. Vontress,** Ph.D., is Emeritus Professor of Counselling Psychology from George Washington University and a licensed psychologist in private practice in Washington, DC. He has published numerous books, book chapters, and articles in cross-cultural counseling, existential counseling, and traditional healing.

**Njoki Nathani Wane,** Ph.D., is Associate Professor at the Ontario Institute for Studies in Education, University of Toronto. Her research and publications include "Black Feminist Thought," "African Women and Spirituality," "African Women and the Question of Development," and "Experiences of Visible-Minority Student Teachers in Teacher Education Programs."

CPSIA information can be obtained
at www.ICGtesting.com
Printed in the USA
FFOW01n0420100315
11691FF

9 780761 930471